E-Political Socialization, the Press and Politics

Labour, Education & Society

Edited by György Széll,
Heinz Sünker, Anne Inga Hilsen
and Francesco Garibaldo

Volume 32

PL ACADEMIC RESEARCH

Christ'l De Landtsheer / Russell F. Farnen /
Daniel B. German / Henk Dekker /
Heinz Sünker / Yingfa Song /
Hongna Miao (eds.)

E-Political Socialization, the Press and Politics

The Media and Government in the USA, Europe and China

PL ACADEMIC RESEARCH

Bibliographic Information published by the Deutsche Nationalbibliothek
The Deutsche Nationalbibliothek lists this publication in the Deutsche Nationalbibliografie; detailed bibliographic data is available in the internet at http://dnb.d-nb.de.

Library of Congress Cataloging-in-Publication Data

E-political socialization, the press and politics : the media and government in the USA, Europe and China / Christ'l De Landtsheer, Russell F. Farnen, Daniel B. German, Henk Dekker, Heinz Sünker, Yingfa Song, Hongna Miao (eds.).
pages cm
Includes index.
ISBN 978-3-631-62834-8 — ISBN 978-3-653-01971-1 (ebook)
1. Political socialization. 2. Social media—Political aspects. 3. Mass media—Political aspects. I. Landtsheer, Christ'l de.
JA76.E15 2014
306.20285'4678—dc23

2014006884

ISSN 1861-647X
ISBN 978-3-631-62834-8 (Print)
E-ISBN 978-3-653-01971-1 (E-Book)
DOI 10.3726/978-3-653-01971-1

PL Academic Research is an Imprint of Peter Lang GmbH.

Peter Lang – Frankfurt am Main · Bern · Bruxelles · New York · Oxford · Warszawa · Wien

This book is part of an editor's series of PL Academic Research and was peer reviewed prior to publication.

www.peterlang.com

Preface

This volume contains several chapters that were previously published elsewhere and several that are published here for the first time.

Chapters that are original to this book are:

- 1 – Introduction by the editors of this volume
- 2 – Political Socialization Defined: Setting the Context by Daniel B. German
- 3 – Youth, Peer Culture, and Everyday Political Consciousness by Heinz Sünker
- 6 – Participation Friendliness of Political Websites by Christ'l De Landtsheer
- 17 – Implications for E-Media, the Press, Government, and Politics in China by Yingfa Song and Hongna Miao.

Chapter 4 Politics, Education, and Paradigmatic Reconceptualism: US Critical Theory in the 1990s by Russell F. Farnen originally appeared in pages 15-43 of *The Politics, Sociology and Economics of Education: Interdisciplinary and Comparative Perspectives*, edited by Russell F. Farnen and Heinz Sünker, published by Macmillan Press (London, UK) and St. Martin's Press (New York, NY) in 1997.

Chapter 5 – Media Use in the US: Electronic Media Dramatically Up and Print Media Down by Daniel B. German and Caitlin Lally first was published as an article titled "A Profile of American's Media Use and Political Socialization Effects: Television and the Internet" in *Futures in Education*, Volume 5, Number 3, pages 327-344, in 2007.

Chapter 12 – Post-Communist Media in Russia by Vitaly F. Konzhukov was titled "Post-Communist Russian Media: Economic Pressures and Government Control in the 1990s" in *Democracies in Transition: Political Culture and Socialization Transformed in West and East*, published by Bibliotheks und Informationssystem der Universität Oldenburg (BIS), Oldenburg, Germany in 2000, pages 171-180. This book was edited by Russell F. Farnen, Henk Dekker, Daniel B. German, and Rudiger Meyenberg.

Chapter 13 – Media and Terrorists by Russell F. Farnen was titled "Terrorism and the Mass Media: A Systemic Analysis of a Symbiotic Process" pages 99-143 in *Terrorism*, Volume 13, in 1990.

The following chapters were first included in *Democratization, Europeanization, and Globalization Trends: Cross-National Analysis of Authoritarianism, Socialization, Communications, Youth, and Social Policy* published by Peter Lang (Frankfurt am Main, Germany) in 2005. The book was edited by Russell F. Farnen, Henk Dekker, Christ'l De Landtsheer, Heinz Sünker, and Daniel B. German.

- 7 – Empirical Evaluation of Government and Websites by Christ'l De Landtsheer, Natalya Krasnoboka, and Conny Neuner was titled "Participation Friendliness of Political Websites in Eastern and Western Europe," pages 325-360.

- 8 – The Internet Upholds the Powers That Be by Henk Dekker and Arie in 't Veld was titled "The Internet and Political Socialization: Political Party Websites and Their Effectiveness," pages 41-68.
- 9 – Metaphors in Euroland Press by Christ'l De Landtsheer and Elisabeth Koch was titled "Metaphors and the Framing of the European Single Currency (the Euro) In and Out of Euroland," pages 429-446.
- 10 – Press Reporting on the Euro by Marianne Law, Jerry Palmer, and David Middleton was titled "The Press Reporting of European Economic and Monetary Union in Four European Countries: A Comparative Analysis," pages 361-378.
- 15 – The Electronic Media Deficit by Mary Hepburn was titled "Electronic Media and Political Socialization in the USA," pages 197-206.

The following chapters were first included in *Political Culture, Socialization, Democracy, and Education: Interdisciplinary and Cross-National Perspectives for a New Century* published by Peter Lang Verlag (Frankfurt am Main, Germany) in 2008. This book was edited by Russell F. Farnen, Daniel B. German, Henk Dekker, Christ'l De Landtsheer, and Heinz Sünker.

- 11 – The Ukraine Media on the Orange Revolution by Natalya Krasnoboka and Christ'l De Landtsheer was titled "Broadcasting the Orange Revolution: Rhetoric of the Ukrainian Media during the Presidential Campaign," pages 219-240.
- 14 – Democracy and Virtual Politics by Andy Koch was titled "Party in the Simulacrum: The German Greens and the Virtual Party Meeting of 2000," pages 253-268.
- 16 – Does the Media Reduce Political Participation? By Daniel B. German and Dragan Stefanovic was titled "Political Socialization and Media Use: Period Effects of 9/ll, 2001 on Political Participation in the 2002 and 2004 Elections: Toward a Theory on Media and Politics," pages 241-252.

Dedication

This book is dedicated to Martha D. Bowman, our copy editor, who has worked tirelessly and faithfully with the International Political Science Association's Research Committee on Political Socialization and Education (R.C. 21) since 1986 to produce many collections of our scholarly output, including books, papers, articles, and other academic products. These works were produced to further the knowledge of democratic politics, civic education, and political socialization worldwide and to encourage the growth of democratic political cultures. What modest efforts we published would not have been possible without her competent, clear, consistent, and professional input from beginning to end. Thank you, Martha, for making us look so good in print.

The Editors

Table of Contents

Chapter 1
Introduction

The Editors

Our lives increasingly are played out in an electronic world. The most recent Kaiser Family Foundation study of youth in America shows that the average amount of time spent with media is 10 hours and 45 minutes. This total includes multitasking (e.g., using more than one medium at a time). If one adds texting, the figure jumps to 12 hours and 20 minutes. That is more time than is spent sleeping, eating, and non-media school and face-to-face family-peer socializing. The 10 hours and 45minutes represent an increase of 3 hours and 16 minutes more than was found in the initial Kaiser study conducted in 1999. Between 2004 and 2009, iPod/MP3 player use went from 18% to 76%. Cell phone use went from 39% to 66%. We are moving toward life in a virtual non-face-to-face electronic world. Immediate implications can be seen in the Kaiser Family Foundation study. Heavy media users get poorer grades in school and, relevant to the socio-political world, are more likely to get into a lot of trouble. Minorities (blacks, and Hispanics) are more likely to be exposed to media; consequently, there is a digital divide. Print consumption, included in the overall figure, has declined while TV content has increased along with music/audio, computer, video games, and movies (Rideout, et al., 2010, pp. 2, 4, 10, 28; Kaiser Family Foundation, 2010, pp. 1-3).

Moreover, studies show that adults are moving in the same direction (German and Lally, 2007, pp. 338-339). Studies show that while adults are using the Internet and other computer related media, their TV consumption has also increased. What implications do these developments have for politics? Worries that virtual world consumption would result in lowered political involvement have not been borne out since voter turnout increased in the 2004 and 2008 US Presidential elections.

The nature of our news consumption has changed possibly for the worse. As newsprint declines and access to news moves online, the type of news we consume has changed. In a quality newspaper (such as *The New York Times* or *Le Monde*), editors/journalists select what goes on the front page and gets more public attention. On the computer, the top stories are not picked by professional media gatekeepers, but by an algorithm process which quantifies the number of hits each news item receives and moves the most frequently hit items to the top. In a sense, this process (e.g., employed by Google) democratizes the news by giving the general public control over topics that move to the top. But is this majority-based selection method the best way to decide what news is most important?

Majority rule without minority rights might be perceived as majority dictatorship. This is an outcome that democratic societies prevent by using all kinds of checks and balances. Letting the public move news stories to the top might just be the wrong way to determine what really is significant. Furthermore, the news popup (which appears when one clicks on a news item) is a very brief one-page summary, complete with advertising and other items. This is what people like. Those who run Google have found that it is what the public wants. It's the news people want to access, not necessarily the news they need to be informed about as citizens. This gets to one of the conundrums of democracy which solves the problem of anything-goes majority rule with minority rights protection or any kind of sage input. And what about the preferred lack of depth?

This book examines the state of print and electronic media in the US, Europe, and China. The latest media developments, such as those mentioned previously, demonstrate that we are living in an increasingly media-centric world. The chapters included here represent theoretical and empirical studies that shed light on the meaning of this development. The trajectory of people's move to electronic communication is a global phenomenon affecting people's daily life throughout the world. Does this development aid or impede democracy? Is there an emerging "digital divide" contributing to an increasing gap between the rich and poor nations?

This book is divided into four parts that explore the various aspects of political socialization and its relationship with various media: Part 1 – Political Socialization Background (chapters 2 through 4); Part 2 – Media Use, Government, and Websites (chapters 5 through 8); Part 3 – The Print Press, Broadcasting, and Politics (chapters 9 through 12); and Part 4 – Critiques of the Emerging Virtual/Media World (chapters 13 through 17).

In Chapter 2, Daniel German looks at the basics of the political socialization process. Media, an agent of socialization, seems to edge out the traditional major socialization agency: the family. The trajectory of more media influence in the formation of our orientations toward society, government, community, and relations with other people are carefully monitored to ensure that we do not move in an unwanted direction, such as the destruction of democracy and/or positive social relationships. Inevitably, there is a lag between technology and the study of its effects, so the effort to chart these interrelationships is never finished. Technological change is not new. Witness the effects of the Gutenberg press and radio on communication. The history of communication technology is a steady increase of print and now electronic transmissions in our lives.

In Chapter 3, Heinz Sünker examines the influence of peer groups on the political socialization of youth. Traditional theories provided a pessimistic outlook for the future of successful political socialization. However, more recent explorations into youth and peer culture provide more hope for the future.

Chapter 4 examines the fundamental assumptions and criticisms from US reconceptualists and their current relevance. Some US critical theorists changed from a Marxist viewpoint to one of social democratic liberalism, with an emphasis on democratic, non-revolutionary reform. In this chapter, Russell Farnen focuses on the need for core processes that emphasize problem solving, decision making, policy analysis, and basic subject matter which discusses political theory, ideology, and systems that help students to both handle and explain their political worlds, regardless of country of origin. This chapter finds political and cognitive sciences, problem solving, socialization, and political education research to be both complementary and mutually reinforcing. American concerns focus on the overly complex nature of such interrelationships, but such studies are mutually productive and useful for future progress in the field.

In Chapter 5, Daniel German and Caitlin Lally document media use among children and adults to show that we are simultaneously moving from less print consumption to more electronic use (including more television, along with a dramatic increase in computer-related activities). In the wake of this development, a digital race-based and socio-economic divide appears to be emerging. Access to information, the computer's promise of democratization, seems to be unequal. They ask, "Does living in a digital world result in a decline in social capital (face-to-face social mobilization)?" Perhaps we are losing ground in associational activities traditionally fundamental to democracy. Whether or not this is a reality seems to be mitigated by the relative salience of political issues which may or may not drive political involvement. In the face of more electronic media use, voter turnout increased in the US 2004 and 2008 elections. We will need to monitor this potential loss of social capital to determine whether or not this is a false conjecture.

In Chapter 6, Christ'l De Landtsheer assesses the quality of political websites. She examines party and public administration websites, personal websites for political leaders and administrators, and websites of non-governmental social and political organizations. By employing a coding scheme, De Landtsheer measures the "participation friendliness" of these websites and offers suggestions for building a qualitatively good political site.

In Chapter 7, Christ'l De Landtsheer, Natalya Krasnoboka, and Conny Neuner created an instrument to empirically evaluate websites. This survey instrument is a multifaceted methodology for measuring government websites, but it could easily be employed to examine private business websites as well. The authors examined websites in seven European nations and determined that the Netherlands has the most overall participation-friendly site and Poland the least friendly. Their scheme judges the transmission of information, the ease of interactivity, user friendliness (including links, search, and help functions), and site aesthetics. As more and more people enter the virtual world, governments should be interested in creating the most useable sites possible to better serve their citizens and create a more effective government.

Chapter 8 looks at how the Internet reinforces the incumbent political powers. In an empirical experiment, Henk Dekker and Arie in 't Veld demonstrate that instead of giving more groups access to people through websites, organizations with more money are able to create better websites that hold the interest of users.

Consequently, the already powerful and financially well-heeled organizations gain access to the voter's minds while the less fortunate drop out of sight.

Metaphors abound in press coverage of politics and politicians, who attempt to "frame" these metaphors to their advantage. For example, a press story might state that an administration has been hit by a "hurricane" and an administration official may state that we have weathered the hurricane and are returning to normal. The metaphorical frame gives the consumer a sense thatthings are not right or a perception that all is OK. In Chapter 9, Christ'l De Landtsheer and Elisabeth Koch suggest that Euroland nations' press used positive metaphors (e.g., emotively and persuasively optimistic) to bolster public support for adopting the Euro currency. In comparison, non-Euroland nations' press was relatively devoid of metaphors. A frame sets the stage for a positive, neutral, or negative view of a political issue and may influence its fate.

In Chapter 10, Marianne Law, Jerry Palmer, and David Middleton show how the United Kingdom press gave a more negative frame to adopting the Euro. This negative frame may have influenced public opinion against joining Euroland.

In Chapter 11, Natalya Krasnoboka and Christ'l De Landtsheer show how traditional media use relatively few metaphors in a crisis. In comparison, the newer online media use metaphors in more abundance in support of a revolutionary mood.

In Chapter 12, Vitaly Konzhukov shows how the Russian government ended the democratization period of print and electronic press following the end of the Soviet Union. The new Russian government resorted to economic deprivation, censorship, and "trumped up" criminal prosecutions to reign in newly developed print and broadcast (radio and television) media.

Several studies cast doubt on the idea of the media's contributions to democracy. In Chapter 13, Russell Farnen notes that terrorists and media are like a "horse and carriage." Writing before 9/11, Farnen states that our response to terrorism (which uses the media to convey its messages) mostly is violent. Our response to 9/11 was three wars: one in Afghanistan, another in Iraq, and a final "War on Terrorism" at home in the US and worldwide. He advocates a less violent response that looks at the causes of the terrorist act and examines ways to deal with the underlying problem without resorting to warfare.

In Chapter 14, Andy Koch argues that the Internet's virtual world should not be a substitute for real-world involvement in politics. Contrary to providing a more democratic avenue for involvement in politics, virtual politics might have the opposite effect by making people lose interest in direct involvement.

In Chapter 15, Mary Hepburn is concerned that television - now combined with the Internet - creates a seductive electronic world. This electronic world encourages people to spend their time there. Hepburn finds this enchantment with the electronic world discourages people from getting involved in the real world of politics. Certainly, this development merits a very careful assessment, which is a primary mission of this book.

In Chapter 16, Daniel German and Dragan Stefanovic question the whole notion of electronic media's dampening political involvement based on the rise of voter turnout in America's 2004 and 2008 elections. Issues played a central role in this increased involvement. They theorize that the salience of issues may move participation up and down and not necessarily the lack of face-to-face relationships. This whole argument may not settle the question since US voter turnout in 2004 and 2008 may have been even greater than it was, being lowered by television and the Internet.

In Chapter 17, Yingfa Song and Hongna Miao examine the influence of the Internet on China's government. The increased use of the Internet has heightened citizens' interest in and capacity for political participation. While breaking down the traditional pyramid structure of Chinese society, the Internet has also formed a new bureaucracy and a widening digital gap. China's quest for cyber democracy is hampered by this digital gap as well as the government's strict control of the Internet's content.

References

German, D. and C. Lally (2007). "A Profile of America's Media Use and Political Socialization Effects: Television and the Internet's Relationship to Social Connectedness in the USA," pp. 327-344 in *Policy Futures in Education*, Volume 5, Number 3.

Kaiser Family Foundation (2010). "Daily Media Use Among Children and Teens Up Dramatically From Five Years Ago." http://www.kff.org/entmedia/entmedia012010nr.cfm.

Neuner, C. and C. De Landtsheer (2005). "Towards a Methodology for Evaluating the Quality of (Public) Websites." http://internetjournals.net/journals/tir/2005/January/Paper%2008.pdf

Rideout, V., U. Foehr, and D. Roberts (2010). "Generation M2: Media In The Lives Of 8- To 18-Year-Olds" in A Kaiser Family Foundation Study, January 2010.

Part 1
Political Socialization Background

Chapter 2
Political Socialization Defined: Setting the Context

Daniel B. German

Professor (Emeritus) of Political Socialization, Appalachian State University, Boone, North Carolina, USA

Abstract

Political socialization is the process by which orientations toward the political system are developed from one generation to another. These orientations include: 1) political knowledge; 2) opinions about specific political issues, deeper attitudes, and beliefs or values; and 3) behavior such as voting. All of the orientations shape an individual, depending on where the process takes place (e.g., in India, the United States, or South Africa). Other influences affecting the unfolding development of political orientations are agents of socialization, including family, media, region, education, ethnic or racial group, and gender. The process begins early in life and continues throughout the life cycle. Out of this process, a political culture which shapes the functioning of a particular political system is formed.

Introduction

The systematic study of what we call scientifically today "political socialization" clearly began with Plato. In the 4th century BC, Plato wrote the *Republic*. In this book, he advocated education and training from early childhood on to develop guardians of the city state Athens. They must be devoted to the city and capable of overcoming temptations and witchcraft. These guardians must be strong; but unlike the disciplined and strong rulers of Sparta, they must not use their strength for purposes of tyranny and plunder. Plato advocated the creation of different roles for the city state. A farmer should be a farmer. A soldier should be a solider. An artisan should be an artisan. They each have a specific role and must be brought up ("socialized") to fulfill a particular function. The soldier must not be surrounded by music or engaged in reading poetry, but instead must be trained in the art of warfare. One might clothe the farmer in glorious robes, but he will cease to be a farmer. Or one might let the potter drink and feast, but then they will cease to be potters. This means that a particular society (whether it is ancient Greece or Russia in the millennium) is the product of upbringing and education.

Knowledge is a product of the socialization process. The level of knowledge in a society has important implications for the development of what type of political system exists. A democratic government requires literacy for its citizens. Democracy could not have developed in ancient Greece without literacy because citizens had to read laws posted outside an assembly area and support or oppose them by direct vote. A critical feature of authoritarian (dictatorships, monarchies, warlords) political systems is to keep the mass of citizens semi-literate to illiterate. Many people in the world (even in the 21st century) do not receive enough education to be considered literate. How could you engage in politics if you do not understand what is going on? Studies of different types of political systems clearly demonstrate that a high level of educational achievement is associated with non-authoritarian political processes and vice versa. Literacy, however, while being an essential ingredient of free and open democratic political systems, is often not sufficient to the existence of democracy. The Third Reich under Adolf Hitler was as authoritarian as a political process can get, yet Germany at that time had nearly universal literacy. The same was true for the Soviet Union under the totalitarian rule of Joseph Stalin.

Combined with knowledge, a certain set of attitudes and values determines what kind of political system exists. The beliefs and values of a society are referred to as culture. Each nation has a political culture, which refers to its political values or political ways of doing things. In America, there is an acceptance by many (not all) of a kind of democratic creed composed of majority rule with minority rights, rule of law, free speech, and free and open elections. Thus, there is a consensus on the rules of the game played in American politics. In many other nations, this democratic creed is not a part of the typical way of doing things. Transparency International lists many nations in the world which are awash in corruption. There is a "take whatever you can get, by whatever means you can use to get it" philosophy. Fairness is not valued. In Russia, today as throughout its history, people value strong-man rule. Russians are socialized to prefer a strong leader due to a history of invasion, whether from the Mongols to the East or Europeans from the West. If a strong leader (whether Czar or Premier) subverts the election process, eliminates media opposition, and otherwise exerts an iron-handed rule, it is fine with the Russian people. In 2006, Russia was listed as 2.5 on a scale of 1 to 10 (10 =low corruption), so it ranks high on corruption.

The US fell prey to corruption during the early 2000s. For example, lobbyist Jack Abramoff bribed members of Congress to pass legislation favorable to his business interests. However, in the 2006 elections, voters threw out of office the party primarily responsible for accepting bribes. Eliminating corruption was listed in polls as one of the primary reason voters gave for overturning the party in power in Congress. Americans consequently showed that they do not accept corruption in political parties and, instead, value a free and open process.

Knowledge, attitudes, and values are connected to political behavior. Studies show that an attitude of efficacy (which is the extent to which one feels that his/her involvement is politically effective or not) is highly associated with political participation. High efficacy is associated with education in democratic political systems; along with trust in the system, it is essential to popular involvement in political processes. If these attitudes fall to a very low level, it is dubious whether a democratic system could function; it might fall prey to an authoritarian or totalitarian alternative, which occurred in the history of Germany, France, Chile, Argentina, Thailand and other nations.

The Agents of Socialization

There are several factors which have an impact on political socialization. These include education, family, media/computer technology, gender, region, religious orientations, as well as life cycle and generations.

Education

Education is a very strong predictor of a nation's political culture. Wealth and investment in literacy was a primary ingredient of ancient Athens' embrace of democracy. In examining the level of educational achievement worldwide, a relationship exists between the type of political system and many related socio-political variables. A popular mass-based educational system is associated with democratic political systems. Low educational achievement is related to authoritarian political systems. Many African, Asian, and Latin American nations do not have high levels of school attendance and rate very low in democratic assessments. On political rights measures, as an example of an undemocratic nation, Bangladesh rates poorly. It has state security laws that give undue power to the government. Demonstrations and street protests are met with excessive police force. Violence against women (including death and rape) are among other violations of civil rights. Freedom House, on a scale of 1.0 to 7.0, rates Bangladesh as a 4.0, which makes it only a partly free nation. The education system in Bangladesh has an abysmal record. A majority of children have never been to school.

By contrast, New Zealand, which was rated high in democratic processes, is rated as 1.0 (free) by the Freedom House; New Zealand has a strong record of guaranteed civil and political rights for all. Educational achievement is universal and compulsory to age 16 and free in state school until age 19. However, New Zealand has problems with its indigenous Maori population, not dissimilar to Australia's aborigine citizens. Education, employment, income, health, housing, and treatment in the criminal justice system lag in comparison with the mainstream population. The Maori are about 15% of New Zealand's population.

Following World War II, there was a great expansion in academic education in Western Europe. For example, in Germany, very few young people went to the academic track gymnasia and on to higher education. Many young people went to technical training schools and were in the workplace by age 16. Level of educational achievements in European nations was closely related to being chosen for political leadership, business ownership, officers in the military, and even being in the clergy. Broadening the education base through comprehensive schools for the masses and free attendance at the university (dependent upon admission) in Germany means more people are involved in all upper power and business echelons in society.

Studies show that students' involvement in other aspects of the educational environment is strongly related to participation in politics. Extracurricular activities (ranging from student government, school newspaper, athletics, and even cheerleading) are predictors of later life political activity.

Family

The nature of family life can have a profound effect on later political activity. A highly disciplined, rigidly patriarchal family structure can result in adherence to authoritarian political structure later in life. Studies show that a more authoritarian personality emerges. The authoritarian personality is intolerant of a diversity of ideas and experimentation with new concepts. It tends to be submissive to authority, obeying without question. Authoritarians tend to be intolerant of ethnic and social minorities. They are more militaristic than non-authoritarian personalities. Needless to say, the authoritarian personality is not conducive to the development of democracy. Asian and African families tend to be very strict with male-oriented decision making. It is said with at least some validity that communism in the People's Republic of China is more compatible with the traditional Chinese Confucian culture with strict rule in everything from family life to government administration.

The effects of family influence (which is probably the paramount agent in the political socialization process throughout the world) can be clearly seen in political party affiliation studies in the US. Studies show that if both parents are of the same political party, chances are great that the children will also belong to that party. Other factors contribute to the successful passing of the party affiliation from parents to child. If politics is a salient topic at home and the offspring know what the parents think, there is more of a chance that not only political partly affiliation will be passed on, but also positions on highly visible issues. The occurrence of a politicized home atmosphere is declining possibly in America more so than anywhere else. With both parents working, parents simply don't spend as much time with their children as they used to. Of great importance is the fact that households are not what they used to be. It is increasingly the case that all family members have their own television sets and they do not spend time with each other. Computers have added to the separation since children have their own personal computers. Television and computer consumption have both increased in American homes; therefore, family members spend more time using electronic communications systems instead of talking with each other. This pattern is affecting the transfer of political orientations from parent to child, resulting in an increase in independent party affiliation.

Family life is undoubtedly more close-knit in developing nations. But, politics may not be very salient in nations where there is not much of a tradition of popular political involvement.

Media/Computer Technology

Undoubtedly the media (particularly television and the general trend toward the use of information technology such as the Internet, instant messaging, and other forms of electronic communication) are not only transforming families, but people and nations in an emerging global world.

In *Bowling Alone: The Collapse and Revival of American Community*, Robert Putnam argues that a key ingredient of democracy is social capital. Social capital is the existence of a connectedness that citizens have to each other; it enables them to engage in social activities, including involvement in political associations. Drawing on the theory of Alexis de Tocqueville (*Democracy in America*, 1835), who felt that a rich associational life in America sustained civic self-government, Putnam is concerned that too much use of media is resulting in an individual disconnectedness, much to the determent of democracy. He noticed that as television consumption goes up, associational involvement goes down. In fact, according to A.C. Neilson surveys, television use is increasing in America. Amazingly, while computer/Internet use is dramatically increasing, US households are watching more television.

The number of Internet users in America is increasing at a phenomenal rate. Under a quarter of households had Internet access in 1997. By 2006, this figure jumped to over two-thirds. As these figures rise, face-to-face social involvement declines. This, according to Putnam, is a tragedy for democracy, which thrives on a face-to face associational behavior. Certainly, the world of electronic communications is transforming the world as we have known it. Young people in America are now almost 100% using the personal computer and are consuming more and more television as well, thus changing the socialization process in ways which really need to be closely monitored.

In the developing world, the media are being harnessed to increase awareness and comprehension of democracy. In South Africa, for example, websites, newspapers, newsletters, television, and cyber cafes are being used to create a democratic community. While information technology is used to draw people in developing nations into political participation, it may be individualizing people in the developed nations into a virtual world and drawing them away from real-world participation. However, voter turnout in the US went up from around 50% in the 2004 presidential election to 60%, indicating perhaps that the increased emersion in information technology may not necessarily have dampened popular participation.

There are enormous variations in media relations between government and citizens throughout the world, ranging from government-owned and -censored to privately-owned, but -censored and, finally, to mostly or entirely privately-owned and free. Which of these circumstances exists in a country has enormous implications for the socialization process.

In totalitarian systems, media are an arm of the political party and serve as a means of propaganda. Under this system, the government owns the media and allows no criticism of government policy. In the socialization process from the earliest years on, there is no development of the idea of toleration of media-supported dissent typical of a democracy. Beginning in 2002, the organization Reporters Without Frontiers has evaluated press freedoms in most of the nations throughout the world. Totalitarian nations fared very poorly, with North Korea being the consistently worst ranked nation. There is no press freedom in North Korea. Criticism is banned and, if it occurs, the dissenters are sent to prison. Foreign media is kept out. The North Korean leader Kim Jong-il personally controls the press. "Uniformity" could be the word which best applies to the North Korean media. Dissenters sometimes are executed in public in North Korea to teach the people a lesson. There is no criticism of Kim Jong-il. During recent years of famine and starvation, especially for North Korean children, there was no mention of this disaster.

All of the worst-rated nations by Reporters Without Frontiers are located in Asia, the Middle East, and Africa, with one exception: Cuba. All of the totalitarian nations (North Korea, Cuba, People's Republic of China, Laos, and Vietnam) are at the bottom of the list. Next to North Korea is Turkmenistan (Asian), Eritrea (African), followed by Cuba (Latin American), Myanmar (Asian), People's Republic of China (Asian), Iran (Middle Eastern), Saudi Arabia (Middle Eastern), and Ethiopia (Africa). The President of Turkmenistan (as an example of a very poor media environment) is willing to use violence, including torture to death, to quash journalistic dissent. In Eritrea, one might be secretly imprisoned. With a press milieu like this, there is obviously no chance for socialization toward the values of a free and open democratic political system.

The best press freedom nations are Northern European: Finland, Ireland, Iceland, and the Netherlands. They all share first place. In these nations, Reporters Without Frontiers found no censorship, government threats, intimidation, or physical action. Other top nations are all West and Central European in 2006, including the Czech Republic, Estonia, Norway, Slovakia, Switzerland, and Hungary. The United States in 2006 fell to53rd from 17th in 2002. In part, the US declined because of a trend of the federal courts to deny reporters the right not to reveal their sources. For example, this resulted in *New York Times* reporter Judith Miller's imprisonment in 2005. These actions are undertaken in the "war on terror." Reporters Without Frontiers points out that a Sudanese cameraman, Sami al-Haj working for *Al-Jazeera*, as another example, has been held since June 2002 at the Guantanamo US military base. Still, the US has a relatively free press.

When it comes to media and political socialization, it is important to examine the varied patterns of Internet use throughout the world. Younger generations are increasingly turning to the Internet for political information. There are dramatic variations in Internet access from one continent to another and within continents. The Internet is believed to be a possible boon to democracy since it gives access to information necessary to understand the political world and it could enable users to establish a website to obtain support for a political cause. The problem is that a worldwide digital divide may create an unequal playing field for those connected to the Internet and those not so advantaged. Internet World Stats shows that, indeed, Africa is particularly disadvantaged in this regard with less than 5% having access, compared to over two-thirds in North America and over 50% in European Union (EU) nations. Even within Europe, EU candidate nations only have a little above one-fifth of their population connected to the Internet. Within Africa, there are variations ranging from 10% access in South Africa (not high, albeit one of the most technologically advanced nations in Africa) to only 3% in Nigeria and less than 1% in Niger. In Asia, access is barely above 10%, with great diversity ranging from nearly 70% in Japan and South Korea (which are considered democracies) to below 10% in the People's Republic of China and almost no access in North Korea (which are communist totalitarian nations). In India, which is considered a democracy, access is only around 5% with great variations, depending on where you live and level of income. In South America, Internet access is about 15% with variations ranging from a high of over 40% in Chile to about 4% in Paraguay. In the Middle East, the overall access level is 10%. Variations of Internet use are great with above 50% access in Israel to about one-third in the United Arab Emirate to only 1% in Yemen. As the world moves into a global information technology age, these variations might seriously diminish the ability of developing nations to keep children and adults abreast with the changing climate of education, business, politics, and life in general. It is worth noting that nations which are totalitarian and have had periods of, or are, authoritarian rule have low popular access to the Internet.

Gender

There are dramatic differences worldwide when it comes to the political status of women. Scandinavian nations have the highest percentage of women in legislatures. The figure is the highest in Sweden, where above 40% of parliamentary members are women. However, even in France, one of the birthplaces of popular rule, the figure is only about 11%, which is roughly comparable to the US. Women did not get to vote in France nationally until after World War II. Throughout the world, not only are women infrequently involved in elected office holding, but especially in developing nations, their status is quite poor. In a country like Nigeria, as an example, women face outright second-class status compared to men. Marital rape is not considered a crime in Nigeria. In Russia, where women fared better under communism, women are abused at home, discriminated against in the workplace, and young women often trafficked abroad (to Western Europe and the US) for prostitution.

Women's opinions on political issues frequently differ extensively compared to men. Women are less approving of collateral damage (inadvertent killing of civilians) in war, less supportive of the death penalty, and more likely to support social services of all kinds. In this regard, women are said to be more nurturing. Both the differences in office holding and opinions are due to differences in the socialization process. Studies show that women engage less in aggressive sports and are less likely to be risk takers. Women engage more in non-combative social relationships with other women and are more prone to be kept at home. Young men engage much more in extreme sports, including riding motorcycles, sky diving, alpine skiing/snowboarding, football, hunting, and other high-risk endeavors to the point that they die in significantly higher numbers in their 20s than women. Consequently, women grow up less interested in the rough-and-tumble political world which includes warfare. They are much less likely than men to even try to get involved in politics. Women often do not run for political office, much less hold office.

Region

Regional differences in socialization often produce variations in political orientations. Studies on the authoritarian personality conclude that the South in the US has more authoritarians, followed by the Mid-west, compared to the Northeast and West. It is clear that voting patterns relate to these differences, with conservative George W. Bush carrying the South and Mid-west in the 2004 presidential elections. In France, the provinces are notably more conservative than Paris.

Religious Orientations

Religious orientations are related to political opinions and behavior. The Jewish population is the most liberal in America. More orthodox religions, including the Jewish orthodox religion, produce more conservative political thought. The Islamic religion teaches women to play a more traditional role in society, including non-participation in politics.

Life Cycle and Generations

Two very important concepts in political socialization research are life cycle and generation. Life cycle refers to the development of political orientations over time, from birth to death. Studies conclude that political changes occur throughout the life cycle; however, generation can be critical to the development of political orientations that crystallize over time. In other words, one does not necessarily get more conservative over time as much as one becomes conservative or liberal early in life and experiences continuity over time.

Socialization begins in early childhood. Children younger than about age 10 to 11 are egocentric. They do not cognize the political world beyond themselves and their immediate family and perhaps an extended tribe if they are part of one. Young children think in concrete terms as opposed to abstract thought. They personalize political thinking, focusing on the police or president. At about age 10 or 11, children begin to cognize a broader world, including community and nation. They develop the ability to think beyond a person (such as a president, prime minister, or king) and develop a comprehension of process, such as elections and legislative activities. Children become sociocentric, understanding that they live in a society broader than just their family.

Two psychologists, Joseph Adelson and Robert P. O'Neil, asked children and adolescents aged 11 to 18 what the purpose of a law requiring vaccination would be. The 11-year-olds said that it would be to keep them from getting sick, whereas the 18-year olds stated that it would be to prevent an epidemic in society. When asked whether or not government should be able to take away a person's property to build a road, the 11-year-olds said "no," while the 18-year-olds were more likely to say that the individual should sell the property for the benefit of the community.

There is a primacy principle in the socialization process that what is learned early is learned best and structures later learning. Young children develop beliefs without a knowledge dimension. Later, adolescents begin to develop knowledge, but it is felt that there is a primacy principle. That is, early developed beliefs filter and shape knowledge learned later. For example, political party affiliations develop in very young children, but they cannot express what the parties stand for. They thereupon shift through information and accept information that supports their attachment to a prior-held orientation toward a political party.

As children get older, they develop knowledge about the political world. The socialization process appears to be largely over by about age 20 or 25. There would be enormous variations in this development depending on different educational opportunities. Attitudes, values, and beliefs persist and crystallize later in life. However, a period effect can alter political thinking. A dramatic political event (such as war or an economic depression) can cause later resocializtion.

Generation is a powerful political force. Political events occurring during the crucial socialization years of about age 10 or 11 to 20 shape new entrants into a political system. Research indicates that party affiliation and subsequent voter trends are affected by the circumstances existing during the pre-adult years. Children growing up in the American "Roaring 20s" in the US became more Republican in party identification than not and have stayed that way throughout life. Young people socialized during the Great Depression in America became Democrats and still largely vote for the Democrat party. One might speculate that Americans who were socialized from 1930 to 1940 (ages 10 to 20), which were years of economic adversity, were able to take the adversity of World War II more easily than some other generation.

Young people socialized during the Ronald Reagan years have been more Republican in political party affiliation. Those socialized during the Bill Clinton years are more liberal in opinion polls on issues like same-sex marriage and abortion; they are more likely to be affiliated with the Democrat party.

There would be variations on this process throughout the world. In nations with very little mass education and media penetration, generational socialization might be minimal since family and village would loom large as the major political input. Under these circumstances, new generational thinking could emerge, but it would be much slower over a long period of time unless some truly major event would rapidly have an impact on everyone.

References

Adelson, J. and R. O'Neil (1966). "Growth of Political Ideas in Adolescence: The Sense of Community," pp. 295-306 in *Journal of Personality and Social Psychology*, Vol. 4.

Freedom House, http:www.freedomhouse.org

International Institute of Democracy and Electoral Assistance (IDEA), http://www.idea.int/resources/

Internet World Stats, http://www.internetworldstats.com

Putnam, R. (2000). *America's Declining Social Capital*. New York, NY: Simon & Shuster.

United Nations. daccess-dds-ny.un.org/doc/undoc/gen/G06/118/36/pdf/G0611836.pdf?OpenElement

Reporters Without (Sans) Frontiers, http//en.rsf.org

Chapter 3
Youth, Peer Culture, and Everyday Political Consciousness

Heinz Sünker

Professor of Social Pedagogy and Social Policy, University of Wuppertal, Wuppertal, Germany

Abstract

This chapter examines theories about the effects of peer culture on the political consciousness of youth. How youth are encouraged to become active participants in the political process is based on the influences of their peers as well as those of the family, their community, and the country's society and government. Theories formulated by Horkheimer and Adorno in Germany's fascist past are contrasted with those developed by more modern researchers who share a more positive viewpoint.

Introduction

Horkheimer and Adorno (1997) argue in their famous chapter "The Culture Industry: Enlightenment as Mass Deception" in *Dialectic of Enlightenment* about a way which mediates questions of socialization and of the constitution of subjectivity. At first glance, their conclusion seems to be very dark with respect to the future of enlightenment and human subjectivity. There are only a few signs showing alternatives (i.e., the perspective of emancipation, liberation, and consciousness). But we must remember that even though their book was written during the dark period of German fascism, they also refer to the possibilities of bourgeois-capitalist societies.

Therefore it is useful to quote and comment on some of their arguments (all taken from Horkheimer and Adorno, 1997):

> Consumers appear as statistics on research organization charts, and are divided by income groups into red, green, and blue areas; the technique is that used for any type of propaganda (p. 123).
>
> What connoisseurs discuss as good or bad points serve only to perpetuate the semblance of competition and range of choice (p. 123).
>
> The man with leisure has to accept what the culture manufacturers offer him. Kant's formalism still expected a contribution from the individual, who was thought to relate the varied experiences of the senses to fundamental concepts; but industry robs the individual of his function (p. 124).
>
> There is nothing left for the consumer to classify. Producers have done it for him (p. 125).
>
> The might of industrial society is lodged in men's minds. The entertainments manufacturers know that their products will be consumed with alertness even when the customer is distraught, for each of them is a model of the huge economic machinery which

has always sustained the masses, whether at work or at leisure - which is akin to work (p. 127).

In the culture industry this imitation finally becomes absolute. Having ceased to be anything but style, it reveals the latter's secret: obedience to the social hierarchy. Today aesthetic barbarity completes what has threatened the creations of the spirit since they were gathered together as culture and neutralized (p. 131).

And so the culture industry, the most rigid of all styles, proves to be the goal of liberalism, which is reproached for its lack of style (p. 131).

In the public voice of modern society accusations are seldom audible; if they are, the perceptive can already detect signs that the dissident will soon be reconciled (p. 132).

Not to conform means to be rendered powerless, economically and therefore spiritually - to be "self-employed." When the outsider is excluded from the concern, he can only too easily be accused of incompetence. Whereas today in material production the mechanism of supply and demand is disintegrating, in the superstructure it still operates as a check in the rulers' favor. The consumers are the workers and employees, the farmers and lower middle class. Capitalist production so confines them, body and soul, that they fall helpless victims to what is offered them. As naturally as the ruled always took the morality imposed upon them more seriously than did the rulers themselves, the deceived masses are today captivated by the myth of success even more than the successful are. Immovably, they insist on the very ideology which enslaves them. The misplaced love to the common people for the wrong which is done them is a greater force than the cunning of the authorities (p. 133).

The connoisseurs and the expert are despised for their pretentious claim to know better than the others, even though culture is democratic and distributes its privileges to all. In view of the ideological truce, the conformism of the buyers and the effrontery of the producers who supply them prevail. The result is a constant reproduction of the same thing (p. 134).

For only the universal triumph of the rhythm of mechanical production and reproduction promises that nothing changes, and nothing unsuitable will appear (p. 134).

But what is new is that the irreconcilable elements of culture, art and distraction are subordinated to one end and subsumed under one false formula: The totality of the culture industry. It consists of repetition (p. 136).

Business is their ideology. It is quite correct that the power of the culture industry resides in its identification with a manufactured need, and not in simple contrast to it, even if this contrast were one of complete power and complete powerlessness. Amusement under late capitalism is the prolongation of work. It is sought after as an escape from the mechanized work process, and to recruit strength in order to be able to cope with it again. But at the same time mechanization has such power over a man's leisure and happiness, and so profoundly determines the manufacture images of the work process itself (p. 137).

No independent thinking must be expected from the audience: the product prescribes every reaction: not by its natural structure (which collapses under reflection), but by signals (p. 137).

The culture industry perpetually cheats its consumers of what it perpetually promises (p. 139).

The secret of aesthetic sublimation is its representation of fulfilment as a broken promise. The culture industry does not sublimate; it represses (p. 140).

There is laughter because there is nothing to laugh at. Laughter, whether conciliatory or terrible, always occurs when some fear passes. It indicates liberation either from physical danger or from the grip of logic. Conciliatory laughter is heard as the echo of an escape from power; the wrong kind overcomes fear by capitulating to the forces which are to be feared. It is the echo of power as something inescapable. Fun is a medicinal bath. The pleasure industry never fails to prescribe it. It makes laughter the instrument of the fraud practised on happiness (p. 140).

. . . but the necessity inherent in the system not to leave the customer alone, not for a moment to allow him any suspicion that resistance is possible (p. 141).

The principle dictates that he should be shown all his needs as capable of fulfilment, but that those needs should be so predetermined that he feels himself to be the eternal consumer, the object of the culture industry (p. 142).

Both escape and elopement are predesigned to lead back to the starting point. Pleasure promotes the resignation which it ought to help to forget (p. 142).

The stronger the positions of the culture industry become, the more summarily it can deal with consumers' needs, producing them, controlling them, disciplining them, and even withdrawing amusement: no limits are set to cultural progress of this kind (p. 144).

The effrontery of the rhetorical question, "What do people want?" lies in the fact that it is addressed - as if to reflective individuals - to those very people who are deliberately to be deprived of this individuality. Even when the public does - exceptionally - rebel against the pleasure industry, all it can muster is that feeble resistance which that very industry has inculcated in it. Nevertheless, it has become increasingly difficult to keep people in this condition. The rate at which they are reduced to stupidity must not fall behind the rate at which their intelligence is increasing. In this age of statistics the masses are too sharp to identify themselves with the millionaire on the screen, and too slow-witted to ignore the law of the largest number. Ideology conceals itself in the calculation of probabilities (p. 144).

In either case they remain objects (p. 147).

The culture industry tends to make itself the embodiment of authoritative pronouncements, and thus the irrefutable prophet of the prevailing order (p. 147).

The new ideology has as its objects the world as such. It makes use of the worship of facts by no more than elevating a disagreeable existence into the world of facts in representing it meticulously. This transference makes existence itself a substitute for meaning and right (p. 148).

The enemy who is already defeated, the thinking individual, is the enemy fought (p. 149).

The attitude into which everybody is forced in order to give repeated proof of his moral suitability for this society reminds one of the boys who, during tribal initiation, go round in a circle with a stereotyped smile on their faces while the priest strikes them. Life in the late capitalist era is a constant initiation rite. Everyone must show that he wholly identifies himself with the power which is belaboring him (p. 153).

In the culture industry the individual is an illusion not merely because of the standardization of the means of production. He is tolerated only so long as his complete identification with the generality is unquestioned (p. 154).

In this way mass culture discloses the fictitious character of the "individual" in the bourgeois era, and is merely unjust in boasting on account of this dreary harmony of general and particular. The principle of individuality was always full of contradiction.

> Individuation has never really been achieved. Self-preservation in the shape of class has kept everyone at the stage of a mere species being. Every bourgeois characteristic, in spite of its deviation and indeed because of it, expressed the same thing: the harshness of the competitive society. The individual who supported society bore its disfiguring mark, seemingly free, he was actually the product of its economic and social apparatus (p. 155).
>
> The most intimate reactions of human beings have been so thoroughly reified that the idea of anything specific to themselves now persists only as an utterly abstract notion: personality scarcely signifies anything more than shining white teeth and freedom from body odor and emotions (p. 167).

Reflections

On the one hand, this theme of "peer group and the political socialization of juveniles" is based on the subject that Krappmann (1983) so aptly presented in his article "Socialization in the Peer Group." There he argued for the unquestionable contribution which the peer group makes in the development of one's personal competence, activity, and identity. This is related to the actual significance of the peer group as part of the socialization process, comparable to the family with respect to its actual efficacy (Krappmann, 1983, p. 433). On the other hand, with regard to a basically socio-theoretical and socio-political reflexion, the theme is connected to questions about the forms and contents for integrating the rising generation into the emerging society. Considering its youth-theoretical, youth-sociological, and youth-political particularities, this question about integration indicates both the socio-theoretical genesis of and the socio-political value of analyzing the overall significance of juvenile peer groups. In its relevance to juvenile peer groups, the intergenerational paradigm – which directed the pedagogical and sociological center of interest in youth from Schleiermacher (1983) to Mannheim (1965) – intersects with a theoretical homogenization at the beginning and an emphasis on the theory of individuality at the end of this century (Sünker and Volkmer, 1990). Schleiermacher's concepts are representations of the dialectics between "preserving and changing" on the socio-evolutionary level, while Mannheim's contribution dealt with the theoretical context of modernizing social processes. With Thrasher's (1927), Cohen's (1986), and Salisbury's (1962) publications, the perspectives of social integration and social control (which is guided by a theory of deviance when treating the topic of age-homogeneous groups of juveniles) are illustrated in the US discussion; for example:

> The modern youth if . . . "youth" is understood as the developmental phase from . . . childhood up to adulthood is "antisocial" in a certain sense and to a certain degree as far as its behaviour is to be related to an intermediate stage which misses continuance and . . . goal orientation in order to be able to be social. This phase is characterized by the partly abrupt transition from the intimate relations of the small family to the deemotionalized relationships of the modern working world which are governed by rational and organizational measures. When the juvenile of our industrialized, bureaucratic society leaves the parental home he [/she] is confronted with social structures in which the be-

> haviour acquired in the family is not appropriate any more. Thus, the research for behavioural structures can be realized as the basic need of the modern youth which is convenient for the "second level'" which the juveniles need to get acquainted with. Furthermore in the course of this transitional phase on the one hand, a strong impulse to perform and to carry [one's] weight and on the other hand a mental, intellectual and social liability converge which bear the possibility of a conflict with the environment having this constellation and by the omission of the behavioural support in the anonymous and deemotionalized structures of the large cities and the large-scale enterprise-like working world (Rausch, 1962, p. 146).

Peer Group and Socialization

Processes that distinguish between social development and youthful life can be described systematically and historically. For example, Eisenstadt (1965) focuses on the structural aspects of peer groups, while Habermas (1987) approaches the theme of "adolescent problems" from a socio-critical perspective.

In her article, "Peers and Political Socialization," Silbiger (1977) hints at an analytical approach which reveals the problematic structure of this theme. It is remarkable that there are no immediately available proofs for (or answers to) questions about the relevance of peers in the field of political socialization. The authors of the newest German contribution on youth, peer groups, and politics also mention a lack of empirical research in this field. Therefore, we rely on Eisenstadt's classical and basic representation of the meaning of age-homogeneous and age-heterogeneous groups in adolescence.

The "socialization" of persons (which ensues from, or breaks with, the principles of a common family life) relates to the important task each society and social system undertakes to assure continuity by replicating its own structures, norms, and values (Eisenstadt, 1965, p. 51). Accordingly, age-heterogeneous and age-homogeneous groups have the same function: "to be the instances of the socialization of the individual and the mechanism of the community in the social system" (Eisenstadt, 1965, pp. 60-61). Safeguarding continuity is no problem as long as the general society's and the family's systems closely correspond with each other. Problems arise if the transition from family principles to those of the external social structure is not conducted smoothly or if certain factors hinder the process for shaping universal relationships. Thus, "the transfer of identification and expansion of solidarity" (Eisenstadt, 1965, p. 67) as a basis for universalism (which mainly helps determine formal principles, in contrast to Eisenstadt's view) is prevented. In this case, Eisenstadt adjusts age-homogeneous groups to the socially produced cleavages. Social dysfunctions which are established in the family lead Eisenstadt to claim "that from the perspective of the social system, the assignment of roles and the formation of groups are not less important on the basis of the homogeneous age than for the personality integration of the individual" (Eisenstadt, 1965, p. 72).

The range of political socialization is based on several considerations. Age-homogeneous groups form the mediating links between the principles of family life and those of the social system. That is, peer groups help complete the personality integration which the family cannot carry out any more. At the same time, they establish the individual's social attitude via group socialization, which is necessary for the maintenance of the social system. In contrast to Eisenstadt's exposition of the problem (at least as far as identity in adolescence is concerned and the question about the family's achievement of socialization), Habermas' (1987) "Theory of Communicative Action" delves into how the prevailing social system affects the family's function as far as the social integration of youth is concerned. Thus, he concludes that the wilful rationalization of the real world is also evident in structural changes in the bourgeois family. Opposed to ignoring the effect of history on the changing social structure, he argues for the possibility "that by the equalized relational patterns of individual bahavioral manners and liberalized educational practices, a part of the rational potential that is [part of] communicative action is also released" (Habermas, 1987, p. 568).

The ambiguity of the social developmental processes which Habermas analyzes is essentially supported by the fact that the family's private world is confronted by external economic and administrative factors "instead of being mediated by them from behind. In the case of the families and their environment, a polarization between communicatively structured and formally organized fields of action [is] observed which establishes the process of socialization under different conditions and which sets out a different type of risks" (Habermas, 1987, pp. 568-569).

The potential increase of communicated rationality in the family's private world directly leads to claimed (as well as susceptible) conditions of socialization which arise when we examine the so-called "adolescent problem." This can be stated as follows:

> If the imperatives of the system do not sneak into the family any longer, if they don't settle down in systematically distorted communication, if they don't intervene with the formation of the self inconspicuously, but come up to the family mysteriously from the outside, then there is a more lively formation of disparities between competence, attitudes and motives on the one hand, [and] functional pretensions of the adult's role on the other hand. Problems arising from the dissociation from the family and development of one's own identity critically tests adolescent development which is seldom secured institutionally in modern societies with respect to the ability of the preceding generation to effectively connect with the succeeding one (Habermas, 1987, pp. 569-570).

This functional rift does not offer a solution to how youth transition from the family's socialization conditions to those they will encounter in external organizations as adults. Methodical and logical research is needed to reinterpret the current findings on peer groups in the life of today's juveniles.

Research Problems and Research Results

The basis of the problem of youth socialization is addressed in a wide range of approaches advanced in the Anglo-Saxon and German literature on youth research.

Let us start with the premise that youth socialization involves trying to make sense of many contradicting socialization theories about class, race, and gender. Cohen (1986, p. 76) deals with these research problems by determining how real economic situations affect the analysis of imaginary relationships (i.e., the codes of reproduction). The latter "form the subject positions in which contradictions, separations, and breaks are experienced as their exact opposites, as the maintenance of clear-cut orientation patterns and stable identities" (Cohen, 1986, p. 78).

As a general basis for analysing juveniles' political socialization processes, Hornstein (1989) describes and critiques the current tendencies used to research adolescents. "In contrast ... a research is desirable that keeps its eye on the whole relations of the life practice and the conditioning social relationships given therewith" (Hornstein, 1989, p. 122).

Habermas (1987) establishes the change of form in the problem of adolescence. Baethge (1986) investigates the structural change in the fields of juvenile experience (with respect to its social and individual meaning) as a transition from a product-oriented to a consumer-oriented paradigm of socialization. The consumer-oriented model is treated ambiguously as both hope and disaster in discussions about individualization (Baethge, 1986). They both relate to the latest statements about the political process of youthful socialization by labelling it "the liability in political securities of orientation" (Heitmeyer and Olk, 1990). Heitmeyer and Olk maintain that we must examine this ambiguity carefully because it is the foundation of basic social developmental processes. They also emphasize that the problem of analyzing juveniles' political orientation conditions already exists at the interpretative level (i.e., how this behavior helps when processing economic-social and everyday experiences plus actual political problems). They also try to describe how the tense relationship which exists between youth and politics developed.

The relevant problem (in the context of our theme) is that the significance of peer groups for political socialization (in terms of political everyday consciousness) is ignored. From today's viewpoint of political socialization (particularly for peer groups) theories, only restricted and valid propositions or research practices are considered relevant.

Statements about speculative or contradictory propositions relate only to ideas about research needs as Krappmann (1983) contends. The perceived lack of interactional studies indicates that there is a need for a socialization model that allows one "to estimate one's own contribution to social relationships among peers in respectively different phases of socialization" (Krappmann, 1983, p. 447). Furthermore, Krappman raises a significant question about the consequence of social developmental processes which explores peer groups' quality as a relevant factor for socialization theory. A loss of this special quality of socialization has consequences for children's development as subjects who, themselves, are able to act (Krappmann, 1983, p. 462).

According to Krappmann (1983), the general framework for a research task that focuses on youth peer-group socialization must deal with the problems of age-groups with respect to politics. Girls' participation in peer groups develops much like the socialization of their male counterparts. Ignoring the political dimension while considering girls, Mitterauer (1986, p. 244) sees the development of the informal group "as the most important social form of youth at the present time [and one considered] as an indication of same general tendencies" (Mitterauer, 1986, p. 236). He emphasizes the following:

> Since the family has developed from an organizational form of work to a social form whose primary mutuality lies in the field of leisure, the family and the peer group became rivals, which they were not in the traditional society by any means. The family and the peer group do not compete only about temporal demands. A rivalry of the orientation of values which might have played a minor role historically, is also essential (28) Mitterauer (1986, p. 124).

In a "careful" argument, Hurrelmann (1985, p. 70) assumes that peer groups begin their socializing functions early in adolescence. The peer groups become identified as forms of social life that depend on leisure. They give their members full opportunities for participation. Thus, they allow one to gather experiences in social contexts which are perceived as being vitally relevant. However, they are prevented from doing so in other social fields of action:

"Most peer groups organize themselves outside the systems of family and education and take it for granted that they are not adult initiated, guided and controlled" (Hurrelmann, 1985, p. 70). From this, the authors reason that peer groups have the potential

> to become the dominating field of orientation and action in adolescence if this result is directed by juvenile life-situations and interest orientations. Thus, the peer group, whose spectrum ranges from spontaneously formed cliques up to tight social groups such as 'juvenile gangs,' is to be considered an important instance of socialization in adolescence (Hurrelmann, 1985, p. 71).

Additionally, the leading researcher on "socialization of youth" develops his hypothesis in a similar direction:

> There is an increased chance, within the age cohort, because of this lost control by adults, for the growth of behavioral patterns which differ from the postulated norms set by parents, educators or the law. This development would not increase young peoples' sense of insecurity. Therefore, age homogeneous relationships produce both protection and a balance for the influence of large social units. At the same time they are an important part of youth socialization that may ease and encourage the transition to adulthood (Wurzbacher, 1978, p. 34).

Moreover, Wurzbacher links this general assessment of the importance of the peer group for youth development with his hypothesis about relationships between organized groups and processes of activating, selecting, and educating "socially active personalities:" "The analysis of biographies of socially active adults leads to the hypothesis that the readiness to engage in the public field, in organs of self-administration, in politics, in civic action groups, in associations, etc. develops according to how a particular person belongs to a juvenile group and, in whose confines, he could become acquainted with social activities and conduct and could practice them" (Wurzbacher, 1978, p. 49).

Political Consciousness, Way of Life, and Adolescent Cultures

Wurzbacher's (1978) limited approach is quite different from those who exclude the dimensions of political socialization either implicitly or explicitly and from those who favour more research in this field. By contrast, Schulze (1977, p. 9) tries to come up with the "latent" conditions of political socialization in his empirical investigation of "Political Learning in Routine Experience" in order to split the relationship between readiness for political activities and everyday reality in adolescence. The target of his investigation is restrictive. Nevertheless, it is interesting for us to consider selected parts of his work and the relevant outcomes and results, especially since his approach and results point to specific difficulties for research in this opaque field.

For Schulze, the leading question is "how the different instances of socialization [the family, the educational system, and peer groups] interact with respect to the political process of activating, in which way therefore, different manifest constellations of conditions cause different manifestations of the readiness for political activity in the three interactional fields" (Schulze, 1977, p. 109). His clear result lies in his estimation that all instances of socialization are manifestly efficient; however, they do not reveal any rank order in this efficacy:

> The results indicate that there is no instance of socialization whose manifest political impulses do not touch the juvenile. For the family, the educational system, and age-homogeneous groups, each instance explains a substantial part of the variance concerning the readiness for political activity if the latent influences of socialization and the manifest influences of the two respectively different areas are controlled (Schulze, 1977, p. 110).

However, Schulze's more general estimation is more decisive for our question about the possible constitutional conditions of political everyday consciousness. According to his assessment, the orientations which juveniles acquire via their immediate everyday relations influence their orientations toward the political field: "Political conformity or non-conformity is partly learned by 'non-political' communication" (Schulze, 1977, p. 143). For the political quality in socialization processes, the politicization of everyday experiences is meaningful because

> the fewer juveniles who are confronted with the political area with respect to their common interaction (process of activation) the less they realize the democratic content

> of problems in such situations. Political experiences do not work only (cognitively) as a stimulus for development of the ability to perceive structurally but also (normatively) as conditions for the formation of pro-democratic values. Foremost, both components together constitute sensitivity for democratic problems (Schulze, 1977, p. 146).

The critical problem for political activation of common experiences in adolescence is clearly recorded in this ambiguous characterization. Perhaps it can only be solved by comparing two texts which are based on pure research. From a critical cultural perspective, Claussen (1993) argues for continuities in "the authoritative social character" in his consideration of juvenile political socialization processes. At the start, he describes a "rather confusing picture" (Claussen, 1993, p. 533) with respect to the relevant findings and theoretical material in this field of juvenile political socialization. He presents the following result:

> All this culminates in political everyday consciousness which absorbs the pattern of acting and thinking that was found as being appropriate for the consideration of politics in earlier family life situations and that mobilizes natural-like ontological, personal, utopian and fossilized-philosophical structures of thinking or social images. With its help, the nature and appearance of the political normally remains inscrutable and affirmatively confirmed in social world-constellations (Claussen, 1993, p. 532).

In contrast to this, Baacke (1987) argues from a position that is culturally optimistic in his characterization and interpretation of "Youth and Adolescent Cultures." His theme is that the formation of adolescent cultures is "also a new variation of the self-assertion of individuality. The brilliant aesthetic [. . .] is not 'from the inside' but rather culturally productive forces which break through mechanisms of commercialization/comodification" (Baacke, 1987, p. 534). For him, it is crucial that youth cultures respond to a common cultural problem. That is to explain "how individuality is to be preserved (in view of the prevalent socialization of personal biographies and life-chances), what subject it is there that wants there to say 'I'" (Baacke, 1987, p. 201). The resistance (that is both subjectively and theoretically motivated) in youth cultures (whose constitution contains classical problems about the peer group and simultaneously is freed from a functional perspective) is confronted with views that are based on the forfeiture, decline, or decay of history (Baacke, 1987, p. 33).

Since these two models/positions react negate each other, we need to look into the development of research investigations. They break down the socio-theoretical and socio-political framework that we are concerned with here and try to use relevant contributions from Anglo-Saxon peer group research. Appropriate considerations and research results are discussed in terms such as "child development," "human development," and "moral development." These are mainly focused on topics regarding the extension of mother-child-centering and problems of the complementary influence of parents and peers on the development of adolescent values and attitudes. The main problem remaining is the generalization of research outcomes.

It is necessary not only to supplement political dimensions and possibilities in this respect, but also to acknowledge their structuring effects.

Back to the Roots: Socialization, Contradiction and Consciousness

Horkheimer and Adorno (1997, pp. 144-145) question if – and for how long – consumer capitalism would be able to keep the people in a condition of alienation and domination. This question is also considered in an American and British study, described by Phil Wexler's (1990) "holy sparks" and Paul Willis' (1991) "common culture."

Wexler deals with the classical problem of critical theory: "the major hegemonic tendency, which is not simply social rationalization but intensified monetization of dynamic connections among all social relations and bonds and their formation as commodities" (Wexler, 1990, p. 160). He is interested in the dialectic of the intensification of control and pathologies and in individual awareness and a sense of life's possibilities and choice.

His "emergency exit" – with respect to social control and liberation – is the use and analysis of the process of "resacralization." He argues that this so-called "religious transference" reopens "an intersubjectivity that has been socially emptied in the institutional rationalization process managed by class-differentiated, defensive selves." He adds: "The religious transference facilitates trust and, therefore, social interaction or intersubjectivity." Wexler focuses on the processes of mutual recognition and a concept of the dialogue (much like the German discourse on "Bildung" or education) (Sünker, 2006).

The "creative potentials of self-transformation and resacralization" could be used against the culture of consumption in a new cultural trajectory which is also based on educational tasks. Promoting processes of self-transforming – within an understanding of teaching as redemption – is the challenge here.

Willis' (1990) approach centers around the sentence: "We are all cultural 'producers' and the idea that we have to see all human beings as 'full creative citizens' and not as lumps of labor power." Especially as regards youth, he is interested in the "vibrant symbolic life and symbolic creativity in everyday life" (Willis, 1990). The everyday life is his vantage point for analysing social action, processes of "the formation and reproduction of collective and individual identities" (Willis, 1990). A pertinent result of his analysis is to acknowledge that the "tasks of symbolic work and creativity may include not only the attempt to retain identity in the face of the erosion of traditional value system but also to forge new resistant, resilient and independent ones to survive in and find alternatives to the impoverished roles proffered by modern state bureaucracies and rationalized industry" (Willis, 1990). He is also interested in the dialectic of consumption: "consumerism has to be understood as an active, not a passive, process" (Willis, 1990). He raises the question of the possibility of creative consumption. "We are interested to explore how far 'meanings' and 'effects' can change quite decisively according to the social contexts of 'consumption,' to different kinds of 'de-coding' and worked on by different forms of symbolic work and creativity" (Willis, 1990). One of the potentials of cultural modernization could be the establishment of "proto-communities" based on some common interests supplying "some of the preconditions for both the 'old' and the 'new' politics" (Willis, 1990).

Wexler and Willis agree about emphasizing the new role of senses and the body, of energy as human power. While Wexler refers to religion and creativity, Willis refers to everyday cultural activities and creativity. Both approach a politics of meanings and identity, especially in relation to questions about youth and peer culture.

To observe societal relations (for an individual or an age group and society) and their consequences, one must first determine the consequences of the capitalist mode of socialization. Generally, it is about the contradiction connected with the socialization pattern between the production and the destruction of the social; sociality comprises a well-known reason for actual debates between communitarians and liberals. We believe that the contradiction between production and destruction of sociability is a reason to consider segmentation when discussing the development of societally made potential for both power/domination and emancipation/consciousness. Against Horkheimer and Adorno's (1997) more pessimistic view of world history, the contributions in the field of peer culture – and especially in the field of social analysis – and youth show reasons to hope for a better human future.

References

Baacke, D. (1987). *Jugend und Jugendkulturen. Darstellung und Deutung*. Weinheim and München, Germany: Juventa.

Baethge, M. (1986). "Individualisierung als Hoffnung und als Verhängnis," pp. 28-123 in R. Lindner and H.-H. Wiebe (eds.) *Verborgen im Licht: Neues zur Jugendfrage*. Hamburg, Germany: Europ Verlag.

Claussen, B. (1993). "Jugend und Politik," pp. 527-541 in H.-H. Krüger (ed.) *Handbuch der Jugendforschung,* 2nd edition., p. 527-541. Opladen, Germany: Leske & Budrich.

Cohen, P. (1986). "Die Jugendfrage neu denken," pp. 22-97 in R. Lindner and H.-H. Wiebe (eds.) *Verborgen im Licht. Neues zur Jugendfrage*. Hamburg, Germany: Europ Verlag.

Eisenstadt, S. (1965). "Altersgruppen und Sozialstruktur," pp. 49-81 in L. Friedeburg *Jugend in der modernen Gesellschaft*. Köln, Germany: Kiepenheuer & Witsch.

Habermas, J. (1987). *Theorie des kommunikativen Handelns*. Vol. 2, Zur Kritik der funktionalistischen Vernunft, 4th edition. Frankfurt am Main, Germany: Suhrkamp.

Heitmeyer, W. and T. Olk (1990). "Jugend und Politik. Chancen und Belastungen der Labilisierung politischer Orientierungssicherheiten," pp. 195-217 in W. Heitmeyer and T. Olk (eds.) *Individualisierung von Jugend.* Weinheim and München, Germany: Juventa.

Horkheimer, M. and T. Adorno (1997). *Dialectic of Enlightenment*. (Translated by J. Cumming. New York, NY: Continuum.

Hornstein, W. (1989). "Auf der Suche nach Neuorientierung: Jugendforschung zwischen Ästhetisierung und neuen Formen politischer Thematisierung der Jugend," pp. 107-125 in *Zeitschrift für Pädagogik*, Vol. 35.

Hurrelmann, K. (1985). *Lebensphase Jugend. Eine Einführung in die soziawissenschaftliche Jugendforschung*, p. 70. Weinheim and München, Germany: Juventa

Krappmann, L. (1983). "Sozialisation in der Gruppe der Gleichaltrigen," pp. 443-368 in H. Hurrelmann and D. Dietrich (eds.) *Handbuch der Sozialisationsforschung*, Sonderausgabe p. 443-468. Weinheim, German and Basel, Switzerland: Beltz.

Mannheim, K. (1965) "Das Problem der Generationen," pp. 23-48 in L. v. Friedeburg (ed.) *Jugend in der modernen Gesellschaft*. Köln, Germany: Kiepenheuer & Witsch.

Mitterauer, M. (1986). *Sozialgeschichte der Jugend*. Frankfurt am Main, Germany: Suhrkamp.

Rausch, R. (1962) "Gefährdete und gefährlich Jugend," pp. 146-150 in H. Salisbury *Die zerrüttete Generation*. Reinbek, Germany: Rowohlt.

Salisbury, H. (1962). *Die zerrüttete Generation*. Reinbek, Germany: Rowohlt.

Schleiermacher, F. (1983). *Pädagogische Schriften I. Die Vorlesung aus dem Jahre 1826*. Frankfurt/ Main, Germany: Suhrkamp.

Schulze, G. (1977). *Politisches Lernen in der Alltagserfahrung: Eine empirische Analyse*. München, Germany: Juventa.

Silbiger, S. (1977). "Peers and Political Socialization," pp. 172-189 in S. Renshon (ed.) *Handbook of Political Socialization. Theory and Research*, p. 172-18. New York, NY: Free Press.

Sünker, H. (2006). *Politics,Bildung, and Social Justice: Perspectives for a Democratic Society*. Rotterdam, the Netherlands: Sense Publisher.

Sünker, H. And I. Volkmer (1990). "Jugendkulturen und Individualisierung," pp. 61-79 in W. Heitmeyer and T. Olk (eds.) *Individualisierung von Jugend*. Weinheim and München, Germany: Juventa.

Thrasher, F. (1927). *The Gang*. Chicago, IL: University of Chicago Press.

Wexler, P. (1990). *Social Analysis of Education: After the New Sociology*. New York, NY and London, UK: Routledge.

Willis, P. (1990). *Common Culture*. Milton Keynes, UK: Open University Press.

Willis, P. (1991). *Jugend-Stile: Zur Ästhetik der gemeinsamen Kultur*. Hamburg, Germany: Argument-Verlag.

Wurzbacher, G. (1978). "Gesellungsformen der Jugend in der Bundesrepublik – Hypothesen über Strukturen und Sozialisationswirkungen," pp. 28-52 in H. Reimann and H. Reimann (eds.) *Die Jugend*. 2nd edition. Olpaden, Germany: Leske & Budrich.

Chapter 4
Politics, Education, and Paradigmatic Reconceptualism: US Critical Theory in the 1990s

Russell F. Farnen

Professor (Emeritus) of Political Science, University of Connecticut, Storrs, Connecticut, USA

Abstract

Within the general context of the US educational "system," this contribution answers three questions: What are some of the recent and significant trends in critical social science or radical educational theory on social structure, culture, and individual or group behavior? Do these trends (such as ethnographic research and everyday politics) coincide with any current developments in the United States in the domains of political science, socialization, and education? Is there any prospect that critical educational studies will have a significant impact on curriculum, research, or theoretical formulations in American political science, education, and/or socialization? The chapter ends with a discussion of such trends and relevant conclusions stemming from them. In this chapter, "critical" educational theory refers to a diverse group of radical democratic, new left, neo-Marxist, and reconceptualist critics of both classic and social "liberal" and "neoconservative" concepts of schooling (that is, opposed to those espousing what Tomas Englund describes as their "patriarchal" and "scientific/rational" discourses on education).

The American Educational Scene: Current Contexts

Just how conservative is contemporary American political culture and how much influence does business have over US schools? Presently, the US is in the midst of yet another educational "revolution," revolving around the development of a national curriculum (Smith, O'Day, and Cohen, Winter 1990). This effort will be enforced with a large measure of nationwide testing and performance "report cards" (the original fear many of those involved had when the National Assessment of Educational Progress [NAEP] began work in the mid-1960s; Anderson, et al., April 1990). However, this has been delayed by the relatively innocuous amounts (less than 1% of total costs) regularly allocated for federal educational funding. The US also enjoyed the beneficence of a chief executive who had pledged to be the "education President." His aim was to make America "number one" in science, math, and other business-directed processes, such as writing and reading skills. Luckily (or unfortunately, with respect to proper funding and public prominence) for political educators, he had not targeted the civic education curriculum for top-down reform. The administration focused on geography and history revisions, which it considered more "solid" subjects than social studies and civics – a trend common to conservative regimes in the UK, Finland, Canada, and within several American states, such as California.

America's conservative climate is also illustrated in popular and administration views on education, achievement testing, and business" role in the schools. It is also evident in the current euphoria about history teaching and unitary notions about CIVITAS, the US Constitution, and calls for education for (historical, not contemporary) democracy. For example, President Bush's "America 2000" educational reform proposals aimed for state and local implementation of conservative programs (such as "core competencies," "literacy," educational "choice," "flexibility," "accountability," and "uniform" national testing). Bush proposed to identify 535 "New American Schools" for reform; this was less than 1% of the nation's 110,000 schools. He also wanted business to "reinvent the American school" so he could "unleash American genius" to redesign them. He also advised educational innovators to ignore "all traditional assumptions about schooling and all the constraints that conventional schools work under." However, this was not supposed to cost any more federal money. Optimistically, he hoped that "By the year 2000, all children in America will start school ready to learn" (Tirozzi, May 19, 1991).

The elite's emphasis in US national educational goals is on science and mathematics achievement. Other competencies in more challenging subject matter (including English, history, and geography instruction, where the abilities "to reason, solve problems, apply knowledge, write, and communicate effectively") are also targeted. The NAEP now publishes its "content frameworks" and "proficiency standards" in these areas. A national curriculum and testing program would be based on NAEP standards, with state-by-state "report cards." The current debate is about creating a national educational model (based on ones from Japan or France or states such as California). Even American Federation of Teachers (AFT) union leaders support a competency-based, confidence-producing, national curriculum. Important issues (such as whose goals, whose curriculum materials, accountable to whom, with what flexibility, with what implications for teaching, and under whose governance?) are only now being discussed.

At issue is the continuing existence of pluralistic (public and private) and democratic (local and state) control over educational decision making in the society. The need to dismantle certain existing educational bureaucracies in states and municipalities is being debated. New public agencies may have to be created to devise frameworks; to develop, revise, monitor, and coordinate standards; to produce models; and to both monitor and report findings. Also discussed is the fact that nationwide standards and tests will prompt teaching for them either directly or by rigid adherence to a curriculum blueprint.

Such blueprints endorse certain pedagogical and educational values plus descriptions of what is to be learned. For example, the California history/social science framework ignores the social studies perspective, favoring the historical approach, corresponding with the national trend. The role of exams in any new system will be critical. Paper and pencil, essay, and multiple-choice exams are not the only available options. Experience with more "authentic" testing formats (in the UK, the Netherlands, and some US states) produced new evaluation formats. These tests measure abilities other than mere factual recall. Open-ended questions evaluate problem solving, data analysis, analytic writing, creative tasks, experimentation, and speaking proficiency. However, the old problems of how to make such tests, how to report results, and how to rank students, teachers, and systems on their results (as well as built-in antiminority biases) are only a few examples of attendant, but seldom-debated, long-term testing conundrums. (For a more complete analysis of America's educational climate, see Farnen, October 1991.)

The Left/Right versus Center Debate

According to Aronowitz and Giroux (1985), these rightist critics have misdiagnosed America's ills, provided the wrong solutions, and wrongly blamed education for current social ills. Schools are not responsible for high unemployment, stagnant productivity, foreign competition, deficit financing, and the growing gap between rich and poor. Even the solutions proposed are irrelevant since the kind of polarized, service-oriented, and unskilled society of America-in-the-making has nothing to do with the conservative educational plan. With America near federal budgetary bankruptcy because of its deficit financing of huge and wasteful military expenditures ($3 trillion from 1980 to 1990), the current educational crisis is as much a cause of local and state impoverishment and shrinking resources as it is a result of philosophical and organizational confusion. The New Right's nostrums for business control of education belie the ethical and public mission of the school as a site for learning about civic participation, social reconstruction, and moral purpose. With their focus on economic goals, conservatives gloss over the schools as arenas for class conflict, sites for lower-class failure, and evidence of the failure of consensus politics. Rightists thereby destroy the moral and political basis for public schooling. Without a democratizing mission, popular support and financing for public schools is at risk. A new public philosophy of education (based on a theory of democratic citizenship education for individual and group empowerment) is needed to provide the necessary antidote for rightist's poisoning of the American educational wells (Farnen, October 1991, pp. 201-206).

The Political Economy of Education: Carnoy's and Levin's Perspectives

Carnoy and Levin analyzed recent educational developments in the US along with changing national demographics and productive capacities. They assert that there are still strong conflicts between the capitalist/reproductive and the democratic/egalitarian dynamics in US society. One example of a social policy time bomb is the fact that more reproductive minority populations now constitute nearly half of the school population in certain states (such as California). Also, at least one-third (a growing number) of the pre-collegiate school population is disadvantaged because of racial, recent immigration, or class factors. Such statistics indicate the existence of a new underclass that is ill-prepared for the demands of work life and a group which state and business interests cannot long ignore in terms of providing either more social justice, equity, and/or equal access to schooling (Carnoy and Levin, 1986, pp. 44-45).

Carnoy and Levin also categorize reconceptual analysts of schooling into autonomous and functionalist varieties which, respectively, assume that schools operate separately from the economy and society (for example, Dewey, Bourdieu, Apple, and Giroux) and those who stress education as producing "human capital," thereby reproducing class relations in correspondence with society's economic and social needs (for example, Carnoy, Levin, Bowles, and Gintis). The critical autonomy analysts also see workplace culture reflected in the school curriculum and ideology; however, they insist that schooling is independent of economic production and, therefore, creates values apart from the rest of society. The critical functionalists stress correspondence and reproduction; yet, they differ over ideas (such as the nature and purpose of man, society, and government as well as the meaning of progress) and simultaneously dismiss observed differences between schooling and society as trivial. Carnoy and Levin claim a paradoxical relationship between schooling and work in that they are both alike and different. Schooling makes a difference because "formal education is the principal source not only of values and norms among youth but also of skills and practices of production." Yet "neither the practices nor the outcomes of schooling correspond directly to the structures and practices of work" (Carnoy and Levin, 1986, p. 37).

The social conflict dynamic pits democratic forces operating through the state to increase the pace of social change, workplace equality, economic security, and participation in decision making. The same forces are at odds in the schools, where the power of competing groups determines which way the balance (capitalist or democratic) will swing. The influence of capitalist production and class conflict is expressed in the hegemonic bourgeois state. Yet, the modern state also plays an important interventionist role in the production process, just as it does in the schools. Education is "responsible for justice and equity in an inherently unjust and inequitable system of production." Education's role is to reproduce inequality while trying to produce equality, thereby creating ideological conflicts over status, property, and power. Since such institutional conflict is system-wide, education can influence (and be influenced by) other social institutions operating under the force of capital accumulation (Carnoy and Levin, 1986, pp. 38-40).

Although democratic schools must prepare citizens for their life roles, teaching students about equal opportunity, human rights, civil liberties, participation, and the law is in direct conflict with job-related "skills and personality characteristics that enable them to function in an authoritarian work regime. This requires a negation of the very political rights that make for good citizens" (Carnoy and Levin, 1986, p. 41). Strong, social movements can influence the trend toward equal rights and opportunities; weak, business interests can predominate by stressing reproduction roles and inequalities. Periods of economic expansion and relative prosperity allow social groups to exert greater influence than do periods of contraction or retrenchment (such as during the 1990s). During the 1980s (and 1990s), education reforms proposed more competition, rigor, excellence, standards, and basic skills as well as improved teacher training, testing, merit pay, longer school schedules, homework, efficiency, and productivity. Gone were the previous emphases on "equity, equality, and access" as well as compensatory education for the disadvantaged, learning-disabled, bilingual, or minority students. Vouchers, tax credits, market competition, aid to private schools, tax reductions, high-tech education, and computer skills were proposed to end previous democratic reforms. Efficiency, competition, discipline, skills, standards, and better management became the new watchwords for the Reagan and Bush years of educational retrenchment and hegemonic control over schooling (Carnoy and Levin, 1986, pp. 41-45).

The Need for a Theory of the State: Macpherson

Critical social scientists" continual emphasis on the state's key role in the production and education sectors led political scientists such as Macpherson (1977) to both raise the question of the need to go beyond the explanation of political processes to the question of the need for a revised theory of the state in the "grand" classical tradition of great theorists like Bodin, Hobbes, or Hegel. Macpherson reported that the 1970s crop of liberal democrats and empirical and normative theorists said we do not, while social democrats and Marxists said we do. His earlier treatment of "contemporary Marxist lessons for liberal-democratic theory" is still instructive. He proposed that "there is a lot to learn from them. For they do see more clearly than most others that what has to be examined is the relation of the state to bourgeois society, and they are examining it in depth." This is quite unlike liberal theory which unquestionably accepted both the bourgeois state and society as a single package (Macpherson, 1977, pp. 61-67). The complementary work of Offe and Ronge (1975), Carnoy (1984 and 1985), and Fischer (1990) are evidence of the significance of this trend.

Some Basic and Contrasting Perspectives in American Reconceptualism: Anyon, Apple, and Giroux

A New Civics and the Hidden Curriculum

In contrasting radical perspectives on schooling and society in the UK and the US, Arnot and Whitty (1982, pp. 93-103) delineate three characteristics of the American approach. These are a critique of schooling combined with educational intervention for social change, a commitment to "intellectual and methodological pluralism," and an interactive relationship between theory and empirical research.

These theoretical constructs are not only linked to, but depend on, European (including British) theoretical underpinnings. In this regard, the work of Anyon, Apple, and Giroux is exemplary.

Both Apple and Giroux criticize the "monolithic" views of the strict correspondence theory. The mediating role of schools and the resistance to dominance practiced there illustrate the active contestation, struggle, and contradictions which emerge in both educational and workplace settings. The social transfunctional role of schooling allows the possibility of change and emancipatory reconstruction of both schooling and society.

Anyon, Apple, and others showed that school textbooks were designed to be conflict-free, legitimated the social order, and stressed stability and social harmony at the expense of "sordid" reality. The distortions, "silences," and misperceptions in textbooks are shaped by social realities in which the powerless play no important role in US history; this reinforces their impotence. School texts present an ideology which is designed to produce meanings and which, itself, must be deconstructed. The commodification process of the text production system involves publishers, textbook writers, readers, and other relevant interactions which are beyond mere reproduction theory (Arnot and Whitty, 1982, pp. 96-97; Anyon, 1979 and 1980)).

Similarly, the hidden curriculum as a socializing influence illustrates the implicit and covert transmission of values, beliefs, attitudes, norms, and behaviors through curriculum structures and the social relations of schooling. Once again, the simple economic correspondence model of Bowles and Gintis did not explain conflicts, contradictions, and discontinuities both within and between schools and the economy they were supposed to reproduce. Willis, Apple, Giroux, and others recognized that the very tensions and contradictions in schooling allowed school to be considered a potential site for innovation, change, and transformation. This allowed Anyon, et al. to develop the more complex theory of "the reproduction of conflict rather than merely the maintenance of domination." For instance, Anyon's study of classes in five US East Coast elementary schools shows the degree to which resistance and struggle to traditional schooling are both alike and different among students from various class backgrounds (Anyon, 1983).

Since a critical pedagogy to resolve such contradictions is still lacking, Giroux proposed moving beyond reproduction and critique to a transformational, liberation, and emancipatory emphasis (which the hidden curriculum concept promises). In this regard, he is joined by Apple, who also sees the possibility of intervention through schooling against the panoply of technical controls which restrict teachers and which are designed to produce professional consumers for the economic system. Anyon's studies of schooling also revealed the transformational possibilities of penetration, resistance, and counterhegemony. Like Apple, Anyon sees these possibilities may be limited to particular classrooms, teachers, schools, and sites since curricula, classes, and social expectations vary according to the "curriculum in use" there. Moreover, gender, race, and class are also relevant when considering such transformational possibilities. These are mainly revealed through ethnographic educational research (Anyon, 1983, pp. 98-102).

Giroux's work tries to move beyond structural-functionalist and reproductive theory to "a radical pedagogy that connects critical pedagogical theory with the need for social action in the interest of both individual freedom and social reconstruction" (Giroux, 1981a, pp. 7-8). Reproductive rationality is useful, but deficient, because of its "one-sided determinism, its simplistic view of the mechanisms of social and cultural reproduction in schools, its ahistorical view of human agency and, finally, its profoundly anti-utopian stance toward radical social change" (Giroux, 1981a, p. 14). The simple correspondence or "black box" model of schooling is too simplistic in that teachers and students produce as well as conserve knowledge. Resistance, the dialectic, human agency, contradictions, mediation, and opposition are part of the process for recreating and changing the social order, not merely mirroring it. Ideological hegemony can be linked to culture and resistance in schools to expose hegemonic practices to explore transformational possibilities, to disclose structural limits, to reveal contradictions in the lived lives of teachers and students, and to develop a radical pedagogy to allow students to explore the sources and limits of meaningful discourse. Giroux finds that modern pedagogy is "atheoretic, ahistoric, and unproblematic" so that its positivistic outputs are technologically sound, but undemocratic and nonemancipatory. A new curriculum must be based on students" everyday lives and historical and societal dialectics. It should also be reflective, critical, demystifying, transcendent, and reconstructive (Giroux, 1981a, pp. 37, 107, 123, 130-132, 143; Wood, Spring 1982, pp. 63-71; Popkewitz, 1983 and May 1985, pp. 429, 436).

As Wood points out, part of the problem with Apple, Giroux, Anyon, and other radical critics is the communication and "translatability" of theory into practical educational language and action. In response, Apple proposes that teachers transform their own work lives. They can then regain control and autonomy over teaching and engage in direct political action against proposals, such as tax credits for educational "choice" in schooling. Sponsoring revisions of the history curriculum, worker democracy, and feminist programs, and encountering "possessive individualism" through tapping students" "lived culture" offer other reform possibilities to challenge "the balance of forces within a specific arena" (Apple, 1982a, pp. 88-90, 130-134).

Apple also endorses the "rediscovery" of the "heuristic power" of history and puts the contemporary form of social relations in an historical context. Responding to classical, elitist, and conservative critics of schooling, he advocates considering "critical literacy," understanding diverse traditions and histories (normally excluded from schooling), and fostering "a democratic curriculum." This includes using knowledge and skill to create and pursue one's own interests while being able "to make informed personal and political decisions; and to work for the welfare of the community." He proposes democratic reforms to insure site management of schooling, more local initiative and control, greater freedom and flexibility, decentralized examination and textbook selection, and less educational bureaucracy. More collective and cooperative teamwork among teachers, sabbaticals and study periods, and teacher control over teaching/learning innovations are other strategies he proposes. To develop a more democratic educational environment, he suggests salary increases, peer reviews, and greater school-university linkages, along with implementing a new assessment and evaluation plan and engaging students in challenging learning settings. Student empowerment, counter-hegemony, and demystification of inequality are still other features of this political awareness curriculum (Apple, 1988, pp. 11, 189-195).

Other Trends in Critical Social Science and Educational Theory

Some General Observations

Critical educational, radical reconceptualist, and neo-Marxian theories of schooling in the US, Sweden, the UK, France, Germany, and elsewhere represent a serious and useful attempt to intellectually disaggregate what schools do in modern industrial and postindustrial societies. While these theorists disagree on details of the economic-political-cultural-educational nexus, certain basic concepts frequently appear and reappear in their writings. These include terms, processes, and concepts such as social reproduction, qualitative and ethnographic methods, correspondence theory, the hidden curriculum, discourses, contradictions, resistance, institutional sites, human agency, penetration, limitations, ideological hegemony, social and cultural capital, deskilling, the critique of modernism, postindustrialism, positivism, structuralism and functionalism, inequality and oppression, the utility of dialectical tensions, enlightenment, liberation, transformational praxis, and the critical importance of community, class, gender, and race as criteria for identifying social oppression in different cultural sites and social practices.

Three major schools of thought use the economic, cultural, and hegemonic-state reproductive models. The political economy model (Bowles and Gintis, 1976, 1986, and 1988) is the dominant one for the "hidden curriculum," educational policy, and ethnographic research studies. Bowles and Gintis use correspondence theory to equate school classroom practices with workplace needs and demands. The social division of labor and the class structure are mirrored in schools. The "hidden curriculum" in schools legitimizes the workplace's authority, rules, values, rationality, and power relationships. Intellectual, hierarchical, and competitive tasks are valued more than manual, democratic, or group/shared processes. Students learn to read, write, and add for productive work, to behave properly to meet job expectations, and to respect the rules and hierarchy imposed by the capitalist order. To this analysis, Althusser (1971) adds an ideological dimension. The day-to-day "culture" of the school is one aspect of this ideology. Its "unconscious" dimension is found in the "meanings, representations, and values" underlying school practices, shared images, structures, and concepts. Christian Baudelot and Roger Establet see schools as sites of ideological conflict, stemming from external sources. Class culture is seen as the primary source for such resistance; yet, ideology actively involves both dominant and oppositional strains. These contradictions may impede both self- and collective-liberation.

Bourdieu's (1973, 1977, 1984, and with Passeron, 1977 and 1979) cultural-reproductive model posits the dominant culture of the ruling class as the hidden basis for maintaining class interests, hierarchy, and domination. Since schools are relatively autonomous, they are perceived as being "neutral" in transmitting cultural capital and rejecting less-valued, lower-class culture. The school's curriculum, language, and positive behaviors are actually those of the dominant culture (that is, the ruling class). The historical conditions ("habitat") and deliberately cultivated, durable, individual dispositions ("habitus") of persons enable schools to dominate the "unconscious" of young workers so completely that they willingly accept their predetermined lot in society. Structural conflict is possible in Bourdieu's theory, but it is rather mechanistic, just as his views of class are overly homogeneous. His rejecting conflict, struggle, and resistance within different classes and his ignoring both the active reconstruction of ideologies and resistance to their imposition through counterideologies are other shortcomings of his analysis, according to Aronowitz and Giroux (1985, pp. 85-86). He is also ignorant of the oppressive burdens of material conditions and other economic constraints which impede the growth of working-class students and, at the same time, limit their possibilities for critical thinking and emancipation (Shirley, 1986).

If the nexus between the state and capitalism was illuminated in Antonio Gramsci's writings, that between the state and schooling is explained by Apple (Spring 1979, Spring 1980, 1982b, 1983, 1985, and with King, 1983, and with Weiss, 1983). They use the state hegemony model to explain the process of class domination over the political and educational system as well as the economy and its cultural superstructure. Gramsci saw hegemony as primarily the expression of the ruling class's and their allies" world view and, then, as the forceful imposition of a dominant ruling ideology over the consciousness, everyday lives, knowledge, and culture of subordinate groups. The state itself consists of both a political and civil society, which use "official" ideology to eliminate opposing views. Ideological hegemony must be continuously maintained by force, consensus, and/or domination. This is true even if it meets resistance from those refusing to be incorporated or unwilling to give "active consent" to the rulers. The state represents class, power, interests, rule, struggle, domination, and divisions, all masquerading as "normality" and "nature." Different ruling class factions may quarrel over specific public policies, but not over fundamental power and economic relationships. These remain unquestionably supportive of the capitalist order. State rulers defend the economic and moral order and engineer the consent of the ruled through false promises of opportunity, democracy, and happiness. They also "rewrite history" and destroy class opponents amidst obvious ideological contradictions found in everyday reality (Aronowitz and Giroux, 1985, pp. 87-92).

Schooling is used to reinforce society's dominant ideology, culture, and economic practices. Schooling highly values positivism, science, mathematics, basic research, competence, credentials, vocational education, national history, and other production-related output products which support economic efficiency and allow for "capital accumulation." Planning, bureaucracy, and rationality keep children in school and off the streets and label deviants (victims) responsible for their own failures. This is the alternative to illuminating the social and economic causes of "failure" or allowing the masses to share in decision and policy making. The capitalist state allows a liberal democratic ethic of individual rights and responsibilities to operate in schools. This philosophy assumes that the state is neutral. Conflict is rationalized at the individual (rather than the more-threatening class) level and is, thus, made more impotent. Laws undergird the school system, force change, ensure conformity and compliance, and indirectly quash resistance. However, such an analysis may also be a bit abstract while ignoring the role of resistance to domination through counterhegemonic practices (Aronowitz and Giroux, 1985, pp. 92-98; Giroux, 1981a, pp. 91-109).

Aronowitz and Giroux (1991) also appropriated elements of the postmodern critique into their explication of class, race, gender, and sexual preference questions in contemporary American and Western societies. For example, Giroux (1991, pp. 1-59 and 217-256) looks to a grand synthesis of liberal freedom, postmodern particularism, feminist everyday politics, and democratic socialist solidarity and civism into a new unity in diversity. This "difference within unity" goes beyond radical critique, intellectual redefinition, and democratic pedagogy to a new form of democratic "cultural politics" devoid of any master narrative or grand discourse and focusing on resistance and the democratic struggle to achieve "justice, freedom, and equality" (Giroux, 1991, pp. 56-59).

A "border pedagogy" of antiracism is needed to empower students to decode knowledge and power relationships within different cultural settings using historical and cultural analysis, lived experiences, democratic authority, justice, and power interrelationships along with redefining constructs such as "the other" and "otherness" both in and out of schools (Giroux, 1991, pp. 247-256). In this setting, schooling becomes one form of "cultural politics" and is linked to democratic public life; teachers become "engaged intellectuals and border crossers" who develop ". . . forms of pedagogy that incorporate difference, plurality, and the language of the everyday as central to the production and legitimation of learning" (Aronowitz and Giroux, 1991, p. 187). However, this postmodernist view of the radical reform project comes under severe criticism for its fashionable amalgam of several popular discourses as well as for its confusing call to politicize teachers in the absence of a well-argued and principled case for redemptive justice, "self-enlightenment," equality, and an ideologically sound conception of "utopian universalism" which will have meaning for many teachers in the US and Canada.

The US: Bowles' and Gintis' Dynamic Views

With Ivan Illich's (1970) notion of deschooling society, Marxist reproduction theorists created a dismal portrait without any hope for reforming schools, either from within or without. As Willis (1981, p. 63) notes, the new convention deals with those proposing radical educational change within the classroom as being optimistic proponents of liberation, praxis, and enlightenment. By contrast, those pessimists adhering to reproduction theory eschew any possibility for educational change in the absence of economic and social reconstruction along truly egalitarian lines. For example, Wood (Spring 1982, pp. 56 and 63) labels the reproductive school of Marxism as the philosophy of "paralysis" and "cynicism." As examples of reproductionists, Bowles and Gintis (1976) accept Althusser's (1971) characterization of schools as "ideological state apparatuses." There, oppressed students accept their fate as products of the "false consciousness" developed through capitalistic schooling. While liberal theories of development, integration, and democracy are content to justify schooling as preparation for later life, reproduction theorists claim that cognitive skills learned in school have little relation to the actual requirements of work life. Capitalistic society uses a hegemonic ideology which persuades students that their job roles are ethical, necessary, "natural," or right. Schools legitimate this nonparticipatory, undemocratic, and hierarchical order while developing a consenting consciousness among their pupils. The schools both reflect and are modeled on the workplace, with its "hierarchical division of labor." This is the "structural correspondence" theory in operation. It promotes "subordination," "powerlessness," inequality, and hegemony. Bowles and Gintis (1976, p. 224) originally perceived "a strong prima facie case for the causal importance of economic structure as a major determinant of educational structure." Economic reform was, consequently, a prior condition for any educational transformation.

Schooling in capitalist societies diverts attention from the need for equality and liberation by imposing a "false consciousness" and ideology of hegemony on students, rather than addressing the need for "a revolutionary transformation of economic life." However, "revolutionary educators" can serve as a vanguard of the proletariat role by pressing for educational democracy, dissolving the workplace-education correspondence, rejecting "simple antiauthoritarianism and spontaneity" as principles, creating "class consciousness," and practicing transformational "political work" for short- and long-run change (Bowles and Gintis, 1976, pp. 127-134, 265, and 286-287; Wood, Spring 1982, pp. 55-63).

Wood's analysis of Bowles' and Gintis' and Althusser's work subscribes to Bernstein's (1978) earlier critique of the latter's neo-Marxism by labeling the lot with terms such as structuralist, positivist, economic determinist, empiricist, and being advocates of pseudo-scientific "laws." As the dominant "educational ideological apparatus," schools join the police and military as a "repressive state apparatus" to ensure capitalist domination and hegemony. Liberal social humanists mistakenly underwrite repressive testing, ordering, and empirical social science positivism, as well as cultural reproduction, according to these radical educators of the American left. In Wood's (Spring 1982, pp. 61-63) view, this verdict encourages "paralysis," cynicism, negativism, disillusionment, and silence among other educational practitioners. It also ignores the democratic, egalitarian, liberating, and social transformation mission of American schooling, as well as the possibility for resistance to hegemonic forces. To fill this gap (between the "authoritarian" impetus of reproduction theory and the realities of schooling), a second group of radical critics (for example, Apple, Giarelli, Aronowitz, and Giroux) has evolved, providing a message of hope, possibility, and social reconstruction.

In fact, Gintis and Bowles (1981, pp. 45-59) restated and re-evaluated the correspondence principle. They also answered charges of alleged radical functionalism and "missionary pessimism," ascribed to their lack of appreciation for the systemic contradictions within education and between it and capitalistic economic processes and social relations. Moreover, with Dewey, they recognize liberalism's egalitarian, developmental, and integrative educational principles, rather than its merely being unequal and repressive schooling which, in the process, produces "good citizens" for an undemocratic capitalist society – without democratic power, participation, cooperation, emancipation, and social and economic relations. However, they still maintain that the correspondence principle has explanatory value, point to the need for systemic reform through democratic socialism, explain school outputs as products of structural social relations (not just content), and identify control over (rather than ownership of) schools as the route to follow for progressive educational reform. Inherent contradictions between education's legitimizing and reproducing roles and advanced capitalism's accumulating and restructuring processes places these two systems "out of synch" with one other. American higher education previously reflected this contrast between the post-1945 needs of the growing white-collar/service economy and the older, liberal, elite education designed for a managerial class on the one hand and the emerging vocationalism and anti-intellectualism on the other. The growing incongruence between inert, "old" schools and the dynamic, "new" service economy established the groundwork for "back to basics" claims which were founded on the apparent cultural lag between less-responsive higher education and the demands of the capitalist economic order.

The social relations (or forms, rather than contents) of liberal education produced and legitimated institutions and communication discourses which are the products of interclass "accords." Therefore, schools remain contradictorily progressive and reproductive. These tensions can only be resolved by democratizing both the school curriculum and its social relations. This could fulfill the liberal promise of equality, democracy, liberty, and emancipation, but without (or with lessened) propertied/accumulative/capitalist hegemony, dominance, and subordination (Gintis and Bowles, 1981, pp. 45-59).

The US: Carnoy and Colleagues on the Political Economy of Education

Between 1977 and 1990, Martin Carnoy (with various coauthors) studied education and employment, educational reform, the political economy of education, economic democracy, and the state and political theory. Much of this work is on third-world countries (such as China, Cuba, Nicaragua, Mozambique, and Tanzania). Its focus is on cross-national and comparative analysis of the politics of/and education.

Carnoy and Levin (1985 and 1986) also study the topic of schooling and work in the democratic state. This includes relationships between theories of the state and education, social conflict, reproduction, and contradictions in schooling and educational reform. They posit that schools and workplaces are both alike and different. Both are "large, bureaucratic, impersonal, hierarchical, and routinized'; both use external rewards as motivators (grades and wages) and allow experts, authority, regulations, and schedules to dominate the same minorities and classes which fail in both sites. Yet, American schools "more than any other major social institution" also "provide equal opportunities for participation and rewards." Workplace gender inequities are not reflected in education nor are the vast differences in societal wealth mirrored in the more-equalized level of educational investment in the society. Educators and students also have more rights and freedoms than do workers (as a result of forces such as politics, law, and democratic "mobilization").

While US schools prepare students for inequality, they are more equal and participatory than offices and factories. The correspondence principle must be qualified since there is a clear conflict between the economic reproduction function and the dynamic for rights, equality, and participation. Schooling reflects the struggles underway in the society at large (that is, between democratic egalitarianism and the demands of capital). This historical "struggle" occurs within the state and is reflected in the schools. In effect, educational change is based on a new theory of politics and the state. The latter is seen as "the condensation of conflictual class and social relations" and both as "product and shaper of such relations." The state has tried to "move class and social conflict" into politics by declassifying and redefining workers, farmers, women, and blacks as "citizens" with equal rights and responsibilities. This thrust for democratic egalitarianism produced social conflict since politics could "drastically alter the conditions of capitalist accumulation." The school is "situated in the heart of sociopolitical conflict," reflecting these "tensions." Educational change is a product of internal conflicts within the state. At different historical periods (partly depending on the strength of social reform movements), either the democratic or reproductive capitalist ethos dominates. Dominated groups can make "authentic" changes and gains. In turn, they produce changes in the basic rules of the political and educational "game," despite the prevailing influence of the capitalist class. In effect, they conclude that "school struggles and outcomes have an impact on the workplace and force change in civil society as well as in political society" (Carnoy and Levin, 1986, pp. 528-541).

Carnoy and Levin (1985) also analyze the relative utility of the progressive (Dewey), critical progressive (Goodman, Holt, Kozol), functionalist (Inkeles), critical functionalist (Althusser and Bowles and Gintis), critical autonomy (Apple, Giroux, and Willis), and their own model of educational change via social conflict. They counterpoise utilitarian, pluralist ("common good"), "class-perspective" (Marxist), structuralist, bureaucratic "third force," and their own "social conflict" theories of the state. For example, Carnoy and Levin summarize Offe's (with Ronge, 1975) views on state autonomy and the "representative" role bureaucracy plays. Bureaucrats must satisfy the interests of the capitalist class. Yet, bureaucrats simultaneously increase labor's power via educational programs while legitimizing themselves by meeting certain demands of labor while ensuring profitability and a smooth-functioning economy. For Offe, the bureaucracy actually coalesces the interests of the capitalist class and serves as an "independent" mediator for struggles over capital accumulation. But the "crisis of legitimation" resulting from performing these bureaucratic roles makes the state a battleground for conflict resolution. Education allows the state to be legitimate, reproduce capitalism, and ensure employability for labor. Carnoy and Levin, however, claim that Offe's and Ronge's analysis of education is too unidimensional, neglects other "ideological apparatuses" (such as mass media), and underestimates the important role of social movements in ideological formation and in setting the state's agenda, rewards, and policies (Carnoy and Levin, 1985, pp. 15-45).

Carnoy's (1985) analysis of the political economy of education "treats education as a factor shaped by the power relations between different economic, political, and social groups." As he says, "how much education an individual gets, what education is obtained and the role of education in economic growth and income distribution are part and parcel of these power relations." Thus, his analysis requires a clear perspective on the governmental sector, the political system, and a functional "theory of the state." As he sees it, the state must mediate between employers and workers as well as between voters and capitalists, using education to provide a skilled workforce, to socialize workers, and to inculcate the appropriate ideology. Sometimes, these contradictory goals can overproduce educated workers or encourage workplace democracy, whether as intended or unintended outcomes of schooling (Carnoy, 1985, pp. 157-158; Carnoy and Levin, Winter 1986).

Critiques of the Reconceptualist Critics from the UK and the US: Cole and Liston

There is no unanimity in critical social science or pedagogical approaches, "schools" of thought, or even in personal theoretical or philosophical consistency over the years. This poses difficulties for the uninitiated reader's understanding of the broad dimensions of critical educational theory. For example, Cole (1988a and 1988b) examines the changing political philosophy of Bowles and Gintis. He makes a convincing case that these two authors' basic orientation in Schooling in Capitalist America (1976) agreed with reductionist Marxism (that is, base/superstructure and economic determinism) and revolutionary socialism. In their later article on "Contradiction and Reproduction in Educational Theory" (1981), they moved away from this position by tempering Marxism in their theory of sites (state, family, and capital production) and the practices which support personal, group, or class "interventions" to maintain or transform certain social realities. They also humanized and pluralized their definition of the state while simultaneously distancing themselves from a neo-Marxist stance, moving toward a liberal democratic formulation of the state as primarily a governmental institution.

Cole claims that Bowles and Gintis (1986) moved even further away from their original position to embrace "postliberal democracy" with its expanded personal economic rights (property) as well as political rights for citizens with "equal" rights, regardless of race, gender, or class. This shift proposes the revision, reconstruction, or destruction of current capitalist institutions through "workplace democracy," "democratic economic planning" through increased power and worker control, "community access to capital," reduced ("equitable") economic inequality, socially directed ("collective") capital "investment decisions," and "democratic accountability." However, these authors identify the most significant flaws in classic liberal theory. These include ignorance of exploitation and oppression, its application of principles (such as liberty and equality) to the state (but only liberty to the economy), its false distinction between a "private" economy and "public" state, and liberals" allowance for private exploitation, dominance, and/or oppression of "learners" in school, of the incarcerated, "uncivilized" races, and of "irrational" wives in the family (Cole, 1988b, pp. 459-460).

This critique, itself, consistently applies neo-Marxian analysis of key concepts (such as state domination and oppression, antipluralism and liberalism, class, gender, racial exploitation, hegemony, labor solidarity, and discourse analysis) to Bowles' and Gintis' writings, theory, and philosophy. As such, Cole may well be more faithful to the British or European school of Marxist analysis, just as Bowles and Gintis are both products of, and are reacting to, the perhaps stronger liberal (both individual and especially social) tradition in American political culture (also see Cole, 1989).

Liston (May 1988, pp. 323-350) analyzes some changing contexts and neo-Marxist positions on schooling and social reproduction theories. For the latter, he says that "little reliable empirical knowledge has been ascertained" to support their functional/logical explanations. These are often stated in tautological terms. Frequently, Liston maintains, the arguments of Bowles and Gintis (1976), Apple (1982a, 1982b, and 1983), and Carnoy and Levin (1985) employ "weak" functional explanations. Thus, effects are noted, institutional or agency functions are attributed, and this course of reasoning is considered equal to (or sufficient for) an explanation for the described social phenomenon. By comparison, "real" functional explanations clearly identify real effects, then prove a practice or institution exists because of, to maintain, and/or as a cause of this given effect (for example, schools exist to maintain the society as it is; or school tracking systems exist to minimize economic crises or to legitimize the capitalist order in capitalist societies). Such "facile" functional explanations are also applied to other assertions. These propose that, while schools exist to maintain the capitalist system, they also conflict with (or contradict) this order. This happens because their capital accumulation and meritocratic or legitimating roles may clash with the social order if those who "strive" in schools do not find jobs and "thrive" later in the economic world. Such explanations would be more soundly based, Liston maintains, if they could show how school affects "products" or if outcomes explain why schools are as they are (causation), not merely their either sustaining or contradicting capitalism and its related effects (Liston, May 1988, pp. 328-330).

Liston also describes the variety of philosophical underpinnings in various neo-Marxist analyses of schooling. Bowles and Gintis are responsible for shared insights, such as "historical correspondence." This theory shows that when major economic transformations occurred, power and class structures and relationships changed and the educational (cultural) superstructure mirrored these altered economic conditions. There is also the more specific phenomenon of school-work-life correspondence where the social division of labor is reinforced in schools by maintaining class structures and cultivating relevant parental expectations. Consequently, professional parents expect self-motivation and a free-wheeling or open work/school atmosphere. The working class "prefers" a restrictive and controlling educational climate because it reflects their personal modes of routinized, meaningless, and orderly work life. Correspondence (Bowles and Gintis, 1976) is also based on an economic determinist model. That is, the forces and relations of production determine the forms, meanings, structures, and processes of schooling as well as other social institutions (superstructures). This model also accounts for contradictions and conflicts (sometimes "muted") in the economic sphere, which are responsible for subsequent educational conflicts and changes as well. Schools also require students to compete, rather than cooperate, with one another for grades and "honors." Since students lack self-motivation, they only respond to external rewards. The credentialing system, the top-down organization of school hierarchy, and the deskilling of teachers (via prepackaged curricula and diminished professionalism) lead to the legitimation of prevailing social norms and rules for work life management.

Because schools reflect the class, race, and gender structures of the general society, they try to respond to a multiplicity of competing demands from employers, workers, educators, parents, and politicians. All help to influence tracking, hierarchy, curriculum, teachers, resource allocation, and other aspects of schooling. Schooling may also be considered a democratic "right" of all citizens. Consequently, a certain amount of excellence and equality through democratic schooling (if properly understood) may be possible. It can result in social transformation through theoretically informed action (praxis), along with an informed understanding of the close connections between capitalism and schooling (Liston, May 1988, pp. 334-342).

Tracking must be examined through empirical and qualitative studies of differential, class-based curricula, which subsequently result in higher social status as well as greater social and economic power. Informed studies (with a proper theoretical base) can produce findings which will help to meet functionalist criticisms as well as to provide grounded underpinnings for the theoretical construct being examined. Historical studies (with case studies of tracking controversies at the urban level) can show the influence and interest of business classes in a tracking system and a differential class-based curriculum. In this way, Liston contends, a structure or procedure can be shown to produce interactive effects which feed back into its maintenance based on these supporting effects (Liston, May 1988, pp. 344-348).

A Comparative (Swedish) Perspective: Englund

Englund provides a useful comparison among patriarchal, scientific-rational, and democratic conceptions of democracy, equality, the good society, rationality, science, individualism, schooling, literacy, and politics. While the neoconservative position is based on the patriarchal conception and includes formal, elite, organic, valuative, idealistic, atomistic, private, nationalistic, reformist, religious, legalistic, and cultural values, the scientific-rational (or what Fischer, 1990, calls the "technocratic rationality") model is based on funtionalism, equal opportunity, the market, positivism, individualism, choice, private values, vocationalism, progress-ivism, empiricism, political neutrality, and utility. He prefers the democratic conception, which is participatory, results- and human-rights-oriented, pluralistic, neopragmatic, communitarian, comprehensive, public-welfare-minded, critical reconstructionist, and devoted to popular political and social education for conflict resolution.

Perceiving civic education as an example of both the politics of education and a case of politics and education allows for an analysis of curriculum as a political problem in Sweden and other countries. Englund (1986) analyzes criticisms of Freeman Butts' unitary approach to American citizenship as historical study by detailing his stress on unum over pluribus in social studies education. Butts" critics affirm that no social consensus exists on unitary values. The educator should reflect social tensions and conflicts (not just some artificial consensus) and increase the public's capacity for civic discussion and the formation of new publics, not parrot state or media-sponsored official ideology. Along with Giroux, he sees the civic educator helping create a new public philosophy of education, learning, and citizenship (apart from the state), raising citizenship to a complete ethical, moral, and social (not merely political) philosophy for "developing democratic and just communities" self-governed via ethical public leadership principles (Englund, 1986, pp. 328-330) Englund shares English and American views of civic education as political involvement, activity, and participation. The goals of citizen "awareness" and "responsibility for political decisions" are highly valued. He agrees with Giroux (1983a and 1984) and Giarelli (1983) that the civic educator should lead public discussions. There, the public can discharge their civic purposes by exercising the "office" of citizen to form new publics. We need new "public spheres" where people can learn and apply their skills to "the wider political, social, and cultural processes." Citizenship should not be viewed as a function of the state, as Giroux maintains, but as a "quality" that applies to all of social life. As Giroux says, the goals of this type of citizenship are "critical literacy," "social empowerment," and "developing democratic and just communities" through an informed citizenry that is "capable of exercising political and ethical leadership in the public sphere" (Englund, 1986, pp. 329-330; Giarelli, 1983, p. 35; and Giroux, 1984, pp. 190 and 192).

Ethnography, Critical Studies, and Politics

Certain "interpretive approaches" also contribute to the study of education and schooling from a comparative perspective on micro systems or "the world of everyday life." This ethnographic perspective focuses on social reality in the schools, observations there, and social interactions, while using videotaped or audio-recorded documentaries (Tobin, 1989, pp. 173-177). "Critical approaches" to the ethnography of schooling "emphasize class conflict, the dissimilar interests of various classes, and their differing relationship to (and benefits from) the workings of the educational system" (Masemann, February 1982, p. 9). "Conflict approaches" also have social (and structural) theoretical underpinnings, but are less compatible with functionalist approaches. These approaches see schools as agents for the "reproduction of society," where personality trait reinforcement prepares different classes for economic roles as workers or managers. They posit a "theory of correspondence," in which "social relations of production are mirrored in the social relations of education." For example, some theorize that schools stratify and produce the "cultural capital" (ideas, ideology, etc.) the dominant class needs. Teachers, like workers, are becoming "deskilled" professionals with ready-made, prepackaged curriculum. Key research topics include student alienation, curriculum packaging, credentialing, required courses, norms of prediction, social control mechanisms, socialization practices, and miscommunication. Student "resistance" to such manipulations include cheating, distancing, absenteeism, mindlessness, inattention, avoidance, or rebellion. Praxis is avoided since schooling, knowledge, and credentials are not usefully applied, only "banked" for future use (Masemann, February 1982, pp. 5-14).

Specific ethnographic research on school socialization and desegregation policy produced much harsher conclusions about democratic socialization and racial equality practices in public schools (Wilcox 1982a and 1982b; Hanna, 1982). Wilcox (1982a) asserts that schools transmit culture and socialize children for "available" adult work roles. Adult work roles are highly differentiated and stratified. Therefore, while US schools are supposed to encourage equal opportunity, they also stratify persons for future jobs by teaching and evaluating those cognitive skills, learning abilities, and technical skills ("human capital") deemed useful for later work life. They also develop appropriate roles for workers and managers through "self-preparation" for the work hierarchy. Personality factors which are appropriate for relating to authority differ from one job role to another, with some being "externally" (assembly line workers) and others "internally" (managers) motivated. These critiques of multidimensional sources and self-image development (anticipatory socialization) have major implications for schooling, the social context of the classroom, the teachers" interactions with students and parents, and vice versa (Wilcox, 1982a, pp. 268-309).

Micro- and macro-level perspectives on schooling and change also interest ethnographers. Teachers often use closed control systems and restricted language, even in "open" classrooms where they monopolize some class time for management. Merely having (or paying lip service to) learning centers and individualized learning practices does not necessarily reduce "authoritarian teacher control mechanisms," which are used more harshly against lower-SES students. Black children in white-dominated classrooms are resegregated by achievement levels, even without tracking. Administrative ignorance and unwillingness to help teachers experiencing difficulty in newly integrated schools was also observed. No conjoint, multicultural curricula developments were supported, nor was outreach to minority parents attempted. (Parents are systematically excluded from schools, as a rule.) Different class members learn similar roles in the schools. But the values of success in the general society predominate when school/societal discontinuities occur. By detailing such relations, ethnography helps us compile a more dynamic view of what happens to whom, and with what lasting effects, in schools (Wilcox, 1982b, pp. 462-478).

Do Current Trends in Critical Educational Theory Parallel and Reinforce or Contradict Recent Developments in US Political Science, Socialization Research and/or Civic Educational Reforms?

Political Science and Decision Making

American political science is still searching for a disciplinary core by discussing methods, processes, and the role of different subfields and concepts. Some relevant and useful unifying concepts include power, influence, authority, political "values," the state, politics, and government. Appropriate accepted research methods and political processes are behavioral, neo-Marxist, statistical, postbehavioral, qualitative, philosophical, psychological, public or rational choice, pluralism, and decision/policy making approaches. Certain subfields of analysis identify political theory, public policy, or the general study of politics or governments as key elements in such a core. While political science remains undisciplined, political scientists intuitively recognize and embrace something or someone as their own and reject that (or someone's work) which is not. In many respects, what is left of a diffuse political science core is merely a shared focus on the process of policy analysis or decision making of a common vocabulary which allows comprehensible discourse to occur in a continuous metadiscourse with colleagues in the same field or subfield (Monroe, et al., March 1990, pp. 34-43; Farnen, 1990, pp. 29-48; Almond, Fall 1988, pp. 828-842).

The "Discipline" of Political Science as an Undisciplined Field of Study

The relevance and applicability of critical social science and radical educational theories to US political science, socialization, and education research and writing are still unclear, undeveloped, tangential, and weak. There are neo-Marxist, radical, or new left political analysts in the academy; but they mainly prod, arouse or act as scapegoats for centrist-oriented colleagues. Mainstreamers often treat them in a condescending way, much like carnival freaks - something human and alive, but bizarrely deformed and sometimes repulsive. Only in certain conceptual areas, political topics, or cultural sites do political scientists and critical social and educational theorists have opportunities to come together. Instances such as discussions about the politics of education, collective union negotiations, social or cultural "capital," civic education, or the "hidden curriculum" provide occasions for mainline political scientists to discuss relevant "left-wing" theoretical and evidentiary constructs. These marginal intersections "mainstream" these ideas into the continuing public discourse about the relevance of political questions to learning, schooling, civic education, and public educational policy.

In this regard, Dryzek and Leonard maintain there is no exclusive tradition in American political science, saying that "disciplinary pluralism is the norm, and the existence of skepticism itself accentuates that pluralism." They claim that the profession has often been involved in "real politics" and just at the right time as well. As they observe, recent currents of disciplinary skepticism very aptly reflect present political realities and "the context of a polity and a discipline that have lost their bearings" (Dryzek and Leonard, December 1988, pp. 1256-1257; Dryzek, May 1986).

Critical Pedagogy, Political Science, and Political Education: Some Developmental Parallels, Clashes, and Collisions

Most recent discussions on core values and appropriate methods in contemporary US political science seem singularly unenlightened about many questions which have motivated political study. These involve the nature and purpose of human beings, society, the state, and government as well as contrasting views about the good society and paths or policy choices which might be taken to achieve the public good either today or tomorrow. Instead, US political scientists are overly concerned about conversational themes such as pluralism, objectivity, political neutrality, and the primacy of classic democratic political theory in their intra-disciplinary discussions.

But which themes of critical educational theory appear most useful for both enlightening and "liberating" American political science, citizenship education, and political socialization research? Critical educational theorists and social scientists add to our knowledge about politics, education, and socialization in several areas. Nevertheless, there are several other areas where conspicuous "silences" in their texts provide few satisfactory answers to still other pressing current problems. A review of these contrasting contributions may help answer this question.

A Workable Theory of the State

The first productive area stemming from trends in critical social science resurrects discussions about a current and viable theory of the modern state. Much of political science, civic education, and socialization research has no clear concept of what the state, government, or civil authority is supposed to do, what it does, or why it does what it does. Vague formulations of popular sovereignty are combined with a penchant for participation to achieve abstract notions of democratic fulfillment. In this regard, critical social scientists clearly oppose the liberal/capitalist state's basic values and manifestations (Offe and Ronge, 1977). These challenges are both radical and essential to an appreciation of the central questions of power, authority, bureaucracy, legitimacy, justice, freedom, solidarity, and equity (Carnoy, 1984 and 1985).

Radical theorists clarify this aspect of their political and educational philosophy while challenging their detractors to debate alternative views with appropriate evidence, knowledge, and value claims. Therefore, as Macpherson (1977) and Finkelstein (1984) observed, radical philosophical critics helped raise basic political and teleological questions about the nature, nurture, and purpose of human beings, society, and government. Alternatively, their self-satisfied liberal and conservative opponents prefer to ignore such questions or to assume answers to them as part of the conventional wisdom. But little in the contemporary debate about the nature of political science is concerned with a viable theory of the modern democratic state. In fact, when the right proposes statist ideas, the left (not the center) has felt most compelled to respond to their undemocratic elitism, self-serving economic and class-based motivations and their reduction of human interaction to self-interest, exchange relationships, and moral/ethical anarchy or conformity.

Using critical social science perspectives to analyze US public policy making, some American scholars questioned the normative, ethical, political, and philosophical basis for neoconservative and liberal notions of efficiency, "the market," and cost benefit analysis (Fischer and Forester, 1987). Fischer's (1990) analysis helps us spot links between the postindustrial economy and the new administrative state. Within a nonpositivist and democratic framework, Fischer proposes redesigning bureaucratic institutions to counter their "managerial bias" by encouraging "participatory expertise" in community cooperatives, democratized work settings, "alternative technology projects," "new social movements," and achieving social reconstruction via a form of "political ergonomics" in policy making (Fischer, 1990, pp. 7-11 and 13-35). This analysis has implications for across-the-board educational reform.

Liberal Culture and Everyday Politics

A second useful area is radical theory's emphasis on practical political culture as "lived culture," the politics of everyday life, and schooling as an actual experience. While frequently argued in abstract terms (for example, resistance, cultural reproduction, and correspondence theory), the basic point of the struggles, the commonplace, the agony and the ecstasy of everyday work, school life, and community interactions is that these chronicles are real experiences. Accounts of them enlighten the reader; evoke empathy, understanding, and compassion for those whose daily lives are very different from political science textbooks or televised soap-opera myths. Thus, there is some congruence with the subfield of political science/behavior which studies political "patterns in everyday life." To illustrate, Peterson (1990) summarized research on "ordinary people" and politics, including the politics of sex, family, workplace, clubs, religion, and media. For example, the person on the street thinks of politics as the government (state), power, and influence; as functions and evaluations; and as political actors. Ordinary people see politics as part of church, family, work, and club life.

In terms of decision making, the family had the greatest effect on participation and efficacy levels and the church the least influence. This study corroborated the powerful effects of education and income on influencing decision making and decision makers, whether in interest groups, clubs, or traditional forms of political participation. Merely acknowledging that politics happens in everyday life translates into greater influence over decision making in such group settings. Peterson concludes that while SES, education, and gender influence civic orientations and political decision-making participation, it is equally true that greater political efficacy and participation in decision making in everyday institutions also influence formal political decision making and increased participation (Peterson, 1990, pp. 39-55).

Politics of/and Education

Also interesting is the concept of politics and education and the politics of education. Reconceptualists propose that politics is an educational process, while schooling is infused with political content, meanings, processes, and structures. Recognizing the state's role in schooling, the correspondence and reproduction theories, and the schools as independent sites for transformative democratic practices and principles all point to the unity of politics and education as well as the politics of the educational process. The formal and informal, overt and hidden, political and social curriculum is just one aspect of this unity in a democratic political polity between politics and education.

Furthermore, as Richard Merelman (June 1980, pp. 319-320) said when criticizing the hidden curriculum's alleged socially harmful effects, the problematic role of the schools in teaching democracy "is not just an educational problem, for education is a major arena of public policy. Educational failures are, ipso facto, policy failures." The failures of democratic education are also those of American politics.

Class, Gender, and "Minority" Status

Political science is also interested in the critical perspective on class, gender, race, and minority status in schools and the society. Though less developed than the class perspective on schooling, the emerging critique of patriarchy, the socially and individually destructive nature of racial and minority discrimination, and the related treatment of the powerless by the economically and politically privileged (in supposedly democratic societies) inform the field of political science. This should subsequently influence its professional agenda, obligations, and acceptable topics for research and analysis. For example, political socialization studies must not only deal with majoritarian values, processes, and knowledge, but also with alternative perspectives. Moreover, the pattern of social, economic, and political discrimination and the public's knowledge, feelings, and behaviors on this topic are necessary components of any new research agenda on political socialization, especially that conducted in a cross-national perspective.

The Social Dimension of Schooling

A related area of critical educational thought involves educational systems and developmental patterns. Certain radically oriented researchers examined patterns of educational growth, development, and experimentation in third-world and developing socialist systems. For example, these studies focused on the collective, group, and social dimensions of schooling as contrasted with the individualized mission of American and capitalist schooling. These findings not only show the degree to which changes in basic educational skills (such as literacy) are possible, but also the extent to which a social dimension to schooling can be successfully planned and developed. Teaching cooperation, teamwork, and group creativity is important. "Team" control over the work, standard setting, problem solving, or decision making tasks and other aspects of schooling (beyond individualism, olympic-style competition, and discriminatory grading practices) is important for both postindustrial capitalistic and developing countries (Carnoy and Werthein, 1977).

Democratic Personalities in Their Social Contexts

Critical pedagogical theory's resurrection and appropriation of the Frankfurt School's and the American social reconstructionist philosophical traditions is significant to political science's renewed interest in pro-democratic and antiauthoritarian personality characteristics as well as their social and cultural manifestations, interactions, and reinforcements. For example, the earlier work of Fromm, Adorno, and Marcuse on empirical-theoretical links, the authoritarian personality's "escape from freedom," and the process of dialectical interrogation across the cultural spectrum (for example, media, politics, aesthetics, and education) is valuable in creating "the sane society." This is especially true with the end of the cold war because the nationalistic imperatives engendered for over 40 years in the West impacted authoritarianism and its cultural correlates (such as antiauthoritarianism and democracy) in the US and other countries. Farnen (July 1991 and 1992), Meloen (1992), and Hagendoorn (November 1991) discussed the relevance of authoritarianism, militarism, nationalism, cultural hegemony, ethnocentrism, and dogmatism to the study of democracy and education.

Ethnography (Cultural Studies)

The progress which radical ethnographers, critical educational theorists, or English practitioners of cultural studies (such as Willis and Anyon) made in combining cultural studies and theoretical constructs with the ethnographic method shows the power of this qualitative approach to "thickly descriptive" analysis of "lived lives" and school "cultures." To unravel the mysteries underlying significant questions (such as "Do schools really make any difference?"), critical ethnographers uncovered the basic outlines of hierarchy, cultural dominance, and class hegemony which operate in capitalist schools. In schools today, the correspondence and reproduction principles function along with strains of resistance and transformative possibility.

Policy Making and Political Socialization

Critical social science research in public/educational policy making and for political socialization research is also valuable. While many critical educational theorists dismiss much of the work on political socialization and educational politics and decision making as theoretically uninformed, liberally biased, and counterproductive for depicting both the reality of schooling and the possibility for reform, they offer few constructive alternatives, models, or actual case studies as a more viable approach. However, the work of Willis, et al. (1988) on the social conditions of youth in Wolverhampton, England provides some insight. This radical policy research and cultural studies project focused on a local economy, youth unemployment, relevant survey findings, and a "qualitative" picture of youth culture and local youth services. Its goal was development of "a policy and institutional framework capable of grasping the full range of needs of young adults and empowered to respond to them in a coordinated and integrated way" (Willis, et al., 1988, p. 3).

Policy proposals based on this research study include coordinating local policy, structuring (not individualizing) concepts of unemployment, combating redundancy and victimization approaches, establishing empowerment through problem self-definition, developing a collective focus on a "policy/services/resources" package, and trying "riskier" and more liberating policies than now exist. Even more specific policy proposals for a local council, enlightened policy statement, bureaucratic restructuring, and a town "youth site" are proposed in accordance with a youth-developed "charter" (Willis, et al., 1988, pp. 231-243). This type of action-oriented and theoretically informed research could be applied to political socialization, multicultural education, and civic education curriculum projects in other research settings.

The Hidden and Explicit Curricula

New left and neo-Marxist discussions of the "hidden curriculum" (as versus the formal curriculum) not only interest political scientists and educators, but they actually provoked a heated debate in American Political Science Review during 1980 and 1981. At that time, two prominent political scientists (Richard Merelman and M. Kent Jennings) engaged in a spirited exchange. Merelman (June 1980) claimed that democratic schooling did not seem to make much difference, whereas Jennings (June 1980) held that it did. (For an evaluation of this exchange, see Farnen, 1990, pp. 54-61; also see Merelman, March 1981, and Jennings, March 1981, for their final views on this subject.)

When this debate continued the following year, it mainly devolved into an argument about which scholar could provide more statistics supporting the influence of education on democratic values. More to the point is Giroux's perspective on the Merelman argument, which he terms part of "the liberal problematic." Giroux (in Giroux and Purpel, 1983) faults Merelman (ignoring Jennings) for not seeing that the intraschool division he describes "may have its roots in the dominant society" (that is, in "the very nature of capitalist society" which restricts democracy to politics and inequality to economics). Instead, Giroux attributes to Merelman characteristics that typify "the liberal perspective in general" (that is, "little or no understanding" of how social conditions create "oppressive features of schooling," as well as "the ideological texture of school life"). There is no room in the liberal view for evaluating "contradictory knowledge claims" or explaining both how such a "reality" emerged or how it may be successfully resisted through "critical thinking or constructive dialogue." The alternative, radical approach to the hidden curriculum does not merely dismiss the phenomenon as a "structural constraint" or consensus-producing techniques, but rather uses it as a "focus on conflict" and "on social structures and the construction of meaning" (that is, it questions reproduction, "dominance," "exploitation," and class "inequality") (Giroux and Purpel, 1983, pp. 54-56; Giroux and Penna, 1981, pp. 209-230).

These three perspectives show that there is both a pluralism in (and division among) political science views about the hidden curriculum. It is also relevant to current disciplinary discourse and its modernistic "great conversation." But radical critics obviously hit a very sore spot by attacking present formulations of democratic schooling. This discussion illustrates the lack of engagement and what Giroux called "constructive dialogue" between the radical and traditional political science communities. The Merelman-Jennings debate lost sight of the radical critique, posed an alternative model, quarreled over the democratic relevance of schooling, and heaped statistical evidence (minus any theoretical underpinnings) on one another without a real debate over the radical critique up by the phrase "the hidden curriculum." None of the information in the American political socialization and ethnographic literature on class and racial divisions (the work of Litt, Jaros, Greenberg, et al., reprinted in Bell, 1973, pp. 91-128 and 189-299; Anyon, 1979 and 1980) was discussed. Nor were the radical critics asked to reply to the terms of this debate. This left a huge silence instead of useful answers. Such deficiencies surely need correction in future encounters of this sort.

Political Education

Finally, we focus on civic education, citizenship, and political education. The utility of the radical critique in this respect is its formulations of both the "hidden curriculum" and other useful constructs (such as resistance and the possibility of transforming schools which may exert a liberating and emancipatory influence on students, teachers, and the society itself). This critique is holistic in its approach because schooling is placed in the context of the home, media, job, and across all groups, institutional, individual, internal, and external agents and levels in a lifelong perspective.

Since the radical critique has mostly been at the theoretical level (because of its roots in classic and neo-Marxist, Gramsci, Friere, Dewey, and Frankfurt School analysis), the details of how one creates a radical curriculum (that is, educational praxis) have not been superabundant. But we now have some indications of what this more mundane aspect of schooling actually means.

As an alternative to traditional models, Apple and King want schools to move beyond mere reproduction of work and rhetorical humanistic models to a Gramscian analysis of the school site as an ideological setting by asking: Whose interests do the schools serve? How are cultural and economic capital distributed? Can institutions "enhance meaning and lessen control?" What are these social interests? But they expect no consensual or monolithic answers (Apple and King, 1983, pp. 82-99). Giroux's "new sociology of curriculum" is also based on the answers to questions about the curriculum, such as: What is such knowledge? How is it produced? How does the classroom reproduce the workplace? Where does its legitimacy come from? In whose interests? How are "contradictions and tensions" over knowledge mediated? And, what legitimizing role does evaluation play? (Giroux, 1981b, p. 104). Giroux's view of citizenship education as evoking civic courage among an active, involved, public-minded citizenry to produce just and democratic communities also sets a context for such interrogations. Still other radical political economists applaud Piagetian active cognitive formulations and reject Kohlberg's moral stages as an irrelevant discourse about moral development without a basis in "the coordinates of social action" (Huebner, 1981, p. 134). Yet, Giroux and Purpel (1983, pp. 61-81) think enough of Kohlberg to include his piece on "the moral atmosphere of the school."

Radical democratic educators have not yet come to terms with stage, developmental, moral, or structural/functional cognitive theory or with decision making, problem solving, or cross-national political socialization findings. An entire generation of recent research in these areas remains beyond the pale of the reconceptualists (Farnen, July 1991 and November 1991). While these findings might benefit from post-hoc critical pedagogical scrutiny, it might be more fruitful for radical educationists to join such cross-national research projects to influence the questions asked of whom as well as when, where, and why we should ask them. In this respect, the more culture-bound Anglo-Saxon theoretical constructs which inform critical social science and educational study in the US, UK, and Germany (for example, the liberal and neoconservative critique) may be quite inappropriate in a former state-socialist-command economic/political system (such as Hungary), whereas the correspondence, resistance, and implicit curriculum concepts may fare better. An Hungarian listening to a neo-Marxian analyze schooling might think these missionaries of the left had arrived 45 years too late since they have only just begun to develop the market, democracy, civil society, or opportunities for choice among competing public philosophies and policies.

Conclusions

In assessing the relevance of reconceptualism to political science, political education, and political socialization, the great virtue of this diverse school of thought (which is united only through a common political economy, social justice, and transformational nexus) is its dialectical and interrogatory approach to schooling, the state, politics, social traditions, and the economy. In performing this controversial and often negative critique, the uninitiated reader has no secure curriculum, evaluation, or teaching technique safety net. Although the neophyte reader is exposed to a myriad of "what's wrongs and what not to dos," there are "silences" about what will work and why. For example, critical pedagogy does not enlighten us about developmental stages or stances or about cognitive psychology, schema theory, and/or whether these ideas can be radicalized, reconceptualized, or made to withstand rigorous interrogation. While not differing much from humanistic evaluators, radical critics often focus on teacher training rather than on the teachers of teachers and/or students, curriculum, and instruction (that is, the latter is perhaps the actual "stuff" of schooling). While an educational philosophy is admirable and an enlightened theory may emancipate us all, there is also a danger of orthodoxy, intolerance, and conformity to one theoretical principle: that espoused by the political economists of schooling. Consequently, the reader must keep track of who is up and who is down on the list of acceptable reconceptualists or "right thinkers." Adding to the confusion, radical theorists score their hits and errors differently.

There is also a potentially dogmatic strain in the radical critique, which itself must be offset through a commitment to honest dialogue and debate. This purpose is not well served when the opposition is demonized as the "enemy," using schools and other "ideological state apparatuses" to spread reproduction-based "myths" of pluralism and liberalism. Excoriating the conservative philosophy of schooling as essentially undemocratic is one thing, but linking the "misguided" liberal innocenti as fellow travelers of the right wing is quite another. While conservatives may be as economically deterministic as the most radical neo-Marxists, 20th century social liberals have merely to reorganize their political views along more social democratic and critical educational lines to reach a working consensus with the critical left.

And so it might go with other topics on the US national agenda. These include the probable critical stand on individuals and teachers determining what both learn in school, the need for commonality in theory, but an appreciation of multi-culturalism while working to offset race/class/gender oppression in both schools and society, and opposing values "transmission" in favor of their mutual development through a liberating curriculum process.

These are just a few of the primary issues in the American educational debate in addition to those previously mentioned, such as parental educational vouchers ("choice"), merit pay, antidiversity, competition, and the America 2000 educational policy agenda (Klein, 25 August 1991, pp. 4-7). To be more effective, the radical critique could be deployed for or against such conservative policy proposals (or partially in favor of certain social liberal alternatives). Not to be more fully involved in this debate is to allow the strong forces of resurgent traditionalism and phoney individualism to go unchallenged and uninterrogated. After all, radical pedagogy and social science are both internally and externally controversial – as both its fundamental nature and developmental designs oblige reconceptualism to be.

References

Almond, G. (Fall 1988). "Separate Tables: Schools and Sects in Political Science," pp. 828-842 in *PS: Political Science and Politics*, Vol. 21, No. 4.

Althusser, L. (1971). *Lenin and Philosophy and Other Essays*. New York, NY: Monthly Review Press.

Anderson, L., et al. (April 1990). *The Civics Report Card*. Princeton, NJ: Educational Testing Service.

Anyon, J. (1979). "Ideology and United States History Textbooks," pp. 21-39 in R. Dale, et al. (eds.) (1981) *Education and the State*, Vol. 1. Lewes, Sussex, UK: The Falmer Press.

Anyon, J. (1980). "Social Class and the Hidden Curriculum of Work," pp. 317-341 in H. Giroux, A. Penna, and W. Pinar (eds.) (1981) *Curriculum and Instruction*. Berkeley, CA: McCutchan.

Anyon, J. (1983). "Intersections of Gender and Class: Accommodation and Resistance by Working Class and Affluent Females to Contradictory Sex Role Ideologies," pp. 19-37 in S. Walker and L. Barton (eds.) *Gender, Class, and Education*. Lewes, Sussex, UK: The Falmer Press.

Apple, M. (Spring 1979). "What Correspondence Theories of the Hidden Curriculum Miss," pp. 101-12 in *The Review of Education*, Vol. 5, No. 2.

Apple, M. (Spring 1980). "Analyzing Determinations: Understanding and Evaluating the Production of Social Outcomes in Schools," pp. 55-76 in *Curriculum Inquiry*, Vol. 10.

Apple, M. (1982a). *Education and Power*. Boston, MA: Routledge and Kegan Paul.

Apple, M. (ed.) (1982b). *Cultural and Economic Reproduction in Education. Essays on Class, Ideology, and the State*. London, UK: Routledge and Kegan Paul.

Apple, M. (1983). "Work, Class, and Teaching," pp. 53-67 in S. Walker and L. Barton (eds.) *Gender, Class, and Education*. Lewes, Sussex, UK: The Falmer Press.

Apple, M. (1988). *Teachers and Texts*. New York, NY: Routledge, Chapman and Hall.

Apple, M. and N. King (1983). "What Do Schools Teach?" pp. 82-99 in H. Giroux and D. Purpel (eds.) *The Hidden Curriculum and Moral Education: Deception or Discovery*. Berkeley, CA: McCutchan.

Apple, M. and L. Weiss (eds.) (1983). *Ideology and Practice in Schooling*. Philadelphia, PA: Temple University Press.

Arnot, M. and G. Whitty (1982). "From Reproduction to Transformation: Recent Radical Perspectives on the Curriculum for the USA" pp. 93-103 in *British Journal of Sociology*, Vol. 3, No. 1.

Aronowitz, S. and H. Giroux (1985). *Education Under Siege*. South Hadley, MA: Bergin and Garvey.

Aronowitz, S. and H. Giroux (1991). *Post-modern Education*. Minneapolis, MN: University of Minnesota Press.

Bell, C. (ed.) (1973). *Growth and Change*. Encino, CA: Dickenson.

Bernstein, R. (1978). *The Restructuring of Social and Political Theory*. Philadelphia, PA: The University of Pennsylvania Press.

Bourdieu, P. (1973). "Cultural Reproduction and Social Reproduction," pp. 487-511 in J. Karabel and A. Halsey (eds.) (1977) *Power and Ideology in Education*. New York, NY: Oxford University Press.

Bourdieu, P. (1977). *Outline of Theory and Practice*. Cambridge, UK: Cambridge University Press.

Bourdieu, P. (1984). *Distinction: A Social Critique of the Judgment of Taste*. Cambridge, MA: Harvard University Press.

Bourdieu, P. and J. Passeron (1977). *Reproduction in Society, Education, and Culture*. London, UK and Beverly Hills, CA: Sage.

Bourdieu, P. and J. Passeron (1979). *The Inheritors. French Students and Their Relation to Culture*. Chicago, IL: University of Chicago Press.

Bowles, S. and H. Gintis (1976). *Schooling in Capitalist America*. New York, NY: Basic Books.

Bowles, S. and H. Gintis (1986). *Democracy and Capitalism*. New York, NY: Basic Books.

Bowles, S. and H. Gintis (1988). "Contradiction and Reproduction in Educational Theory," pp. 16-32 in M. Cole (ed.) *Bowles and Gintis Revisited: Correspondence and Contradiction in Educational Theory*. Lewes, Sussex, UK: The Falmer Press.

Carnoy, M. (1984). *The State and Political Theory*. Princeton, NJ: Princeton University Press.

Carnoy, M. (1985). "The Political Economy of Education," pp. 157-173 in *International Social Science Journal*, Vol. 37, No. 2.

Carnoy, M. and H. Levin (1985). *Schooling and Work in the Democratic State*. Stanford, CA: Stanford University Press.

Carnoy, M. and H. Levin (1986). "Educational Reform and Class Conflict," pp. 35-46 in *Journal of Education*, Vol. 168, No.1.

Carnoy, M. and H. Levin (Winter 1986). "But Can It Whistle?," pp. 528-541 in *Educational Studies*, Vol. 17, No. 4.

Carnoy, M. and J. Werthein (1977). "Socialist Ideology and the Transformation of Cuban Education," pp. 573-584 in J. Karabel and A. Halsey (eds.) *Power and Ideology in Education*. New York, NY: Oxford University Press.

Cole, M., ed. (1988a). *Bowles and Gintis Revisited: Correspondence and Contradiction in Educational Theory*. Lewes, Sussex, UK: The Falmer Press.

Cole, M. (1988b). "From Reductionist Marxism and Revolutionary Socialism to Post-Liberal Democracy and Ambiguity . . .," pp. 452-462 in *British Journal of Sociology*, Vol. 39, No. 3.

Cole, M. (1989). "Race" and Class or "Race" Class, Gender, and Community," pp. 118-29 in *British Journal of Sociology*, Vol. 40, No. 1.

Dryzek, J. (May 1986). "The Progress of Political Science," pp. 301-20 in *The Journal of Politics*, Vol. 48, No. 2.

Dryzek, J. and S. Leonard (December 1988). "History and Discipline in Political Science," pp. 1245-1260 in *American Political Science Review*, Vol. 82, No. 4.

Englund, T. (1986). *Curriculum As A Political Problem*. Stockholm, Sweden: Almqvist & Wiksell.

Farnen, R. (1990). *Integrating Political Science, Education, and Public Policy*. Frankfurt am Main, FRG: Verlag Peter Lang.

Farnen, R. (1993a). "Cognitive Political Maps: The Implications of Internal Schemata (Structures) versus External Factors (Content and Context) for Cross-National Political Research," pp. 212-281 in G. Csepeli, L. Keri, and I. Stumpf (eds.) *State and Citizen*. Budapest, Hungary: Institute of Political Science, Hungarian Academy of Sciences.

Farnen, R. (1993b). "Reconceptualizing Politics, Education, and Socialization: Cross-National Perspectives on Cognitive Studies, Problem Solving, and Decision making," pp. 375-459 in R. Farnen (ed.) *Reconceptualizing Politics, Socialization, and Education: International Perspectives for the 21st Century*. Oldenburg, FRG: University of Oldenburg BIS.

Farnen, R. (1994a). "Politics, Education, and Reconceptualism: Current Trends in Critical Theory, Political Science, and Socialization in the United States" (published in German as "Politik, Bildung und Paradigmenwechsel: Jüngste Trends in der Kritischen Pädogogik, in den politischen Wissenschaften, in den politischen Socialisation und in der politischen Bildung in den Vereinigten Staten," pp. 338-384 in H. Sünker, D. Timmermann, and F. Kolbe (eds.) *Bildung, Gesellschaft, Soziale Ungleichheit* (Education, Society, and Social Inequality). Frankfurt am Main, FRG: Suhrkamp Verlag.

Farnen, R. (1994b). "Nationality, Ethnicity, Political Socialization and Public Policy: Some Cross-National Perspectives," pp. 23-101 in R. Farnen (ed.) *Nationalism, Ethnicity, and Identity: Cross-National and Comparative Perspectives*. New Brunswick, NJ and London, UK: Transaction Publishers.

Farnen, R. (1994c). "Political Decision making, Problem Solving, and Decision making: American and Cross-National Perspectives," pp. 129-53 in S. Miedema, et al. (eds.) *The Politics of Human Science*. Brussels, Belgium: VUB Press.

Farnen, R. (1996). "Politische Sozialisation, Erziehung und kritische Theorie: Politik und Erziehung in den Vereinigten Staten" (Political Socialization, Education, and Critical Theory: Politics and Education in the United States), pp. 135-69 in W. Helsper, H. Krüger, and H. Wenzel (eds.) *Schule und Gesellschaft im Umbruch: Theoretische und internationale Perspektiven* (School and Society in Upheaval: Theoretical and International Perspectives), Vol. 1. Weinheim, FRG: Deutscher Studien Verlag.

Finkelstein, B. (November 1984). "Thinking Publicly about Civic Learning: An Agenda for Education Reform in the "80s," pp. 23-24 in A. Jones (ed.) (1985) *Civic Learning for Teachers: Capstone for Educational Reform*. Ann Arbor, MI: Prakken.

Fischer, F. (1990). *Technocracy and the Politics of Expertise*. Newbury Park, CA: Sage.

Fischer, F. and J. Forester (eds.) (1987). *Confronting Values in Policy Analysis*. Newbury Park, CA: Sage.

Giarelli, J. (1983). "The Public, The State, and Civic Education," pp. 33-36 in A. Bagley (ed.) *Civic Learning in Teacher Education*. Minneapolis/St. Paul, MN: College of Education, University of Minnesota

Gintis, H. and S. Bowles (1981). "Contradiction and Reproduction in Educational Theory," pp. 45-59 in R. Dale, et al. (eds.) *Education and the State*, Vol. 1. Lewes, Sussex, UK: The Falmer Press

Giroux, H. (1981a). *Ideology, Culture, and the Process of Schooling*. Philadelphia, PA: Temple University Press.

Giroux, H. (1981b). "Toward a New Sociology of Curriculum," pp. 98-108 in H. Giroux, A. Penna, and W. Pinar (eds.) *Curriculum and Instruction*. Berkeley, CA: McCutchan.

Giroux, H. (1984). "Public Philosophy and the Crisis in Education," pp. 186-194 in *Harvard Educational Review*, Vol. 54, No. 2.

Giroux, H. (ed.) (1991). *Post-modernism, Feminism, and Cultural Politics*. Albany, NY: State University of New York Press.

Giroux, H. and A. Penna (1981). "Social Education in the Classroom: The Dynamics of the Hidden Curriculum," pp. 209-230 in H. Giroux, A. Penna, and W. Pinar (eds.) *Curriculum and Instruction*. Berkeley, CA: McCutchan.

Giroux, H. and D. Purpel (eds.) (1983). *The Hidden Curriculum and Moral Education: Deception or Discovery*. Berkeley, CA: McCutchan.

Hagendoorn, L. (November 1991). "Authoritarianism, Education, and Democracy." Paper presented at the International Conference on "How To Be A Democrat In A Post-Communist Hungary," Center for Political Science, Hungarian Academy of Sciences, Balatonföldvár, Hungary.

Hanna, J. (1982). "Public School Policy and the Children's World: Implications of Ethnographic Research for Desegregated Schooling," pp. 316-355 in G. Spindler (ed.) *Doing the Ethnography of Schooling*. New York, NY: Holt Reinhart and Winston.

Huebner, D. (1981). "Toward a Political Economy of Curriculum and Human Development," pp. 124-138 in H. Giroux, A. Penna, and W. Pinar (eds.) *Curriculum and Instruction*. Berkeley, CA: McCutchan.

Illich, I. (1970). *Deschooling Society*. New York, NY: Harper and Row.

Jennings, M. (June 1980). "Comment on Richard Merelman's "Democratic Politics and the Culture of American Education"," pp. 333-337 in *American Political Science Review*, Vol. 74, No. 2.

Jennings, M. (March 1981). "Comment on the Merelman-Jennings Exchange," pp. 155-156 in *American Political Science Review*, Vol. 75, No. 1.

Klein, E. (August 25, 1991). "We're Talking About a Revolution," pp. 4-7 in *Parade Magazine*.

Liston, D. (May 1988). "Faith and Evidence: Examining Marxist Explanations of Schools," pp. 323-350 in *American Journal of Education*, Vol. 96, No. 3.

Macpherson, C. (1977). "Do We Need a Theory of the State?," pp. 61-75 in R. Dale, et al. (eds.) (1981), *Education and the State*, Vol. 1. Lewes, Sussex, UK: The Falmer Press.

Masemann, V. (February 1982). "Critical Ethnography in the Study of Comparative Education," pp. 1-15 in *Comparative Education Review*, Vol. 26, No. 1.

Meloen, J. (1992). "A Critical Analysis of Forty Years of Authoritarianism Research," pp. 128-165 in R. Farnen (ed.) *Nationalism, Ethnicity and Identity: Cross-National and Comparative Perspectives*. New Brunswick, NJ and London, UK: Transaction Publishers.

Merelman, R. (June 1980). "Democratic Politics and the Culture of American Education," pp. 319-332 in *American Political Science Review*, Vol. 74, No. 2.

Merelman, R. (March 1981). "Reply," pp. 156-158 in *American Political Science Review*, Vol. 75, No. 1.

Monroe, K., et al. (March 1990). "The Nature of Contemporary Political Science: A Roundtable Discussion," pp. 34-43 in *PS: Political Science and Politics*, Vol. 23, No. 1.

Offe, C. and V. Ronge (1975). "Theses on the Theory of the State," pp. 77-85 in R. Dale, et al. (eds.) (1981) *Education and the State*, Vol. 1. Lewes, Sussex, UK: The Falmer Press.

Peterson, S. (1990). *Political Behavior. Patterns in Everyday Life*. Newbury Park, CA: Sage.

Popkewitz, T. (May 1985). "Intellectuals, Sciences, and Pedagogies: Critical Traditions and Instrumental Cultures," pp. 429-436 in *American Journal of Education*, Vol. 93, No. 3.

Shirley, D. (1986). "A Critical Review and Appropriation of Pierre Bourdieu's Analysis of Social and Cultural Reproduction," pp. 96-112 in *Journal of Education*, Vol. 168, No. 2.

Smith, M., J. O'Day, and D. Cohen (Winter 1990). "National Curriculum American Style," pp. 10-17 and 40-47 in *American Educator*.

Spring, J. (1993). *Conflict of Interests: The Politics of American Education*, 2nd. Edition. New York, NY: Longmans.

Tirozzi, G. (May 19, 1991). "Bush's Education Plan is Too Limited to Have a Real Impact," p. E3 in *The Hartford Courant*.

Tobin, J. (1989). "Visual Anthropology and Multivocal Ethnography: A Dialogical Approach to Japanese Preschool Class Size," pp. 173-187 in *Dialectical Anthropology*, Vol. 13.

Wilcox, K. (1982a). "Differential Socialization in the Classroom: Implications for Equal Opportunity," pp. 268-309 in G. Spindler (ed.) *Doing the Ethnography of Schooling*. New York, NY: Holt Reinhart and Winston.

Wilcox, K. (1982b). "Ethnography as a Methodology and Its Application to the Study of Schooling: A Review," pp. 456-488 in G. Spindler (ed.) *Doing the Ethnography of Schooling*. New York, NY: Holt Reinhart and Winston.

Willis, P. (1981). "Cultural Production Is Different from Cultural Reproduction is Different from Social Reproduction is Different from Reproduction," pp. 48-67 in *Interchange on Educational Policy*, Vol. 12, Nos. 2-3.

Willis, P., et al. (1988). *The Youth Review: Social Conditions of Young People in Wolverhampton*. Aldershot, Hants, UK: Avebury, Gower.

Wood, G. (Spring 1982). "Beyond Radical Educational Cynicism," pp. 55-71 in *Educational Theory*, Vol. 32, No. 2.

Part 2
Media Use, Government, and Websites

Chapter 5

Media Use in the United States: Electronic Media Dramatically Up and Print Media Down

Daniel B. German

Professor (Emeritus) of Political Science, Appalachian State University, Boone, North Carolina, USA

Caitlin Lally

Communications Assistant for the National Governors Association, The George Washington University, Washington, DC, USA

Abstract

This research project traces the media use habits of children and adults. Over time, television consumption is increasing even though computer and Internet activities are also rapidly increasing. The American people are consuming greater amounts of electronic media while traditional newspaper use is declining. It appears that people are not connecting face to face as much as in the past and live more and more in the individualized world of media. Furthermore, a digital divide based on socio-economic status and race is evident. Blacks use television more than Whites and Hispanics and African Americans and Hispanics use the computer less than Whites. Both of the developments of increased media use and the digital divide do not bode well for 1) building the social capital of connectedness, and 2) widening access to political information which fuels democracy. The political socialization process and hence American political culture are developing new patterns which should be carefully monitored in the future.

Introduction

The most comprehensive media study in existence for children is administered and distributed by the Kaiser Family Foundation. The first comprehensive report released was in 1999, called Kids and Media at the New Millennium, which was the primary data source used for our previous research project, "Television and the Internet's Effects on the Socialization of American Children" (German and Lally, 2005). As the Kaiser Family Foundation found it necessary to update their report in 2004 due to significant changes in media technology, it is important to continue to write about what types of implications these significant changes have for the future of American society. Furthermore, it is necessary to examine the patterns of media use by all Americans – not just children – as the current trend in the US has become particularly focused on a consumer society in which the individual reigns supreme and participation in community activities is increasingly absent. To supplement what the Kaiser Family Foundation has done for children, the US Department of Commerce has put together "A Nation Online," a two-part publication exploring how Americans use the Internet and the effects of the rapidly growing broadband technologies on media consumption, and a study released by the Pew Research Center entitled "Internet News Takes Off" (Pew Research Center, 2005). Although these studies are not as comprehensive as the Kaiser project, they serve as a good indication about who is accessing what types of media and what they are concerned about while searching information. The issues most prevalent in American society related to media use tend to be 1) access, 2) amount of daily media use, and 3) content of media. These three factors are extremely important because not only do they result in a lack of participation in community activities (social capital), but also access and information quality may be a major contributing factor in what is known as the "digital divide" between socio-economic classes. This chapter begins with a discussion of the previous research and conclusions of several scholars, followed by a profile of American children's and adults' media consumption habits and access, and ends with a brief discussion of the implications these trends have for American society and politics.

Past and Present: Where Does American Society Stand Today When Compared to the Past?

In 2000, Robert Putnam released his book *Bowling Alone: The Collapse and Revival of American Community*. Since then, he has been considered one of the premier scholars on the issue of the waning fund of social capital in the US: "Civic engagement and social capital entail mutual obligation and responsibility for action" (Putnam, 2000, p. 21). He and many other scholars believe that the only way to repair social connections in the US is "to ask how the positive consequences of social capital – mutual support, cooperation, trust, institutional effectiveness – can be maximized and the negative manifestations – sectarianism, ethnocentrism, corruption – minimized" (Putnam, 2000, p. 22). According to Putnam, one form of social capital that is important to look at is participation in politics. While Americans participate at roughly the same levels as other democracies worldwide, albeit a bit lower in voter turnout, the important differences appear when examining what Putnam calls "inter and intra generational cohorts" (Putnam, 2000, pp. 32-27). Putnam says that while it is true that there are wide gaps in voter participation and general interest in politics both between generations and when comparing people of similar ages in differing decades, he believes that these are just the most visible symptoms of a larger problem that faces the American nation. While voting and information gathering can be done relatively alone, things like party identification and volunteering in political campaigns are more community-based activities that add to social networks. Party identification has dropped from around 75% in the 1960s to lower than 65% in the 1990s (Putnam, 2000, p. 38). The levels at which people worked for a party in the 1980s and 1990s have dropped by nearly 50% from the 1950s and 1960s; however, the number of people contacted by the parties was nearly 2.5 times greater in 1996 than in 1968 (Putnam, 2000, p. 39). Putnam notes that it is very hard to reconcile this fact and the growing intake of capital by the political parties, but he concludes that this is an indication of the "professionalization and commercialization of politics in America" and that this growth of money in politics simply has created professional politics aimed at mass marketing strategies (Putnam, 2000, pp. 39-49). Another important aspect of social capital is civic participation – in what numbers and how often are Americans participating in groups? Alexis de Tocqueville famously wrote:

> Americans of all ages, all stations in life, and all types of disposition are forever forming associations. There are not only commercial and industrial associations in which all take part, but others of a thousand different types – religious, moral, serious, futile, very general and very limited, immensely large and very minute … Nothing, in my view, deserves more attention than the intellectual and moral associations in America (cited in Putnam, 2000, p. 48).

However, the associations of today are truly a different beast from what de Tocqueville observed over 170 years ago. Increasingly, groups that have been founded after 1965 have mass membership and are what Putnam calls "mailing list organizations" (Putnam, 2000, p. 51). His example is the American Association of Retired Persons (AARP) in which fewer than 10% of its 33 million members actually attend any type of meeting. For many associations in the US today, there is little to no interaction; the only type of involvement necessary is writing and mailing a check (Putnam, 2000, p. 51). Putnam believes that it is important that we differentiate between these new types of organizations, which he refers to as "tertiary associations" where there is no social contact, and organizations like prayer groups or gardening clubs, which are called secondary associations. In tertiary associations, members' ties are to common beliefs and leaders but not to each other (Putnam, 2000, p. 52). As an example of the decline in participation of Americans in chapter-based organizations, Putnam cites the case of Parent Teacher Associations (PTAs). During the late 1950s and early 1960s, Parent Teacher Associations were at the height of their membership, with nearly 50% of parents with children under the age of 18 in school attending PTA meetings. Today, that membership level has decreased to less than 20% of parents with school-aged children participating in PTA meetings (Putnam, 2000, p. 57). So, Putnam points out that while many people look at growing membership trends in organizations, this may not be an accurate predictor of Americans' levels of civic engagement (Putnam, 2000, p. 58). We must look at active and involved membership encompassing face-to-face contact with members of a community.

A third type of social capital that Putnam discusses is religious participation. Members of religious groups are more likely to participate in other civic and political organizations. About 50% to 60% of churchgoing members volunteer at some organization as opposed to 30% to 35% of non-members (Putnam, 2000,

p. 67). Religious organizations have been at the cornerstone of many historic American movements – in particular the civil rights movement:

> The Black church functioned as the institutional center of the modern civil rights movement ... Churches provided the movement with an organized mass base; a leadership of clergymen largely economically independent of the larger white society and skilled in the art of managing people and resources; an institutionalized financial base through which the protest was financed; and meeting places where the masses planned tactics and strategies and collectively committed themselves to the struggle (Putnam, 2000, p. 68).

While there is much debate about what should be classified as church membership and which records are right – Gallup polls or church records – Putnam (2000, p. 72) concludes that claiming church membership and actual attendance have two different measures. While Americans are 10% less likely to claim church membership now than in the 1950s and 1960s, they are anywhere from 25% to 50% less likely to actually attend any church services. Some of the gaps in this data come particularly from people who claim a religion, but do not attend church (Putnam, 2000, p. 72). Again, as discussed in relation to political and civic engagement, significant religious participation can be seen between generational cohorts. People today are attending church in fewer numbers than people in similar age categories in the 1950s and 1960s and American churches today are far less engaged in the community, which only contributes to the declining social connectedness within communities (Putnam, 2000, p. 79). Specifically, "the boomers" born in the years immediately after World War II where an estimated two-thirds who were raised religious, "dropped out" of their religious tradition, as described by Wade Clark Roof and William McKinney:

> Large numbers of young, well-educated, middle class youth ... defected from the churches in the late sixties and the seventies … Some joined new religious movements, others sought personal enlightenment through various spiritual therapies and disciplines, but most simply 'dropped out' of organized religion altogether ... [The consequence was a] tendency toward highly individualized religious psychology without the benefits of strong supportive attachments to believing communities. A major impetus in this direction in the post-1960s was the thrust toward greater personal fulfilment and quest for the ideal self … In this climate of expressive individualism, religion tends to become 'privatized,' or more anchored in the personal realms (cited in Putnam, 2000, p. 74).

Why is American Society Losing Social Capital?

Most of the time when pollsters ask Americans why they tend not to participate in civic activities, the answer is "I don't have time." The number of Americans who "always feel rushed" has more than doubled since the 1960s (Putnam, 2000, p. 89). While there is still much debate, most economists fall into one of two categories when discussing whether or not Americans work more today than they did in the 1950s and 1960s. Some economists, such as Ellen McGrattan and Richard

Rogerson, say that Americans are working about the same number of hours per week as they have been since World War II (Putnam, 2000, p. 190). However, there are some economists, such as John Robinson and Geoffrey Godbey, who say that Americans actually have about 6.2 more hours of free time on average than they did in the 1950s. These economists attribute this figure to improved technology for housework, fewer children, and early retirement (Putnam, 2000, p. 190). While it may seem that some free time has been gained, scholars believe that this gain in leisure time seems only to affect less educated classes of people. In 1969, highly educated people worked an average of six hours more per week than high school educated people and in 1998, they worked 13 hours more per week. However, even if certain segments of the population seem to be busier than others, there is actually a positive correlation between number of hours worked and civic engagement (Putnam, 2000, p. 191).

As society progresses, technology, specifically the technology of communication, has become more and more present in our daily lives. Since 1948, television has increasingly become an important aspect of Americans' lives. Putnam (2000, p. 217) quotes T.S. Elliot as having observed television as "a medium of entertainment, which permits millions of people to listen to the same joke at the same time, and yet remain alone." However, the first forms of mass communication were not visual or audio mediums like television and radio, but newspapers. Alexis de Tocqueville described the importance of the newspaper in civic engagement:

> When no firm and lasting ties any longer unite men, it is impossible to obtain the cooperation of any great number of them unless you can persuade every man whose help is required that he serves his private interests by voluntarily uniting his efforts to those of all the others. That cannot be done habitually and conveniently without the help of a newspaper. Only a newspaper can put the same thought at the same times before a thousand readers. So hardly any democratic association can carry on without a newspaper (cited in Putnam, 2000, p. 218).

Still today, newspaper readers continue to be the most well-educated and the citizens most likely to participate in civic life. However, the number of people who read newspapers has declined rapidly in the past couple of decades as people turn more and more to electronic media (Putnam, 2000, pp. 218-219). Further, while Americans spend a great deal of time watching the television, like people who read the news, the number of people who watch the news is also on the decline.

Putnam says it is important to consider the fact that nothing has had a more profound effect on leisure time in the US than television, and the longitudinal effects the Internet will have on our society have only just begun to appear (2000, p. 221). The proliferation of mass communication technology such as television and the Internet has dramatically changed the way Americans live their lives. Statistics compiled by analysts tell us that annually, Americans watch 250 billion hours of television each year and the average number of hours a day per household that the television is switched on is 6 hours and 47 minutes. We also know that each year, the average American child will spend about 900 hours in school and about 1,500 hours watching television. This intrusion of television into our lives is creating a consumerist culture in which by age 65, an American will have seen over 2 million commercials. The top 100 television advertisers spent over $15 billion selling products to the American people (Herr, 2001). Research on how television is affecting the American public has been going on for some time and leaders of the medical community have long voiced their opinions on the negative consequences television may have. Critics blame television for the nation's violence epidemic, poor self-image, and the sedentary nature of American society. A child will see nearly 8,000 murders on television before they leave elementary school and that number reaches 40,000 by the age of 18 (Herr, 2001). Experts say that television has become an addiction among the American public, with many "high television" watchers expressing five symptoms of dependency upon television, which is two more than needed to classify something as clinical substance abuse (Herr, 2001). A survey in 1995 also blames television for the 4.7 million children found to be "severely overweight" in the US. This same group watches an average of 22 hours of television per week and consumes a high-calorie diet – experts found 200 junk food commercials within a four-hour period of Saturday morning cartoons (Herr, 2001). Children are not the only ones to suffer from the obesity epidemic in the US; adults who watch three hours or more of television a day are much more likely to be severely overweight than those who watch less than half an hour a day (Herr, 2001). According to Nielsen Media Research (2005), Americans are watching television today in record levels.

While television viewing rates have increased across the US, the number of households with Internet access has also risen dramatically, from 54.6% in 2001 to 61.5% in 2003, and continues to grow (US Department of Commerce, 2004, p. 5). Americans use their Internet connections to communicate via e-mail, play games, listen to music, watch television or movies, purchase goods, bank, and get information. The Internet has allowed Americans to continue their consumerist ways without every having to leave their home. This is a trend that seems to be affecting young people the most; A Nation Online: How Americans are Expanding Their Use of the Internet (US Department of Commerce, 2002, p. 42), says that "by the age of 10 young people are more likely to use the Internet than adults at any age beyond 25." The Internet is increasingly being used in the classroom. Some 84% of children aged 5 to 9 use the Internet at home, school, or both (US Department of Commerce, 2002, p. 44). However, in spite of pervasive Internet use in the classroom, major usage gaps exist between different age, racial, and socio-economic status groups. The Internet is a wonderful tool for education due to the wealth of information it provides, but as with television, it is not without concerns among parents. Parents continue to be worried about the types of inappropriate or dangerous material their children may be exposed to through Internet use. Of parents surveyed in A Nation Online (US Department of Commerce, 2002, p. 54), 46.9% indicated a concern about materials their children were being exposed to from the television and the Internet equally.

Doris A. Graber (2002) has found that African American households as well as Hispanic households are more reliant on television than are White families. However, she finds the greatest differences in how Americans use media between income levels: "High-income families, who usually are better educated than poor families, use print media more and television less than the rest of the population" (Graber, 2002, p. 202). However, Chadwick (2006, pp. 73-77) says that when explaining the digital divide in particular Internet usage, it is important to look at the variables of income, race, and education level as they are all strong indicators of the types of media consumed and the quality of the information being obtained. Chadwick (2006, p. 73) points out that it is important to note that demographic variables can be very closely related and these three in particular are strongly intercorrelated. Through an analysis of these variables from each study, income followed by education and then closely followed by race seems to be the most statistically significant variable when determining who has access to quality information and the Internet. However, Chadwick points out that these broad demographic variables do not necessarily explain why certain Americans are accessing the Internet and others are not. A study done by the University of Southern California indicates that those who access the Internet more often (typically younger, White, highly educated and upper income) use the Internet for a broad range of activities that shape their social, personal, and professional networks while expanding their knowledge, as opposed to those who access the Internet less often (who typically are in lower socio-economic groups), who do so mostly for entertainment (Chadwick, 2006, p. 75).

Television and the Internet: Important Sources of Political Socialization?

What role do the media play in shaping the identity of individuals? According to Huntemann and Morgan, media, particularly television, influence children's "values, beliefs, dreams, and expectations" (2001, p. 311). Huntemann and Morgan (2001, p. 312) say that adolescence is the time the media play the largest role in helping to shape individuals' identity. Studies show that media play a large role in shaping the identity of adolescents, who are searching for independence from family and society. A great deal of content analysis of television programs and commercials has been done and common findings report that media provide a quick way for children to learn what it means to be a boy or a girl (German and Lally, 2005). Despite progress in television in providing women with non-traditional roles, gender stereotypes still exist which are picked up in television use beginning in early childhood years. Huntemann and Morgan give as an example the use of teen magazines to define young girls' femininity (2001, p. 314). It is alarming to think that there is a lack of studies of media effects on the sexual behaviors of adolescents, but there is a large pool of analysis of television programming with sexual content. Further, Huntemann and Morgan (2001, p. 315) perceive that sexual attractiveness is critical and for the majority of people, the comparisons that this invites are not healthy. In the development of an identity within society, this can lead to isolation, self-rejection, and an obsession with body image among adolescents. Content analysis of television programming also reveals that "sex" in the media refers to an unmarried, heterosexual couple. Gay and lesbian teens are excluded completely from the perceived television audience (Huntemann and Morgan, 2001, pp. 315-316).

Media portrayals also affect the socialization of minority children. Walter Gerson (1966) explores this in his article "Mass Media Socialization: Negro–White Differences." Gerson suggests that African American children are in fact more socialized by mass media than are White children. They may even be using media, in particular the television, to learn how to behave more like White people. Gerson believes that this behavior is only perpetuating social segregation, a poor self-image among African American children, and highlighting the differences between communities (Gerson, 1966, pp. 40-50). The portrayal of minorities has deep historical roots, but negative images of minorities are repeated and normalized by keeping certain groups invisible (Huntemann and Morgan, 2001, p. 316). Statistics published by the Common Sense Media Poll report that, of the characters shown on prime time television, 3% are Asian, 4% are Latino, and 16% are African American; the remaining 74% are White. Also, 19% of prime time television characters are non-human, while only 17% are women (Key Findings, 2003). Content analyses have shown that, typically, minorities are associated with crime, violence, and substance abuse and are rarely seen in interracial interactions, unless it is with an authority figure. Researchers have found that because of the negative portrayal of minorities, minority children who watch a lot of television have a poor self-concept and do not want to participate in society outside of their community. As a result of the distorted view of African Americans in the media, African American children often reject their non-White, non-European heritage (Huntemann and Morgan, 2001, p. 316). The negative portrayal of minorities has come under much criticism by minority group leaders, yet minorities still remain some of the most active consumers of media. One theory as to why this occurs is what Oscar Gandy calls the "social construction of risk" (Gandy, 2001, pp. 600-618). Using content analysis and surveys, Gandy concludes that the depiction of both minorities and women in the media leads them to believe that the world is a dangerous place. Both women and African Americans feel they are more at risk in society for some type of crime or prejudiced treatment than White males (Gandy, 2001, pp. 600-618).

Many African Americans see racial biases in American media as a long-term trend. Michael Ryan (1982, pp. 276-289) tries to determine how minorities choose their media in order to avoid what they see as an emphasis on bad news and a suppression of good news in urban, minority, and low-income neighborhoods. This unfair depiction of minorities causes a negative self-image and may lead to a rejection of American culture as a whole and, therefore, poor socialization of minority citizens. It is plausible that the way the television media depict gender roles, sexuality, violence, and minorities could be contributing to the loss of social capital in the US as television increasingly grows to be a major aspect of socialization in the lives of Americans (German and Lally, 2005). Many experts believe that media portrayals of minorities are responsible for race-oriented political activities in the US (German, 1994; Chaffee and German, 1998). German (1994, pp. 285-297) observed the evident policy shift away from minority civil rights toward different types of policy by the Reagan administration and which led the American population to agree that minority groups were no longer disadvantaged in society. Using a content analysis of major news networks (ABC, NBC, and CBS), German determined that minority groups' inability to remain in the media spotlight has caused problems with race relations in the US and has led to the attitude that these groups are no longer disadvantaged (1994, pp. 285-297). In 1998, Chaffee and German carried out a content analysis of three major newspapers (the *New York Times*, the *Los Angeles Times*, and the *Chicago Tribune*) to determine what types of coverage minority citizens are receiving. They determined that the small amount of news coverage given to minorities, especially Hispanic Americans, coupled with the negative subject matter of the majority of this coverage, has provided a base for extremely negative attitudes among Americans toward minority groups (1998, pp. 312-320). Further, Kellstedt (2000) determined that the quality of media relations with minority groups determines political policy dynamics of race relations. Typically, an emphasis on individuality leads to conservative racial policy and an emphasis on egalitarianism leads to more liberal racial policies (Kellstedt, 2000, pp. 245-260). Individuality is more often the favorably portrayed media role today.

The portrayal of families in the media has also developed the socialized attitude of American youth toward problem-solving. Often, quick solutions to conflict create a sense of immediate gratification in the eyes of children and distort their view of commitment to a relationship. According to Kubey and Donovan (2001, p. 331), "People have been conditioned to expect quick and easy solutions," and this may be a key reason why many people are not prepared for the roles of parent and spouse. Content analysis of television programs by experts in psychology, communication, and sociology clearly indicates that television has a large effect on the education of children (German and Lally, 2005).

What follows is a profile of the American public and their use of television and the Internet: who has access, how much they are using it, and what they are accessing. The increasing widespread use of television and the Internet by almost every American for both information and entertainment can help us to explain the decline in US face-to-face social connectedness.

Media Use Patterns: A Profile of American Children

What is important to note in Table 1 is that access to television has reached almost total saturation, with 99% of households having at least one television. Also, although questions about instant messaging programs were not asked in the Kaiser 1999 survey since it had not yet become popular, almost 60% of households surveyed in 2004 had an instant messaging program. Internet subscription has risen 27% between 1999 and 2004, with 74% of households surveyed having access in the home. Table 1 indicates that American youth are heavy media users.

*Table 1: In-home media availability in 2004 and 1999 (Source: Roberts, et al., 2005) *Indicates unavailable data*

Medium	*n* =1+		*n* =3+	
	2004 %	1999 %	2004 %	1999 %
Television	99	99	73	70
Computer	86	73	15	8.0
Cable/satellite television	82	74	*	*
Premium channel	55	45	*	*
Internet	74	47	*	*
Instant messaging program	60	*	*	*

When access is broken down by race and ethnicity there are some important trends to examine in Table 2. While 99% of all ethnicities own at least one television, African Americans have access to the most television sets, with 81% owning three or more, which is almost 10% more than Whites (73%) or Hispanics (72%). However, when looking at computer ownership, Blacks and Hispanics are 12% and 10% (respectively) behind Whites and when ownership of three or more computers is taken into account the percentage of Whites (15%) who own three or more computers nearly doubles compared to Blacks (9%). Perhaps the most important characteristic to take from Table 2 is the difference in access to the Internet across races. Eighty percent of Whites have access to the Internet at home, but only 61% of Blacks and 67% of Hispanics.

Table 2: In-home media availability by race and ethnicity (Source: Roberts, et al., 2005)
**Indicates unavailable data*

Medium	n = 1+			n = 3+		
	White %	Black %	Hispanic %	White %	Black %	Hispanic %
Television	99	98	99	73	81	72
Computer	90	78	80	15	9	11
Cable/satellite television	83	83	78	*	*	*
Premium channel	56	65	55	*	*	*
Internet	80	61	67	*	*	*
Instant messaging program	63	47	55	*	*	*

As indicated in Table 3, level of education, the greatest predictor of social class, is correlated with who has access to the Internet in the home. Sixty-eight percent of children of parents with a high school education have access to the Internet at home while 82% of children of parents who graduate from college (or more) have access.

Table 3: In-home media availability by parental education (Source: Roberts, et al., 2005)
**Indicates unavailable data*

Medium	n = 1+			n = 3+		
	High school %	Some college %	College or more %	High school %	Some college %	College or more %
Television	99	99	99	74	68	75
Computer	82	84	91	8	9	22
Cable/satellite television	80	84	83	*	*	*
Premium channel	55	58	57	*	*	*
Internet	68	74	82	*	*	*
Instant messaging program	56	59	67	*	*	*

One of the most interesting changes in the data comes from the report of differences between boys' and girls' access to all multimedia categories, as seen in Table 4. In 1999, boys and girls reported usage of television, the Internet, and the computer in general at roughly the same levels give or take a few percentage points. However, in 2004, there are substantial differences in reports usage, with 8% more boys than girls having access to their own personal television. The difference between boys and girls remains about the same for access to a personal computer (9%) or Internet connection (7%).

Table 4: Gender and changes in ownership of selected personal media: 1999-2004 (Source: Roberts, et al., 2005)

Medium	Year	Boys %	Girls %
Television	2004	72	64
	1999	70	70
Computer	2004	35	26
	1999	22	27
Internet connection	2004	24	17
	1999	14	16

The number of rules that parents have greatly affects what type of content children are exposed to and how much time they allot daily to each medium. In Table 5, it is very interesting to note that a very small number of the total sample of children in the Kaiser study report (2005) have rules about the amount of time spent watching television and even fewer have rules about what is being viewed. Across genders, children experience about the same number of rules. However, when it comes to looking at rules by race, more Whites (13%) and Hispanics (19%) have rules about television viewing than African Americans (8%). Also, children of parents with some college education or college education and beyond are twice as likely to have some types of rules dealing with watching television.

Table 5: Television rules: percentage of children with television-related rules (Source: Roberts, et al., 2005)

	Rules about amount of time %	Rules about type of content %
Total sample	14	13
Gender		
Boys	15	14
Girls	12	12
Race/ethnicity		
White	13	13
African American	8	7
Hispanic	19	15
Parent education		
High school	9	10
Some college	15	12
College or more	16	14
Household income		
Under $35.000	11	14
$35.000-$50.000	17	13
Over $50.000	12	12

While rules associated with watching television apply to a very small percentage of the sample population, the proportions grow when talking about computers and the Internet (see Table 6). Parental filters are typically in low use across the board. The issue of protecting children from objectionable content on the

Internet first appeared in the early 1990s when the Internet began to increase in popularity. The Child Online Protection Act became law in 1998 and it made it a criminal act to allow children to view harmful material on the Internet. Objectionable sites were able to defend themselves by putting into place a system in order to verify a viewer's age, such as credit card numbers or access codes.

New technology allows for different types of filters to be applied while accessing the Internet. The two main types of filters are "client side" and "server side." Client side filters, the more flexible of the two, are software programs that are loaded onto individual computers. Many of these programs are designed specifically for children and work in conjunction with popular web browsers like Internet Explorer or Netscape. The two most popular "client side" filters are Net Nanny and Cyber Patrol (Lenhart, 2005). "Server side" filtering works in one of two ways: ISP (Internet Service Provider) filtering is when an Internet company allows clients to activate controls that block unacceptable sites on their account and web filtering is when clients hire an organization to filter their Internet access for them. Generally, web-based filtering requires a monthly subscription fee. Either method, ISP or web-based, requires Internet access to be filtered through a third party and is less flexible than "client side" filters (Lenhart, 2005). Most of the time, filters have to be paid for and we see that Hispanics are 10% behind Whites and 9% behind Blacks in the use of such filters. Also interesting to note in Table 6 is that for every category of rules, children of parents with a college education are 9% more likely to have rules than children of parents with a high school education.

Table 6: Computer rules: percentage of children with computer-related rules (Source: Roberts, et al., 2005)

	Rules about amount of time %	Rules about what can be done on the computer %	Parents usually know which websites are visited %	Parental filters on computers %
Total	28	32	30	25
Gender				
Boys	26	35	27	24
Girls	32	28	33	26
Race/ethnicity				
White	30	33	34	27
African American	25	31	24	26
Hispanic	25	31	24	17
Parent education				
High school	23	26	23	24
Some college	27	31	30	26
College or more	32	35	34	25
Household income				
Under $35.000	30	33	28	27
$35.000-$50.000	29	32	31	25
Over $50.000	27	31	30	24

One might argue that the freedom given American children translates into more democratic political orientations as adults than if the children were strictly supervised. But, it does appear that many children's freedom of choice represents too much of an abdication of parental responsibility.

While new technology is emerging every day, children are not cutting back on television time to fit the newer mediums into their day (see Table 7). They view television just as much today as they did in 1999. However, it is interesting to note that African Americans watch television over an hour more each day than do White children.

Table 7: Television exposure by gender, race, parent education, and household income (Source: Roberts, et al., 2005)

	Average daily television use (hours and minutes)
Gender	
Boys	3:04
Girls	3:04
Race/ethnicity	
White	2:45
African American	4:05
Hispanic	3:23
Parent education	
High school	3:12
Some college	2:48
College or more	3:03
Household income	
Under $35.000	3:16
$35.000-$50.000	2:55
Over $50.000	3:08
Year	
2004	3:04
1999	3:05

While we can see that television usage has not gone down between 1999 and 2004, computer and Internet usage has increased significantly, as indicated by Table 8. Children are being exposed to the computer and Internet over a half an hour more in 2004 than they were in 1999.

Table 8: Computer exposure by hours per day by gender, race, parent education, and household income (recreational) (Source: Roberts, et al., 2005)

	Total computer use	Total Internet use
Gender		
Boys	0:60	0:44
Girls	1:04	0:53
Race/ethnicity		
White	1:02	0:48
African American	0:52	0:37
Hispanic	0:54	0:42
Parent education		
High school	0:55	0:44
Some college	0:57	0:44
College or more	1:12	0:55
Household Income		
Under $35.000	0:55	0:43
35.000-$50.000	0:58	0:45
Over $50.000	1:11	0:56
Year		
2004	1:02	0:48
1999	0:27	0:11

When adding up the time children spend with different types of media (watching television, listening to music, watching movies, using the computer, and playing video games), we see that they spend over 7.5 hours using media every day (see Table 9). While some of this media use takes place during the school day, much of it occurs outside of school.

Table 9: Media time vs. time doing other activities (Source: Roberts, et al., 2005)

Activity	Time (hours and minutes)
Watching television	3:04
Hanging out with parents	2:17
Hanging out with friends	2:16
Listening to music	1:44
Exercising, sports, etc.	1:25
Watching movies/videos	1:11
Using a computer	1:02
Pursuing hobbies, clubs, etc.	1:00
Talking on the telephone	0:53
Doing homework	0:50
Playing video games	0:49
Reading	0:43
Working at a job	0:35
Doing chores	0:32

Another important factor is that children who have their own television watch it almost an hour and a half longer each day than children who do not have their own television set (see Table 10). Those who have their own computer use it an hour and twenty minutes more than children who do not have their own personal computer.

Table 10: Personal media vs. media exposure (Source: Roberts, et al., 2005)

Television		Computer	
Yes	No	Yes	No
3:31	2:04	1:30	0:47

For many years now, child activists and pediatricians have been speaking about the negative effects that television content has on children's self-esteem and here the Kaiser family foundation has asked some very interesting questions about how content a child is with their appearance in relation to the amount of exposure they have to television and the computer on a daily basis. It is quite obvious from Table 11 that the least content children watch television nearly a half an hour longer each day than those who are most content and they use the computer around 20 minutes longer each day.

Table 11: Media exposure in hours and minutes by contentedness (Source: Roberts, et al., 2005)

Medium	Low contentedness	Moderate contentedness	High contentedness
Television	3:25	3:02	2:57
Computer	1:16	1:01	0:55

Media Use Patterns: A Profile of American Adults

When the Internet became popular, it was said that it could save the ever-increasing levels of apathy among the American public toward politics. However, according to Chadwick (2006, p. 25), in the early years of the Internet, it was the conventional wisdom that those who were looking for political information on the Internet were those citizens who were already active. The 2004 presidential elections and the use of blogs and other types of what is becoming known as e-politics are certain to have long-term effects and new trends are sure to appear (Chadwick, 2006, p. 26).

Table 12 provides a profile of who uses the Internet in the US. It can be seen that many of the lower socio-economic groups use the Internet in the lowest numbers, creating what has been described as a digital divide between the haves and the have-nots in American society; and the gap between people with less than a high school education and those who have a college degree (or more) is more than 50%. It is quite evident from past research that education is one of the greatest predictors of social class. Thus, we can also see the differences in the degree of access to the Internet according to income, race, and age. While lower socio-economic groups have a lesser degree of access to the Internet, television has saturated the market, with 99% of households owning a television. Table 13 is from a Nielsen Media Research News Release in 2005 entitled "Americans Watch TV at Record Levels." Television consumption is increasing in the face of increased Internet use.

Table 12: Demographics of US Internet users 2004 (Source: Chadwick, 2006, p. 73)

Demographics	Percentage Online
Women	61
Men	66
Age	
18-29	78
30-49	74
50-64	60
65 +	25
Race/ethnicity	
White, non-Latino	67
African American, non-Latino	43
Latino	59
Community type	
Urban	62
Suburban	68
Rural	56
Household income	
Less than $30.000 per year	44
$30.000-$50.000	69
$50.000-$75.000	81
More than $75.000	89
Education	
Less than high school	32
High school	52
Some college	75
College +	88

Table 13: Average hours/minutes of television consumption per day by broadcast year (Source: Nielson Media Research, 2006)

Broadcast year	Average hours/ minutes per day
2004-2005	8:11
2003-2004	8:01
2002-2003	7:55
2001-2002	7:42
2000-2001	7:39
1999-2000	7:31
1998-1999	7:24
1997-1998	7:15

Table 14 shows the digital divide using several different databases. While the Kent State figures are somewhat different from the other studies, Chadwick (2006,

p. 74) points out that Kent State used some controls that actually make them more accurate. However, the figures seem to be in agreement across all of the studies. They show that education and income seem to be the greatest indicators of who is accessing the Internet. Education and income are closely followed by age and race. This leads to the question, what types of activities are Americans using the Internet for?

Table 14: The access divide in the USA: a survey of surveys (Source: Chadwick, 2006, p. 74)

Internet access	Department of Commerce/NTIA, September 2001	Pew, May 2002	Kent State Survey, July 2001	Mean
Education gap (high school diploma vs. college education	41	37	21	33
Income gap (below vs. above $30.000 a year)	35	37	24	25
Age gap (B: 18-24 vs. over 50; C: 18-29 vs. 50-64; D: average 28 vs. average 61)	28 B	22 C	24 D	25
Race gap (African American vs. White)	20	15	17	17
Ethnicity gap (Latino vs. White)	28	6	13	16

The National Telecommunications and Information Administration (NITIA) and the Economics and Statistics Administration (ESA) of the US Department of Commerce use the US Census Bureau's Current Population Survey in A Nation Online (US Department of Commerce, 2002) and an update focusing on broadband technology in 2004 (US Department of Commerce, 2004). It is one of the most comprehensive reports on how Americans are using the Internet. As indicated in Figure 1, Americans who have access to the Internet use it for a variety of reasons. Of those who use the Internet, over 60% use it to find out the news, weather, or sports information, even more use it for some type of product search (i.e., online shopping), but the largest category (84%) use it for e-mail. A poll done by the Pew Research Center in 1998 shows what Americans are interested in when they watch the news – particularly the local news.

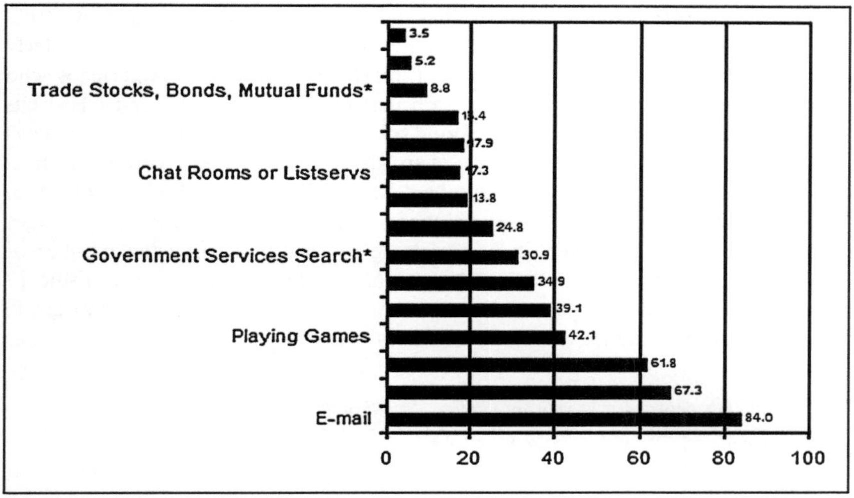

Figure 1: Online activities, ages 15+ (Source: US Department of Commerce, 2002)

So, of the small percentage of Americans who get their news in some way, the largest interest is crime and the second largest interest is in health and community. It is important to note in Table 15 that local government and domestic policy are about 11 and 15 percentage points behind community. Americans have more of an interest in their immediate community than in local or national government.

Table 15: General news interest, June 8, 1998 (Source: Pew Research Center, 1998)

	% who follow very closely
Crime	36
Health	34
Community	34
Sports	27
Local government	23
Science and technology	22
Domestic politics/policy	19
Religion	18
Business and finance	17
International affairs	16
Entertainment	16
Consumer news	15
Culture and the arts	12

However, overall news viewing has declined steadily since a May 1993 benchmark. Table 16 shows a trend among Americans who say they regularly watch the nightly news. As indicated by Table 16, the number of Americans who regularly watch nightly news on the main networks (ABC, NBC, and CBS) has declined from 60% to 38% in a time period of only five years. While network news viewing among Americans has seen a sharp decline, cable news stations such as CNN enjoyed a rise in viewing numbers until 1998, when the percentage of Americans who watched cable news plunged to 23%, lower than the percentages for any other year. However, it is interesting to note that while the number of Americans who never follow the news in nightly bulletins is rather low, Table 17 indicates that the percentages of Americans who never follow cable news are in many cases higher than for those who regularly watch.

Table 16: Nightly network news viewing (Source: Pew Research Center, 1998)

% who watch	May 1993	March 1995	April 1996	May 1998
Regularly	60	48	42	38
Sometimes	28	28	29	28
Hardly ever	5	14	15	15
Never	6	10	14	19
Don't know	1	*	*	*

Table 17: Cable news network viewing (Source: Pew Research Center, 1998)

% who watch	May 1990	May 1993	March 1995	April 1996	May 1998
Regularly	27	35	30	26	23
Sometimes	25	34	28	33	34
Hardly ever	7	7	13	14	13
Never	40	24	28	27	30
Don't know	1	*	1	*	*

As the "Cable news network viewing" Pew report (Table 17) suggests, the decline in viewing within the news viewing segment of the American population can be compared to a newer way to access news – the online newspaper. This new medium is especially in evidence among the young and those who are in what Pew terms the "working years" (i.e., ages 30 to 49). Twenty-three percent of the population surveyed by the Pew Research Center report getting their news online every day. Those figures are higher in the 30 to 39 and the 40 to 49 age groups, where the percentages move to 33% and 27% respectively, and rapidly decline to only 7% for the 70+ age group. The authors predict that new generations will produce entirely different patterns, with the elderly being even more involved in the future with electronic news gathering compared to younger age categories since they are the heaviest newspaper consumers today.

In Table 18, it is interesting to note that the audiences who watch nightly news, morning shows, cable news, sports, and weather, and who use the Internet for news all possess different demographic characteristics in American society; they have different interests that are fulfilled by the type of news medium they choose. While Americans today are clearly not as interested in community events and government politics as the generations before them, they also claim that one more aspect of their lives has disintegrated with their increased television and Internet use: "The Internet could be the ultimate isolating technology that further reduces our participation in communities even more than did automobiles and television before it," says Dr. Norman Nie of the Stanford Institute for the Quantitative Study of Society (SIQSS Press Release, 2000). People report that they feel their conversations on the telephone and in person have been reduced due to increased levels of Internet use. As can be seen from Figure 2, more than a quarter of survey participants claim that they are spending less time on the telephone with family and friends due to the Internet.

Table 18: The growing trend of online newspapers (Source: Pew Research Center, 2005)

Main source	Total	18-29	30-39	40-49	50-59	60-69	70+
Television	74	70	63	74	76	85	83
Papers	44	37	39	41	52	50	57
Internet	24	36	31	29	18	9	3
Radio	22	18	26	24	22	19	19
Magazines	5	5	7	4	5	5	6
Get news online everyday	23	23	33	27	24	15	7

Analysis and Conclusions

Television and the Internet are increasingly suspected to have a profound effect on the development of identity and the depletion of social capital in American society. Even though the Federal Communications Commission has set guidelines for television through the Children's Television Act of 1990 and the Telecommunications Act of 1996, it lacks the power to truly enforce these guidelines. However, there is a lack of research on whether the favorite and often provocative television shows and websites of Americans really do have negative effects on children's socialization. Many experts believe that television and the Internet are strong agents of socialization, especially citing relationships between violent or sexual content on television and violent behavior or sexual promiscuity in individuals; however, there is disagreement as to what should be done. Under the leadership of Senator Joseph Lieberman, the Committee on Health, Education, Labor, and Pensions reviewed a bill known as the Children and Media Research Advancement Act or CAMRA (see Lieberman, et al., 2004). This bill, which never became law, called for the National Academy of Science to work with the Institute of Medicine to explore the cognitive, physical, and socio-behavioral effects of media on childhood socialization, and for $90 million to be appropriated. The effect of long-term television and Internet use by Americans is increasingly becoming an issue within American politics, particularly with the loss of social capital in the US. In the next few years, beginning with the CAMRA Act, experts in many fields should need to begin to do more in-depth research on how the explicit themes of television and its consumerist undertones affect the behaviors and opinions of US citizens. As of now, all we can examine is who has access, what are they accessing, and how much time they are spending accessing these media (German and Lally, 2005). Researchers also need to seek answers to the question of how television and the Internet affect the physical health of Americans, which the CAMRA Act calls for. Perhaps, when the research is done and Congress knows how television and the Internet are affecting the socialization of Americans, we can use these media to create a more active political culture.

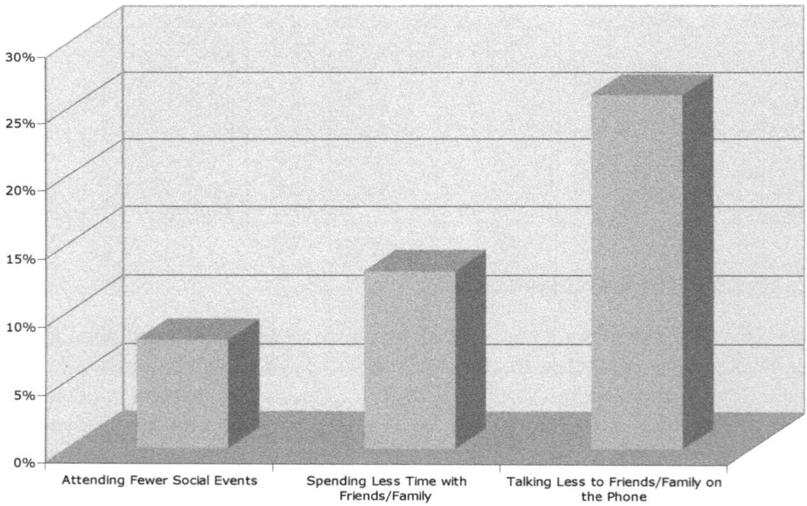

Figure 2: Internet users spend less time in social activities (Source: Stanford Institute for the Quantitative Study of Society, 2000)

The Internet is increasingly being used by children and adults in the United States. However, there are dramatic differences in accessibility in the home between higher and lower socio-economic status groups and between racial groups. Hence, the democratization opportunities of free information for all are compromised by the huge digital gap between those who have computers (Asian and

White racial groups and those with high incomes and education) and those who do not (African American, Hispanic, poorly educated, and low-income populations). Many scholars hoped that the Internet would open up the political process and be a check on the influence of big money, and afford poorer groups political access to many people. So far, as the data in this article imply, lower-income, poorly educated, and minority groups still do not have access to this outlet to voice their opinions and gain political ground (Purvis, 2001, p. 327). Congress has begun to use the Internet as a way of communicating with constituents and we are beginning (in particular with the 2000 and 2004 elections) to see a new type of campaigning that may lead to more grass-roots efforts. But the results of this type of campaigning remain to be seen (Purvis, 2001, p. 309). Furthermore, as with television, there are, in the case of the Internet, no studies that actually analyze the social and political development of children and adults resulting from Internet use. It is interesting that the social/political sciences too often ignore these media and often forget the socialization process itself. The genesis of adult behavior begins early in life and these electronic media are increasingly present in children's lives (German and Lally, 2005). However, some studies conclude that the enormous time spent by individual Americans watching television and accessing the Internet has led to a cutback in the time they spend in face-to-face contact with other people (SIQSS, 2000). The dramatic differences we see between income, educational level, and race contribute to social and information gaps in our society. In conclusion, as the Internet reaches the market saturation levels that television has reached and Americans become even more consumed by this media trend, social capital as we have known it may continue to disintegrate. A new kind of individualized, virtual connectedness will evolve. Can this be good for what is left of the democracy which de Tocqueville saw in the 1830s?

References

Chadwick, A. (2006). *Internet Politics: States, Citizens, and New Communication Technologies*. New York, NY: Oxford University Press.

Chaffee, R. and D. German (1998). "New Frontiers in Political Socialization Research: Media and Racial Minorities in the USA," pp. 312-320 in K-P. Hufer and B. Wellie (eds.) *Sozialwissenschaftliche und bildungstheoretische: Reflexionen*. Berlin, Germany: GAM Media.

Gandy, Jr., O. (2001). "Racial Identity, Media Use, and the Social Construction of Risk among African Americans," pp. 600-618 in *Journal of Black Studies*, Vol. 31, No. 5.

German, D. (1994). "The Role of Media in Political Socialization and Attitude Formation toward Racial/Ethnic Minorities in the U.S.," pp. 285-297 in R. Farnen (ed.) *Nationalism, Ethnicity, and Identity: Cross-national and Comparative Perspectives*. New Brunswick, NJ: Transaction.

German, D. and C. Lally (2005). "Television and the Internet's Effects on the Socialization Processes of American Children." Paper presented at the International Political Science Association Research Committee on Political Socialization and Education, Wuppertal, Germany.

Gerson, W. (1966). "Mass Media Socialization Behavior: Negro–White Differences," pp. 40-50 in *Social Forces*, Vol. 45, No. 1. http://dx.doi.org/10.2307/2575776

Graber, D. (2002). *Mass Media and American Politics*. Washington, DC: CQ Press.

Herr, N. (2001). "The Sourcebook for Teaching Science: Television and Health. http://www.-csun.edu/~vceed02/health/docs/tv&health.html

Huntemann, N. and M. Morgan (2001). "Mass Media and Identity Development," pp. 309-219 in D. Singer and J. Singer (eds.) *Handbook of Children and the Media*. Thousand Oaks, CA: Sage.

Key Findings: The 2003 Common Sense Media Poll of American Parents. 2003. http://www.commonsensemedia.org/resources/polls.php (accessed December 6, 2004).

Kellstedt, P. (2000). "Media Framing and the Dynamics of Racial Policy Preferences," pp. 245-260 in *American Journal of Political Science*, Vol. 44, No. 2. http://dx.doi.org-/10.2307/2669308

Kubey, R. and B. Donovan (2001). "Media and the Family," pp.323-336 in D. Singer and J. Singer (eds,) *Handbook of Children and the Media*. Thousand Oaks, CA: Sage.

Lenhart, A. (2005). *Protecting Teens Online. Pew Internet and American Life Project*. Washington, DC: Pew Research Center for People and the Press.

Lieberman, J., S. Brownback, H. Clinton, R. Santorum and M. Landrieu (2004). "Children and Media Research Advancement Act, S. 2447." Thomas Legislative Information on the Internet. http://thomas.loc.gov/cgi-bin/queiry/C?c108:./temp/~c108DNBGws (accessed December 5, 2004).

Nielsen Media Research (2005). "Nielsen Reports Americans Watch TV at Record Levels." News Release, September 29.

Pew Research Center for the People and the Press (1998). "Internet News Takes Off." http://people-press.org/reports

Pew Research Center for the People and the Press (2005). "Public More Critical of Press, But Goodwill Persists." http://people-press.org/reports

Purvis, H. (2001). *Media, Politics, and Government*. Orlando, FL: Harcourt College Publishers.

Putnam, R. (2000). *Bowling Alone: The Collapse and Revival of American Community*. New York, NY: Simon & Schuster.

Roberts, D., U. Foehr, and V. Rideout (March 2005). *Generation M: Media in the Lives of 8-18 year-olds*. Washington, DC: The Henry J. Kaiser Family Foundation.

Ryan, M. (1982). "Media Attitudes and News References: An Analysis of Demographic Variables for a Sample of the Urban Poor, pp. 276-289 in *Journal of Black Studies*, Vol. 12, No. 3. http://dx.doi.org/10.1177/002193478201200303

Stanford Institute for the Quantitative Study of Society (SIQSS) (2000). "Study Offers Early Look at How Internet is Changing Daily Life." http://www.stanford.edu/group/siqss/Press_Release /press_release.html

US Department of Commerce (2002). "A Nation Online: How Americans are Expanding Their Use of the Internet." Washington, DC: US Department of Commerce: Economic and Statistics Administration and the National Telecommunications and Information Administration.

US Department of Commerce (2004). "A Nation Online: Entering the Broadband Age." Washington, DC: US Department of Commerce: Economic and Statistics Administration and the National Telecommunications and Information Administration.

Chapter 6
Participation Friendliness of Political Websites

Christ'l De Landtsheer

Professor of Communications Science, University of Antwerp, Antwerp, Belgium

Abstract

This chapter focuses on the quality assessment of political websites. It introduces a special coding scheme which enables one to evaluate and compare the quality of websites in the political sphere. These websites include party and public administration websites and personal websites of political leaders and administrators, as well as sites from non-governmental social and political organizations. Maybe even more important is that the criteria of the coding scheme may further the building of a qualitatively good political site in terms of "participation friendliness."

Introduction

Websites form a new and additional political communication channel in a virtual and worldwide environment, which introduces new features into relations between writing and reading, between verbal and visual media. This creates a new model of political communication that has a potential to improve existing forms of political participation as well as to introduce new forms for those who are inclined to benefit from digitalization.

As we all know, creating a successful website is not easy. This is an obvious conclusion when looking at sites that are difficult to navigate, find information from, or interact with. As users, we are struggling with poorly designed and implemented sites. As researchers, we need to tackle the problem in a new way. It is important to understand that it is not enough to make a website functional, but the site should also be usable, appealing, compelling and engaging from a user's point of view. The "art" of creating engaging websites needs new interdisciplinary approaches, presenting perspectives from communication studies, film and media analysis, graphic design, architecture, development of digital technologies and computer science, etc., as well as a psychological understanding of the human being as an emotive, sensuous, cultural, intellectual and social being (Neuner and De Landtsheer, 2005).

This chapter will first in a general part, introduce e-politics, the use of the Internet as a means of communication in politics. It will discuss the debate between believers and non- believers in e-politics. Can we consider the Internet as a new means of more equal communication? This chapter will detail the role of political websites and e-campaigning and give an overview of research results.

The chapter will then introduce, more specifically, a method for assessing the quality of political websites or websites in the public sphere. This method is entitled "the participation-friendliness index for political websites" (De Landtsheer,

Krasnoboka, and Neuner, 2007). A final section will explain that the coding scheme is based upon political participation theory. The method was, until now, used to evaluate websites in the European Union countries, in the Unites States, and in South Africa. Most of the websites were analyzed at the event of political elections. Besides, the coding scheme was applied to governmental sites and sites by non-governmental (social) organizations, or even by terrorists, in order to get an insight in their communication strategies.

General Part

Within the last decennia, the Internet has evolved from the pale copy of the traditional media to the full-scale virtual public sphere, the meeting place of different actors. The world of politics could not stay away from the options offered by the Internet. The new prospects of digital information and communication did not pass unnoticed by political spin doctors. From this point of view, the Internet provides cheap but effective forms of infotainment, which, while bypassing the traditional filters of mainstream mass media, connect political actors directly with their voters. However, as different research projects demonstrate, despite the obvious advantages that the Internet communication offers for political actors, not all politicians and political parties have realized and acknowledged the importance of having an online presence.

E-politics

While the Internet has become a standard means of information and communication in advanced nations, the rest of the world lags far behind. Similar to challenges in other areas of social, economic, and political development, the African continent, for instance, continues to be the least affected by technological innovation. The North-South divide, reinforced in recent years by the "digital divide," is primarily associated with Africa's challenges. Even a continent as digitally challenged as Africa is not, however, completely homogeneous. Levels of social development are relatively low compared to more advanced world nations, but there are significant and consistent differences across the continent. As in many other areas of societal development, both the Northern African countries and South Africa are pioneering Internet use on the African continent.

The role of the Internet in political and social affairs is hotly debated in the literature. Scientific views vary from "cyber optimists" to "cyber pessimists." In its pure, uncontrolled form, the Internet has all chances to develop into the proper public sphere (Bennett, 2003), where variety of ideas and comments can be relatively easily and quickly exchanged throughout the world, bypassing the channels of more traditional mass communication. This leads to "one-to-one," "one-to-many," and "many-to-many" types of communication, freed from any form of control, geographical, or time barriers.

Norris (2001) distinguishes two forms of Internet communication. The "top-down" communication enables practically unlimited stream of information from online actors. This form of Internet communication leads to the enrichment of the public with socially and politically relevant information and facts, which in its turn leads to the emergence of "bottom-up" communication, including exchange of ideas, inauguration of debates, and mobilization of public opinion.

The Internet is a cheap means of communication understood in relative but not absolute terms of the efficiency of the message dissemination. The price of the global message dissemination via more traditional channels considerably exceeds the price of the digital channel. Such convenient economic aspect of the Internet communication attracts ever growing numbers of social and political actors willing to spread their message as wide as possible. Bennett (2003) also stresses the importance of Internet communication for "global activism." The ever growing number of world-wide networks makes possible the phenomenon of "global thinking."

Such an often utopian vision of virtual communication is particularly attractive for the marginal and marginalized organizations and actors who embrace the Internet's possibilities of anonymity and breadth of their message circulation despite limited financial resources. So, in the early 1990s, the Zapatista rebels in Mexico have used the Internet to mobilize their supporters. During the war in Bosnia-Herzegovina, the opposition to the Milosevic regime received an additional boost and support through the Internet-based radio station. Emerging African organizations for women's wellbeing use the chance to establish Internet contact with similar organizations worldwide. For some disappearing aboriginal communities, such as the Cherokee Indians in the US, the Internet has become the essential tool to preserve and protect their cultural identity (Arnold and Plymire, 2000). And in countries like Tunisia and Egypt, the Internet helped to bring some of the power back to the citizens.

Although the Internet looks like the world of equal chances in terms of variety of opinions and possibilities for mobilization, there is no equality in terms of Internet access or intellectual and technical skills connected with Internet use. In this respect, the Internet reinforces the chances of those with necessary skills and equipment to create an e-fluential elite (Accone, 2002). Thus, only this elite can really enjoy the advantages of the new digital medium, while less fortunate actors are only further marginalized. Further widening of the gap between material and intellectual possibilities of different groups, now on the basis of Internet access, has received the name of digital divide.

The arguments of cyber optimists and cyber pessimists are also heard on the digital landscape. Optimists see in the Internet the potential for further democratic development which can bring an uncensored transnational public sphere by the means of equal access to the Internet technologies. In their turn, pessimists refer to the digital divide theory, stressing the unequal chances based on race, gender, and socio-economic status.

Believers versus Non-believers

There is no consensus in the literature for the relevance and significance of political websites. While practically all authors agree on the role political websites may potentially play in their parties' or group's propaganda, rationality of such involvement and its added value are often questioned.

Believers: Advantages of the Political Internet Compared to Traditional Media

In their analysis of the political websites in New Zealand, Conway and Dorner (2004) list five ways in which, according to the authors, political parties may improve their communication by the means of the Internet and to reach greater mobilization effects than traditional media may have. They talk about increased volume of the information transmission; speed of intercommunication; diversity of technoformats (audio, video, text); multidirectionality of communication and information flows; and decentralization of control.

Similar arguments appear in the work of McLaughlin (2003) on the use of the Internet by dissident organizations and parties, such as the Muslim Brotherhood in Jordan and Egypt. The guarantee of publication freedom by the means of control's decentralization is of particular importance here, taking into account the level of censorship in the Middle East authoritarian regimes.

Norris (2001) distinguishes top-down and bottom-up (vide supra) communication. The author stresses that the potential advantage of the Internet as a communication medium in comparison with traditional media is the free spreading of different types of information. This can combine posting the full text of the governmental report next to the summaries of audio and video materials from press conferences and debates. The spreading of information occurs directly and simultaneously and is available to the broader Internet public in an efficient, equal, and cheap way. Next to such examples of top-down communication, political parties can initiate additional bottom-up communication exchanges between citizens or interest groups on one side and the politicians and governmental officials on the other side. Many political websites also employ interactive tools such as chat rooms and feedback forms as well as comments pages.

These and other advantages are particularly pronounced in smaller parties which previously did have proper means for political communication due to the costs involved. Bimber (1998) stresses the bridging of the financial gap between groups and parties as one of the most important outcomes of Internet communication. The Internet offers easier ways to mobilize funds and votes for those political groups which previously were unable to enjoy such mobilization through more traditional means of communication. The principle that smaller parties (left out by the traditional media) acquire via the Internet a cheap platform for spreading their political message and, in this way, get more equal chances with bigger parties, has received the name of "leveling of the playing field" (Norris, 2003;Tkach-Kawasaki, 2003; Gibson, et al., 2003).This fact can be seen as an explanation why smaller parties are often more enthusiastic about the potential offered by digital political communication compared to bigger parties.

Non-believers: No Visible Advantages of the Internet Compared to Traditional Media

According to Coleman (1999), "The e-campaigning hype has far exceeded any real political effects." Compared to the generally accepted professional standards of Internet design, the majority of political websites remains considerably behind (Norris, 2003). This is particularly noticeable in terms of user-friendliness and interactive possibilities: many sites lack proper search options, site maps, or graphic illustrations. Often, official information is presented in a very dry, formal, and technical style, which requires a certain degree of prior knowledge and acquaintance with official procedures. Readability of online texts often becomes yet another challenge for regular citizens due to the usage of the simple techniques of "copy-paste" of official documents directly onto websites without any elementary adjustment, technical and cognitive alike. In many cases, the informative function of the website (top-down communication) exceeds its interactive (bottom-up) possibilities.

Norris (2003) concludes that while the Internet possesses a variety of possibilities, it should be seen rather as an addition to and not as a replacement of more traditional forms of political communication. Also, while the advantages of Internet communication before the more traditional means promoted by the "believers" are acknowledged, not all of them are realized in practice. Websites and emails are additional ways in which political actors may reach citizens, not as substitutes for more traditional ways of engagement. One of the possible explanations here is that citizens have to be stimulated in the first place to start using the Internet for political reasons (Hansen, et al., 2005). This means, among other things, that the government, the administration, political parties, and NGOs need to promote their websites first via conventional offline communication channels.

Also the argument about "leveling the playing field" has been critically approached by many authors (Margolis, et al., 1997; Gibson, Nixon, and Ward, 2003; Gibson, Rommele, and Ward, 2003). There are no signs of more even balance between different parties and interests online than what exists offline. Discrepancies and inequalities between political actors are now reflected online. Politics on the Internet is politics as usual (Margolis and Resnick, 2000), bigger parties are more present online than smaller ones (Norris, 2000; Pew Research Center, 2000). Big parties, which previously reached big numbers of voters via traditional means of communication, now are able to reach bigger numbers of voters online as well (Bimber, 1998). Websites of big political parties are also richer, content-wise and visually, than the websites of smaller parties (Hansen, et al., 2005) because big parties have more resources to recruit the personnel to update and design their websites. Richer parties are also capable of greater offline promotion of their websites. In other words, the arrival of the Internet does not break down financial and institutional barriers. Despite this fact, there are still a certain number of smaller parties (primarily green and left parties) that succeeded in breaking through the existing pattern, launching successful political websites. Different empirical analyses demonstrated that precisely such parties have the most user-friendly and interactive websites (Gibson and Ward, 1998, 2000, 2001, 2002; Voerman and Ward, 2000; Ward, et al., 2003; De Landtsheer, et al., 2004; De Landtsheer, et al., 2001).

Research Results

Based on the previous empirical analysis of political websites in various countries, we can establish a number of empirical findings. These include that big political parties are more inclined to be present online, that newer parties will have a greater online presence, and that ideology also plays some role (Norris, 2001; Gibson, et al., 2003; Ward, et al., 2003; Margolis, et al., 1997; De Landtsheer, et al., 2005; Cuevas, 2004).

Despite the great enthusiasm that smaller parties have shown to the arrival of the new medium, it is the bigger parties which researchers find present online (Norris, 2001). There are hardly many signs of the "leveling of the playing field" (Gibson and Ward, 2001 and 2002). More recently, De Landtsheer, et al. (2001 and 2004) confirm this hypothesis in the study of the last European elections, and Cuevas (2004) finds support for the same claim in her analysis of the Filipino political websites. This fosters the conclusion that bigger political parties have more and better chances to be present online. The data from the 2001 UK elections show that bigger parties are able to invest more time and resources for maintaining their websites, often offering extra search and fundraising options (Ward, et al., 2003). Similar results come out of the studies of the 1998 and 2000 US election campaigns (Gibson, et al., 2003): websites of bigger parties are more functional and offer extra options in comparison with smaller parties. Also Norris (2001) in her analysis of 399 websites concludes that smaller parties offer less content and often lack interactive options. De Landtsheer, et al. (2001 and 2004) registered a strong correlation between the size of political parties and participation-friendliness of their websites. Similarly, Carlson and Kjupsund (2001) suggest that websites of smaller parties in the 1999 Finnish elections had lower quality compared to the websites of bigger parties. Furthermore, Conway and Dorner (2004) argue that bigger parties in New Zealand use their websites and online presence more effectively and efficiently. De Landtsheer, et al. (2004 and 2007) reported similar results in their study of Belgian websites, stating that overall quality of smaller parties' websites is lower than that of bigger parties.

Gibson and McAllister (2005) suggest that political groups which stress the importance of political participation and decentralization of powers and who rely on support of the more educated middle class are more inclined to engage in online campaigning. In another analysis of the 2000 US presidential elections, it was discovered that the websites related to the Democratic party had scored better than those related to the Republican party (De Landtsheer, et al., 2001). The Democrats put efforts into interactive features of their websites, while the Republicans use the Internet primarily for self-presentation and public relations. As far as the study of the Belgian political websites is concerned, the ecologist and leftist parties score better than others. The later study, however, shows that the differences between left and other parties are diminishing, with right-wing and conservative parties rapidly catching up.

Websites in Political Campaigning

Only ten years ago, the use of the Internet in a political campaign was seen as a strange and questionable innovation. Today, practically no important political campaign in Western societies is organized without the development of a suitable Internet strategy. Politicians, media, and civic groups employ diverse online means to present, defend, and promote their ideas and choices. Some of them dare to use highly interactive applications, others prefer to stick to the safe haven of (merely) information spreading. Election campaigns in particular have seen a dramatic increase in Internet use. Today, practically any politician or political party that competes in elections runs at least one political website. Additionally, support and partisan groups launch their own online presence. In their turn, media organizations and think tanks develop expert websites, where visitors may not only find sufficient analytical material and compare candidates' programs, but even determine their own political preferences in case they are not sure which candidate may represent their interest in the best possible way. Alongside more "traditional" forms of online presence (such as websites and forums), newer Internet applications such as YouTube and LiveJournals are widely used for political ends.

Despite the rapid innovation of the Internet space, websites continue to be the major means of political representation online. They contain the fullest information on the parties, groups, and candidates who run in elections. Websites are directly controlled by the political actors themselves so that the (in)famous complaints about media framing and agenda setting are no longer a challenge in the case of Internet communication.

American political life has seen the most profound impact of the Internet on its conduct. The Internet has become not only the additional communicative tool for well-known candidates but also an irreplaceable means for the lesser known candidates to spread their message and to gain voters' support. In particular, the

Internet has become an important fundraising tool. In Europe, use of the Internet for political purposes is less pronounced and intense. Nevertheless, also here the Internet plays an ever-growing role in political and, particularly, in election campaigns.

The first prominent use of the Internet by political parties and candidates had been launched during the 1996 presidential election campaign in the United States. Many political parties lacked any sound strategy for the effective use of the Internet (Selnow, 1998; Roper, 1998). Often, parties had to begin using the Internet simply so they would not look outdated. However, the lack of a clear web strategy had become the important characteristic of political websites of the first generation. In many cases, the material which could be found then on the political websites was "copied and pasted" from the newsletters and party papers, which were first and foremost available offline. In a 2005 study of Danish websites, Hansen, et al. (2005) refer to those first-generation websites as the "telephone book generation" because the majority of websites primarily contained addresses and telephone numbers of party bureaus as well as old and new party programs and press releases.

Websites of the second, "information-broadcasting generation" (Hansen, et al., 2005), are characterized by the development of specific web strategies which differed from the general campaign strategies. The primary goal was to inform potential voters on different aspects of party politics, while there was no real trust yet in the advantages of digital communication as such. Where first-generation websites were mainly known for providing administrative information (and that primarily for the party members), second-generation websites were more focused on voters and providing them with relevant information. Thus, at that stage, the Internet began to be seen as a new way to supply information. Although at that stage, a separate, specific Internet strategy emerged (different from the general campaign strategy), the message sent through the digital channel remained unchanged compared to that sent through other communication channels.

The online campaign of Howard Dean for the nomination as the Democratic presidential candidate in the 2002 US elections became a catalyst for the emergence of third-generation websites. This new type of website became known for its three major goals: to convince instead of simply to inform voters, to boost fundraising, and to mobilize supporters. Such proactive functioning of the websites was named the "integrated image generation" (Hansen, et al., 2005). Online donations, personalized blogs of candidates, coordination of online communication, and a political activism events calendar are only a few attributes of this new generation of websites.

Methodology Part

Several attempts have been made to evaluate the quality of political websites. Qualitative and quantitative methods were applied to investigate how efficiently and appropriately politicians, parties, and candidates filled their sites with content

(Davis, 1999; Klinenberg and Perrin, 2000; Norris, 2003; Cullen and Houghton, 2000). Some studies focused on counting certain features (Hill and Hughes, 1998; Gibson and Ward, 1998; LaPorte, et al., 2000; West, 2001; Foot and Schneider, 2002; Schneider and Foot, 2002; Rosenstiel, et al., 2004) while others also included the evaluation of quality (Davis, 1999; D'Alessio, 1997). Even though the analysis of party and campaign websites is not novel, only a few studies offer a comparative perspective. Before detailing the participation-friendliness coding scheme, we will discuss the theory on which the scheme is built.

Political Participation and Political Websites

Political participation can be seen as any kind of (political) communication processes to try to influence the selection of governmental personnel and the actions they take (Verba and Nie, 1972). Scholars tried to systemize the possible forms of political participation (Milbrath, 1965). For the purpose of our assessment scheme, we focus on a categorization regarding content. Building on Hagen (1997), we distinguish four main forms of political participation:

1. Active information seeking. Diverse information about the political processes and the political actors is a base for opinion formation and activity in political life.
2. Active political discussion. Discussion between citizens and between citizens and institutions is another important act of political participation. According to Etzioni (2003) a reasoned, informed, and broadly shared position requires dialoguing. In order to influence the selection and actions of representatives, one has to build an opinion first.
3. Voting. As the most direct activity to select governmental personnel, voting is the third dimension of political participation and, in the views of scholars, the central one. In order to deepen public actions, citizens must at least participate in the choice of their public officials. In this context, political parties function as important participation channels for citizens. Parties decide about the available candidates to vote for and formulate the "supports" and "demands" of citizens as an input into the political system (Milbrath, 1965).
4. Political activity. As any activity that is directed at securing or opposing any change in the law or in the policy or decisions of central governmental or local authorities (whether inside the country or abroad), political activity is the fourth dimension. Conventional and unconventional activities include volunteering in campaign work, participating in a community forum, demonstrating, or even mobilizing fellow citizens (Barnes and Kaase, 1979).

Especially in the context of the European elections (where politics seems to be removed from citizens), political websites can extend and enhance these forms of political participation. The next part of this chapter presents a short, exemplary sketch of possibilities for improving citizens' participation with the help of the Internet.

Political Websites

Given the four types of citizens' political participation, how can a political website's design and content enhance these activities from a citizen's perspective? In order to address the question, we try to identify the Internet's potential to support and improve these four dimensions of citizens' political participation. Regarding the four categories of political participation, we argue that websites should be informative, interactive, user-friendly, and aesthetically stimulating.

The "information" quality of websites relates to information seeking by citizens. The Internet enables an information transfer with a much higher volume and speed compared to traditional mass media (Neuner and De Landtsheer, 2005). The often-claimed lack of transparency and access to the traditional media channels by citizens and minor political actors can be compensated by information provision and exchange via websites (Mambrey, et al., 1999). The new possibilities for combined text, audio, images, and hyperlinks enable new styles of multi-media messages, which can enrich and stimulate communication processes. The political parties, therefore, are expected to offer political information in an adequate format on their websites (e.g., background information downloadable as a pdf-file, downloadable speeches, linking important information).

The "interactive" quality of websites concerns the political discussion function. Websites should support citizens for information activation and documentation (e.g., download papers and forms). Moreover, they should enable citizens to directly communicate with the candidates and parties in a reciprocal way or even enable citizens to mobilize other citizens. The interactive features of the Internet enable two-way communication (synchronous or asynchronous and in horizontal and lateral directions) between fellow online citizens, interest groups, political parties, candidates, and so on. These features of websites make interaction possible between users and a website interface (e.g., navigation, download). A user has more control since the limitations of time and space and the borders between authors and receivers of information are blurring (Neuner and De Landtsheer, 2005). Online, citizens can discuss and reflect their viewpoints, everybody can become an editor or a publisher, and community connections (e.g., online forums) can be fostered. Websites can (online) expand and optimize the existing channels of communication (e.g., political parties, mass media, and public sphere).

"User-friendliness" of websites relates to the voting dimension of political participation. The term "user-friendliness" embraces the extent to which a website supports its users in completing their tasks efficiently, effectively, and satisfactorily (Nielsen, 2000). Citizens will be encouraged to use political websites if they are user-friendly. While newspapers and electronic mass media tend to provide mostly the coverage of the major candidates and the hottest issues, websites can help to compensate for the deficits. Appropriate information and communication services (beyond the 30-second advertisements, sound bites, and horse race campaign coverage) can engage voters by providing more substance. In addition, candidates can contact the electorate personally via e-mail or discussion forums and try to convince or mobilize them. In this way, the gap between politicians and their electorate could be narrowed. A cleverly constructed website can target many audiences and even attract new ones, especially young people (Norris, 2001).

The "aesthetics" applied to websites relates to the dimension of political activity. The aesthetic quality of a website is directly connected to its persuasive and mobilizing functions that are based on the emotional appeal of the site. Our definition of "aesthetics" embraces the entire perception of a website by the citizen users. It addresses the arrangement and style of written words, elements of visual communication (e.g., pictures, empty space, body language), as well as the use of sound with which a website invites and challenges a user to follow its lead. It refers to the mediated tone and mood of a website's content (Schirmacher, 1999). There are many ways to become politically active. For a brief overview, people can join a range of direct (e.g., petition for a referendum) and indirect (party membership, volunteer party work, etc.) conventional forms, as well as direct (e.g., participating in actions of social movements, NGOs) and indirect (participation at citizen forums and networks) unconventional forms of political activities (Kaase and Marsh, 1979; Norris, 2003). It is often claimed that the growing popularity of unconventional "grassroots" forms of political activities exists due to an increasingly perceived "weakness" of citizens against the distanced and alienated apparatus of the state (including political parties) (Norris, 2003). Against such a background, websites can function as a "bridge" (a direct and interactive communication channel) between the MPs, party officials, candidates, and citizens. Moreover, issues can be launched by intellectuals or by advocates with limited resources and be taken up by journalists or associations off- and online. Issues, subsequently, can even turn into social movements or into new subculture; and they can finally reach the mass media and appear on the political agenda.

Participation-friendliness Scheme

The coding scheme we present here was developed and primarily applied in the comparative study of political websites in Eastern and Western Europe (De Landtsheer, et al., 2005). The term "participation-friendliness" emphasizes how the design and the content of a website can enhance, motivate, and encourage citizens to become active participants in the political communication processes on- and offline.

We have developed the criteria which take into account a wide range of factors supposedly crucial in this context. The criteria are based on the latest literature (books, case studies, articles, and web design guidelines) from the different fields of study: political science, educational and information science, communication and commercial studies, graphic design, and psychology. The coding scheme is easily adaptable for the study of other public actors' websites, such as social movements, candidates, governments, interest groups, media organizations, etc.

Participation-friendliness is the major evaluation parameter of the coding scheme. It is based on the assumption that a political website can become an important information, communication, and participatory tool in election campaigns and other forms of politicians-citizens interactions only if it satisfies certain criteria. The coding scheme includes the four main categories: information, interactivity, user-friendliness, and aesthetics (for a detailed description of all categories, see Appendix 1).

Information pays attention to the quality and type of information. Interactivity deals with the possibilities offered to be an active citizen, contrasted to an unengaged recipient of information. Building on Rafaeli (1988), we consider interactivity as not just a technological feature, but also as a communication concept by itself. User-friendliness refers to the ease with which users can navigate the site and find information and services. Even if the Internet technologies carry a high potential to foster citizen's participation possibilities in impressive new ways, scientists should not forget that it is still an interaction between humans and a machine. And the website interface as a mediator of this interaction plays a significant role (Norman, 2002; Dillon, 2000; Schneiderman, 1998). Since for many citizens, the computer is still a confusing or even frightening tool, it is important while assessing the participation-friendliness of political websites to consider how citizens will best interact with the website interface. Theories and research from interface design, human-computer interaction, and cognitive science provide a valuable contribution for improving political website interfaces concerning their potential to foster citizens' engagement. Aesthetics addresses the arrangement and style of written words and visual elements with which the medium invites and challenges a user to follow its lead.

Measurement of Criteria

From a great range of possible conditions of political and electoral success of websites, we have chosen information, interactivity, user-friendliness, and aesthetics as the key characteristics of websites' participation-friendliness. Each main category includes five subcategories. We give each subcategory a weight factor, according to its estimated power to support civic engagement. Within each category, a maximum of four points are given to each of the subcategories (0 = not present, 1 = scanty presence, 2 = average presence, 3 = above-average presence, 4 = very good presence). These points are multiplied with the corresponding weight-factors. Their sum gives points for each category. A website can score a maximum of 60 points per category, which in total gives a maximum of 240 points for the index of Participation Friendliness. The more points a website gets, the more participation-friendly it is assessed (see Table 1 for the coding scheme). For better comparisons, we have also given "low-average-high" labels for these points (see Table 2).

Table 1: Assesment scheme for participation-friendliness of political websites

not present	scarcely present	average present	above average	overwhelmingly present
(0 points)	(1 point)	(2 points)	(3 points)	(4 points)

Categories	Weight Factor
1. Information	
1 self-representation and public relations	(value 1)
2 extern information	(value 2)
3 general 'boulevard' information	(value 3)
4 political information for citizens	(value 4)
5 political background information	(value 5)
2. Interactivity	
1 read-only-service	(value 1)
2 read-and-just-write-service	(value 2)
3 electronic correspondence	(value 3)
4 forums/discussion groups/virtual communities	(value 4)
5 self-presentation possibilities for citizens	(value 5)
3. User-friendliness	
1 actuality	(value 1)
2 compactness	(value 2)
3 search/navigation help	(value 3)
4 investigation/documentation help	(value 4)
5 links	(value 5)
4. Aesthetics	
1 humor/parody	(value 1)
2 symbols/political propaganda	(value 2)
3 pictures	(value 3)
4 visual attractiveness/appeal	(value 4)
5 design/structure	(value 5)

Table 2: Participation-friendliness of websites

	Low	Below average	Above average	High
Points for Information, Interactivity, User friendliness, Aesthetics	0 – 15	16 – 30	31 – 45	46 – 60
Points for Participation Friendliness	1 – 60	61 – 120	121 – 180	181 – 240

The qualitative and quantitative aspects are equally important for all categories. They should be used to construct a good website, which serves users' needs in a satisfactory way. It always depends upon the purpose of the website and the target group.

Conclusion and Discussion

The intention of this chapter is to show the need for bringing single areas together in one framework to provide a broad picture of the quality of a website. The suggested categories can still be better theoretically underpinned, conceptualized, and categorized. Moreover, their proper application always depends on the purpose and nature of the website and the cultural context. Especially, the aesthetics should no longer be ignored when talking about useable and engaging websites since they can play a crucial role in motivating the citizens to get engaged with the content of the site. The movement from book to screen, from print to digital with changed concepts of space, time, togetherness, and communication provides so many surprises, opportunities, hopes, and fears that none of us can say how it will play out. Our experiences in the "virtual world" will affect our perceptions and activities in "real world." With changed media and communication, the concept of the public sphere and democracy also changes. But how we judge these changes is less important than combining our expertise to actively create this new public space/new part of our public sphere. A shared common world (with public and private discourse) requires the people's participation. In order to design meaningful and attractive websites, designers must understand how citizens use and perceive the sites they visit. Therefore, the user should be in the center of the design. Moreover, users and perceptions may vary among various types of websites and tasks, so we should start with specific contexts before we draw general conclusions.

It is clear that the potential of the Internet to enhance citizens' participation not only depends upon the design and content of their websites, but on a number of factors, such as an institutional framework of a political system, access to the websites, electronic literacy of citizens, resources, and the goodwill of the political actors.

Acknowledgements

This chapter was earlier published in pages 99-124 in Marczewska-Rytko, M. (ed.) 2012, *Democratic Thought in the Age of Globalization*. Lublin, Poland: University Maria Curie Sklodowska Press. It was delivered as a lecture at China University of Mining and Technology (CUMT) Xuzhou, China, as the guest of Professor and Dean of Graduate Affairs, Song Yingfa, on May 13, 2011. The author thanks Cornelia Neuner for her contribution to an earlier version of this chapter (Neuner and De Landtsheer, 2005).

Appendix 1. Criteria for the Assessment-Scheme

Information

This category focuses on the general utility of the information in terms of its volume, quality, and type. It is not intended to evaluate how democratic and reliable the actual content is.

1.1. Self-Presentation and Public Relations (value 1)

Does the website provide information about the organization, its purpose and belonging? Is the Internet used as a vehicle for appropriate public relations (the purpose of the website, major events and dates, self-presentation)? Is the news service well organized (press releases, press and picture archives, contact person)? Does the website provide enough information to form opinion about the people and institution behind it (curriculum vitae, point of view about actual issues, present political position, etc.)?

1.2. External Information (value 2)

It concerns additional information service (e.g. actual news, situation abroad, links to other organizations, information about the actions of social movements, and members of the constituency). Mobile information services about upcoming events, weather, etc., are also included here. We assume that citizens can benefit from this in an indirect way by gaining broader knowledge in their preparation of activities. It may change their position or spur them to action or at least attract their interest. It gives them a good overview of actual political and public processes and allows them to get more detailed information about the subjects and organizations they are interested in.

1.3. General/Boulevard Information (value 3)

Information can be made available online from or about government departments, citizens' advice bureaus, libraries, council offices, and many other (public) institutions, particularly at the local level (e.g., opening hours, job offerings, contact-addresses, associations, registered societies, statistical data, information about the use of the public purse, events and cultural offerings, other information which helps to organize daily life of active citizens).

1.4. Political Information for Citizens (value 4)

This criterion considers whether political information contributes to the transparency and facilitates political participation. During elections, the following would be of special interest: candidates with their personal aims and point of views, statements, speeches, articles, interviews, publications, and other information on actual issues reflecting the (partisan) viewpoints as well as other opinions, election results, political agendas, information about elections, and planned actions in the constituency, information focused on local issues.

1.5. Political Background Information (value 5)

This subcategory examines whether diverse opinions of citizens, media, or opponents are shown as well as comments and polls. Can citizens find a range of different opinions, origins, reasons, and expectation of the political message that are not found on the evening news? Is there any information which contains comparisons between candidates, messages, issues, party policies?

Interactivity

This category deals with the possibilities which a website offers citizens to use and debate the supplied information. Does the site treat users as passive recipients of information rather than as active citizens?

2.1. Read-Only-Service (value 1)

Websites can simply post essays to provide citizens with (political) information without giving the possibility for any kind of interactions like comments, requests, reaction, or deliberation. Does the website give pure passive information without input or feedback possibilities for the citizens? This one-way communication is better than no information, but it would not meet the needs of a politically interested user and does not exploit the potential of the Internet.

2.2. Read-And-Just-Write-Service (value 2)

Does a website offer possibilities for sending an e-mail (e.g., for further information, complaints or direct contact with a politician, a party member, candidate, or activist, etc.)? Is there a feedback possibility via e-mail? Contacting the e-candidate might be the first step of getting involved in politics.

2.3. Electronic Correspondence (value 3)

Does the website promote online transaction services with regular feedback loops? Do they guarantee that communication can be reciprocal? For example, are there e-mailing lists, a guest book, newsletter, and online campaigns to join on the website? Does the website link political experts or administrators with "ordinary" citizens? Can citizens, for example, attend online consulting hours, fill in feedback forms about the site, register online for a campaign or party membership, make reservations and order brochures online, conduct or participate in opinion polls, enroll for a course, or apply for a job online?

2.4. Forums, Chat Groups (value 4)

Does the website provide a chat room so that the newly assimilated information can be discussed vertically as well as horizontally (e.g., with the owner of the site), linking citizens directly to one another? Are there forums for different (partisan) citizens/groups to find a public voice? For how many topics does the website offer discussion groups? Are these groups moderated and are political actors also joining them?

2.5. Self-presentation Possibilities (value 5)

Self-presentation possibilities center on whether a website helps citizens to organize common activities by themselves. The websites of political parties, politicians, or civic organizations can, for example, offer citizens to make their own page. In this way, people can present and discuss actual information that is, in their opinion, interesting for their fellow citizens (e.g., local issues, building plans, activities). Especially people who are not so familiar with buying a domain and building own website would feel supported and encouraged by these possibilities.

User-friendliness

This criterion concerns how easy it is to use a political website.

3.1. Actuality (value 1)

Does the website provide citizens with the latest (election) news, press-releases, forthcoming events, hot topics, major political news, news from the region, etc.? How often is the information updated and how many dead sites/pages exist?

3.2. Compactness (value 2)

Is the information well-structured and is it linked so that one can click further without surfing through the entire website? Is the site quickly readable and understandable? Is there superfluous information or is the most important political information is brought to the forefront?

3.3. Search/Navigation Assistance (value 3)

The navigation system and the menu points are crucial for the user to get the required information easily and quickly. Furthermore, there should be a sitemap which provides a general overview and contains pictures to snap/click on. How understandable is the chosen name for the presented menu point? Are all pages included in the navigation?

3.4. Investigation and Documentation Assistance (value 4)

Especially beginners may need additional help to find the required information, documentation, and comments. Therefore, it is important to offer appropriate possibilities for investigation like databases, searching machines, archives, and possibilities to bookmark the site, print, or download the documents. Are there search engines? Do the results correspond to the typed keywords? Are there other language versions? Are innovative technologies used to download videos, speeches, or slide shows quickly (also inexpensively)?

3.5. Links (value 5)

Links contain information or recommendations beyond the context of the current text. They should be organized to help a user, but not to distract or disorientate. Therefore, the text/name of the link and its placement is very important. A special links section should be arranged by topic and be commented. Strategically connected links can facilitate citizens' interest in political participation.

Aesthetics

Aesthetics appeals to our senses and to our intellect. It is about how creative, innovative, and appropriate the sites/messages are designed to attract citizens' attention.

4.1. Humor/Parody (value 1)

Even politically active citizens like to be entertained. It is about the style and language of the presentation. Does the site use tools of political humor (e.g., parodies, political cartoons and caricatures, funny pictures, ironic or polemic ways of writing, funny/sarcastic comments about the life and love of political actors, anecdotes)? Are there additional offerings, for example, the possibility to send funny e-cards about politicians, or animations, etc.?

4.2. Symbols/ Political Propaganda (value 2)

Symbols can help make abstract topics more concrete. In this context, it is about whether there is appropriate political propaganda (not an overload at the cost of useful political information). Do websites use typical and well-known (national) symbols, like the colors of the American flag, to strengthen the feeling of unity and identity? How attractive is the language? Are the used metaphors and symbols understandable and constant?

4.3. Pictures (value 3)

Photos, illustrations, or graphics can help visualizing the topic/problem, simplify complex connections, and facilitate reading. Moreover, pictures can communicate their own message. Through their appropriate design, they should help form the right impression.

4.4. Visual Appeal/Attractiveness (value 4)

This criterion deals with the general style of the website. The pages should be appropriate in length, clearly laid out, and readable. The appeal and friendliness of the website depends on the colors, typography, unity of single sites, appropriate use of multimedia elements, etc.

4.5. Design/Technology (value 5)

This focuses on interface design and the technology that was used. Concerning the used technology, crucial issues are: compatibility for older browsers, loading speed, offer of alternatives for missing plug-ins (e.g., a flash and html version), the absence of frames in order to find the site via search engines, using of the site without changing the settings (e.g., screen resolution, enabling cookies).

References

Accone, T. (2002). "Digital Dividends for Journalism in Africa," pp. 67-70 in *Nieman Reports*, Vol. 54, No. 4.

Arnold, E. and D. Plymire (2000). "The Cherokee Indians and the Internet" in D. Gauntlett (ed.) *Web Studies*. London, UK: Arnold.

Barnes, S. and M. Kaase (eds.) (1979). *Political Action: Mass Participation in Five Western Democracies*. Beverly Hills, CA and London, UK: Sage.

Bennett, W. (2003). "Communicating Global Activism: Strengths and Vulnerabilities of Networked Politics," pp. 143-168 in *Information, Communication and Society*, Vol. 6, No. 2.

Bimber, B. (1998). "Toward an Empirical Map of Political Participation on the Internet." Paper presented to the American Political Science Association, Boston, MA, September 3-6.

Carlson, T. and G. Kjupsund (2001). "Old Wine in New Bottles? The 1999 Finnish Election Campaign on the Internet," pp. 68-87 in *Harvard International Journal of Press/Politics*, Vol. 6, No. 1.

Coleman, S. (1999). "The New Media and Democratic Politics," pp. 67-74 in *New Media and Society*, Vol. 1, No. 1.

Conway, M. and D. Dorner (2004). "An Evaluation of New Zealand Political Party Websites." http://informatinr.net/ir/9-4/paper196.html.

Cuevas, A. (2004). "The Internet and 2004 Philippine Elections: Analysis of Election Campaign Websites." http://www.thephilippines.org/.

Cullen, R. and C. Houghton (2000). "Democracy Online: An Assessment of New Zealand Government Web Sites," pp. 243-267 in Government Information Quarterly, Vol. 17, No. 3.

D'Alessio, D. (1997). "Use of the World Wide Web in the 1996 US Election," pp. 489-500 in *Electoral Studies*, Vol. 16, No. 4.

Davis, R. (1999). *The Web of Politics: The Internet's Impact on the American Political System*. New York, NY: Oxford University Press.

De Landtsheer, C. N. Krasnoboka, and E. Gomezllata (2001). "Userfriendliness of US Presidential Election Websites." Paper presented at Etmaal Communicatiewetenschap, Free University, Amsterdam, the Netherlands.

De Landtsheer, C., N. Krasnoboka, and C. Neuner (1999). "Participation-friendliness of Political Websites in Eastern and Western European Countries," pp. 325-360 in R. Farnen, et al. (eds.) *Democratization, Europeanization, and Globalization Trends: Cross-national Analysis of*

Authoritarianism, Socialization, Communications, Youth, and Social Policy. Frankfurt am Main, Germany: Peter Lang.

De Landtsheer, C., C. Neuner, and N. Krasnoboka (2007). "The Top Ten of Europe: How to Predict the 2004 European Election by the Quality of Websites?" Paper presented at the ECPR Conference in Pisa, Italy, September 5-8.

De Landtsheer, C., D. Vertessen, and T. De Vree (2004). "Participatievriendelijkheid van politieke websites in België," in D. De Landtsheer *Politik impresiemanagement in Vlaanderen en Nederland*. Leuven, Belgium: Acco.

Dillon, A. (1990). "Edsigning the Human-Computer Interface to Hpermedia Applications," pp. 185-197 in D. Jonassen and H. Mandl (eds.) *Designing Hypermedia for Learning*. New York, NY: Springer-Verlag.

Etzioni, A. (2003). *The Monochrome Society*. Princeton, NJ: Princeton University Press.

Foot, K. and S. Schneider (2002). "Online Action in Campaign 2000: An Explanatory Analysis of the US Political Web Sphere," pp. 222-244 in *Journal of Broadcasting and Electronic Media*, Vol. 46, No. 2.

Gibson, R. and I. McAllister (2005). "Does Cypber Campaigning Win Votes? Online Communication in the 2004 Australian Election." http://repositories.cdlib.org/cgi/viewcontent.cgi!article=1064&context=csd.

Gibson, R., P. Nixon, and S. Ward (eds.) (2003). *Political Parties and the Internet: Net Gain?* London, UK and New York, NY: Routledge.

Gibson, R., A. Rommele, and S. Ward (2003). "German Parties and Internet Campaigning in the 2002 Federal Election," pp. 79-108 in *German Politics*, Vol. 12, No. 1.

Gibson, R. and S. Ward (1998). "UK Political Parties and the Internet," pp. 14-38 in *Harvard International Journal of Press/Politics*, Vol. 3, No. 3.

Gibson, R. and S. Ward (2000). "A Proposed Methodology for Studying the Function and Effectiveness of Party and Candidate Web Sites," pp. 301-319 in *Social Science Computer Review*, Vol. 18, No. 3.

Gibson, R. and S. Ward (2001). "Open All Hours? UK Political Parties and Online Technologies." Paper presented at the Digital Seminar, IPPR in London, UK, June 20.

Gibson, R. and S. Ward (2002). "Virtual Campaigning: Australian Parties and the Impact of the Internet," pp. 99-129 in *Australian Journal of Political Science*, Vol. 37, No. 1.

Hagen, M. (1997). "A Typology of Electronic Democracy." No longer available online.

Hansen, K., K. Pedersen, and D. Wahl-Jorgensen (2005). "Cyber-campaigning: The Character, Development and Consequences of Parties' Electioneering in Cyber-space." Paper presented at the Nordic Political Science Association's Conference in Reykjavik, Iceland.

Hill, K. and J. Hughes (1998). *Cyberpolitics: Citizen Activism in the Age of the Internet*. Lanham, MD, Boulder, CO, New York, NY, Oxford, UK: Rowman & Littelfield.

Kaase, M. and A. Marsh (1979). "Political Action: A Theoretical Perspective," pp. 27-56 in S. Barnes and M. Kaase (eds.) *Political Action: Mass Participation in Five Western Democracies*. Beverly Hills, CA and London, UK: Sage.

Klinenberg, E. and A. Perrin (2000). "Symbolic Politics in the Information Age: The 1996 Republican Presidential Campaigns in Cyberspace," pp. 17-38 in *Information, Communication & Society*, Vol. 3, No. 1.

LaPorte, T., et al. (2000). "Democracy and Bureaucracy in the Age of the Web: Empirical Findings and Theoretical Speculations." Cyberspace Policy Research Group (CyPRG), http;/www.cyprg.arizona.edu.

Mambrey, P., H. Neumann, and K. Sieverdingbeck (1999). "Bridging the Gap Between Parliament and Citizen: The Internet Services of the German Bundestag," pp. 480-492 in *Parliamentary Affairs*, Vol. 52, No. 3.

Margolis, M. and D. Resnick (2000). *Politics as Usual: The Cyberspace Revolution*. Thousand Oaks, CA: Sage.

Margolis, M., D. Resnick, and C. Tu (1997). "Campaigning on the Internet: Parties and Candidates on the World Wide Web in the 1996 Primary Season," pp. 59-78 in *Harvard International Journal of Press/Politics*, Vol. 2, No. 1.

McLaughlin, S. (2003). "The Use of the Internet for Political Action by Non-state Dissident Actors in the Middle East." http://firstmonday.org/issues/issue8_11/mclaughlin/index.html.

Milbrath, L. (1965). *Political Participation: How and Why Do People Get Involved in Politics?* Chicago, IL: Rand McNally.

Neuner, C. and C. De Landtsheer (2005). "Towards a Methodology for Evaluating the Quality of (Public) Websites," pp. 57-64 in *The IPSI BgD Transactions on Internet Research*, Vol. 1, No. 1.

Nielsen, J. (2000). *Designing Web Usability*. Indianapolis, IN: New Riders Publishing.

Norris, P. (2000). "The Global Divide: Information Poverty and Internet Access Wordwide." Paper presented at the Internet Conference International Political Science Word Congress, August 1-6, 2000, in Quebec City, Canada. http://www.pippanorris.com.

Norris, P. (2001). *Digital Divide: Civic Engagement, Information Poverty and the Internet in Democratic Societies*. New York, NY: Cambridge University Press.

Norris, P. (2003). "Preaching to the Converted? Pluralism, Participation and Party Websites," pp. 21-46 in *Party Politics*, Vol. 9, No. 1.

Norman, D. (2002). "Emotion and Design: Attractive Things Work Better," pp. 36-42 in *Interactions Magazine*, Vol. ix, No. 4.

Pew Research Center (2000). *Internet Election News Audience Seeks Convenience, Familiar Names*. Washington, DC: Pew Internet & American Life Project http://www.pewInternet.org.

Rafaeli, S. (1988). "Interactivity: From New Media to Communication," pp. 110-134 in R. Hawkins, J. Wiemann, and S. Pingree (eds.) *Advancing Communication Science: Merging Mass and Interpersonal Processes*. Thousand Oaks, CA: Sage.

Roper, J. (1998). "New Zealand Political Parties Online: The Word Wide Web as Tool for Democratization or for Political Marketing?" in C. Toulouse and T. Luke (eds.) *The Politics of Cyberspace: A New Political Reader*. New York, NY: Routledge.

Rosenstiel, T., et al. (2004). "E-Politics 2004: How Online Campaign Coverage has Changed in Four Years," http://www.journalism.org/resources/research/reports/campaign2004/epolitics-/epolitics.pdf.

Schirmacher, W. (1999). "Media Aesthetics in Europe." http://www.egs edu/faculty/schirmacher/aesth.html.

Schneider, S. and K. Foot (2002). "Online Structure for Political Action: Exploring Presidential Campaign Web Sites from the 2000 American Election," pp. 43-60 in *Javnost – The Public*, Vol. 9, No. 2.

Schneiderman, B. (1998). *Designing the User Interface: Strategies for Effective Human-computer Interaction*. Reading, MA: Addison-Wesley.

Selnow, G. (1998). *Electronic Whistle-Stops: The Impact of the Internet on American Politics*. Westport, CT: Praeger.

Tkach-Kawasaki, L. (2003). "Politics@Japan: Party Competition on the Internet in Japan," pp. 105-123 in *Party Politics*, Vol. 9, No. 1.

Verba, S. and N. Nie (1972). *Participation in America: Political Democracy and Social Equality*. New York, NY: Harper and Row.

Voerman, G. and S. Ward (2000). "New Media and New Politics: Green Parties, Intra-party Democracy and the Potential of the Internet (An Anglo-Dutch Comparison)," pp. 192-215 in F. Ankersmit, et al. (eds.) *Jaarboek 1999 DNPP*. Groningen, Germany.

Ward, S., R. Gibson, and P. Nixon (2003). "Parties and the Internet: An Overview" in R. Gibson, P. Nixon, and S. Ward (eds.) *Political Parties and the Internet: Net Gain?* London, UK: Routledge.

West, D. (2001). "State and Federal E-government in the United States 2001." http://www.InsidePolitics.org/egovt01us.html.

Chapter 7
Empirical Evaluation of Government and Websites

Christ'l De Landtsheer, Natalya Krasnoboka, and Conny Neuner

University of Antwerp, Antwerp, Belgium

> With the networks in place an interactive technology to hand, people can vote on issues, inform themselves on government policy, and interrogate their representatives: they can become the active, effective citizen of the democratic dream (Street, 1997, p. 28).

Abstract

This chapter argues that websites can be useful to improve democratic citizenship. Since political participation is crucial to democracy, political websites should be constructed to enhance citizens' participation. Political websites form a particular case, so does their participation friendliness. Therefore, the participation friendliness of political websites is of great importance. This study explores websites' characteristics that could improve active citizenship. It develops an assessment scheme for the participation friendliness of political websites that takes into account participatory characteristics that are relevant from the point of view of political communication. It also presents an application of this scheme to some political websites in Western and Eastern European countries in 1999. The study reveals profound distinctions between political websites in various Central and Eastern European (CEE) countries as well as distinctions between political websites of CEE countries and EU countries.

User-friendliness for the Citizen

The Internet shows great promise for democracy in terms of revitalized patterns of political communications from a citizen's point of view. It is often said to be the perfect instrument for returning (at least some) power to citizens. It is considered to have great participatory potential, enlarging and improving possibilities for "ordinary citizens" (not only privileged ones, such as candidates, journalists, rich and influential people, and organizations) to participate in the public sphere of a representative democracy. In established democracies, it is increasingly claimed that citizens are distracted with inefficient participation activities, while important plans and decisions are made elsewhere out of their reach.

The citizens' political role is increasingly considered too minimal (Barber, 1984). Traditional media (such as press and television) are supposed to be guides for citizens in politics and decision making. They also act as watch dogs to ensure democratic and accountable performances by elected politicians. But they have long been criticized for their inability (even lack of interest) to serve political needs of civil society in any appropriate way. Thus, the arrival of a new, "unmediated" medium (such as the Internet) may reestablish these links between society and politicians as well as bring citizens closer to and better acquaint them with political issues, bypassing and/or supplementing traditional media functions.

Potentially, the Internet offers even greater opportunities for transitional societies and new democracies. In these countries, the possibilities for political participation and free speech were very limited for decades because of the well-known and vigilant activities of the single party and security service apparatus (Krasnoboka, 2002). Here, the Internet can establish a new type of political participation, devoid of the interference of these previous political regimes and traditional wrongdoing of established capitalist democracies.

All in all, the Internet (with its participation-friendly characteristics like interactivity, world wide and free accessibility, and new user-control features) seems to be quite welcome in different parts of the world. But what would such an "electronically enhanced democracy" look like? The term "electronically enhanced democracy" means any democratic political system in which computers and computer networks are used to carry out crucial functions of the democratic process, such as information and communication, interest articulation and aggregation, and decision-making, including deliberation as well as voting (Hagen, 1997). In general, increasing the level and quality of citizens' political participation possibilities is a major goal (Barber, Mattson, and Peterson, 1997). Therefore, our main questions are: Does the use of the Internet make it possible to improve the existing representative democratic system by making it more responsive, transparent, and accessible for citizens? Can the Internet really help to enhance the flow of information and communication between and among political institutions, citizens, and politicians? Can websites in the public sphere help to improve citizen participation?

In theory, the democratic potential of the Internet seems appropriate to optimize "role-fulfillment"' of public actors as well as citizens. That is at least what one group of Internet researchers, the so-called cyber optimists (Norris, 2000) suggest. They hope that the Internet can provide new opportunities for facilitating active citizenship in a representative democracy. With the help of the Internet, people from all over the world can communicate with each other; everyone can access any public actor, institution, or politician to discuss and clearly understand which decisions are made on their behalf and to influence their decisions (Rheingold, 1993; Coleman, 1999; Mambrey, et al., 1999; Bonchek, 1995).

More pessimistic voices claim that the Internet cannot be expected to transform existing disparities of power and wealth, to facilitate increased access to policy makers, or to make political processes more transparent to increase the level of citizens' political participation. They emphasize the importance of technical and economic problems in accessing computers (Ward, et al., 2003).

Who is right? Strong claims from both sides are not scientifically well founded and research often has not gone further than popular rhetoric. The Internet is a complex and changing medium. Research thereon remains fragmented, not presenting any general and logical picture. So, the answer is currently unclear and requires that we weigh many factors in addition to those stressed already.

This study lays no claim to accounting for all possible views and criteria concerned with the "democratic" impact of cyberspace. Neither does it take a firm cyber-optimist position. The study starts from the moderate assumption that to make the representative democratic system more responsive and to enhance citizens' political participation, websites (as an additional channel of political communication) should at least be designed in a participation-friendly way. Besides controversial questions like universal access, media competence, organizational structures, and the people's willingness to increase their political engagement, one major problem is the design and content of websites in the public, party, and political spheres (Löfgren, et al., 1999; Mambrey, et al., 1999).

Eurobarometer data reveal that only 10% of those with access to the Internet in EU countries visited a party website in 2000. Other data suggest that in the 2000 US and in the 1988 Danish elections, only 7% to 8% visited candidates' sites. In the 2001 UK elections, only 2% visited party sites (Ward, et al., 2003; Norris, 200lb; Crabtree, 2001). The dominance of dead, dated, and unsatisfying political websites raises doubts about the potential of the Internet to promote a better-informed and more active citizenry (Resnick, 1998; Davis, 1999; Sassi, 2000). We argue that citizens will only be encouraged to use websites if they are easy to access, contain current and engaging content, and are "user-friendly."

User-friendliness refers to how useable a website is or the extent to which a website supports its users in completing their tasks efficiently, effectively, and satisfactorily (Preece, 2002; Graber and White, 2001). Therefore, the participation friendliness of political websites has user-friendliness as a base, but it also emphasizes how the design of the website can motivate and encourage citizens to become active or to participate in the public sphere both on- and offline.

We next turn to the concept of active citizenship and people's participation in the public sphere. Then, we introduce our applied assessment scheme. In the section after that, our key research findings for CEE countries as well as EU countries are summarized.

The Internet and Political Participation

Why improve political participation possibilities at all? How can the Internet help accomplish that goal? In a democracy, the main function of citizens' political participation is to keep the political system balanced by legitimating the actions of the politicians through citizen support (Milbrath, 1965; Barber, 1984). Political participation can be seen in terms of communication concerned with influencing public opinion or participating in the political life of a democracy. Nowadays, in European countries, the prevailing model is representative democracy. Considering the shrinkage of the nation state and the growing importance of (worldwide) social movements (Norris, 200 la and b), the target for such participation has widened beyond national governments. There are various definitions of political participation (Verba, et al., 1978; Milbrath, 1965). For our purpose, we distinguish among four different dimensions of political participation that could be improved through the political use of the Internet.

First, the basic dimension of political participation is information-seeking. With the Internet, far more information can be made available, which thus can increase e-political knowledge and awareness of political issues. Any kind of political documents (such as political news, submissions from interested parties, and speeches of representatives as well as arguments from private individuals) could be made instantly available. Directly through their websites, parties can provide citizens with much more information than before. The same holds true for candidates, local parties, and individual party members who now can produce their own sites. Dissenting voices can also profit from the electronic platform. Citizens who felt (because of the role of media gate keepers like TV and radio) excluded can autonomously interact as communicators online, spread active information, and react to any article or event (Hague and Uhm, 2003; Ward, et al., 2003; Bowie, 2003). The effect of the opportunities for information seekers that the Internet provides is, indeed, highly dependent on the willingness of public actors to make political processes more transparent. Therefore, the politicians as well as the intermediary systems have to put required political information in an appropriate form on their website (Barber, Mattson, and Peterson, 1997, p. 38).

Active political discussion with one's family, friends, colleagues, neighbors, and elected representatives is the second dimension of political participation. Perhaps one of the best ways to increase citizens' participation in the public sphere is to foster community connections. Civic networks can provide discussion groups on community issues ranging from children's playgrounds to local politics. The Internet can give more opportunities for collective public discussion (on- as well as offline) and reflection on issues of importance among citizens, interest groups, and political parties. Such virtual communities are not supposed to replace face-to-face meetings, but rather to complement them (Miller, 1996, p. 35). Moreover, elected representatives can be asked to explain political issues or to report back on their own voting record or speeches. Discussions about progress within legislatures can be held instantly among citizens as well as with politicians. Until now, most communications from party websites were not really interactive. Parties are sparing in their interactivity because opening up one's site to comment with bulletin boards and chat rooms is a risky gambit (Ward, et al., 2003; Hague and Uhm, 2003; Margolis, et al., 1997, 1999; Davis, 1999). Again, the impact of the Internet in this respect depends on the willingness of public actors to make their sites more responsive.

Voting is the third dimension of political participation. Many scholars believe it is the central, most important one. Traditional mass media (like newspapers and television) are increasingly blamed for not fulfilling their public task by covering prominent and influential candidates/parties and by distorting and trivializing political information instead of making political processes more transparent

(Oberreuter, 1982). Anyhow, there is a widespread decrease in levels of partisan attachment among voters for political parties. The finding from the Dutch 1998 elections that there was a consensus that if a website does not do any good, it does not do harm either, may be worth noting (Ward, et al., 2003; Erik-Lane and Ersson, 1996). The Internet (with its varied interactive information and communication possibilities) can compensate for some of these deficiencies. The new services can engage voters on matters of substance rather than style or symbolic politics, getting beyond 30-second advertisements, sound bites, or the usual horse-race campaign coverage and narrow the distance between representatives and the electorate (Abramson, Arterton, and Orren, 1988, p. 91). Candidates can contact their potential electorate directly and personally and try to convince and mobilize them as Bob Dole in the 1996 US presidential campaign did, "This is an important business - this election is important. I ask for your support, I ask for your help . . . if you really want to get involved, just tap into my homepage."

Political activity is the fourth dimension. It includes political activists working on campaigns, organizing local party events or citizen initiatives, participating in community forums, and managing or participating in interest groups, social movements, and similar activities. For social movements, the Internet is increasingly useful for overcoming the problem of collective action. And younger voters are more likely to use the web politically because they are the computer-literate generation (Ward, et al., 2003; Coleman, 2001). As a direct and interactive channel of communication, the Internet provides additional ways to prepare political actions on- and offline. Citizens can tell their representatives their demands and needs at length, without fighting for a role as a minor communicator in the mass media system. It may be true that most survey evidence testifies to the dominance of major parties in cyberspace, just as in traditional media (Ward, et al., 2003). Interest groups (including the smaller and less influential ones) now have more opportunities to inform, recruit, and motivate citizens. Lots of other participatory activities (like parliamentary hearings, building-plans, community work, and citizens' initiatives) can be optimized with these new interactive information and communication possibilities (Gotze, 1998; Barnett, 1997, p. 206). The Internet can facilitate their political expression and engagement (McGookin, 1995; Wilhelm, 2000). The following section deals with identifying the criteria for "participation-friendly" political websites and explains our applied assessment scheme.

Assessing Participation-Friendliness of Political Websites

Our assessment scheme for public websites (De Landtsheer, Krasnoboka, and Neuner, 1999) aims to cover the previously mentioned dimensions of political participation. The main categories of the scheme (see Table 1 in Chapter 6) assess how much political websites contain elements that facilitate citizens' political participation. Furthermore, the criteria we distinguished are based on the latest relevant literature (books, articles, case studies, guidelines) of diverse fields (psychology, sociology, political science, media studies, human-computer interaction, web design, computer science, information systems, marketing, entertainment, and business).

This assessment scheme includes four main categories/criteria. These criteria include information, interactivity, user-friendliness, and aesthetics. Each main category includes five subcriteria. The category of Information pays attention to the amount, quality, and type of information. Interactivity deals with the possibilities offered to be an active citizen rather than a disengaged recipient of information. User-friendliness refers to the ease with which users can navigate the site as well as find and use information and services. Aesthetics covers the audience's whole perception of the website. It addresses the arrangement and style of the written words and of the visual elements with which the medium invites and challenges a user to follow its lead. The criteria and subcriteria are intended to represent minimum standards only, not best practice, so they slightly overlap.

How Informative are Websites?

The first evaluation category is entitled Information. It deals with the general utility of the information, focusing on amount, quality, and type of information. It is not intended to evaluate thoroughly how democratic and reliable the actual site content is. We distinguished the following subcategories for this criterion:

- Self Presentation and Public Relations (value 1). Does the website provide some information about the organization, its purpose, and the institutions to which it belongs? Does the sender use the Internet as a vehicle for appropriate public relations (major events and dates, philosophy, services)? Is the news service well-organized (press releases, press archives, picture archives, contact person)? Does the website provide the citizens with enough information (curriculum vitae, point of view about actual issues, present political position) to form their own opinions about the main persons or institutions of the website? The value 1 is given as a weight factor because this kind of information is basic and crucial for users entering a website; they need to quickly establish its purpose, receive orienting help, and access legal information (such as from whom, why, and for whom the site is made).
- External Information (value 2). Does the site provide for additional information services (e.g., news, the situation abroad, links to other organizations, information about the actions of social movements or related issues such as a link to community activities in the constituency)? Up-to-date information services about upcoming events, about the weather, etc. are included in this category. We assume that the citizens can benefit from this in an indirect way like gaining broader knowledge to prepare to act. It might change how they see the world, spur them to action, or at least attract their interest. It gives them a

good overview about actual political and public processes and allows them to get more detailed information about the subjects and organizations they are interested in. That is why the weight factor here is valued as a 2.

- General/Boulevard Man-on-the-street Information (value 3). This subcategory refers to information that can be made available online from (or about) government departments, citizens' advice bureaus, libraries, council offices, and many other (public) institutions, particularly on the local level. It should be useful for citizens (e.g., opening hours, job offerings, contact addresses, associations, registered societies, statistical data, information about the use of public funds, events, and cultural offerings, or other kinds of information which might be helpful to active citizens). Also, general information concerning the privacy and security implications of site use is found in this category. The value 3 reflects the importance of matters of interest to the public in general. especially on the local level. Even with increased global/transnational public sphere activity, it is the local level where people's sense of communal identity tends to be the strongest. Furthermore, activities at the local level might foster latent citizen appetite for political involvement.
- Political Information for the Citizens (value 4). This subcriterion considers whether the supplied political information contributes to the transparency of democratic processes and facilitates deliberation and political participation. During elections, the following would be of special interest: candidates' personal aims and point of views, statements, speeches, articles, interviews, publications, and other information on actual issues reflecting (partisan) viewpoints as well as various open opinions, election results, political agendas, information about elections and planned actions in the constituency, and local issues. This could encourage citizens to react (e.g., through opinion-building, discussing information with fellow citizens, establishing priorities, and organizing political action). Political information about actual issues is vital for participation; therefore, the weight factor's value is 4.
- Political Political Background Information (value 5). This subcategory examines whether diverse opinions of citizens, media, or opponents are shown as well as editorial judgment, in-depth analysis, comments, and polls. Does the website provide citizens with issue-specific information of the kind that is not limited by the formal and general presentation of the issue you find in the mass media? Can citizens find a range of different opinions, reasons, and political messages that are not found in. the evening news? Is there any information which compares candidates, messages, issues, or party policies? Such information is essential for understanding politics, for forming your own point of view, and thus engaging in political actions. This reflects the value 5.

Are the Websites Interactive?

This category deals with the questions: Which possibilities do political websites offer citizens so they can debate with other citizens as well as with politicians, candidates, media, and communities? Does the website treat users as passive recipients of information rather than as active citizens? It was not intended to provide evidence concerning turnaround times or limitations on the service.

- Read-Only-Service (value 1). Does the website give purely passive information without input or feedback possibilities for the citizens? Read-only based websites simply post essays to provide the citizens with (political) information, without giving them a chance to make any kind of comments, requests, reaction, or deliberation. This one-way communication is better than no information but would not meet the needs of the politically interested user; it does not exploit the full potential of the Internet at all. Therefore, we give the value 1 as the weight factor.
- Read-And-Just-Write Service (value 2). One may assume that institutions offer certain opportunities for two-way communications via the Internet This service may include sending an e-mail for further information, filing complaints, or directly contacting a politician, a party member, candidate, or activist. At the end of each single page of the site is there a feedback opportunity via e-mail (e.g., to contact the author) or does this exist only on the starting page or not at all? A personal contact address (on- and offline) at the end of each page gives the citizen a feeling of support and credibility. Contacting the e-candidate might be the first step in getting involved in politics. Thus, the value 2 seems appropriate.
- Electronic Correspondence (value 3).The first two interactive services mentioned previously cannot be seen as original possibilities offered by the Internet. They are relatively often used in traditional political campaigns as well as by traditional media. However, the Internet can be used to intensify and broaden interactive contacts between political actors and citizens. Online guest books and feedback, newsletters, and e-mailing lists allow an increased amount and quality communication as well as its frequency and intensity. Does a website promote online transaction services with regular feedback loop? Do they guarantee reciprocal communication? For example, are there e-mail lists, a guestbook, a newsletter, and online campaigns to join on the website? Does the website link political experts or administrators with "ordinary" citizens? For example, can citizens attend online visiting hours, fill in feedback forms about the website, register online for campaign or party membership, make reservations and order brochures online, conduct or participate in opinion polls on current topics, enroll for a course, or apply for a job online? Value 3 for the weight factor refers to the fact that facilitating such kinds of civic activities via the Internet may motivate citizens for further political engagement.

- Forums, Chat Groups (value 4). This subcategory concerns possibilities to communicate political information inside or outside elections. Does a website provide a chat room, so that the newly assimilated information can be discussed vertically as well as horizontally (e.g., with the owner of the site) and link citizens directly to one another? Are there forums for different (partisan) citizens/groups to find a public voice? For how many topics does the site offer discussion groups? Are these groups moderated and are political actors joining them? Forums or chat groups that are only provided via a link do not count in this category. Fostering community connections (on- and offline) is said to be helpful for encouraging citizens' participation. The value 4 for the weight factor reflects this.
- Self-Presentation Possibilities (value 5). This subcategory centers on whether the website helps citizen to engage in, as well as to organize, common activities by themselves. The websites of political parties, politicians, or civic organizations provide a wide range of activities. For example, they can offer citizens an opportunity to make their own pages within a website to present themselves, to share their viewpoints, and to mobilize others. In this way, people can present and discuss actual information that is, in their opinion, interesting for their fellow citizens (e.g., local issues, building plans, activities). For many people, it is still a barrier to buy their own domain and create their own websites. Thus, offering them a "web space" where they can publish content easily can foster their engagement on- and offline. They will feel more involved and can motivate others in a powerful way; therefore, the value is 5.

How User-friendly are the Sites

This criterion concerns how easy it is to use political websites. It concerns the effectiveness, efficiency, and satisfaction with which users can achieve their tasks. The category also encompasses adapting the website's design to the needs of handicapped people (e.g., ability to enlarge the text, alternative texts, or additional pictorial descriptions).

- Actuality (value 1). Does the website provide citizens with the latest or major (election) news, press releases, upcoming events, hot topics, regional news, etc.? How frequently is the information updated and how many "dead" sites and links exist? The date of the latest review or content on each page should be stated. It is very important to keep the public informed and interested in elections, even if the news is not directly related to a particular election campaign. This is the basis for establishing credibility and trust; therefore, we use the value l for the weight factor.
- Compactness (value 2). Is information prepared in an appropriate way for publication on the Internet? According to surveys, online readers prefer small information units, presented in a clear way, and they do not like scrolling. On a

website, distracting advertising banners or pop-up messages should be limited. Is information structured well and is it linked so that one can click further when it is appropriate, without surfing through the entire website? Does a website contain quick and understandable units of information and news or does a reader find long articles or copies of printed ones on it? Is there too much superfluous information? Is the most important political information up to the date? The value 2 refers to the necessity for easily readable sites to keep a user motivated and satisfied.

- Search/Navigation Assistance (value 3). On-site search engines and navigational devices are crucial for users to find the information and services they require from the site. There should be assistance with searching and an indication of exactly what the search engine will seek. The results should be according to the keywords the users entered, avoiding too many irrelevant items. The browser system should provide navigation options to the users; these options should be used consistently throughout the site. Good navigation devices (for example, Home>About>Party Leader) display the current page's context within the site structure, keep users aware of their location on the site, and make it obvious how information is grouped (allowing users to move easily between these groups). Furthermore, there should be features designed to assist browsing, such as site maps, menus with unambiguous button names, and help options. Are all sites included through site navigation or are there "one-way streets?" Without properly working navigation devices and search engines, the users will quickly become frustrated and leave the site; therefore, weight factor 3 seems appropriate.
- Investigation and Documentation Assistance (value 4). Beginners might need some additional help to find required information and services and learn how to use the site. Therefore, it is important to offer appropriate and diverse possibilities for investigation (e.g., databases, search machines, archives), ways to bookmark the site, as well as print or download documents. Different areas (e.g., archives, job section, surveys, interviews, press) should be accessible to the public, not just be restricted to "members only." Do they offer the content of the website in different languages (English, Spanish)? Does the site provide the option to download or print longer articles? Do providers use innovative technologies to download videos, speeches, or slide shows quickly? Can you bookmark the most interesting sites (no frames)? Good applications for documentation and help will have a supportive effect on the user's further activities. In this respect, value 4 seems appropriate.
- Links (value 5). Links are characteristic for hypertext; they contain information or recommendations beyond the context of the current text. They should be organized to help the users, but not to distract or disorient them (especially external links). Therefore, the text/name of the link is very important as is its placement. Ideally, a special links-section should be arranged by topic with

instructions. For example, the clever use of hyperlinks can give citizens a good overview of actual political processes and allow them to get (via a "mouse click") more detailed information. Or they bring together the most important (election campaign) related websites to compare and connect citizens, politicians, and institutions in various combinations. Links can lead citizens back to related on- or offline media resources or to local face-to-face networks that might be better at building social trust and nurturing democratic practices. Strategically connected links through the Internet could facilitate as well as increase citizens' interest in political participation by guiding them through the site and encouraging political action; therefore, we give it value 5.

Are the Sites Aesthetically Pleasing?

Aesthetics plays an important role in how citizens perceive websites. Aesthetics covers the experience that involves and appeals to our senses and intellect. The mediated feeling of what people are reading, seeing, and hearing makes them stay or click away. It is about how creative, innovative, and appropriate the sites/messages are and if they are designed to attract citizens' attention.

- Humor/Parody (value 1). Even politically interested citizens prefer to be entertained (the notion of infotainment), rather than be subjected to purely formal, dry political information. It is about the style/language of the information. Does a website use political humor (e.g., parodies, political cartoons and caricatures, funny pictures, ironic or polemic ways of writing, funny/sarcastic comments about the lives and loves of political actors, anecdotes)? Are there. additional offerings? We ascribe this category the value 1 because style, tone, humor, emotion, and vocabulary are basic for citizens' motivation to participate.
- Symbols/Political Propaganda (value 2). This category aims at judging the persuasiveness of political communication and the language used (e.g., metaphors) or presentation of symbols. Symbols can help make abstract topics more concrete. In this context, it is about whether there is an appropriate use of political propaganda and symbols to help citizens engage with the website. Do they often use typical (national) symbols (like the colors of the American flag) to strengthen the feeling of unity and identity? In what way do they try to convince citizens of the importance of their help/support as well as benefits for citizens? How attractive is the language to appeal to or recruit new fans/members? Are the metaphors and symbols used on the website understandable and consistent? Appropriate symbols and persuasiveness make it easier to motivate citizens for political action; value 2 for the weight factor reflects this. But if there is an overload of political propaganda instead of useful political information, the site is not rated as participation-friendly.

- Pictures (value 3). "One picture is worth a thousand words." Pictures have always been popular means to convey messages and to persuade people. Photos, illustrations, or graphics can help to visualize a topic/problem and can simplify complex connections. An appropriate design should help form the right impression about the politician, institution, or situation at hand (e.g., pictures of members of parliament or of planned public buildings). Since we think in pictures and they cause effects and construct visual images, this category is very important for enhancing participation. Value 3 reflects this. But if the site only shows pictures of certain politicians ("personalization") or has manipulated pictures, it would not be judged as "appropriate" because it hardly provides citizens with useful information. This is the same for pictures which have long loading periods because they make users click away. It is more about the quality of design pictures than about quantity. Too many pictures could even conflict with valuable written information.
- Visual Appeal/Attractiveness (value 4). In today's world, our perception is almost always mediated and all forms of mediation are equally important. There is power in communication beyond written or spoken words (visuals like signs, colors, videos, sound, and body language); nonverbal communication delivers its own message. This subcategory deals with the general style of the website, assuming that the style is inviting and challenges citizens to follow its lead. The pages should be appropriate in length, clearly laid out, and readable. Using headings and the right color and font aid visibility. They should create a space where people feel stimulated and comfortable, reflecting an atmosphere beneficial for building up communities. The site should appeal to the target audience (e.g., a "games for the kid" section). The appeal and friendliness of the website depends on the colors used, typography, unity of single sites, and appropriate use of multimedia elements. These factors influence how much citizens feel encouraged to participate. In this context, important questions include: Are text versions accompanied by parts of video/audio files or pictures/eye-catchers? How funny, fascinating, and colorful is the website? Does it have a unified layout? The value 4 reflects the power of visual communication to raise citizens' interest to participate.
- Design/Technology (value 5). This subcategory refers to the interface design and technology used. Concerning the technology used, crucial issues are: compatibility with older browsers, loading speed, a supply of alternatives for missing plug-ins (e.g., a flash and html version), the absence of frames to find the site via search engines, and the ability to work the site without changing settings (e.g., screen resolution, enabling cookies). Online readers follow other principles than when reading a print article (e.g., their reading is more superficial, the first eye fixations are different, and they do not like long articles). Therefore, the way the site is set up and structured is very crucial (unifying site structure, arranging elements logically, putting the most important

information on top). Only logically categorized content based on users' needs will enable citizens to participate without expressing frustration; therefore, we assign the value 5.

How Can We Assess Websites?

The quality of websites is measured according to the previously mentioned four main categories, each of which can attain a maximum of 60. Thus, a perfect website could receive 240 points. We have given each subcriterion a weight factor based on its estimated strength to support civic engagement. The higher value of a subcategory in regard to participation-friendliness, the higher the weight factor. The weight factors are a result of discussion among the co-authors.

Within each main category (information, interactivity, user-friendliness, and aesthetics), a maximum of 4 points is given to each of the subcategories (0 point = not present, 1 point = scarcely present, 2 points = average present, 3 points = above average present, 4 points = overwhelmingly present). These points are multiplied with the corresponding weight factors. After summing up, one gets the points for each main category. The general sum of all categories (information, interactivity, user-friendliness, and aesthetics) presents us with a general indicator of the participation-friendliness of the political website. The more points a website gets, the more participation-friendly it is assumed to be.

Political Websites in Various European Countries

This case study compares certain European political websites from January 1999 to the end of May 1999. In January 1999, we analyzed various political websites in Germany, the Netherlands, and the UK within the framework of a pilot study. During Spring 1999, we examined an extensive sample of political websites in Russia, the Ukraine, Poland, and former Yugoslavia. Then, we compared the results of our websites' survey within and between Western and Eastern Europe to gather information regarding the development of electronic democracy in Europe.

International statistics (http://www.nua.ie/surveys/how_many_online/europe.-html) show that Europe is the second continent after North America to have broad and intensive Internet penetration. Compared to other continents, Europe represents the rich end of the digital divide. However, distribution of and Internet penetration within European countries is far from being equal. On the one hand, a majority of the European Union states can not only compete with the most digitalized country (United States) but on the other hand, can also produce (even better than can the US) positive results on the issue of bridging the gap between Internet have's and have-not's. Many countries of the former Soviet Union and Socialist Block have Internet penetration rates equal to African countries. It is more than obvious that on the issue of Internet accessibility, citizens of Sweden (with its high Internet penetration rate and diversity of online services and providers) can not be properly compared with Albania. In this respect, we can clearly see a serious digital divide within the European continent (Norris, 200la, 2001 b). However, this explains only the economic and technical side of the problem. At the same time, we may think about other parameters related to Internet use which can bridge certain differences between Europeans in the East and West. For example, this concerns levels of general and higher (primarily technical) education in the former Socialist bloc's countries. Quality of education can be seen as an advantage both on the side of potential Eastern European Internet users and on the side of potential website creators in these countries. We may assume that once technology is available there, Eastern European citizens will then develop sufficient skills to use it for their own benefit.

For each country we investigated, we assessed the websites of the main political parties. For the EU countries (the UK, the Netherlands, Germany), we also analyzed the main governmental website and five social movement websites (Greenpeace, Amnesty International, one trade union, one youth organization, and one electronic democracy movement). For the Eastern European countries (Russia, Ukraine, Poland and former Yugoslavia), we analyzed some politicians' websites as well as a few civil movements. The empirical material for the case study was collected during 1999 when the republic of Yugoslavia still existed. Throughout the text, we therefore continue to refer to Yugoslavia, even though Serbia and Montenegro replaced former Yugoslavia

The European Union Countries

We have evaluated 34 political websites for three EU countries according to the previously mentioned assessment scheme. The United Kingdom (10 sites), the Netherlands (12 sites), and Germany (12 sites) were our test countries. Thes.e Northern European countries were chosen as being among the most technologically advanced democracies in the world. The Netherlands, one of the smallest EU countries, is considered a "consensus" society. The United Kingdom has a highly polarized political system. Germany is a country in which the unification of the former Western (Deutsche Bundesrepublik, DB) and Eastern Germany (Deutsche Demokratische Republik, DDR) provided for economic and political problems and for two types of citizens. Results of our EU test cases are presented in the following paragraphs and in Figure 1.

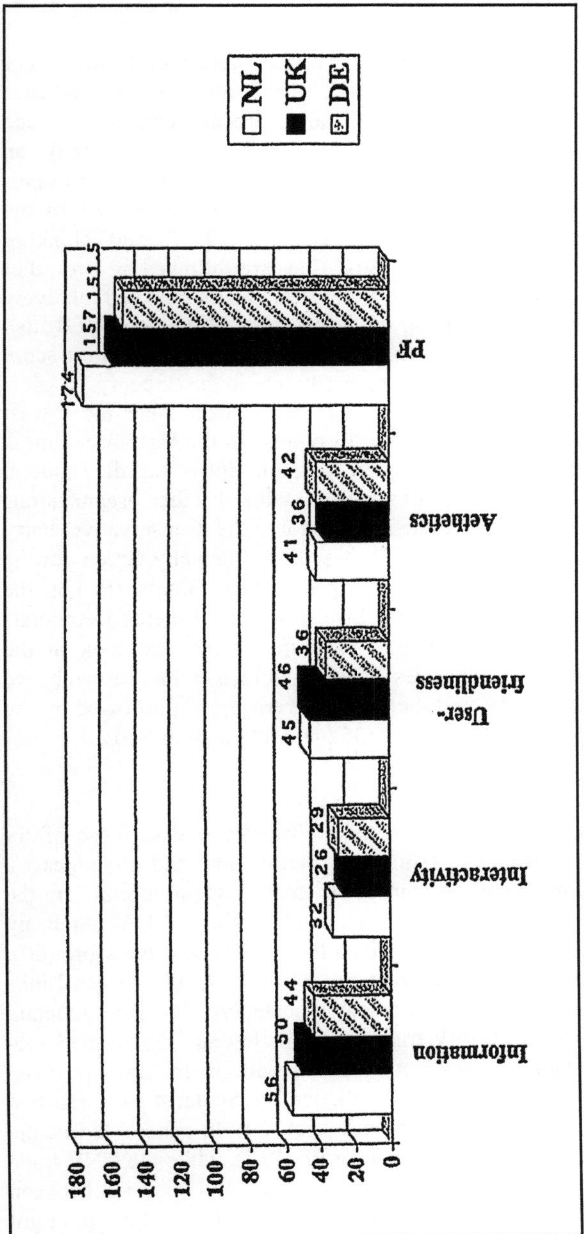

Figure 1: Participation friendliness (PF) of 1999 political websites in the European Union: average for each country

The United Kingdom

For this country, we analyzed the governmental website, websites of three major political parties (including Liberal Democrats), three movements' websites (Fundamentally Green, Amnesty International, and Greenpeace), TUC trade union's website, a website of the youth group Thinking Politica, and finally, an online democratic portal, UK Citizens Online. Websites vary among themselves in points they scored on major categories of participation friendliness (PF). In the "Information" category, three civil websites (Greenpeace, TUC, and Thinking Politica) received the highest possible score (60). They are followed by two other civil websites (57) and an online portal (54). All political parties received relatively low scores, with the Labour .Party receiving the lowest core (29) among all British websites. In the Interactivity category, Thinking Politica had the highest score (56), with the majority of other websites scoring pretty low in the category.

A governmental website and political parties here again have the lowest scores, with the Labour Party warranting only 13 points. In the User-friendliness category, only Greenpeace scored the highest possible (60) and the Liberal Democrats have the lowest (21) among all websites, with all other organizations ranging between these two. In the Aesthetics category, the Conservative Party received the highest score (53) among all websites; Fundamentally Green got the lowest (16). Overall, the total score for Participation Friendliness (PF) is the highest for Thinking Politica (217) and the lowest for the Liberal Democrats (98), with all websites scoring on average 157 points. When we look at the distribution of scores among four categories of PF examined in this research, we see that the Information category scored the highest average (50), followed by the categories of User-friendliness (46), Aesthetics (36), and Interactivity (26).

The Netherlands

For this country, we analyzed one governmental website as well as those of six main political parties, two movements (Amnesty International and Greenpeace), one trade union (CNV), one youth organization, and a social portal. In the Information category, four websites (a governmental website, CDA, Amnesty International, .and a student organization) received the highest possible score (60). The remaining websites scored in a range between 51 and 59, with Groen Links receiving the lowest score (49). In the Interactivity category, the governmental website scored the highest (52) and CNV trade union the lowest (13). In the User-friendliness category, the Socialist party got 60 points and Groen Links received the lowest among websites (32). In terms of Aesthetics, the Socialist party reached the highest score (57) and the CNV trade union lowest (29). In general terms, the governmental website received the highest total for PF (214), while the CNV trade union scored the lowest total (129). In terms of average score distribution between different categories, the situation here is similar to one in the UK: Information got the highest score (56), followed by User-friendliness (45) Aesthetics (41), and Interactivity (32).

Germany

In the case of Germany, we looked at the governmental website websites of the six main political parties in the country, Greenpeace and Amnesty International as social movements' websites, a website of the OTV trade union RCDS student movement's website, and a social portal, Politik Digital. In the Information category, an online social portal scored the highest (60). Scores for other websites in this category vary dramatically, with Amnesty International having the lowest (18). The same diversity of results is characterized for our second category Interactivity. Here, the German SPD took the lead (51). The student movement's website scored lowest (9). The gap between the best and the worst scoring websites in the User-friendliness category is also very big, with Greenpeace getting 60, but Amnesty International only 13. Aesthetics has become prominent on the SPD website (54). Once again, Amnesty International scored the lowest (22). In general terms, two international social movements became the best and the worst scored websites for Germany: Greenpeace took the lead (219), while Amnesty International got only 65 points for its Participation Friendliness (PF). In terms of average score distributions among four categories of PF in the scheme, the German case slightly differed from two other EU countries. Here, the Information category (44) was followed by Aesthetics (42). User-friendliness came in third (36), with Interactivity bringing up the rear (29).

Key Findings

If we now compare our results among the three countries, we see that the Netherlands had, on average, the highest PF (174), followed by the United Kingdom (157) and Germany (151.5). To a large extent, the average results across four categories do not differ a lot among the countries. For all of them, Information was the category with the highest score and Interactivity, the lowest. For the Netherlands and the UK, User-friendliness was the second best scoring category and Aesthetics, the third. For Germany, the last two categories were reversed. Having looked at the individual websites across the countries, we found that German-based Greenpeace scored the highest (219) among all investigated websites, just a bit lower than the maximum possible 240 points. It was closely followed by the British youth website, Thinking Politica (217) and the Dutch governmental website (214). Germany also had the website which scored the lowest: Amnesty International (65), followed by the UK's Liberal Democrats (98).

The Dutch governmental website scored the highest not only in its own country, but among all governmental websites and higher than any political party in these three countries. Among political parties, the Dutch Socialist Party (210) took the lead, followed by the German Social Democratic Party (199). All international social movements scored rather well and quite equally, with the exception of Germany, where the Amnesty International website had the lowest score among all websites (65). At the same time, Germany's Greenpeace website had the highest score among all websites (219). Other social movement websites received relatively average scores, neither outscoring other websites nor lagging far behind. However, it is worth repeating that the British youth website had the highest score in its country (217) and the second highest among all websites used in our analysis. At the same time, the Dutch trade union got the lowest domestic score (129) which actually was not very low at all. If we divide websites into two groups (official politics and civil society), official websites scored on average higher in the Netherlands and Germany; in the UK, civil websites got higher scores. However, the difference between two groups was not considerable and, taken together, the average scores for all countries was 157 for official sites and 160 for civil websites.

Central and Eastern European Countries

After our test analysis of the EU websites, we evaluated political websites in four CEE countries according to the same assessment scheme. We chose Russia, Poland, the former Republic of Yugoslavia, and the Ukraine. Russia is the largest European country and a center of the former Soviet Union. Poland is one of the most successful new democracies; additionally, it is a recent NATO member state and a future member of the European Union. The Federal Republic of Yugoslavia has undergone dramatic political and social changes during the time of analysis; this provoked our particular interest in political uses of the Internet in a country in a period of crisis. The Ukraine is the second largest country in Europe (in geographic terms) and a former Soviet Union republic; it held presidential elections in 1999. While Poland joins the EU in May 2004, Russia, Yugoslavia and the Ukraine will become the new neighbors of the enlarged EU. Results for CEE websites are presented in the following paragraphs and in Figure 2.

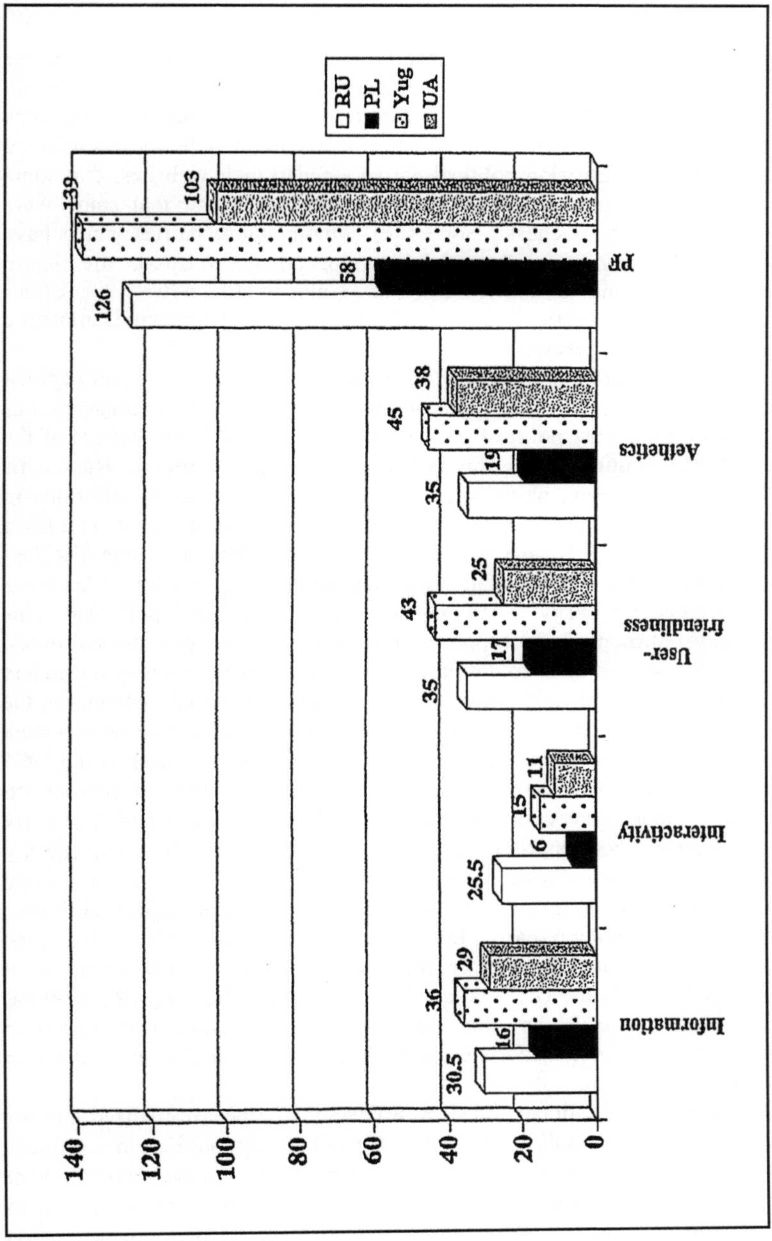

Figure 2: Participation friendliness (PF) of 1999 political websites in Central and Eastern European countries: average for each country

Russia

This country is one of the most representative Eastern European countries on the Internet. It has the greatest number of political parties with websites, nearly 20. This means that almost all leading Russian political parties realized the importance of this new medium. Nevertheless, our choice and scoring of websites was affected by the fact that not all Russian political parties opened their websites, that some websites were under construction (Nash Dom Russia site), or that some were recently revised (Democraticheskij Souz site). Among those parties which have their "pages" on the Internet, we chose the eight most popular in Russia: the Liberal Democratic Party, Communist Party, Democratic Union, Yabloko Party, NDR (Our Home is Russia), Democratic Choice of Russia, Russian Christian Democratic Party, and Constitutional Democrats.

The Liberal Democratic Party (LDPR), headed by the charismatic and populist Vladimir Zhyrinovsky, is a popular party in the country. It can be characterized as one of the most nationalist political parties in Russia. CPRF is the heiress of the former USSR Communist Party. This is one of the largest parties in Russia; its leader, Gennady Zyuganov, participated in the Russian presidential elections in June 2000. Democratic Union of Russia is one of the few Russian parties that takes a pro-Western position. This party was created around the famous Soviet dissident Valeria Novodvorskaya. The Russian social-democratic party Yabloko (Apple) is headed by Grigory Yavlinsky, a famous Russian economist and politician. This party is mainly represented and supported by intellectual and professional elites. The party name was created from the first letters of the family names of its leaders (Yavlinsky, Boldyrev, and Lukin) and the party position is social-democratic; the official symbol of the party is an apple. Another party, NDR, one of the most famous Russian parties of power, was created to support Boris Yeltsen in the 1996 presidential elections. The party occupies a centralist position; it focuses on domestic issues, social protection, and the role of Russia in the world. The party leader was Viktor Chernomyrdin, the then Prime Minister. Demokraticheskiy Vybor Rossij (Democratic Choice of Russia) is another party of intellectuals and reformers as well as a former party of power, headed by Egor Gajdar. However, unlike Yavlinsky's Yabloko party, DVR tries to speak not only to its target electorate, but also to much broader groups of the population. For this purpose, it uses some populist methods. The Russian Christian Democratic Party (RChDP) has Aleksander Chuev as a leader; this party operates very similar to European Christian-Democratic parties. Cadets is the Party of Constitutional Democrats; their leader is Alexander Krutov.

While investigating political websites in Eastern Europe, we realized that the phenomenon of individual political websites is as popular among Eastern European politicians as websites of political parties and movements (if not even more popular than the latter two). Even when the party or political movement has a website, its leader prefers to have his/her own page as well. Considering the poor navigation help through Russian political websites and the lacking links to other sites, we were only able to find the websites of four Russian politicians. They are the websites of Irina Hakamada, Alexander Lebed, Boris Nemtsov, and Sergey Kirienko. Sergey Kirienko was a former Prime Minister of Russia during the financial crisis in Summer 1998. He had structured and mobilized a reform project for the Russian economy, but was dismissed as Prime Minister and got a very negative evaluation from the Russian population. Hakamada is a famous Russian economist and one of the few female members of the Russian Parliament. Alexander Lebed is a former general of the Soviet Russian army, the governor of the Krasnoyarsk region. Boris Nemtsov is the former Vice Prime Minister of Russia.

Finally, we looked at three websites for social movements: .Revolutionary Young Communist League, National Patriotic Front Pamyat, and the Russian National Unit. Among the three social movements chosen for our analysis, two (Pamyat and Russian National Unit) have a very strong nationalistic position. The third movement (Revolutionary Young Communist League) is a radical leftist youth movement which operates in several former Soviet Union republics.

Russian political websites differ with respect to visual appeal and exploitation of the Internet's interactive potential. The average score of the political sites was 126. However, if we evaluate separately websites of political parties and movements, on the one hand, and personal websites of politicians, on the other, we come up with an average of 104 for parties and movements and 187.5 for personal websites. The winner is the Kirienko's website (221) with Hakamada's site as a well-scoring second (211) and Yabloko party's website coming in third (207). (This was the best score for political parties and movements.) Yabloko had the most properly and successfully developed website among Russian political parties. In comparison with others, Yabloko was characterized by the most interactive usage of the Internet's communication facilities (for example, connecting the electorate and their representatives via e-mail). The party chose the "newspaper" (tabloid) design of their website, but in a clearly structured way. The Internet is primarily used by the party for two reasons: self-presentation and improving the communication flow among party members. The party is planning to create the first virtual party primary organization in Russia. Their website contained several interactive forums, numerous discussion groups, permanent opinion polls and small surveys, separate pages of its youth organization, and sites of regional organizations. Moreover, it has a virtual library (consisting of the most famous Russian and Soviet philosophical, sociological, and political books and articles since the end of the sixth century), which is remarkable.

Also the following websites scored above average: the Liberal Democratic Party (129), Russia's Democratic Choice (133), and the Cadets (134). From an online marketing viewpoint, LDPR was probably the most successful example. Out of several interactive possibilities offered by the party's site, only the discussion group failed since it was not moderated and lacked serious participation. The currency of the website is visible from the starting page; instead of the usual party logo, they used pictures to portray the latest events, accompanied by slogans such as "Peace in the Balkans! No Bombs!" This is the most appropriately illustrated website among Russian political parties. Liberal Democrats even offer a song about Russia, sung by the party leader. People can send a letter to any LDPR member of the Parliament, read party announcements, and check schedules of radio and TV programs about LDPR or other related subjects. "Our news," which presents and explains the current events (from the party's viewpoint), is the brightest and most promotional part of the website.

The worst-scoring party website was the Russian Christian-Democratic Party (30). Three other party sites scored well below the average: the Communist Party of the Russian Federation (CPRF) (53), The Demokraticheskij Souz Rosij (Democratic Union of Russia) (40), and Nash Dom Rosija (Russia is Our Home) (50). The information on the Communist Party website is only about the party, itself. The site provides complete information about the party, its political publications, actions, events, and activity. Bibliographical references are poor; the English version is almost undeveloped and not up-to-date. The design gives a strict impression; although well structured, the website is stingy with visuals.

In contrast to the websites of the political parties, individual politicians use the interactive channels of the Internet to a much higher degree. Sergey Kirienko (whose website takes the lead among Russian political sites) realized the idea of an Internet parliament. Visitors to the Kirienko website can discuss the goals and tasks of the e-parliament. In addition, there are many different types of discussion groups and voting possibilities on current issues of Russian political and social life. Kirienko is probably the only Russian politician who is not "afraid" to tell funny stories about his life and political activity and who invites the visitors to join him, telling jokes and anecdotes about Kirienko, himself. Irina Hakamada and Kirienko have permanent discussion groups and virtual communities on their pages; visitors can read questions to and answers from politicians, talk to each other, and suggest new forms of communication. On these pages, one can find not only articles (written by the politicians) and their biographies from other media, but also stories about them, told by the members of their families and their friends. These websites contain real photo albums, which tell stories about the private lives of "real" people. Politicians' websites that score around the average are the ones by Lebed (158) and Nemtsov (160).

We also evaluated websites of several Russian movements. The server of Pamyat (Memory), Russian Orthodox Monarch National Movement, scored best (156). The most remarkable element of the site is a photo collection of the Russian Orthodox icons, a library of books devoted to Russian history, and a collection of Russian church and folk music.

If we look at the best and worst individual scores of the websites through the subcategories of Participation Friendliness, we see the following picture. In the

Information category, Yabloko got the highest score (56), while the Democratic Union Party received only 2. Other scores are distributed rather unequally between different websites. In the Interactivity category, two personal political websites (those of Hakamada aud Kirienko) got the highest score (60), followed by Yabloko (58). At the same time, the Democratic Union received only 2 points in this category; two other websites, the NDR and Revolutionary League, had 3 each. Kirienko's website also scored the highest (60) on the topic of User-friendliness, while the Russian Christian Democratic Party got only 1 point. In the Aesthetics category, the Liberal Democrats and Lebed's personal website received 56, while the Democratic Union got only 8. If we look at the distribution of average scores between different PF categories, we find that the Aesthetics and User-friendliness categories are the most prominent, scoring an average of 35. They are followed by Information (30.5) and Interactivity (25.5).

Poland

Political websites in Poland scored 58 points on average. Poland has the highest number of "dead" sites. Most of them were used during previous parliamentary/presidential election campaigns and were not updated subsequently. Polish websites hardly use any channels of interactivity. Electronic correspondence devices, self-presentation possibilities for citizens, and forums/discussion groups are rarely found. There is one site that has relatively good scores compared to the others; the Polish People's Party (PSL) (131). It is the only site that contains any navigation/investigation help. The other sites belong to the Social Democracy of the Republic of Poland (SDRP) (67), Conservative People's Party (55), Christian Democracy of the Third Polish Republic (50), Movement for the Republic and Patriotism (45), and Solidarity Electoral Action (42) as the coalition of centre-right forces, the heiress of the famous Polish trade union "Solidarnosc" headed by the first Polish president, Lech Walesa. The lowest scores are for the Movement for the Reconstruction of Poland (17), which is a right-wing European-oriented party with roots in the Polish independence movement.

Looking at scores of individual websites in different categories, we see that the Polish People's Party scored the highest for all categories, with 40 for Information, 12 for Interactivity, 46 for User-friendliness, and 33 for Aesthetics. By contrast, the Movement for Reconstruction of Poland scored the worst for all categories, with 6, 2, 1, and 8 points, respectively. The average distribution of scores through different PF categories is similar to that in Russia, although it is much lower. Aesthetics scored the highest (19), followed by User-friendliness (17), Information (16), and Interactivity (6).

Former Yugoslavia

As mentioned earlier, dramatic events in Yugoslavia during Spring 1999 conditioned our choice of this Central European country. We wanted to see whether the Internet was used by political forces in the country under such special crisis circumstances. We looked at the websites of the six main political parties in the country: New Democracy, Serbian Socialist Party, Serbian Renewal Movement, Democratic Party, Civic Alliance of Serbia, Congressional National Party, New Communist Party of Yugoslavia, and the Serbian Unity Congress.

The average score of Yugoslavian political parties is rather high (139). It is mainly achieved through the Aesthetics and User-friendliness categories, with a majority of the websites displaying extensive photo reports from the war and providing their visitors with different tools for searching and navigating. For example, the Serbian Unity Congress website contains numerous links to political/governmental/independent media websites all over the world to give people access to different viewpoints. They also introduced an interesting interactive service where people can send their questions and suggestions not only to the party members, but also to members of the parliament and even to the American president and vice president. Several Serbian websites also introduced fast news service, mainly to update users on current military developments, new targets, and war casualties.

The average score for Yugoslavian parties is 139. The Serbian Unity Congress received the highest score (208), followed by the Congressional National Party (181). The latter is a right-wing Serbian party, headed by Serbian professors and other representatives of the intellectual elite. Further websites that received above-average scores were the Serbian Socialist Party of Slobodan Milosevic (162) and the Democratic Party (158). Party sites that scored below the average were the New Communist Party (123), the Civic Alliance Serbia (97), New Democracy (96), and the Serbian Renewal Movement (81).

In the Information category, the Congressional National Party received the highest score (54). New Democracy scored only 5. The Serbian Unity Congress scored the best in the Interactivity and User-friendliness categories (39 and 60, respectively). The Congressional National Party also got 60 for User-friendliness. The Civil Alliance of Serbia got the lowest score for Interactivity (4) and the Serbian Renewal Movement received the lowest score (24) for its User-friendliness. In the Aesthetics category, the Serbian Socialist Party of Slobodan Milosevic obtained the highest score (56), while New Democracy scored the lowest (37).

The average distribution of scores through different PF categories is similar to the first two CEE countries we analyzed. Aesthetics scored the highest average (45), followed by User-friendliness (43), Information (36), and Interactivity (15).

Ukraine

In the Ukraine, we discovered five political websites for our analysis. Three of them are websites of political parties (Hromada, Edyna Rodyna, and Zeleni) and two are the personal websites of famous national politicians (Olexander Moroz and

Evhen Marchuk). In former times, Hromada was the second strongest opposition party in the Ukraine (after the Communist Party of Ukraine), but it lost popularity since the 1998 parliamentary elections due to a criminal process initiated against its leader, Pavlo Lazarenko. The Green Party (Zeleni) resembles Western Green parties. It has a large number of seats in the parliament and proclaims that it will do its best for the ecological future of the country and that it will stay independent. Three other sites had been newly created because of the approaching presidential elections in the Ukraine. Two of these sites are personal websites of the presidential candidates (Moroz and Marchuk), the third one (Edyna Rodyna), is a party website intended to present one more presidential candidate, namely its leader, Olexander Rzhavsky.

On average, political websites in the Ukraine scored 103. Overall, the use of the Internet by the Ukrainian political parties is similar to the Polish case. Political websites are mainly created and used there during elections. Hromada and the Green Party of Ukraine are good examples of this. Both sites were created before the last parliamentary elections in the Ukraine and were not subsequently updated or changed. These sites received the lowest scores: Hromada (76) and the Green Party (64). Both personal websites of the politicians have become the country's best websites, with Marchuk's scoring the highest (137) and Moroz second (127). These sites are doing quite well with presenting diverse information about politicians, but they are disappointing in terms of interactivity.

The following results were achieved in the separate PF categories. In the Information category, the Moroz (45) website scored the highest and the Green Party (9) the lowest. Interactivity is poorly represented at the Hromada website (2). The website of Evhen Marchuk scored the highest (16). Both Marchuk and Edyna Rodyna scored the highest (32) in the User-friendliness category, with Zeleni (17) lowest. Aesthetics is managed best on the Moroz website (52), while the Green Party was lowest (17).

The distribution of average scores between different PF categories differs slightly in the case of Ukraine compared to other CEE countries. Although Aesthetics is again the best scored category (38), it is followed by Information (29), then User-friendliness (25), and Interactivity (11).

Key Findings

Over the considered period (Spring 1999), the scores for Participation Friendliness of the political websites in CEE countries range from 139 (Yugoslavia) and 127 (Russia) down to 103 (Ukraine) to 58 (Poland). No website reached the maximum score of 240. The best websites were the Russian sites of the politician Kirienko (221) and the party Yabloko (207) as well as the Yugoslavian site of the Serbian Unity Congress Party (208).

Also the Information category scored less than half of possible points with an average of 28 for all countries. Scores for Information range from 36 (Yugoslavia),

31 (Russia), and 29 (Ukraine) to 16 (Poland). While the subcategory "General boulevard information" scored weakly, "Self-presentation" was pretty well presented. Interactivity (actually introduced in our research as the paramount category) is the weakest one, with average scores of only 14.5. Scores range from 26 (Russia), 15 (Yugoslavia), and 11 (Ukraine) to 6 (Poland). Several websites offer nothing beyond their read-only-service. Electronic correspondence and especially chats/forums are unknown for the majority of the parties' websites or remain scanty at present. Equally average for all countries were the criteria for User friendliness. User friendliness scores ranged from 43 (Yugoslavia), 35 (Russia), and 25 (Ukraine) to 17 (Poland); all the CEE countries together reached an average score of 30. The Aesthetics category refers to visual appeal, design/structure, symbols/propaganda, and pictures. Scores ranged from 45 (Yugoslavia), 38 (Ukraine), and 35 (Russia) to 19 points (Poland). All websites (except those from Poland) differed in the form of visual appeals, but managed to achieve a satisfactory level. They present their sites with a consistent layout; separated "personal," "party," and "external" issues visually; they used pictures and text in a balanced way. Only the subcategory "humor" was usually absent on each site. Regarding the assumption that citizens will only use political websites if they are efficient and easy to use/navigate and if the content is current, the key findings in this category are disappointing. But at least Russian and Yugoslavian websites put news about the situation in Kosovo as the main subject on their site during the conflict Each of these websites contained a political position and a party declaration on this question. Nothing like this could be found on Ukrainian and Polish websites. The hyperlinks between websites were varied (concerning diversity), but most of them provided links to the government of the country, the parliament, or foreign parties with the same political orientation. Remarkable is the fact that several Russian and Yugoslavian parties created digital libraries, giving citizens a chance not only to look through their catalogue of publications, but also to read and print many of the books and articles using PDF files.

Unfortunately, only a minority of the politicians/political parties is using the possibilities of the Internet to its full potential. Although Russia is the winner concerning the "proper" use of the Internet among CEE countries (Yabloko for parties; pages of Hakamada and Kirienko for all websites), Russian sites still offer limited opportunities to connect the electorate with their representatives. There is also a lack of self-presentation possibilities for citizens. All parties see self-presentation as the main reason for their appearance on the websites. But self-presentation is realized very narrowly. That is, in general, there is information about party history, activities, documents, congresses, etc. Links to other pages include only the pages of fellow parties within the country and abroad, under the name "addresses of our friends." Visual attractiveness is understood from the position of party symbols and propaganda. Humor is absent almost everywhere. Biographies of party leaders are serious and "dry." Only Yavlinsky has some comments from his friends and relatives about his childhood. Moreover, only two out of eight parties use the interactive channels of the Internet in an appropriate way. This low level of interactivity can have diverse reasons: first, parties have not yet realized this magnificent opportunity on the Internet; second, most of them are afraid of a torrent of feedback/criticism from citizens; and third, they are unsure about how to deal with it.

All the politicians' sites are friendly and not very politicized. They invite visitors to consider and communicate with them as a "normal" person, instead of merely politicians. Therefore, the main aim of the private websites of Russian politicians can be characterized as a desire to present their "human face." All Yugoslavian websites are current and favorably compete with the Russian sites when it comes to quality and amount of information. They also have the highest level of personalization. Nevertheless, they share the same weakness as the remaining sites: low level of interactivity, lack of humor, and general boulevard information. The Ukrainian websites have more in common with the Polish sites concerning the reasons and goals of their use. Actually, most CEE sites were created during the last election campaign. While Russia and Yugoslavia try to update them and even change their appearance occasionally, Polish and Ukrainian politicians use the sites for elections alone. They seem to have forgotten about them thereafter.

Among the political websites, the ones of individual politicians are more "open" for contacts with citizens. However, such websites exist only in Russia and the Ukraine; they are completely absent in Poland and Yugoslavia. At the same time, the Ukraine and Poland have the highest number of "dead" sites. (This means the sites that are used in the pre-election period are not updated afterwards.) The read-and-just-write service is the most commonly used interactive element. Another practice of many parties is to give a direct answer to citizens' questions on the websites, themselves.

East-West Comparisons

This analysis was aimed at discovering features of the Internet used by political parties in Europe. At the same time, we also wanted. to see whether any considerable differences exist between the political Internet in Western and Eastern Europe. In very general terms, our results show that the Internet is used by diverse political forces throughout Europe. There seems to be no connection between the use of the Internet and the political position (right, central, or left) of a party or group. Similar to their Western European colleagues, CEE political parties are familiar with the new medium and its exploitation for political needs. What is common for all countries and parties across Europe is the use of the opportunities the Internet provides as an additional channel to influence and attract the voters. However, the Internet means used for this aim by Western and Eastern European political actors differ in their quality and intensity. We believe that our assessment scheme clearly shows these differences in Internet use. It has not come as a big surprise that all Western European countries perform on average much better throughout different Participation Friendliness categories (Figure 3). There are more than 100 points difference between the country with the best average score for political websites (the Netherlands) and the one with the worst (Poland). At the same time, there is only 12 points difference between Germany and Yugoslavia. Paradoxically, a personal website of Russian politician, Sergey Kirienko, got the highest score (221) among all the websites we analyzed. However, there are also many CEE websites which scored less than 10 in different categories. Moreover, the category of "dead" websites seems to be a rather Eastern European "phenomenon." Thus, while certain political websites can compete with Western colleagues, the average score for the East is lower.

It is also worth considering differences in the priority given to different PF categories in East and West. While Information is undoubtedly the most prominent PF categories for Western political websites, Aesthetics is the most prominent category for Eastern political websites, with Information coming third as a rule (with the exception of the Ukraine). It can be concluded that Eastern European politicians consider visual attractiveness and broader, symbolic, and visual language to be as important as (or even more important than) the printed word. Such an approach may be related to very recent political transformations in the CEE countries, each country's search for a new identity, and quest for united national factors. In this respect, prominence of the same category (Aesthetics) in the case of Germany compared to two other Western countries seems to be particularly interesting.

Practically all European political parties experience one common challenge: to use the interactive possibilities provided by the Internet. For many proponents of greater political participation, deliberation, and strong democracy, interactivity is the very feature which distinguishes the Internet from other mediated forms of politician-citizen communication. Via interactive communication, an almost equal dialogue can re-emerge between citizens and politicians and a stronger sense of accountability can be re-established. However, Interactivity has become the weakest category for both EU and CEE political websites

The low level of interactivity can be explained in several ways. We believe that politicians may fear or be unwilling to display any other than their own opinions on the Internet. They may not even be fully aware of the Internet's possibilities nor recognize the importance of interactive dialogue. It is also true that online communication is time- and means-consuming. It may even require additional personnel involvement on a permanent basis. Additionally, many political actors (particularly in CEE countries) may not have sufficient financial funds for such activities. Moreover, many CEE parties may have simply not yet developed any particular communication strategy since the average age of these parties is 10 years. As a result, many politicians choose the easiest way and use the Internet as they use any other mean of communication and propaganda. However, it is very important to stress that there are two Russian personal websites which have scored 60 in the Interactivity category and one party's site merited 58.

Our particular focus on political websites in Yugoslavia was provoked by the desire to see whether conditions of political unrest and military crisis may affect the use of the Internet by political parties. If we are to evaluate the use of the Internet by Yugoslavian political parties in one word it would be "creative." The political unrest and military aggression has forced politicians to use all information means available to them. Yugoslavia got the highest average score among CEE countries. Its political websites were filled not only with up-to-date information and impressive photo collections, but also they developed many rather successful and user-friendly applications. It is constructive to imagine for a while in which conditions (the war) Yugoslavian parties used their websites appropriately to support their positions.

Finally, two CEE countries (Russia and the Ukraine) presented us with a new type of political websites which we have not been able to find/identify in other European countries. These are personal websites of prominent politicians. In addition to the fact that such websites promote political personalization online, they have become the most effectively developed websites in Eastern Europe and have reached the levels of the Internet use for politics similar to those in the European Union countries.

Conclusions

We are aware that our explorative analysis will leave some open questions and can only provide a general overview. We hope to inspire future examinations to look more closely at how and why people access and use political websites and to base the design of a website on thorough consultation with its potential users to find out more about their needs and wishes as well as difficulties encountered when visiting the website.

Some suggestions for a higher "participation-friendliness" are the following:

- Maintain a greater focus on users' needs in site design and content (e.g., develop and organize the site content around user groups, provide content in relevant community languages).
- Help users determine the legitimacy of the information and the consequences of their use of the site (e.g., provide the name of the agency, responsibility for content, disclaimer, date of last review or update, detailed and user-friendly information on privacy, security).

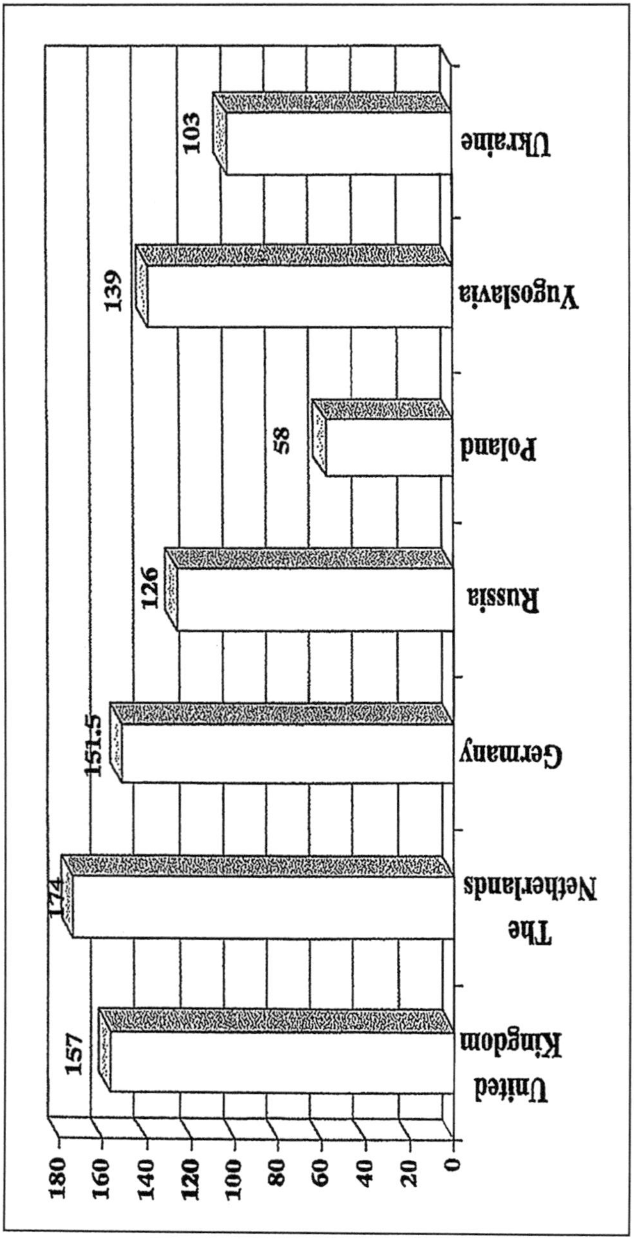

Figure 3: Participation friendliness (PF) of 1999 political websites in various European Union and Central and Eastern European countries: average for each country

- Exploit the interactive capacity of the web for participation in government processes (e.g., provide features for two-way communication between individual members of the pubic, community groups, business and other organizations, and government agencies).
- Improve accessibility to site content for all users, including those with disabilities and those with less advanced technology and skills (e.g., provide a text equivalent for all non-text elements and provide alternatives to high level technology).
- Make sure representatives adapt their work practices so that they can manage these new additional channels of connection with the public. All jobs are conducted within structures; if the structure does not adapt to accommodate new technologies, there is no point in blaming those trapped within it.
- Develop e-democracy into an integral part of representative democracy. To do this, we must devise mechanisms for promoting public deliberation, embedding it within the constitutional process, and demonstrating real links between public input and policy outcomes. Citizens will soon tire of contributing their thoughts if no apparent account is taken of them.

Acknowledgement

Earlier versions of this chapter have been presented at the conference on "Technological Innovation and Political Communication" at the University of Perugia, Perugia, Italy, December 2-4, 1999 and at the Annual Conference of the International Communication Association, Washington, DC, May 24-28, 1999. One other version has been published in Spanish (De Landtsheer, Krasnoboka, and Neuner, 1999, 2001a, 2001b).

References

Abramson, J., F. Arterton, and G. Orren (1988). *The Electronic Commonwealth. The Impact of New Media Technologies on Democratic Politics*. New York, NY: Basic Books.

Barber, B. (1984). *Strong Democracy*. Berkeley, CA: University of California Press.

Barber, B., K. Mattson, and J. Peterson (October 1997). "The State of 'Electronically Enhanced Democracy.' A Survey of the Internet. A Report for the Markle Foundation." Submitted by the Walt Whitman Center for the Culture and Politics of Democracy.

Barnett, S. (1997). "New Media, Old Problems. New Technology and the Political Process," pp. 193-218 in *European Journal of Communication*, Vol. 12, No. 2.

Bonchek, M. (1995). "Political Uses of the Internet." Political Participation Project http://www.ai-.mit.edu/projects/ppp/home.htrnl.

Bowie, N. (2003). "Voting, Campaigns, and Elections in the Future; Looking Back from 2008," pp. 143-167 in H. Jenkins and D. Thorburn (eds.) *Democracy and New Media*. Cambridge, MA and London, UK: The MIT Press.

Coleman, S. (1999). "The New Media and Democratic Politics," pp. 67-74 in *New Media and Society*, Vol. 1, No. 1.

Coleman, S. (ed.) (2001). *2001 Cyberspace Odyssey: The Internet in the UK Election*. London, UK: The Hansard Society.

Crabtree, J. (2001). *Whatever Happened to the E-lection: A Survey of Voter Attitudes towards New Technology during the 2001 Election*. London, UK: The Industrial Society.

Davis, R. (1999). *The Web of Politics. The Internet's Impact on the American Political System*. New York, NY and Oxford, UK: Oxford University Press.

De Landtsheer, C., N. Krasnoboka, and C. Neuner (1999). "User friendliness of Political Websites in Some Eastern and Western European Countries (1999)." Paper for the Expert Meeting on Political Communication and Technological Innovation, organized by Political Communication/Communicazione Politica, The University of Perugia, Perugia, Italy, December 2-4, 1999.

De Landtsheer, C, N. Krasnoboka, and C. Neuner (2001a). "La Facilitad utilizaci6n de los 'web sites' de partidos politicos. Estudio de algunos paises de Europa del Este y Occidental (1999)" (User friendliness of Political Websites in Some Eastern and Western European Countries (1999)), pp. 107-140 in *Cuadernos de lnformacion y Communicacion*, No. 6.

De Landtsheer, C., N. Krasnoboka, and C. Neuner (2001b). "User friendliness of Political Web Sites in Eastern and Western European Countries (1999)." Paper presented at the Annual Conference of the International Communication Association, Washington DC, May 24-28, 2001.

Dole, R. (1996). Http.//www.dole96. com/message (not available online anymore).

Erik-Lane, J. and S. Ersson (1996). *European Politics*. London, UK: Sage.

Gotze, J. (1998). "Participation in the Information Age." Http://www.gotzespace.dk/pzhd/it.html (not available online anymore).

http://www.nua.ie/surveys/how _many_online/europe.htrnl

Graber, D. and B. White (2001). "Medios interpersonales y Comunicaci6n Politica: Comunicaci6n Politica y Redes Electr6nicas" (Interpersonal Media and Political Communication: Political Communication and Technological Innovations), pp. 63-86 in *CIC, Cuadernos de Informacion y Communicacion, Ciberdemocracia*, No. 6. Madrid, Spain: Servicio de Publicaciones. Universidad Complutense.

Hagen, M. (1997). "A Typology of Electronic Democracy." Http.//www.uni-giessen.de/fbo3/vinci/labore/netz/hag_en.htm (not available online anymore).

Hague, R. and S. Uhm (2003). "Online Groups and Offline Parties: Korean Politics and the Internet," pp. 195-217 in R. Gibson, P. Nixon, and S. Ward (eds.) *Political Parties and the Internet. Net Gain?* London, UK and New York, NY: Routledge.

Krasnoboka, N. (2002). "Real Journalism Goes Underground: The Internet Underground. The Phenomenon of Online Media in the Former Soviet Union Republics," pp. 479-499 in *Gazette, The International Journal for Communication Studies*, Vol. 64, No. 5.

Löfgren K., K. Andersen, and M. Sørensen (1999). "The Danish Parliament Going Virtual," pp 483-502 in S. Coleman, J. Taylor, and W. Van de Donk (eds.) *Parliament in the Age of the Internet*. Oxford, UK: Oxford University Press.

Mambrey, P., H. Neumann, and K. Sieverdingbeck (1999). "Bridging the Gap between Parliament and Citizen - the Internet Services of the German Bundestag," pp. 480-492 in *Parliamentary Affairs*, Vol. 52, No. 3.

Margolis, M., D. Resnick, and J. Wolfe (1999). "Party Competition on the Internet: Minor versus Major Parties in the UK and USA," pp. 24-47 in *Harvard International Journal of Press Politics*, Vol. 4, No. 4.

Margolis, M., D. Resnick, and C. Tu (1997). "Campaigning on the Internet: Parties and Candidates on the World Wide Web in the 1996 Primary Season," pp. 59-78 in *Harvard International Journal of Press Politics*, Vol. 2, No. 1.

McGookin, S. (December 27, 1995). "Internet 'May Give Stimulus to Democracy'" in *Financial Times*.

Milbrath, L. (1965). *Political Participation. How and Why do People get Involved in Politics?* Chicago, IL: Northwestern University.

Miller, S. (1996). *Civilising Cyberspace. Policy, Power, and the Information Superhighway*. New York, NY: ACM Press.

Norris, P. (200la). "Digital Parties: Civic Engagement and Online Democracy" (online). http://ksghome.harvard.edu/' .pnorris.shorenstein.ksg/articles.htm.

Norris, P. (200lb). *Digital Divide: Civic Engagement. Information Poverty and the Internet in Democratic Societies*. New York, NY: Cambridge University Press.

Norris, P. (2000). *Democratic Phoenix: Reinventing Political Activism*. New York, NY: Cambridge University Press.

Oberreuter, H. (1982). *Uebermacht der Medien - Erstickt die demokratische demokratische Kommunikation?* (Media Dominance - Is Democratic Communication in Danger?). Zurich, Switzerland: Edition Interfrom.

Preece, J. (2002). *Interaction Design. Beyond Human Computer Interaction*. New York, NY: John Wiley & Sons.

Resnick, D. (1998). "Politics on the Internet: The Normalization of Cyberspace," pp. 48- 68 in C. Toulouse and T. Luke (eds.) *The Politics of Cyberspace: A New Political Science Reader*. New York, NY: Routledge.

Rheingold, H. (1993). *The Virtual Community: Homesteading on the Electronic Frontier*. Reading, MA: Addison-Wesley.

Sassi, S. (2000). "The Controversies of the Internet and the Revitalization of Local Political Life," pp. 90-104 in K. Hacker and J. Van Dijk (eds.) *Digital Democracy. Issues of Theory and Practice*. London, UK: Sage.

Street, J. (1997). "Remote Control? Politics, Technology and 'Electronic Democracy,'" pp. 27-42 in *European Journal of Communication*, Vol. 12, No. 1.

Verba, S., H. Norman, and K. Jae-on (1978). *Participation and Political Equality: A Seven-Nation Comparison*. New York, NY: Cambridge University Press.

Ward, S., R. Gibson, and P. Nixon (2003). "Parties and the Internet: An Overview," pp. 11-38 in R. Gibson, P. Nixon, and S. Ward (eds.) *Political Parties and the Internet. Net Gain?* London, UK and New York, NY: Routledge.

Wilhelm, A. (2000). *Democracy in the Digital Age: Challenges to Political Life in Cyberspace*. London, UK: Routledge.

Chapter 8
The Internet Upholds the Powers That Be

Henk Dekker and Arie in 't Veld

Leiden University, Leiden, the Netherlands

Abstract

Information and Communication Technology (ICT) innovations and the Internet in particular transform society and politics a good deal. ICT and the Internet also change political socialization because political elites and middle-level political actors use the Internet for political information, communication, persuasion, and mobilization. These political Internet messages reach a growing number of citizens who rate the credibility of Internet information quite high. They also consider the Internet a convenient, attractive channel for political information. Whether political websites achieve their desired effects cannot easily be assessed. We invited young people to participate (under clinical laboratory conditions) in a 40-minute political party website surfing/browsing session. Time spent on the sites is considered an important condition to measure the influence of political party sites. Our goal was to explain observed variance in the amount of time our subjects spent on political party websites. The independent variable was the variance in sites' quality. All 10 quality indicators refer to two motivation stimuli: self-efficacy and curiosity. To avoid distortions in our analyses due to unequal distribution of party preferences, we weighted the data for party preference. The hypothesis that the higher the site quality, the longer the site is used could not be falsified: users respond positively to higher-quality sites.

Political Socialization

Political socialization is the whole of those processes and structures through which people develop particular political behaviors and acquire particular political orientations, including political behavioral intentions, emotions, values, attitudes, opinions, beliefs or perceptions, and knowledge. “Processes” include the ways in (and the conditions under) which people receive, process, and more or less accept political messages. “Structures” include the sources/channels and contents of their informative and affective political messages. “Through” means influence. Political socialization research aims to answer the question: What are the origins of individuals' political behaviors and orientations (i.e., how and due to the influence of whom or what do people develop and perform political behaviors and acquire their personal political orientations)? Political socialization research helps to explain the establishment, maintenance, or change of polities, policies, and politics. Political systems, policies, and political processes are influenced by and are dependent on the acquisition, continuity, or change in the political behaviors and orientations of their members, subjects, and participants. These are, themselves, mainly the effects of political socialization processes (Dekker, 199la, b).

The so-called intellectual elites may have an independent, critical contribution to political socialization, but they may also help the political elites legitimize their personal preferences and policies. The various individual agencies and the socializers within them possess a relative autonomy. To understand individuals' socialization, we must study all possible socialization agencies and socializers active therein (Farnen, 1993; Washburn, 1994; Niemi and Hepburn, 1995; Sigel, 1995; Farnen, et al., 1996, 2000; Conway, 2000).

Theoretically, the most influential messengers for information, feelings, and emotions are the ones who first exert influence on the subject with respect to the object under investigation (e.g., grandparents, parents, peers, television programs), who exert influence for the longest period of time (e.g., parents, best friend, spouse), whose credibility the subject believes to be the highest (e.g., parents, teachers, television news), who have the most power over the subject (e.g., parents, teachers, spouse, employer), who have most power to prevent oppositional influences from other socializers (e.g., parents, elites), and who have the most resources and skills to influence and manipulate the subject (e.g., elites in cooperation with public relations and political advertising and marketing experts).

The new Information and Communication Technologies (ICT) and the Internet in particular have changed politics and society a great deal (Hill and Hughes, 1997; Holmes, 1997; Street, 1997; Hague and Loader, 1999; Barney, 2000). One of the benefits over traditional media is that digital hypermedia allow for a greater volume of information to be transmitted across space at faster speeds; the Internet practically eliminates the barriers of time and place. Another of its benefits is the integration of audio, video, graphic, and textual information, including datasets, interactive graphs, and movies. Another important difference is that the web is a solicited method of communication. The targeting is automatic because those customers interested in political information will visit the site. E-mail allows political elites to transmit a great volume of information across space at faster speeds to multiple recipients with minimal costs. Have ICT and the Internet also changed political socialization? Does the Internet have an influence on users' political behaviors and orientations? There can only be a political socialization "influence" when there is a political message, when that message reaches the individual, and when that individual is receptive to the message. We explore this topic next.

The Internet and Politics

ICT, the Internet, and the World Wide Web particularly enjoy a growing interest among political elites and middle-level political actors (Barber, et al., 1997; Connell, 1997; Horrocks, et al., 2000). In many countries, the head of state, government, ministries, parliament, individual members of parliament, political parties, interest groups, and (opposition) socio-political movements have one or more websites. All urge citizens to visit them on these sites. Norris (2000) used common search engines to gage the amount of politics occurring on the Internet and monitored the frequency that eight common keywords are found. The terms "computers," "sex," and "television" proved the most popular keywords. "Politics" came next, slightly outweighing "movies," "religion," and "investing." One in 10 sites referred to "politics." This probably represents a conservative estimate of political sites because many of them are indexed under other terms such as government, parliament, elections, political parties, and interest groups,

Heads of state and governments/administrations use the Internet as an additional agency of political information, public relations, and public diplomacy. Web-enabled government substantively changes public administration across all advanced industrial countries (Prins, 2001). Dunleavy and Margetts (2000) state that informatization of government and public administration makes central control and manipulation of populations potentially much easier (Macpherson, 1998).

Parliaments also distribute many different types of information directly and simultaneously: the daily agenda for parliamentary business, complete versions of official documents (such as the full text of pending legislation and government reports), streaming audio-visual feeds of debates in the legislative chamber, and political education spreads for teachers and students. Members of Parliament have a home page and e-mail address to "keep in touch," "meet," and influence their voters and possible future supporters. As of April 1, 2000, parliaments in 101 countries have established their presence on the Web (57% of the total number of parliaments). While Europe leads the way with 87% of its national parliaments operating websites, Africa lags behind with a mere 33%. The overall number of parliaments with websites has nearly tripled within two years (Inter-Parliamentary Council, 2000). Critical evaluations of current practices point to their relatively poor quality (e.g., features for searching, feedback pages, MPs' personal web pages and e-mail contact addresses are missing) (Norris, 2000; Inter-Parliamentary Union, 2000). Moreover, many MPs foolishly do not respond to constituents' e-mails (Meeks, 2000).

Internet voting is being integrated into the electoral process. The goal is increasing voter turnout. People will not have to make separate trips to an election site to cast a ballot. This means easier registration, no traveling costs, and less time. Moreover, Internet voting is expected to spark the interest of people who are not so much attracted by politics and bring them into the electoral process. However, there are some serious technical and social problems that need to be solved to ensure the security and reliability of the voting process (Gibson, 2002). The 2000 Arizona Democratic primary election was the first binding Internet election to ever occur. While turnout was small, it was substantial. It demonstrated an increase of 575% over 1996; Arizona had the highest percentage increase in turnout in Democratic primary elections. Voting methods (preference for Internet voting versus voting through mail in advance or via machine or paper balloting on election day) was moderately associated with education, income, and age; Internet voting is more popular among well-educated voters, those coming from higher income households, and younger voters. Ideology, "race," gender, and location of residence failed the test of statistical significance. Logistic regression analysis showed that age and education contributed most to the voting method decision, while income was not a significant predictor (Solop, 2000). There is also some speculation that Internet voting may favor US Democrats because Republicans have always had a very high turnout rate, despite the fact that more people are registered as Democrats.

Political parties use the Internet for their intra-party and inter-party communication and their interaction with members and possible future members/voters. Party elites have an additional access to their followers to convince them of particular views. The Internet allows smaller parties more opportunities to get their messages across. They can compete on an equal footing with the major parties to communicate their message to the wider Internet electorate. New members are recruited from categories that are less reached by the traditional media. Parties can invite non-members to take part in Internet discussions to start building a relationship with these possible future members.

Parties have invested heavily in online campaigns. Although accurate figures are not available, it is estimated that the three parties in the UK (by 2001) have put over a million pounds of their funds into websites, e-mail campaigning, and associated new media innovations (Crabtree, 2001). An important element is image marketing and management. Now, leaders like to show off their computer skills to convey an image of a modem, computer-literate leader. Opponents spread online rumors that can keep the accused away from governing; "dirty" Internet tricks and e-"smear" campaigns hurt leaders' and candidates' images. The Internet allows candidates for public office and parties to disseminate quickly retrievable and up-to-date information without interference or "mediation" (e.g., by critical journalists). Instead of merely trying to influence, direct, and manipulate the traditional media, political parties now also go directly to voters with their online efforts.

Parties have new opportunities to raise funds for their campaigns. Partisans are invited to actively participate in the campaign via the Internet. Some parties offer voters the opportunity to make "your own party homepage" (e.g., "your own Gore homepage" in 2000). They provide texts on the party and/or candidate; users can choose from links files what they want to send by e-mail to their own separate distribution lists. Friendly partisans are also invited to order campaign materials.

Political party websites share many elements. All three main parties in the 2001 parliamentary election campaign in the UK had a homepage with identifying features; the party manifesto/program; information about the candidates; daily news stories; full versions of speeches; cartoons, screen savers, and posters to be downloaded; calendars of events; invitations to contact and interact with the party via an online e-mail form or e-mail address to join the party and donate money; and a password-protected area for party members (a members-only "extranet"), including downloadable campaign material, graphics, and advice on how to respond to voters' questions about the day's events and news (Coleman and Hall,

2001). There were also clearly identifiable differences. Each site of the three main parties in the UK during the 2001 parliamentary election campaign had one or more unique elements. These included Frequently Asked Questions (FAQs), games, audio/video clips (of press conferences, interviews), live interviews (for which site users could use e-mail for questions), pop-up boxes (a small screen that "floats" over a site page, drawing one's attention to particular content or to solicit members), and online petitions (Coleman and Hall, 2001). Party sites also differed in sophistication (Earnshaw, 2001) and level of interactivity (e.g., whether the e-mail is answered, answered late, or specifically answered) (Hansard Society, 2001). Differences in the overall quality of party/candidate campaign sites in the US by 1996 and 1998 positively correlated with campaign resource level (Sadow, 2000; Sadow and James, 2001).

Social-political movements (human rights defenders, environmentalists, anti-globalists, but also terrorists, anti-democrats, racists, anti-Semites, neo-Nazis, sexists, and anti-gays) use Internet opportunities to inform and mobilize fellow citizens on a neighborhood, local, regional, national, and even global scale. The Internet gives today's activists an information-gathering network that their predecessors lacked. "Bearing witness" webcam reports alarm and mobilize their viewers. A "NetStrike" consists of a massive and simultaneous access to the same website until it can no longer bear the demand and becomes unavailable. "Rogue" (joke or cyber-squatter) sites try to undermine the effectiveness of their original sites. An increasingly important (and probably effective) grassroots tool is the e-mail petition. In this case, the organization writes the text to make it easier for people to contact their representatives in parliament and other public officials. There are online grassroots calendars where any political group can post its calendar in a centralized location for free and that notify activists when events are added to calendars which interest them. A new technique is to use e-mail to propose grassroots lobbying efforts which then employ handwritten and mailed previously-prepared text to ensure the message will be properly weighed in the representatives' office, where a canned e-mail would not be so highly valued.

ICT and the Internet have also affected the traditional socialization agencies such as mass media and school. Many traditional mass media have developed an additional Internet version (e.g., CNN.com). There are new online news"papers" and weeklies and daily political news and commentary sites. ICT and the Internet have also affected schools and political education (Filzmaier, 2001). Internet political education projects aim to narrow the political digital gap and to improve political competence and interest (for examples of projects, see the politeia.net site of the Politeia Network for Citizenship and Democracy in Europe). NGOs and private organizations provide services to voters and aim to help select a party/candidate in elections, to make informed political choices, and to notify them about relatively simple but important practical matters such as when, where, and how to vote. Online voter guides offer information about the various parties and candidates (e.g., their biography, qualifications for office, policy statements, speeches, and previous performance on fulfilling election promises). Voter guides offer clear voting advice. After answering questions about the relative importance of issues and about the user's own issue opinions, the computer links the user's opinions to party programs and informs the user about which party comes closest to his/her opinions (a voter matching site). In the US in 2000, youth were able to participate in a national (non-binding) online election for president (see the youthevote.com site). In Germany, young people could vote for state and federal parliament parties (see the Juniorwahl.de site). In the Netherlands, young people could vote for parties in the national parliament (see the publiek-politiek.nl site).

Since there can only be political socialization "influences" from the Internet when there are political messages on the Internet, when these messages reach the individual, and when that individual is receptive to the messages, we may conclude that the first requirement is met. Political elites and middle-level political actors use the Internet for political information, communication, persuasion, and mobilization. But now we must ask, do these messages reach many individuals and are they receptive to them?

Political Internet Sites and Citizens

How many people have Internet access? Never before did a new communication medium evidence such a fast growing number of users as has the Internet (Bell and Tang, 1998). However, only 7% of the world's population (mostly in the West) uses the web (Sussman, 2001). In most EU countries, less than half of the population uses the Internet. In Autumn 2000, on average, 26% of EU citizens used e-mail and/or the Internet. Use varies greatly among the 15 EU member states (from 61% in Sweden to 11% in Greece). Managers are most likely to use the Internet and/or e-mail (61%), followed by people who left full-time education at the age of 20 or older, and people who are still studying (both 57%). It is lowest among the elderly; only 4% of retired people use it (European Commission, 2001). There is a digital divide due to the costs of Internet access and/or becoming computer literate in the linguafranca, English. Not all users are frequent visitors. There are more "sensors" (who prefer the real over the virtual) and "hoppers" (who pop in and out of the Internet) than "assimilators" (who absorb the Internet into their lives). "Sensors" fear that the Internet holds its users back from social interaction, do not believe the Internet is the final authority for information, think it is easier to call or go out to shop, are irritated with the abundance of information available online, and do not like junk mail (Lee and Anderson, 2000).

How many citizens see the Internet as an important source of political information? In the US, low (though growing) percentages of Internet users say they view the Internet as very or somewhat important as a source of information about elections. In the presidential election of 2000, half of the Americans viewed the Internet as very (19%) or somewhat (32%) important as a source of information about the election. The figures among actual Internet users are higher (very = 23%, somewhat = 41%) (American University, 2000). In the UK, many fewer Internet users say they are "certain" or "likely" to use it to find information about the election (respectively, 2% and 13%). More than 8 in 10 express no interest in using the Internet during the election: 39% are "not likely" to use it and 45% will "definitely" not use the Internet (Crabtree, 2001; Industrial Society, 2001a).

How many citizens have in fact accessed the Internet for information about politics? In the US, low (though growing) percentages of Internet users say they have actually accessed the Internet for information about politics. In the 2000 presidential election, nearly 1 in 5 Americans said they went online for "election news," compared to fewer than 1 in 10 during the 1996 campaign (Pew, 2001). One-third of the Americans who use the Internet said they obtain information about "politics, candidates, or political campaigns" online. Veteran online users (who have been online for at least three years) were far more likely to get election news (45%) than Internet "newbies" (who began going online in the past six months) (17%) (American University, 2000). Two-thirds of the youth ages 12 through 17 have searched for news online (Lenhart, et al., 2001). Interest in US online campaign news peaked around election day; fully 12% of Americans went online for political news on November 7, 2000. That figure rises to 28% among those who voted on November 7 (Pew, 2000a). Users do not spend much time on political websites: in the presidential election year 2000, more than half of US Internet users who accessed information about politics, candidates, or political campaigns have spent no more than one hour doing so during a "typical" week (53%) (American University, 2000). In the UK, another 1 in 5 respondents who had access to the Internet used it for any 2001 election-related activities. Young people were much more likely to use the Internet to find out about politics than older citizens (Coleman and Hall, 2001).

Why do people use the Internet? The Internet's main appeal is as a campaign news source. It is its convenience that motivates, rather than a desire to tap new or different information sources because users were not getting all the news they wanted from traditional media (respectively, 56% and 29%) (Pew, 2000a). Why do people not use the Internet for political information? A self-evident primary cause is no access to the Internet. Second, people are largely ignorant of political Internet content. Third, people have negative perceptions: they think political information online is aimed at party activists, not at them. Fourth, people do not feel they have the ability to make use of the Internet and its political content. Fifth, people feel they are already overloaded with information on the election. There is no evidence that gender and socio-economic status have an influence on using or not using it. If voters do search for political information, popular expectations are often reversed; they are likely to find the Internet a useful political tool and prefer it to much offline media (Crabtree, 2001).

What are people doing on and with the Internet when it comes to politics and public affairs? Most political Internet users are likely to use it to get information about various issues and candidates (respectively, 36% and 35%) rather than to communicate or chat with others about issues (19%), forward voting-related information via e-mail (17%), communicate or chat with a candidate (7%), donate money to a candidate (5%), or volunteer for a campaign (5%) (American University, 2000). Another study made clear that when it comes to politics and public affairs, Internet users turn to e-mail more than the web. They also prefer humor to action; more than half of Internet users say they have sent or received e-mail jokes about the candidates or campaign (George Washington University, 2000). Political website users are partisan information seekers and/or issue-oriented seekers, but also uncertain information seekers who follow a visual attraction strategy or a browsing strategy (Kern, et al., 1999). In the UK, voters who consider using e-mail during the election are also likely to discuss the election with friends and family, but avoid parties and politicians. Whereas 32 % said they might send e-mail to friends or family about the election and 34% said they might send a joke, fewer than 10% said they would e-mail a candidate, party, or politician (Crabtree, 2001).

What kinds of websites are used? Focus group participants in the Just, et al. (1997) study visited many sites. They spent much of their time at such sites. In 2000, the American campaign sites were used much less frequently than other media-sponsored sites (Pew, 2001). In the UK, traditional news media sites (such as the BBC website) also are the overwhelming choice for reliable information about the election. Political party websites are significantly less popular; only a third of those who considered using the Internet to find information about the election thought they would visit a national political party site. However voters who do search for political information online favor information on policy presented by parties online to offline (Crabtree, 2001). It is difficult to obtain data about the numbers of visitors to party and candidate websites. Most of the party and candidate sites have removed their counters (which would indicate how many hits the sites were receiving) or have simply hidden or not installed them. The few remaining counters (and anecdotal data from campaign managers) indicate that there were not too many hits overall (Dulio, et al., 1999). One of the reasons for relatively low party website hits is that low (though growing) percentages of Internet users access the Internet for political information in general. Another reason is that the voters habitually prefer mediated content that is mostly provided by traditional media. A third reason is that political party websites are hard to find; the web is "about as well organized as a bookstore after a hurricane" (Toulouse, 1998, p. 3).

How do users evaluate political websites? In general, users are pleased with their political Internet experiences. The reasons that US focus group participants gave for liking their experience with the Internet were that the Internet provides access to a lot of information, the experience is interesting ("exciting," "fascinating," "appealing," and "fun"), the web is easy to use, it offers diverse views, and it is accessed quickly. The comments that participants gave about the web were that there was not enough information or that it was not current, reliable, or interesting. Inexperienced users found the Internet slow (Just, et al., 1997). In general, Internet users prefer websites of major news organizations as sources of political information. For election news, CNN.com received the highest percentage approval of any website tested; those users rated that site as very useful. Just over one-third of online users who visited the Bush/Cheney and Gore/Lieberman sites (respectively 7% and 6% of online users) found them very useful (Pew, 2001). In the UK, voters who search for political information online seem impressed with the medium and its usefulness. They are likely to be critical of parties and candidates without an Internet presence, are highly demanding in terms of web content and are extremely critical if their demands are not met. These voters express consistent and definite preferences for styles of web presence and content. They have little tolerance for amateurish websites (Crabtree, 2001).

One might think that the low percentages of Internet users who say they are certain they will use the Internet to get election information has something to do with a possible low rating for the credibility of Internet information. However, available data show the opposite. Credibility (believability) ratings for the online sites of the major national news organizations in the US are substantially higher than ratings for the news organizations themselves. The figures for ABCNews.com and ABC News were 44% and 29% respectively, for CBSNews.com and CBS News 41% and 27%, for USAToday.com and *USA Today* 37% and 21%, and for FoxNews.com and Fox News Channel 34% and 21%, respectively (Pew, 2000a). A possible explanation for this important phenomenon is that people consider information more credible the more they have personally (experienced or) looked for or found it. In Arizona, more than half of adults supported Internet voting being added as an option to all future Arizona elections. Younger people, higher income earners, and more well-educated people expressed stronger levels of support for Internet voting there (Solop, 2000).

How do users estimate the effects of their using political websites? Most focus group participants in the Just, et al. (1997) study believed they learned something about politics from their Internet experience. After people experience using the Internet for voting (e.g., in Arizona), many more Internet voters said they would be more likely to vote if Internet voting was an option in future elections (Solop, 2000). A growing number of US online election news consumers say online election news affected their voting decisions (1996: 31%; 2000: 43%). This subjective effect of online campaign news has been particularly pronounced among young people. Half of the online election news consumers under age 30 say the information they received made them want to vote for or against a particular candidate (Pew, 2000b). However, only 6% of those UK voters who were online said that the Internet was very or fairly important in providing them with information that helped them determine their vote. More younger (17%) than older people (5%) reported this subjective Internet influence upon their vote (Coleman and Hall, 2001). UK voters who search for political information online are likely to judge political parties by their Internet presence. They felt that their image of the party/candidate with the "best" site had improved their image of the party/candidate. The reverse was also true: bad sites translate to a bad image. Having a "bad" website can be a dangerous liability for parties (Crabtree, 2001).

In short, (almost) a majority of the population in industrialized countries uses the Internet. A small, though growing, minority regularly accesses Internet information about politics. Political website users are partisan and issue-oriented, but also uncertain, information seekers. They prefer websites of major news organizations as sources of political information, compared to political party and campaign sites. Credibility ratings for the online sites of news organizations are substantially higher than ratings for the news organizations themselves. Voters who search for political information online are likely to be critical of parties and candidates without Internet presence, are highly demanding in terms of web content, and are extremely critical if these demands are not met. We may conclude that political Internet messages reach a small, though growing, number of citizens and probably influence these citizens' political behaviors and orientations. They rate the credibility of Internet information quite high and consider the Internet a convenient and attractive channel of political communications. It is worth our effort to study the Internet in the context of political socialization (Groper, 1996; Ward and Gibson, 1998). Crucial research questions relate to the intended and unintended effects of political Internet activities. How much influence do political websites have on their users? How can we explain variance in this influence?

Political Party Websites and Their Effectiveness

Our empirical study focuses on political party websites. We selected sites of political parties because parties are integral to the operation of political systems. Moreover, elections are the very heart of democracy and voters vote for a party list in many countries; the list system is the most common method applied in proportional representation systems. The elector votes for a party and its list of candidates, rather than for a single candidate. The research project aimed to answer the question: How can we explain observed variance in effectiveness of political party websites?

Whether political party websites are effective and have their desired effects cannot easily be assessed. Behavioral effects are the least complicated to measure (e.g., the number of e-mails sent by users, orders to send a printed party program, and new membership enlistment). Much more difficult to measure is the sites' influence on political knowledge, beliefs, opinions attitudes, emotions, and behavioral intentions, including party preferences. The main reason for this is that one cannot easily isolate the site's effects from the effects from other political socialization agencies.

Our study is based on the assumption that for any effect and influence, the site needs to be used for at least some time. The longer a site is visited, the more stimuli the user probably receives and the higher is the chance that the desired effects are actually reached (Briggs and Hollis, 1997). A relatively long visit time is a necessary, though not a sufficient, condition for such influence. Time spent on the site is just one (albeit important) indicator of success. Other scholars have used the number of pages read as the dependent variable. However, this number is not easy to observe in a reliable way due to the use of "frames" (two pages within one page), the presence of pop-up windows, and other factors.

How do we explain variance in time spent on political party websites? Why is one website used longer than another? We hypothesize that there is a lot to the quality of the site: a higher quality website is used longer.

What makes for high quality? To answer this question, we apply the Hypermedia Interaction Cycle and the Psychological Model of the Internet-User developed by Fredin (l997) and Fredin and David (1998). Here, the key question is: what intrinsically motivates the user to stay at a particular website? What drives people to continue with the next interaction with a website?

The Hypermedia Interaction Cycle model is an iterative, self-regulatory model that captures the dynamics of hypermedia interaction from a user's perspective. In many ways, it is based on Bandura's 1989 general social learning theory regarding motivation and self-efficacy. It has two dimensions: cycle stages and motivational components. A cycle is the period between leaving a main menu (e.g., a menu on a home page) and returning to a main menu after a successful or failed search. There are three cycle stages: preparation, exploration, and consolidation. The preparation phase includes making a choice from a menu of options. The user makes an estimate of a good choice, taking into account his/her goals. The exploration phase starts when the choice has been made and the user is presented with a variety of information. The consolidation phase occurs when the user reached his/her goal or failed to do so and has decided to try another option. Then the cycle starts again. The time spent on a website is longer the more cycles are started and the longer the cycles are.

Motivation has two components: goals and self-efficacy. Goals motivate by providing the potential of satisfaction (or dissatisfaction). Goal foreshadowing occurs during the preparation phase of the interaction cycle, while goal evaluation occurs during the consolidation phase. Goal evaluation includes the degree of success in finding something good and the degree of liking what was found. Self-efficacy is the conviction that one can do what is required to accomplish a particular outcome (Bandura, 1989). In the preparation phase, the self-efficacy factor is confidence in finding something specific to the immediate task at hand (e.g., useful information). In the consolidation phase, the self-efficacy factors are confidence in finding other interesting information and the degree of surprise with the information found. Self-efficacy is supported by a high quality of the site's information and technology. Surprise is an emotion, resulting from the violation of expectations; it has immediate effects, including motivational ones. Goal conditions and self-efficacy factors act in a cyclical pattern. Achieving a goal strengthens self-efficacy, while self-efficacy, in turn, affects goal foreshadowing.

The three key words in the Psychological Model of the Internet-User are "self-efficacy," "curiosity," and "flow." Self-efficacy is the sense that one can do what is required to accomplish a particular outcome. Curiosity (i.e., the goal is to know more) is raised by stimuli that are novel, somewhat complex, and surprising or ambiguous. In the presence of such stimuli, people may arrive at serendipitous experiences (i.e., emotionally satisfying discoveries). Moreover, emotional satisfaction derived through curiosity often leads to further curiosity. Self-efficacy and curiosity contribute to arriving at a state of flow. Flow is "a state of often intense concentration" and "the experience of exercising control in a complex, difficult activity." It gives an intrinsic motivation because in flow, the reward for achieving a goal, is largely intrinsic; performing the action well is largely its own reward (Fredin, 1997, pp. 5-6; Csikszentmihalyi and Csikszentmihalyi, 1988). A person in a state of flow often forgets the time; if a state of flow ends, one is embarrassed about not knowing the real time involved. Self-efficacy, curiosity, and flow result in self-sustaining actions, which, in their turn, motivate the user to spend more time on any site that encourages these feelings of satisfaction. Websites have a higher quality the more they strengthen the user's feeling of self-efficacy, the more they evoke curiosity, and, as a result, the more they provide a strong sense of satisfaction or the feeling of "flow."

What site characteristics strengthen the feeling of self-efficacy, evoke curiosity, and provide flow? The relevant literature suggests several different quality indicators (Fredin, 1997; Just, et al., 1997; Day, 1997; Schneiderman, 1997; Buchanan and Lukaszewski, 1997; Fredin and David, 1998; Lu and Yeung, 1998; Nielsen, 2000). We selected 10 of these indicators. The first indicator is the first impression the home page of the site makes upon its users. A positive first impression of the site is expected to evoke curiosity. The second indicator relates to the site's appearance/looks and includes layout (e.g., symmetry and visual elements such as colors, illustrations, typeface, and background). A visually pleasing (attractive) site is expected to evoke curiosity. The third indicator relates to site content. The content can be more or less informative, relevant/useful, up-to-date and fresh, reliable and objective, easily accessible (thanks to a clear structure, short paragraphs, and summaries), made to measure, and interesting. The higher the quality of the information the site offers and the more understandable the information is, the more the site strengthens one's feeling of self-efficacy. The fourth indicator relates to the site's navigation opportunities. A clear and consistent navigation menu throughout the entire site (including frames, "hyperlinks," and a search feature) will help the users to find their way and, as a result, will give them a feeling of self-efficacy. Speed of downloading is the fifth indicator. Waiting too long for site content to download annoys the user. A "speedy" site satisfies the user's feeling of self-efficacy. The sixth indicator relates to interaction opportunities, allowing for two-way communication and vital feedback. Thanks to interaction with the site owner/maker, fellow visitors, and/or with elements of the site itself, the user may make fortunate and surprising discoveries that strengthen his/her curiosity. The next two indicators are the presence of video fragments and audio snatches. Opportunities to watch video or to listen to spoken words or music are expected to evoke curiosity. The ninth indicator is the number of missing elements. The more a site offers the things the users are looking for, the more the site is expected to strengthen the user's feeling of self-efficacy. The tenth indicator is the number of elements that do not function well. Possible examples are "links" to pages that are absent or "back"' keys that do not function due to "automatic referral." Ill-functioning elements are expected to undermine the users' self-efficacy.

The Experiment

To explore the relationship between times spent on political party websites and their quality, we invited young people in the Netherlands, aged 18 to 21, to take part in a research study under clinical laboratory conditions in a 40-minute session. This young population had the right to vote in national parliamentary elections for the first time. We also focus on young people because surveys found that the Internet is more likely to be used for political information and discussion among the young and young adults (together with those with higher education degrees and people in higher income categories). We also had to limit our study to party websites from just one country. The Netherlands offers good opportunities for research in this field: its electoral system is a proportional representation system; votes are cast for parties and their lists of candidates rather than for single candidates; there are a large number of political parties; almost all parties have their own website (Voerman, et al., 2002); and the Internet has a rapidly growing number of users.

We recruited participants via a website dedicated to our study and another youth website with a link to our research site. We also publicly displayed posters with a reference to our website. The website and corresponding posters invited youth to participate in "research into the evaluation of websites." The word "political" was excluded purposely to recruit those respondents with low or no political interest. Computer skills and website surfing experience were not required. We wanted to attract other than "dotcom generation" representatives. We made an appointment with the first 41 youngsters who responded by e-mail. We had to limit the number of participants because of a lack of funds. The number 41 corresponds with the "n" in Kern's study, which largely inspired and motivated us to design our own research project (Kern, 1997; Kern, et al., 1999). The personal reward for participation was 15 Dutch guilders (7 Euros).

The respondents formed a highly selective group. Almost all participants were university or higher vocational education students (38 and 2, respectively); one participant attended secondary school classes. Women were over-represented (27). The average age was 20. Nine participants had no website surfing experience. Almost all intended to vote in the upcoming parliamentary elections. A large majority said they had voted for the local council last year and most had a relatively high level of political interest. The various limtations with respect to population and sample size limit the generalizability of our research.

Each session followed a set procedure. Upon arrival at the lab (Leiden University, Department of Political Science), the subjects were given a short briefing. The researcher also provided ample opportunities for participants to clarify their doubts. Then the respondent was invited to write answers for 12 closed-ended questions. These questions tapped, among others: subjective political knowledge, political interest, party preference, party attachment, and voting intention.

After completing the questionnaire, each participant was invited to sit in front of the monitor and keyboard. If necessary, participants were given a demonstration of the basic features and introduced to basic commands. The respondent was told that he/she could make a choice on the websites of six parties (PvdA = Labour Party, CDA = Christian-Democrats, D66 = Liberal-Democrats VVD = Liberal-Conservative Party, SP = Socialist Party, and GL = GreenLeft).

These six sites were the only "bookmarks" available in the browser. Each bookmark referred to the "root" of the site. The bookmark opened either the site's homepage or introductory page. All participants were presented with the same menu of choices. One could start with any party he/she chose, was free to visit any number of sites, and could revisit a site. One was also free to stay at a particular page as long as the respondent wanted. The only limitation was a maximum allowed computer session time of 40 minutes. In practice, 35 of the 41 participants used all six sites.

The researcher sat behind the research subject; the researcher's position did make the subject feel he/she was kept under constant surveillance but at the same time, was close enough to help the respondent immediately in case of technical problems and to closely watch the screen. The researcher made notes about the order in which the sites were visited, the site elements that did not function, the respondent's use of interaction opportunities, and the respondent's viewing of video fragments and listening to audio snatches. The "Surfing Spy" program made a log file (i.e., an electronic account of activity on the research site) for each respondent. The "cache" included all pages that the respondent downloaded, including all elements such as illustrations.

Following the computer session, a structured debriefing interview was held with the respondent to determine his/her evaluation of the sites' characteristics. During this interview, we showed the home- or intro-pages of the party sites that the respondent had visited as a memory aid on the screen. The interviews lasted approximately 25 minutes. The interview questions relate to all 10 quality indicators. For the first impression (appearance, contents, and speed), the respondents were invited to give each site a grade between 0 and 10. Next, they were asked for amplification. Regarding missing elements, the respondents were asked whether they thought particular things, elements, or opportunities were lacking and, if so, what they missed. The answer options for the question about navigation were: very clear, clear, not clear, and not clear at all. The interviews were tape recorded and transcribed. The transcripts (in Dutch) are available for review.

We expected that party website use would positively correlate with party preference and party attachment. Respondents preferring party x were expected to use the site of party x longer than respondents who did not prefer party x. Kern, et al. (1999) demonstrated this correlation in the US. In three of the six cases, the correlation between website use (in seconds) and party preference (a dichotomous variable) was statistically significant (sites 3, 4, and 6), while in the other three cases, this significance was almost reached (sites 1, 2, and 5). The Pearson's r varied from .20 to .50 (site 1 PvdA: r=.21, p=.10, N=39; site 2 CDA: r=.26, p=.07, N=36; site 3 D66: r=.50, p=.00, N=35; site 4 VVD: r=.29, p=.05, N=35; site 5 SP: r=.20, p=.12, N=38; site 6 GL: r=.40, p=.00, N=40; we considered not visiting a site to be a missing value). We also explored the correlation between party site use and subjective political knowledge, political interest, voting intention, and voting or abstention in the past. No correlation was found, with the exception of the time spent on one of the six sites and subjective political knowledge (site number 1; r = .35, p = .02, N = 33). Almost none of the respondents expressed any party attachment.

Party preference was unequal in the group of respondents (site 1 party PvdA: 10 participants; site 6 party GreenLeft: 10 participants; site 3 party D66: 7 participants; site 4 party VVD: 5 participants; site 2 party CDA: 2 participants; and site 5 party SP: 1 participant; no party preference had 6 participants). To avoid distortions in our analyses aiming at exploring the effects of the sites' quality, we weighted the data for the time spent on the party sites for party preference. To illustrate this weighting, we use the data about the fifth (SP) site, visited by 38 respondents. Out of these, 32 preferred one of the six parties. Out of these, 1 preferred the party SP, while the other 31 respondents who visited the SP site, did not prefer the SP. The data from the 1 SP sympathizer counts much more than the data from the other 31 respondents. In case of an equal distribution of party preference (32 respondents with a party preference/6 parties = 5.333), respondents would have had an SP preference and 32.666 another party preference. To reach an equal distribution, the data of the SP sympathizer was weighted with (5.333/1 =) 5.333, while the data of the others were weighted with ((38- 5.333=)32.667/37=) 0.883.

Table 1: Average time spent on six party websites in minutes and seconds (weighted)

Website	Average time in minutes	Average time in seconds	N
No. Party			
1 PvdA	7'39"	459	39
2 CDA	6'45"	405	36
3 D66	6'27"	387	35
4 VVD	6'11"	371	35
5 SP	5'41"	341	38
6 GL	4'45"	285	40
PvdA = Labour Party, CDA = Christian-Democrats, D66 = Liberal-Democrats, VVD = Liberal-Conservative Party, SP = Socialist Party, and GL = GreenLeft			

The average time spent on the six party websites differed considerably. The first site received longest attention. The difference between the time spent on this site and the second most popular site was almost one minute. The shortest time was spent on the sixth site. The difference between this site and the site on the next to final place in the rank order was also almost one minute.

We made 2-by-2 comparisons to determine whether the sites statistically significant differ with respect to average time. The same weighting procedure was followed for the comparisons of two sites. To illustrate this, we use the data about the first (PvdA) site and fifth (SP) site. In total, 36 participants visited both sites. Out of these, 3l preferred one of the six parties. In case of an equal distribution of party preference (31 participants/6 parties=), 5.167 participants would have had a PvdA preference, 5.167 participants a SP preference, and so forth. In reality, there were 9 participants with a PvdA preference and 1 with a SP preference. To reach an equal distribution, the data of the PvdA sympathizers were weighted with (5.167/9 =) 0.574, the data on the SP sympathizer with (5.167/1 =) 5.167, and the data of the others with ((36-5.167-5.167=) 25.666/26=) 0.987. The 2-by-2 comparisons show that the differences in five combinations are statistically significant (t-tests, $p<.05$). Four clusters can be identified: first, the first site to which more time was spent than the fifth and sixth sites. Second, the second, third, and fourth site to which more time was spent than the sixth site. Third, the fifth site to which less time was spent than the first site. Finally, the sixth site to which less time was spent than the first, second, third, and fourth site.

Table 2: Difference in average time spent on six political party websites in two by two comparisons (weighted)

Websites (A)-(B)	Average time spent to A	Average time spent to B	Average time difference	T	P (two-way)	N
1-6 PvdA-GL	433	276	157	4.19	.00*	38
1-5 PvdA-SP	454	335	119	3.01	.00*	36
1-4 PvdA-VVD	445	360	85	1.91	.06	33
2-6 CDA-GL	407	279	128	2.33	.03*	36
2-5 CDA-SP	422	330	92	1.63	.11	34
3-6 D66-GL	382	277	105	2.28	.03*	35
5-6 SP-GL	345	277	68	1.72	.09	38

Table 3: Average scores for 10 characteristics of six party websites (weighted)

Website	First impression	Appearance	Contents	Navigation	Speed
1 PvdA	7.2 (38)	7.5 (39)	7.6	(39)	7.4 (38)
2 CDA	7.3 (36)	7.3 (36)	7.3 (34)	3.4 (36)	8.1 (35)
3 D66	6.6 (35)	6.5 (35)	6.9 (34)	2.7 (35)	7.7 (34)
4 VVD	6.8 (35)	7.0 (35)	7.3 (32)	2.8 (34)	7.5 (34)
5 SP	6.6 (38)	6.6 (38)	6.4 (38)	3.0 (38)	7.7 (38)
6 GL	6.2 (40)	6.0 (40)	6.7 (38)	2.8 (40	7.6 (39)

Website	Interaction	Video	Audio	Missing elements	Not well functioning elements
1 PvdA	0.29 (39)	0.03 (39)	0.06 (39)	0.54 (35)	0.25 (39)
2 CDA	0.30 (36)	0.00 (36)	0.00 (36)	0.77 (35)	0.27 (36)
3 D66	0.00 (35)	0.20 (35)	0.000 (35)	0.75 (32)	0.23 (35)
4 VVD	0.17 (35)	0.06 (35)	0.06 (35)	0.92 (32)	0.32 (35)
5 SP	0.39 (38)	0.00 (38)	0.00 (38)	0.66 (33)	0.00 (38)
6 GL	0.00 (40)	0.00 (40)	0.00 (40)	0.92 (37)	0.06 (40)

We used the 10 indicators mentioned previously to measure respondents' evaluations of the websites' general quality. Average grades were counted for respondents' first impression of the site plus its appearance, contents, and down1oad speed (using a 1-10 scale). The navigation assessment is the average level of clarity (using a 1-4 scale). Interaction, video, and audio are measured as the average number of times respondents used the opportunities. For the missing elements and those not functioning well, we counted the average numbers. We weighted the data about the individual indicators the same as for the average time spent at sites. Some indicators received clearly different average scores for the various sites (e.g., appearance varied from 6.0 to 7.5). Other indicators received almost the same average scores (e.g., average number of audio fragments the respondent listened to). In general, sites on which respondents spent the longest time also received high quality scores. The low time score for the GreenLeft site is also coupled with low quality scores.

The general quality of a party site is the sum of the average scores for the first seven characteristics, minus the average scores for the last two indicators. We excluded the average numbers of audio fragments the respondents listened to because they were extremely low for all six sites. For example, one respondents' scores were: (first impression: 8 + appearance: 7 + contents: 6 + speed: 5 + navigation: 2 + interaction: 2 + video: 1 -) 31 - (missing elements: 1 + not well functioning elements: 1-) 2 = 29. Together, the nine indicators formed a reliable scale (Cronbach's alpha .70; N = 6 party sites). The first two sites received the highest scores; the third, fourth, and fifth sites were in the middle, while the sixth site appeared last.

Table 4: Average general quality scores for six party websites

Website	Quality
1 PvdA	31.76
2 CDA	32.66
3 D66	29.42
4 VVD	30.39
5 SP	30.03
6 GL	28.32

The 2-by-2 comparisons showed that the differences in eight combinations were statistically significant. Four out of the five combinations of sites that differ in time they were visited by the participants also differ with respect to the evaluation of the general quality (1-6, 1-5, 2-6, 3-6). The remaining combination of sites (4-6) differs with respect to the time they were visited, but not with respect to the evaluation of the general quality. This may be due to the relatively small number of respondents that answered all relevant questions for these two sites (n = 25). Four other combinations of sites also differ with respect to general quality, but have not differed in the time they were visited by the participants (2-3, 2-4, 2-5, 3-1). The remaining six possible combinations of two websites (which are not mentioned in Table 5) do not differ with respect to time or to general quality (1-2, l-4, 3-4, 3-5, 4-5, 5-6).

There is a strong correlation between the average time spent on a party website and its average score for quality (Pearson's r .80, p .03*, n = 6). Quality explains 63.7% of the variance in average time spent on the sites. This analysis relates to six cases: the six party sites. There are 12 scores: six scores for the dependent variable (i.e., the average time spent on the six sites) (see Table l, third column) and six scores for the independent variable (i.e., the average quality score for the six sites) (also see Table 4). Note that we do not use the 41 subjects as the cases to be analyzed because we do not intend to explain differences among these subjects. Rather, we want to explain differences among the six party sites. The conclusion is that the higher the quality of the site, the more time the participant spent on it. There are a few combinations of sites that do not fit in this pattern (e.g., the 1-2 sites) (Figure l). The first site received more time from the subjects than the second site, although the latter received a higher quality score. The second site scored higher than the first site on only two out of the nine indicators: navigation and speed. It may be that some quality indicators are more important than others (e.g., appearance and content compared to navigation and download speed).

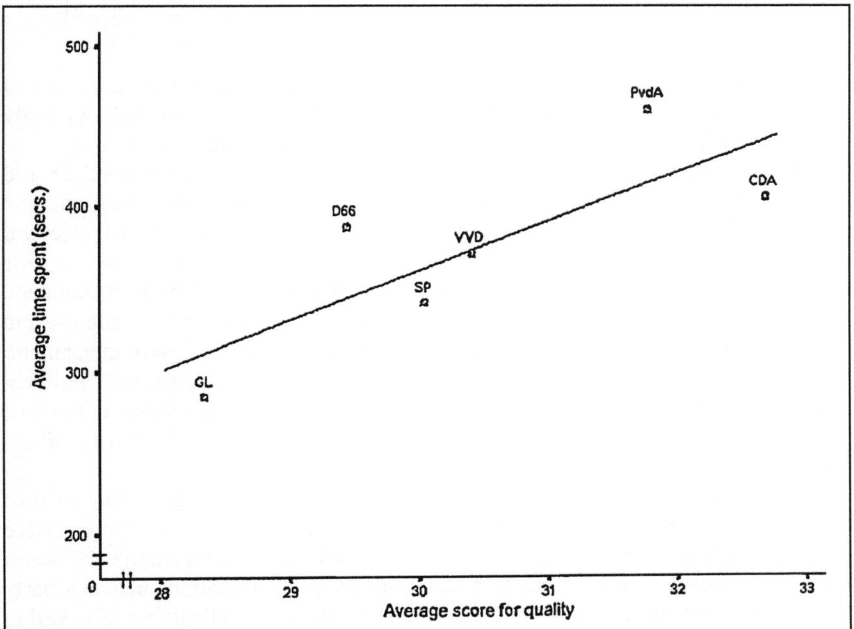

Figure l: Correlations between the average times spent (in seconds) on political party sites and average score (range of 27-33) for their quality

Table 5: Difference in general quality between six political party websites in two by two comparisons

Websites (A)-(B)	Average quality score for A	Average quality score for B	Average quality score difference	T	P (two-way)	N
1-6 PvdA-GL	32.02	27.75	4.28	5.83	.00*	31
1-5 PvdA-SP	32.33	30.28	2.05	2.58	.028	30
1-3 PvdA-D66	32.24	29.60	2.64	3.67	.00*	26
2-6 CDA-GL	32.46	28.25	4.22	4.35	.00*	30
2-5 CDA-SP	32.52	29.92	2.59	2.55	.02*	29
2-4 CDA-VVD	33.26	31.01	2.25	3.08	.01*	24
2-3 CDA-D66	33.30	30.17	3.13	4.04	.00*	26
3-6 D66-GL	29.55	27.89	1.66	2.19	.04*	27
4-6 VVD-GL	30.42	28.29	2.13	1.56	.13	25

Our comments address three main points, each related both to the limitations of the present work and to directions for future work. First, we had to limit our study to party websites from just one country (the Netherlands). That country's electoral system is a proportional representation system. Future comparative research should include party sites from other countries with the same proportional representation system and sites from countries with plurality, majority, and mixed electoral systems. Second, we expected a positive correlation between the amount of time spent on party websites and the subject's party preference and party attachment. We found empirical evidence for the positive correlation between party site use and party preference. Almost none of the respondents expressed any party attachment. No correlation was found between party site use and subjective political knowledge, political interest, voting intention, and voting or abstention in the past (with the exception of the time spent on one of the six sites and subjective political knowledge).

The absence of correlations might be explained by the absence or low level of dispersion of values for these variables. In turn, this is caused by the selective composition of the group of subjects. In future studies, a random sample (of youth and young adults) may allow us to better analyze such correlations between party website use and party attachment, political knowledge, political interest, voting intention, and voting behavior in the past. Third, we gave all quality indicators the same weight in our analysis. There are some indications that users consider appearance and content more important than navigation and speed. In our study, both appearance and content were covered by just one indicator. More specific appearance indicators may relate to typeface, colors, and background. More specific content indicators may be the sites' levels of comprehensibility and conciseness. We may obtain a higher percentage of explained variance in time spent on party sites by weighting quality indicators differently and using more specific appearance and content quality indicators.

Epilogue and Conclusions

There are two competitive hypotheses about the overall political influence of ICT on representative democracies. First, the "mobilization thesis" predicts that ICT will facilitate forms of direct democracy, allowing more opportunities for citizen decision-making (initiatives and referenda), grassroots mobilization, and community organization. ICT reduces the need for indirect representation (Macpherson, 1998). ICT will contribute to shrink the distance between politics and citizens. Political Internet activities will strengthen citizens' political competence and activism. In April 2001, I received an e-mail "View from the Harvard Yard: It Is a Revolution" from Phil Noble, President of PoliticsOnline and Resident Fellow of the Institute of Politics at Harvard University's John F. Kennedy School of Government. The message was "More than ever, I am convinced that the Internet is causing a revolution in politics and government. We may only be at 10am in the morning on day one of the revolution, but it is here. It is happening now."

Second the "normalization hypothesis" predicts that the major traditional offline institutions and interests (such as governments, strong political parties, established media, and corporations) will increasingly dominate the Internet (Coleman and Hall, 2001). Core political institutions and middle-level actors will be thereby strengthened (Norris, 2000). The gap between political elites and large groups of citizens will widen due to a growing digital divide. Access to the Internet will be sharply uneven because economic and technological resources/access and computer skills are unequally distribued, creating an information underclass. Offline inequalities are being replicated in cyberspace (Resnick, 1998).

Third, a separate version of the normalization hypothesis says that new computer networks are an essentially conservative technology that strengthens the prevailing liberal and capitalist global order. Computer networks produce greater elite control over citizens, tighten the screws, and make global economic and political elites richer and more powerful. Computer networking is the Trojan horse for democracies; it is the ultimate capitalist tool due to its predominant control function (Barney, 2000).

But "revolution" is probably an incorrect term; the Internet has transformed politics, but it is currently not a medium that destroys or replaces existing political systems and their power distributions. ICT seems to support the maintenance of pre-existent basic power structures (Bovens, 2003). Autocracies are helped by economic growth due to ICT (Taubman, 1998; Hachigian, 2001; Sandschneider, 2001). Representative democracies (which suffer from a serious crisis due to lowering election turnouts) may be helped by Internet voting because it may bring young first-time voters (who have consistently low rates of election turnout) back into the electoral process.

ICT offers more opportunities to political actors who have more power and financial resources (among other power factors) to buy Internet management expertise, but with an interest in maintaining the status quo. There is also reason to speculate that parliaments will lose influence and power to ministries and public agencies that have more expertise in managing Internet activities. Private companies may also acquire more political influence thanks to their ICT resources and expertise.

At the moment, there seems to be more evidence for the stability thesis than the revolution thesis and more evidence for the normalization thesis than the mobilization thesis. Political socialization in existing political systems plays fundamentally a conservative role; the status quo is maintained. Individuals are led to develop actual behaviors and orientations that are according to, and fit into, the existing political culture and system. The two Internet sites which received the longest participant/subject attention in our research belong to the major Dutch political parties. The shortest time was spent on the oppositional political party site. The first two sites also received the highest quality scores, while the oppositional site arrived in last position. Parties with many members have more financial resources to buy website expertise. ICT and the Internet particularly offer new opportunities for promoting the classic stability and supportive nature of traditional political socialization.

Acknowledgements

The authors thank Montague Kern (Rutgers University) and Rudy Andeweg (Leiden University) who inspired and motivated us to design this research project. We are grateful to Russell F. Farnen (University of Connecticut), Katerina Pouliasi (ERCOMER, Utrecht University), Hsuan Chou (University College Utrecht), and participants in the 2001 IPSA Research Committee on Political Socialization and Political Education Conference, the 2001 Netherlands Institute of Government seminar, the 2001 Annual Conference of the Netherlands Association of Political Science, and the 2001 General Conference of the European Consortium for Political Research for their comments on drafts of this chapter.

References

American University Center for Congressional and Presidential Studies, School of Public Affairs (June 12, 2000). *Public Attitudes. Toward Campaigns and Campaign Practices.* http.//-www.american.edu/acadenuc.depts/spa/ccps/campaignconduct/publications.html.

Bandura, A. (September 1989). "Human Agency in Social Cognitive Theory," pp. 1175-1184 in *American Psychologist*, Vol. 44.

Barber, B. (1984). *Strong.Democracy: Participatory Politics for a New Age*. Berkeley, CA: University of California Press.

Barber, B., K. Mattson, and J. Peterson (1997). *The State of "Electronically Enhanced Democracy": A Survey of the Internet*. New Brunswick, NJ: Walt Whitman Center.

Barney, D. (2000). *Prometheus Wired. The Hope for Democracy in the Age of Network Technology*. Chicago, IL: The University of Chicago Press.

Bell, H. and N. Tang (1998). “The Effectiveness of Commercial Internet Web Sites: A User’s Perspective,” pp. 219-228 in *Internet Research: Electronic Networking Applications and Policy*, Vol. 8, No. 3.

Bovens, M. (2003). *De digitale republiek* (The Digital Republic). Amsterdam, the Netherlands: Amsterdam University Press.

Briggs, R. and N. Hollis (1997). “Advertising on the Web: Is There Response Before Click-Through?,” pp. 33-45 in *Journal of Advertising Research*, Vol. 37, No. 2.

Buchanan, R. and C. Lukaszewski (1997). *Measuring the Impact of Your Web Site*. New York, NY: Wiley.

Coleman, S. and N. Hall (August 10, 2001). “Spinning on the Web: E-campaigning and Beyond,” pp. 7-24 in S. Coleman (ed.) *2001: Cyber Space Odyssey. The Internet in the UK Election*. The Hansard Society. http://www.hansardsociety.org.uk.

Connell, M. (1997). “New Ways to Reach Voters and Influence Public Opinion on the Internet,” pp. 64-68 in *Campaigns & Elections*, Vol. 18, No. 8.

Conway, M. (2000). “Some Alternative Political Socialization Research Designs,” pp. 259- 270 in R. Farnen, H. Dekker, D. German, and R. Meyenberg (eds.) *Democracies in Transition: Political Culture and Socialization Transformed in West and East*. Oldenburg, Germany: BIS.

Crabtree, J. (June 11, 2001). *Whatever Happened to the E-lection. A Survey of Voter Attitudes towards New Technology during the 2001 Election*. London, UK: Industrial Society, Futures Department. http://www.indsoc.co.uk/whats_new/press/010601. -htrn.

Csikszentmihalyi, M. and I. Csikszentmihalyi (eds.) (1988). *Optimal Experience: Psychological Studies of Flow in Consciousness*. New York, NY: Cambridge University Press.

Day, A. (1997). “A Model for Monitoring Web Site Effectiveness,” pp. 109-115 in *Internet Research: Electronic Networking Applications and Policy*, Vol. 7, No. 2.

Dekker, H. (1991a). “Political Socialization Theory and Research,” pp. 16-58 in H. Dekker and R. Meyenberg (eds.) *Politics and the European Younger Generation*. Oldenburg, Germany:BIS.

Dekker, H. (1991b). “Political Socialization in Europe,” pp. 318-349 in H. Dekker and R Meyenberg (eds.) *Politics and the European Younger Generation*. Oldenburg, Germany: BIS.

Dulio, D., D. Goff, and J. Thurber (March 1999). “Untangled Web: Internet Use during the 1998 Election” in *Political Science and Politics*. Also on APSA’s PS Online: http://www.apsanet.org/PS/march99/thurber.cfin (accessed 16 August 2001).

Dunleavy, P. and H. Margetts (November 9, 2000). “The Advent of Digital Government: Public Bureaucracies and the State in the Internet Age.” Paper prepared for delivery at the 2000 Annual Meeting of the American Political Science Association, Washington, DC. http://pro.harvard.edu/abstracts/024/024002MargettsHe.htrn.

Earnshaw, B. (August 10, 2001). "Winning a Seat in Cyber Space: Candidate Web Sites in the 2001 General Election,” pp. 47-60 in S. Coleman (ed.) *2001: Cyber Space Odyssey. The Internet in the UK Election*. The Hansard Society. http://www.hansard-society.org.uk.

European Commission, Directorate-General Press and Communication (2001). *Eurobarometer. Public Opinion in the European Union. Report Number 54. Fieldwork: November-December 2000*. Brussels, Belgium: European Commission, Directorate-General Press and Communication (http://europa.eu.int/comm/dg10/epo).

Farnen, R. (ed.) (1993). *Reconceptualizing Politics Socialization and Education*. Oldenburg, Germany: BIS.

Farnen, .R., H. Dekker, R. Meyenberg, and D. German (eds.) (1996). *Democracy, Socialazation and Conflicting Loyalties in East and West: Cross-national and Comparative Perspectives*. New York, NY: St. Martin's Press and London, UK: Macmillan.

Farnen, R., H. Dekker, D. German, and R. Meyenberg (eds.) (2000). *Democracies in Transition. Political Culture and Socialization Transformed in West and East*. Oldenburg, Germany: BIS.

Filzmaier, P. (June 11, 2001). "Netzgeneration und Politische Bildung: Wissen Kompetenz, und Qualifikation in der 'Cyberdemocracy' als digitale Klassen gesellschaft" (The Net Generation and Political Education). Paper prepared for the Institute of Political Science, University of Innsbruck, Austria. http://www politeia.net/semmar/Papers/ONLINE-Filzmaier.htrn.

Fredin, E. (1997). *Rethinking the News Story for the Internet: Hyperstory Prototypes and a Model of the User. Journalism and Mass Communication Monographs, 163*. Columbia, SC: Association for Education in Journalism and Mass Communication.

Fredin, E. and P. David (1998). "Browsing and the Hypermedia Interaction Cycle: A Model of Self-efficacy and Goal Dynamics," pp. 35-54 in *Journalism & Mass Communication Quarterly*, Vol. 75, No. 1.

George Washington University, Graduate School of Political Management, Democracy Online Project (2000). *Post-Election 2000 Survey on Internet Use for Civics and Politics*. http://-democracyonline.org/databank/dec2000survey.shtrnl.

Gibson, R. (2002). "Elections Online: Assessing Internet Voting in Light of the Arizona Democratic Primary," pp. 561-583 in *Political Science Quarterly*, Vol. 116, No. 4.

Groper, R. (1996). "Political Participation and the Internet: A Review Essay," p. 247-249 in *Political Communication*, Vol. 13, No. 2.

Hachigian, N. (March/April 2001). "China's Cyber-Strategy," pp 118-133 in·*Foreign Affairs*.

Hague, B. and B. Loader (eds.) (1999). *Digital Democracy; Discourse and Decision Making in the Information Age*. London, UK: Routledge.

Hansard Society (August 10, 2001). "E-mail Test," pp. 29-30 in S. Coleman (ed.). *2001: Cyber Space Odyssey: The Internet in the UK Election*. The Hansard Society. http://www.hansardsociety.org.uk.

Hill, K. and J. Hughes (1997). "Computer-mediated Political Communication: The Usenet and Political Communities," pp. 3-27 in *Political Communication*, Vol. 14, No. 1.

Holmes, D. (ed.) (1997). *Virtual Politics. Identity and Community in Cyberspace*. London, UK: Sage.

Horrocks, I., J. Hoff, and P. Tops (eds.) (2000). *Democratic Governance and New Technology*. London, UK: Routledge.

Industrial Society (June 11, 2001). *iSociety*. London, UK: The Industrial Society Futures Department. http://vyww.mdsoc.co.uk/isociety/press release htrn

Industrial Society (June 11, 2001). *Whatever Happened to the E-lection. A Survey of Voter Attitudes towards New Technology during the 2001 Election*. London, UK: The Industrial Society, Futures Department. http://www.indsoc.co.uk/whats_new/press/010601.htm.

Inter-Parliamentary Council (May 6, 2000). "Guidelines for the Content and Structure of Parliamentary Web Sites." Approved by the Inter-Parliamentary Council at its 166th session in Amman. http://www.ipu.org/cntr-e/web.pdf.

Just, M., A. Crigler, and M. Kern (1997). "Citizens and the Internet: Diversifying Information Sources in Cyberspace." Paper presented at the Annual Meeting of the National Speech Communication Association, Chicago, IL.

Kern, M. (1997). "Social Capital and Citizen Interpretation of Political Ads, News, and Web Site Information in the 1996 Presidential Election," pp. 1238-1249 in *American Behavioral Scientist*, Vol. 40, No. 8.

Kern, M., M. Just, A. Crigler, and I. Xie (July 18, 1999). "Patterns of World Wide Web Use in Election Campaigns: Evidence from Interactive Interviews." Paper presented at the Annual Meeting of the International Society for Political Psychology in Amsterdam, the Netherlands.

Lee, B. and J. Anderson (June 12, 2001). "Current Attitudes of Internet Users." Paper submitted for presentation at the Association for Education in Journalism and Mass Communication, The Communication Technology and Policy Division, Washington, DC, 2001. Elon, NC: Elon University, School of Communications. http://www. elon.edu/pew/oneweek and http://-www.pewinternet.org/papers/paper.asp?paper=8.

Lenhart, A., L. Rainie, and O. Lewis (2001). *Teenage Life Online. The Rise of the Instant-message Generation and the Internet's Impact on Friendships and Family Relationships.* Washington, DC: Pew Internet & American Life Project. http://www.pewinternet.org.

Lu, M. and W. Yeung (1998). "A Framework for Effective Commercial Web Application Development," pp, 166-173 in *Internet Research: Electronic Networking Applications and Policy*, Vol. 8, No. 2.

Macpherson, M. (December 7, 1998). "Some Applications of Information Technology to Citizen Participation in Politics." Online paper. http://www.snafu.de/- mjm/miercurea.html.

Meeks, B. (2000). "Most E-mail to Congress is Ignored; Lawmakers Overwhelmed, Study Says. Flooded by Spam, Politicians Reply by 'Snail Mail' If at All." http://www.msnbc.com/news-/540014.asp (11 June 2001).

Nielsen, J. (2000). *Designing Web Usability: The Practice of Simplicity*. Indianapolis, IN: New Riders.

Niemi, R. and M. Hepburn (1995). "The Rebirth of Political Socialization," pp. 7-16 in *Perspectives on Political Science*, Vol. 24, No. 1.

Norris, P. (November 9, 2000). "Democratic Divide? The Impact of the Internet on Parliaments Worldwide." Paper prepared for delivery at the 2000 Annual Meeting of the American Political Science Association, Washington, DC. http://pro.harvard.edu/abstracts/038/038010-NorrisPipp.htm.

Pew Research Center For The People & The Press (June 11, 200la). "Internet Sapping Broadcast News Audience." Section V: Media Credibility. http://www.peoplepress.org/media00sec-5.htm.

Pew Research Center for The People & The Press (June 11, 2001b). "Youth Vote Influenced By Online Information." http://www.people-press. org/onlineOOrpt.htm.

Pew Internet & American Life Project (June 12, 2001). "Internet Election News." Report 27. http.//www.pewinternet.org/reports.asp?Report=27&Section=ReportLevel1&Field=LevelIID &ID=9.

Prins, J. (ed.) (2001). *Designing E-government; On the Crossroads of Technological Innovation and Institutional Change*. The Hague, the Netherlands: Kluwer Law International.

Resnick, D. (1998). "The Normalization of Cyberspace," pp. 48-68 in C. Toulouse and T. Luke (eds.) *The Politics of Cyberspace*. New York, NY: Routledge.

Sadow, J. (2000). "A Uses and Gratifications Theory of Internet Campaigning." Paper prepared. for delivery at the 2000 Annual Meeting of the American Political Science Association, Washington, DC.

Sadow, J. and K. James (June 11, 2001). "A Theory of Internet Political Campaigning: A Revolution that Isn't, Yet." Paper presented at the 2000 Annual Meeting of the Southwest Political

Science Association, Galveston, TX. http://www.people.uis.edu/jsado1/uis/cwsp/swp-sa00.htm.

Sandschneider, E. (2001). "The Internet and China's Political System," pp. 23-26 in *European Political Science*, Vol. 1, No. 1.

Schneiderman, B. (1997). "Designing Information-abundant Websites: Issues and Recommendations," pp. 5-30 in *International Journal of Human-Computer Studies*, Vol. 47, No. 1.

Sigel, R. (1995). "New Directions for Political Socialization Research," pp. 17-22 in *Perspectives on Political Science*, Vol. 24, No. 1.

Solop, F. (November 9, 2000). "Digital Democracy Comes of Age in Arizona: Participation and Politics in the First Binding Internet Election." Paper prepared for presentation at the 2000 Annual Meeting of the American Political Science Association, Washington, DC. http://pro.harvard.edu/abstracts/036/036015SolopFrede.htm.

Street, J. (1997). "Remote Control? Politics, Technology and 'Electronic Democracy,'" pp. 27-42 in *European Journal of Communication*, Vol. 12, No. 1.

Sussman, L. (2001). "The Internet in Flux," pp. 1-4 and 41 in *Press Freedom Survey 2001*. New York, NY: Freedom House. http://www.freedomhouse.org.

Taubman, G. (1998). "A Not-so World Wide Web: The Internet, China, and the Challenges to Nondemocratic Rule," pp. 255-272 in *Political Communication*, Vol. 15, No. 2.

Toulouse, C. (1998). "Introduction," pp. 1-16 in C. Toulouse and T. Luke (eds.) *The Politics of Cyberspace*. New York, NY: Routledge.

Voerman, G., A. Keyzer, F. den Hollander, and H. Druiven (2002). "Archiving the Web: Political Party Web Sites in The Netherlands," pp. 68-75 in *European Political Science*, Vol. 2, No. 1.

Ward, S., and R. Gibson (1998). "The Potential of the Internet: Issues for Research," pp. 6-8 in *ECPR News*, Vol. 10, No. 1.

Washburn, P. (1994). "A Life Course Model of Political Socialization," pp. 1-26 in *Politics and the Individual*, Vol. 4, No. 2.

Part 3
The Print Press, Broadcasting, and Politics

Chapter 9
Metaphors in Euroland Press

Christ'l De Landtsheer

Professor of Communications Science, University of Antwerp, Antwerp, Belgium

Elisabeth Koch

Reuters Amsterdam Bureau, Amsterdam, the Netherlands

Abstract

This chapter aims to find some indications of how and to what extent the Euro (European Single Currency) is portrayed in media coverage from various countries. It investigates the use of metaphors in Euronews. Metaphor is a powerful style form; the way a metaphor is used in public speech reveals citizens' and elites' interests and emotions toward public issues. This was confirmed in several case studies that applied the metaphor model which De Landtsheer (1994, 1998, 2004) developed. The current study focuses on the six months that preceded the public introduction of the Euro in 2002. It examines a 110,435-word sample of media discourse on the Euro from northern and southern Europe and the US covering the period between October 1999 and April 2000. Metaphor use in Euronews by countries that were willing to participate in the Euro was compared with Euronews from countries that were not planning to participate. The results suggest that media discourse on the Euro in so-called Euroland countries was more metaphorical (therefore, emotive and persuasive) than the Euro discourse in the non-Euroland countries.

Introduction

One study (Taran, 2000) on the use of metaphor in the Ukrainian Parliament concluded that metaphors concur with elements of mythical thinking. Other metaphor research suggests that the "European myth" may currently be more coherent than one could imagine and that the political integration of the EU already exists to a large degree in European mentalities. In fact, the "mapping" of metaphors in the European Parliament reveals the divisions found when they are broken down by political functions, rather than by nationalities, countries, or particular languages (De Landtsheer, 1998).

This chapter considers the topic of metaphor in relation to European integration. It contributes to examining these metaphors that represent the "European Myth." Metaphor can be studied as a powerful style form that is often employed in print media in relation to the Euro (the European Single Currency), which is the main feature of the European Monetary Union (EMU) (Farell, et al., 2002). Metaphors are important tools for opinion formation vis á vis the EMU. Metaphor affects citizens' and elites' perceptions of political and economic events (e.g., the introduction of the European single currency). Here, we use the metaphor research method developed by De Landtsheer (1998, 1994) to investigate persuasive and emotive efforts in press reporting about the Euro (De Landtsheer and De Vrij, 2004).

How important is the Euro for European Union member states that were willing to join the Euro zone and for others that decided not to join? In May 1998, participation in the Euro zone was confirmed for 11 EU member states: Belgium, Germany, Finland, France, Ireland, Italy, Luxemburg, the Netherlands, Austria, Portugal, and Spain. At that time, two members (Greece and Sweden) were not admitted because they did not fulfill the convergence criteria. In May 2000, the Commission admitted Greece beginning in January 2001 because it fit the criteria. The Commission decided that Sweden could not be admitted then because the Swedish legislation had not adopted the rules of the EU treaty and its currency did not meet the fluctuation margins set by EMU (http://www.eu.ac.be). The aim of this research is to find (through metaphors alone) some indications of how and to what extent the Euro is portrayed in media coverage from various countries both in and out of "Euroland."

The sample of newspaper articles for this study covers: the period October 1999 to April 2000. The empirical analysis was performed in Spring 2000, so it falls within the time frame January 1, 1999 (the introduction of the. Euro for transactions between banks only) to January 1, 2002 (the actual adoption of the Euro currency for the citizens in the Eurozone countries) (Boles, McDonald, and Healey, 2002; Fella, 2002; http///www.eu.nl). Metaphor use in public speech will be compared for two groups of countries: those that accepted the Euro's circulation and those that did certainly not.

We begin with answers to these questions: What is metaphor? How can we identify metaphor? Next, we focus on our samples. Then, we detail the coding and interpretation of metaphors. Finally, we present our results.

What is Metaphor?

Metaphor is omnipresent in our life, in language, on television, and in the newspapers. One is usually not aware of such metaphors because they are like eyeglasses. One is aware of them only if they obscure vision. Metaphors describe nouns, reduce complexity, and represent facts from a specific perspective. Metaphors fulfill specific tasks (Luczak, et al., 1997, p. l; De Landtsheer, 1998, p. 32). Metaphors can "clarify" things, while retaining the ability to "mystify." Since metaphors often use incorrect analogies, they may transmit certain desirable, but inaccurate, connotations. Metaphors have indisputable manipulative capabilities which help persuade audiences. In this sense, metaphors rely on their inferences and emotive power. They are figures of speech, in which a word (group) symbolizes an idea by using an implicit comparison, rather than a directly stated idea. Most importantly, metaphors seem to function as emotive components of language. De Landtsheer confirmed the longitudinal and cyclical evolution of emotionality in society with her metaphor methodology (Gaus, 2001, p. 122; De Landtsheer, 1987, 1988, 1991, 1992a, l992b, 1994).

All of these qualities make metaphors extremely useful for political purposes. It can be concluded from the relevant literature that metaphors can be used to sensitize audiences about political issues. At the same time, the use of metaphors in public speech obviously can contribute considerable information about public policy developments and public opinion formation (Beer and De Landtsheer, 2004). As many linguistic theorists, from Richards (1936) to Lakoff and Johnson (1980), have argued, metaphors shape our conceptual systems. Metaphor is a "constitutive form" and "an omnipresent principle" not only in language, but also in politics and international relations. Metaphor is an essential part of communications theory and may be used in the social sciences in an expansive way (Richardson, 1994, p. 519).

Aristotle initially formulated the first questions about metaphors: How can we identify and interpret them? What exactly are they? Metaphors go as far back as language itself. They are central to language and ubiquitous in communication (Hahn, 1998). Therefore, many scholars and philosophers have discussed metaphors since Aristotle's time with a variety of replies. Aristotle's substitution theory is based on the idea of similarity between two elements, the subject in question and the substitute expression from another sphere of life that is used to describe it. According to a modern formulation of this theory, metaphors are, "...merely figure[s] of speech in which a word for one idea or thing is used in place of another to suggest a likeness between them, as in 'the ship ploughs the sea'" (Hahn, 1998, p. 133). *The Concise Oxford Dictionary of Current English* (1959, p. 748) says that metaphor is basically an "application of name" or a descriptive term for an object to which it is not literally applicable (the dictionary's example is "a glaring error"). It is an implied comparison or description. Metaphor differs from simile since the latter usually contains the words "like" or "as. "

According to Black (1962, p. 39), metaphors are sentences, not isolated words. A metaphor clearly consists of two components. The metaphorical sentence is "the frame" or the "tenor" and the word or words used metaphorically are the "focus" or the "vehicle" (Richards, 1936). The two basic parts of metaphors are characterized differently by various scholars. For example, Lakoff and Johnson (1980, p. 230) say "we understand experience metaphorically when we use a gestalt from one domain of experience to structure experience in another domain." Kittay (1998, p. 229) speaks of two "semantic fields"; a notion based on de Saussure's and Baily's earlier concepts.

"One has to ride a bicycle in order to keep it moving," Jacques Chirac, the French president, suggested in an interview with the newspaper Figaro. The metaphor helped him present his views on Europe's political unification. Chirac used a metaphor, which is a form of speech or language that consists of an implicit comparison between the topic that is discussed (the political unification of Europe) that is the primary subject (the "frame" or "tenor" of the metaphor) and a topic that belongs to a completely different domain of knowledge (riding a bicycle), which is the secondary subject (the "focus" or "vehicle" of the metaphor).

According to Black, the two subjects (principal and secondary) that metaphors have should be seen as two "belief systems." The secondary subject (e.g., riding a bicycle) consists of a set of beliefs that help construct a set of beliefs about the principal subject (i.e., the European political integration). The two subjects interact in the interpretation, where some features of the secondary subject are highlighted (One has to ride a bicycle in order to keep it moving) to fit the principal subject (the European political integration) and to produce the meaning the speaker aims to convey (which is that "one should energetically proceed with the European political integration in order not to destroy it"). Understanding a metaphor involves comprehending the literal meaning called upon in the vehicle of the metaphor (riding a bicycle) and grasping the vehicle's contrasting relations that are being transferred to a new domain (European political integration).

A commonly used identification criterion for metaphors is "strangeness of the expression to the context." Dobrzynska (1995, p. 597) thought it a fact that metaphors are images and not notions, because they put together unlike, contrasted, and "unfixed semantic elements," causing an aesthetic result for the audience. This aesthetic result is crucial to the attention-attracting qualities and the persuasive effects of metaphor. But Black (1962) formulated the currently used metaphor theory: "interaction theory." According to this theory, the interaction of two ideas produces a new meaning (i.e., one plus one equals three). The conflict or contrast between the two different domains of knowledge or two semantic fields ("politics" and "bicycle"), two subjects, two parts that are often too dissimilar to allow our beliefs about the one to characterize the other directly (Black, 1979, p. 31) produces the metaphorical effect. This effect includes creating new meanings; it is also responsible for the "priming" effect of metaphors. The decision to interpret an utterance metaphorically depends on the "frame" or context: there must be "incongruity" within the utterance itself and its situational context (Kittay, 1987, p. 76).

We assume that the meaning of language is entirely content-dependent (dependent on its use), but that this holds much more for non-literal language, in general, and metaphors, in particular, than for literal language and stereotypes (Kittay, 1987, p. 97). Different kinds of basic frames can be distinguished other than the simple "situational" or "sentence" "frame." These include the "text frame," the "author's frame," the "geographical frame," the "common interests frame," the group frame," or the "language frame" (Kittay, 1987, pp. 55-57).

A substantial body of literature has been published on metaphors and their meanings in certain contexts (for an overview, see Beer and De Landtsheer, 2004). Political metaphors show what could be said for metaphors in general: most works deal with metaphor in relation to a particular topic and its siguificance. Chilton's

(1996) *Security Metaphors: Cold War Discourse from Containment to Common House* is one of these works. Unfortunately, few works were helpful for this rudimentary research and exploration of the meaning of EMU metaphors in various countries. Works of practical value to this investigation of metaphors in newspapers from countries within and outside of the EMU proved to be those dealing with political language, political psychology, political communication, and European integration (Beer and De Landtsheer, 2004; De Landtsheer and Feldman, 2000; Feldman and De Landtsheer, 1998). The Internet contains much data on metaphors. Lakoff and Johnson's book *Metaphors We Live By* (1980) placed metaphor on the agenda for communications and social sciences consideration. It convincingly demonstrated the overall importance of metaphor for our lives and for public discourse. However, our emphasis is on conventional metaphors and how these structure and confirm traditional social values, rather than not on original metaphors or their power to alter political processes.

Sample

This study mainly explores possible differences in trends in reporting about the Euro within and outside of Euroland. Indeed, due to the way the study was set up, it was not possible to compose an equilibrated, random, or stratified sample in terms of countries and newspapers. So our mass media language sample consists of 110,435 words representing 183 days of discourse on the Euro and the EMU in Danish, Dutch, Greek, Norwegian, Spanish, Swedish, and American newspapers.

We chose these countries partly because of practical purposes. To perform a metaphor analysis, one must work with coders who are native speakers. The data collection and coding was set up as a research and take-home exam for De Landtsheer's class of 27 international students taking an international communications course at the University of Amsterdam. The nationalities of the students in the class played a role in the choice of countries and the number of newspapers. Prominent papers from northern and southern Europe as well as one paper from the US were included in the sample. The metaphors come from a variety of newspapers from different countries. Dutch and American newspapers dominate, although Danish, Greek, Norwegian, Spanish, and Swedish papers are also included and play substantial roles. Papers from countries that at that time were supposed to be prepared to participate in the Eurozone include the Greek *Eleftherotypia*, the Spanish *El Pais*, and the Swedish *Dagens Nyheter*. When we conducted this research, Greece and Sweden were not yet allowed to participate in the EMU because they did not fulfill or meet the criteria; nevertheless, they were considered as eventual candidates for participation in the Euro. The Netherlands, a "Euroland country," provided four main newspapers: *Het Parool*, *De Volkskrant*, *NRC Handelsblad*, and *De Telegraaf*.

From the non-Euroland countries, Denmark (an EU country that decided not to adopt the Euro) and Norway (a European non-EU member) were represented by

Politiken and *Aftenposten*. We further analyzed *The International Herald Tribune*, a US newspaper published in Europe. The metaphors were taken only from those articles on or mentioning the Euro or the EMU. Each of the 27 students was assigned a newspaper (in his/her first language) to look through for certain months. Their first job was to search the newspapers for all articles mentioning the European Single Currency, disregarding articles that used the word "euro" only as a currency (e.g., "Sales rose 13 percent to 6.74 million euros from 5.98 million euros on Wednesday") (*The IHT*, January 28, 2000).

Their second job included coding and calculating how many and what type of metaphors appeared in newspaper articles for every 1,000 words on the EMU in a particular time frame. These different interpretations of just one metaphor made it hard to perfectly code each and every one of them in the various newspapers. For this reason, the authors read every metaphor (the foreign ones were translated into English) that was received to make sure that the coding corresponds to what the coder wrote. Once the metaphors were coded by the theory and processes explained later in this chapter, it became possible to say how the print media depicted the European Single Currency over the same six-month period (October 1999 through March 2000).

It can be concluded from earlier studies (De Landtsheer, 1994, 1998; De Landtsheer and Recchi, 2000; De Landtsheer and De Vrij, 2004) that several factors other than interest in the Euro may affect the use of metaphor in public discourse in various countries. These include serious economic, political, or military crises; political extremism; and nationalistic events. But these factors are not dealt with in this study; besides, they may not be that significant. Within certain limits, the use of metaphor is affected by the ideology and scope (popular or elitist medium) of selected news media. These are factors that we tried to control as much as possible in our sample by way of our choices of certain newspapers.

Analyzing Political Metaphors

The method used in this study assessed the metaphor power of a given text corpus. Some of the information that the metaphor power provides us with concerns the emotional loading of a text and the persuasive efforts political elites exert in the process of forming public opinion. Metaphor power is expressed in a metaphor coefficient. Coding schemes (De Landtsheer, 1991, 1992a, 1992b, 1994, pp. 70-71, and 2004) used in these processes produce two metaphor coefficients, one for studied countries in the EMU and another for those outside the EMU.

The hypothesis that has been formulated is as follows. It is more probable that countries inside the "Eurozone" will have a higher metaphor coefficient since they want to promote their new currency (which is what metaphors help them to do in their use of language). Also, the Euro is a very important issue among those countries and is expected to have more frequent mentions in member countries. The United States, Norway, and Denmark (which are not part of the EMU) would most probably have a lower metaphor coefficient because the Euro is not expected to be as important a topic in their newspapers and, therefore, was likely to be mentioned less frequently. But there is no doubt that the new currency has and will have effects on these countries. Considering the actual times in which the coding took place, we expected that Euroland would have a greater total metaphor coefficient in comparison to the non-Euroland countries. Euroland countries in our sample are those which at the time of the research had applied to join the Eurozone; these included the Netherlands, Greece, and Spain (or even Sweden).

The following explanation describes how the metaphor coefficient was conceived and how metaphors were coded The metaphor coefficient (symbolized by C) is the product of three variables that respectively relate to frequency (symbolized by F), intensity (symbolized by I), and content (symbolized by D). Coding metaphors is a process not easily explained in writing; therefore, the following description and information is given in clear, simple, step-by-step fashion.

The first step is that every article with a mention of the Euro and with at least one metaphor had its words counted. This is how we started to calculate the frequency variable (F). It is simply the total number of metaphors per 1,000 words. For example, of the 25 articles on the Euro in the *Aftenposten* (the Norwegian newspaper) coded during these months (November 1999 through March 2000), there were 11 articles with at least one such metaphor. The total words of these articles amounted to 4,617, which would make the equation look like this: 11 divided by (total of 4,617 divided by 1,000) equals 2.382. (Or 11/(4,617/1,000)=2.382). The frequency coefficient (F) has been rounded off to the third decimal place. For this Norwegian newspaper, F is a bit more than two metaphors per 1,000 words. The same coding was done for the other countries and they were compared with these results

Two further steps followed in that each metaphor was then "coded." This meant (in this particular case) that each received two different classifications to detail their metaphoric "power." In the second step, a strength or intensity value is given to each metaphor: s (strong), n (normal), or w (weak). Each of these variables represents a number: a strong metaphor is designated 3 points, normal is 2 and weak is 1. The intensity value that each metaphor is given is based on the coders' own common sense and knowledge. A strong metaphor is presented as original and new, while its literal meaning and emphasis is still quite applicable and current. A normal metaphor is not very creative or unique anymore, although it continues to incorporate distinct implications for its literal meaning. A weak metaphor is popular and frequently used and rarely concerns its literal meaning. To construct the Intensity variable (I), all weak metaphors are tallied and multiplied by 1, every normal metaphor is multiplied by 2, and each strong one is multiplied by 3; the sum of all these is divided by the total number of metaphors. To clarify this procedure, we used the Norwegian *Aftenposten* as an example (Table 1). The 22-point total is divided by the total number of metaphors in the articles to sum/reach one I (the total Intensity). This paper had 22 points/11 (total metaphors) = 2 (total intensity of metaphors for Norway). The same formula was used for the remaining countries.

Table 1: Metaphor Intensity of Euro news in the Norwegian paper Aftenposten (November 1999-March 2000)

Intensity	Total number of metaphors	Total Points
W = 1	X 2 =	2
N = 2	X 7 =	14
S = 3	X 2 =	6
Total	11	22

After the intensity variable coding is done, another symbol is given to each metaphor (this is the third step). This second series of categories and symbols is used to calculate the content variable or content power (D). Since metaphors are widely recognized as a framework for classifying or assorting behavior, different semantic fields of focus are added. An m is given if the metaphor is related to medical issues or illness; sp for sports or theatre; d for death or disaster; po for political or intellectual issues; na for nature; and p for popular subjects or those from everyday life. These categories and symbols represent various degrees of power: m (the strongest of all) is worth six points. It goes down one point respectively, until p (the weakest degree of strength) is left; it is worth just one point. Metaphors that mention body parts (m) and those that refer to sports or theatre (sp) are the most important in speech and print (Beer and De Landtsheer, 2004, contains a taxonomy of metaphorical sources and their possible weight factors).

Metaphors dealing with death, disaster, or violence (d) attract the attention of the audience, but also tend to generate fear. As far as the political and intellectual (po) metaphors are concerned, they do not appeal greatly to mass audiences because the average viewer/reader is not very "intellectual" and has no interest in politics. Metaphors on the topic of nature (na) have an obvious utility since everyone can associate with it. The popular (p) metaphors pertain to everyday life's material aspects (e.g., in the home). These have an inclination to be authentic and genuine and are less associated with the conception of "myths" or "escape" than any of the previously stated classifications of metaphors (De Landtsheer, 1998).

Much of the rhetorical strength of most metaphor categories is that they come from occurrences. or events that all audiences can associate with and understand. Hahn (1998) gives examples of these (e.g., air, fire, earth, water, human anatomy, the animal world, seasons, gardening, planting, growing, decaying, and so on). The fact that these are customary and familiar to audiences means that the writer (in this case) need not use much time or space to convey what he/she is trying to say. Hahn (1998, p. 114) uses this example: if someone writes or says, "he's a bear of a man," most readers/listeners easily understand the gist of the message being communicated. Basic metaphors are not as simple as one may first believe them to be. In

Hahn's example metaphor, the receiver might have one of four different interpretations. Most people would simply envision a large man. Others who had experienced disagreeable encounters with bears might be convinced that the man is potentially dangerous or dangerously powerful. Some receivers could think of bear cubs and determine that the man is playful, cuddly, and clumsy. Lastly, some people may reflect on the differences between human beings and "lower" life forms (e.g., animals) and decide that the communicator is classifying the man as something of a brute or as less than human.

The content power or content variable (D) is discovered in a fashion comparable to the way intensity is calculated. To find D, every metaphor from one country that has been coded with an "m" must be counted and multiplied by 6, then added to every "sp" metaphor multiplied by 5, then added again to all "d" metaphors multiplied by 4, plus the number of "po" metaphors times 3, and so on. This number is then divided by the total number of metaphors (t) in the relevant press articles in that particular country. It becomes clearer in Table 2, using the *Aftenposten* example, if closely examined. We can make it easier to understand by writing the formula (De Landtsheer 1994, p. 71) like this:

$$D = \frac{1p + 2na + 3po + 4d + 5sp + 6m}{\text{Total number of metaphors (t)}}$$

The final step involves calculating C, the metaphor coefficient. C is the product of F, D, and I, which is how the study is set up, always starting with the frequency, then the intensity, then the content power, and finally, the metaphor coefficient. We calculate one metaphor coefficient for the press articles on the EMU from countries that are within it and another for countries outside it.

Table 2: Content power of metaphor in Euro news of the Norwegian paper Aftenposten (November 1999-March 2000)

Content power of metaphors	Total number of metaphors	Total points
P = 1	X 3 =	3
na = 2	X 2 =	4
po = 3	X 0 =	0
d = 4	X 0 =	0
sp = 5	X 3 =	15
m = 6	X 3 =	18
40/11 = 3.636	Total: 11	40
p = popular, na = nature, po = political and intellectual, d = death and disaster, sp = sports, m = medical		

Results

The formulas and equations used in this research are based on the model that De Landtsheer (1994, pp, 69-72) devised to calculate the metaphor coefficient. As mentioned before, the results should be considered only of exploratory interest because of the selective nature of the experiment.

What results do we see in Tables 3 and 4? The US and Greece ranked the highest, while Denmark and Spain ranked the least frequent. Euroland countries have more metaphors in their newspaper articles on the Euro per 1,000 words than non-Euroland countries. These results seem to confirm the hypothesis that news about the Euro in Euroland countries has more emotional impact than that in non-Euroland countries. Since we know that metaphors are figures of speech which help speakers/writers get a point across more easily, it must mean that the more metaphors there are per 1,000 words, the more easily the receiver understands the speaker/writer. Generally, in this sense, more metaphors are better than fewer in newspapers. The countries that are not in Euroland are not necessarily against the EMU, it is just not a major media concern. Norway and Denmark are part of Europe, but voted against changing their currencies to the Euro (Sweden did the same in 2003). As far as the United States is concerned, the Euro could make trading, import, and export with EMU countries much easier; this could make the US pro-Euro. But, of course, the US/Euro trade/exchange rate would have to be considered as well.

Table 3: Frequency of metaphors in Euro news inside Euroland (November 1999-March 2000). These countries wanted to adopt the Euro at the time of the study

Country	Total of words, articles with at least one metaphor	Total of metaphors	Metaphors per 1,000 words (F)	Rank
Sweden	8,660	27	3.118	3
Greece	9,114	72	7.899	1
Netherlands	31.294	218	6.966	2
Spain	4,197	11	2.621	4
Total	58,265	328	6.158	

Note: Every number in Tables 3 through 10 has been rounded either up or down to the third decimal place.

Table 4: Frequency of metaphors in Euro news outside of Euroland (November 1999-March 2000). These countries were not willing to adopt the Euro at the time of the study

Country	Total of words, articles with at least one metaphor	Total of metaphors	Metaphors per 1,000 words (F)	Rank
Norway	4,617	11	2.382	2
Denmark	5,520	12	2.174	3
USA	2,387	113	5.048	1
Total	32,524	136	4.182	

These three non-Euro countries (Norway, Denmark, and the US) had fewer metaphors in their newspapers per 1,000 words (see Table 4). Needless to say, since they are not part of the EMU, the Euro has less importance. This may be substantiated with various quotes, like these from the *International Herald Tribune*: "Euroland is a big question mark" (February 29, 2000) and "Traders ignored a raft of bullish economic news in the Euro bloc that should have breathed new life into the currency" (January 25, 2000). It would be reasonable for non-Euro bloc countries to give priority to articles that are more culturally significant to their particular country. But they cannot avoid writing about the Euro since it is a huge step for the EMU and will make an impact not just on Europe, but also the rest of the world. However, the frequency of metaphors included would be less when they do write about the Euro.

Table 5: Intensity power of metaphors in Euro news inside Euroland (November 1999-March 2000). Countries willing to adopt the Euro at the time of the study

	Sweden	Greece	Netherlands	Spain	Average
Intensity Power	2	2.256	1.651	1.455	1.84
Rank	2	1	3	4	
Total Words in all articles on Euro	9,575	16,037	23,824	15,122	64,558
Total number of weak metaphors	7	12	98	8	
Total number of normal metaphors	13	29	59	1	
Total number of strong metaphors	7	30	32	2	

Table 6: Intensity power of metaphors in Euro news outside Euroland (November 1999-March 2000). Countries that were not willing to adopt the Euro at the time of the study

	Norway	Denmark	USA	Average
Intensity Power	1	1.667	1.982	1.55
Rank	3	2	1	
Total Words in all articles on Euro	9,955	9,315	26,607	45,877
Total number of weak metaphors	2	8	14	
Total number of normal metaphors	7	0	69	
Total number of strong metaphors	2	4	24	

The results of this analysis in regard to the intensity variables of countries within and outside of Euroland are shown in Tables 5 and 6. The first rank is the country with the most intense metaphors. In this case, Greece again ranked as most intense among the countries inside the Euro zone; the US ranked highest for the non-EMU countries. The lower ranks show the least intense countries: in this case, Spain (again) and Norway. The highest degree of the presence or intensity of metaphor power can be detected among countries inside the Euro zone. This is also in line with our hypothesis and makes sense since the countries in Euroland want to promote the Euro as a good thing that will help, support, and benefit Europeans, making Europe a better place to live. Journalists would be expected to avoid putting the Euro down as a currency that will not do well in the future or to relate it to negative happenings. Setting the Euro in a bad light would help neither the EMU nor the morale of the people living there.

Some examples of metaphors from Euroland countries help to substantiate the theories mentioned previously. The Swedish paper *Dagens Nyheter* (March 2, 2000) writes, "To begin with, the rise [of the Euro] had a strengthening effect." The Greek paper *Eleftherotypia* mentions, "The Euro is waiting for a goal to set the score even" and "attack the American currency" (November 27, 1999) and "the markets will not be thirsty anymore" (March 8, 2000). These are very powerful and intense metaphors. From the Spanish *El Pais* we read, "if we cook it [the Euro] with a little mimo, everything will taste as delicious as always" (November 6, 1999). Lastly, some metaphorical examples from the Dutch papers are: "interest fever" (*Het Parool*, February 8, 2000); "the Euro is like dice game" and "Should have ripened the land for the EMU" (both from *NRC Handelsblad*, March 2000); "it's not easy for sand to get caught in the machine" (*De Telegraaf*, December 20, 1999); "Euro-concern ruins fun" and "the stench of crisis blows through the stock market" (both from *NRC Handelsblad*, November 30, 1999).

On the other hand, the lowest degree of metaphor intensity power is in the non-Euroland countries. Again, this should not be a surprise since non-Euroland papers are distributed in countries that will obviously not join the EMU and may depict the Euro as something of lesser value when compared to other countries' treatments. This could suggest that the Euro is not seen as a top priority; rather, it is just a topic they must report with other issues that they consider more important. Countries that are not going to join the Euro club see the currency as a good and positive change for the EMU, but this is not the most meaningful or substantial story for their newspapers. However, the difference between the two groups of countries is not very sizeable.

To exemplify the previous statements, we present some metaphors from outside the Euro zone that were coded. These include “hand in hand,” “make or break,” and “divided roles” from the Danish paper *Politiken* (March 2000). The Norwegian *Aftenposten* used the metaphors “slow journey toward the Euro” (November 2, 1999) and “Euro climbs upward” (November 25, 1999). The US includes metaphors like “sinking Euro,” “driving down the Euro” (both from *IHT*, October 9-10, 1999) and “the Euro must recover” (*IHT*, January 5, 2000). All are quite weak metaphors and not very significant.

The number of words per country and their totals in Tables 5 and 6 are there for reasons of comparison. Obviously, countries that adopted the Euro had the most relevant words because there were more countries coded and more newspapers involved. Only three countries coded at that time were supposed to stay outside the EMU; therefore, they have a smaller word count. But they average out like this: countries inside Euroland 64,558/4 = 16,139.5, countries outside Euroland 45,877/3 = 15,292.3. This makes the amount of words in articles on the Euro (regardless of whether there are any metaphors in the articles) from countries that at the time were and were not to be members of the EMU more or less even.

Table 7: Content power of metaphors in Euro news inside Euroland (November 1999-March 2000). Countries that were willing to adopt the Euro at the time of the study

Countries	Sweden	Greece	Netherlands	Spain	Average
Content Power	2.37	2.887	3.413	2.273	2.736
Rank	3	2	1	4	

Table 8. Content power of metaphors in Euro news outside Euroland (November 1999-March 2000). Countries that were not willing to adopt the Euro at the time of the study.

Countries	Norway	Denmark	USA	Average
Content Power	3.636	2.583	3.355	3.191
Rank	1	3	2	

Table 9: Number of metaphors in content categories in Euro news within and outside Euroland (for D) (November 1999-March 2000). Countries that were and were not willing to use the Euro as their currency at the time of this study

Countries	Medical	Sports	Death	Politics	Nature	Popular	Total metaphors
Sweden	2	0	0	11	5	9	27
Greece	7	7	8	1	5	33	71
Netherlands	28	3	9	0	7	52	189
Spain	1	0	0	4	1	5	11
Norway	1	1	3	0	1	6	12
Denmark	1	1	3	0	1	6	12
USA	14	5	6	8	8	26	107

The content power or variable (D) is found only by putting all relevant metaphors in one out of six content categories (m, sp, d, po, na, or p) and, therefore, adding the appropriate symbol to all metaphors coded which stand for particular values (De Landtsheer, 1998). The results of the content variable are interesting because it is higher for the countries outside Euroland. So far, the results for F and I were higher for Euroland countries. Why is this so? The reason may be that Norway, Denmark, and the US use more metaphors with higher valued symbols, such as m, d, and po. These metaphors deal with medical issues or illness, death, disaster, politics, or intellectual topics. The other countries (Sweden, Greece, the Netherlands, and Spain) use "softer" metaphors, dealing mostly with popular subjects that everyone understands, like nature, sports, theater, and everyday life situations. Some examples here are: "the Euro searches for new depths" (*De Volkskrant*, December 4, 1999); "the Euro has been itching" (*Het Parool*, December 3, 1999); "analysts could smell the increase in interest" (*De Telegraaf*, February 19, 2000); "the Prime Minister isn't putting his cards on the table" (*De Volkskrant*, February 19, 2000); "the boiling of the markets" (*El Pais*, December 5, 1999); "they see the bright side of the moon" (*Eleftherotypia*, November 30, 1999); "a wave of sales" (*Eleftherotypia*, March 24, 2000); and "the [Swedish] crown is tied to the German mark" (*Dagens Nyheter*, October 16, 1999).

The metaphor coefficient is the product of the metaphor variables frequency (F), intensity (I), and content (D), which are indicators of the metaphor power of a text (De Landtsbeer, 1998). It is obvious in Tables 9 and 10 that C is the last calculation for this research. The overall ranking that shows which group of countries has the highest and lowest degrees of metaphorical presence is also included. This metaphorical base, in correspondence with the hypothesis, is highest among countries that (at the time of the research) were willing to be part of the EMU and lowest among those that were outside the EMU. The average for Table 10 is calculated by the total divided by the number of countries 114.1/4 = 28.525; the average for Table 11 is 51.589/3 = 17.196.

Table 10: Metaphor coefficient in Euro news inside Euroland (November 1999-March 2000). Countries that were willing to adopt the Euro at the tune of the study

Countries	F x	I x	D=	C
Sweden	3.118	2	2.37	14.779
Greece	7.899	2.254	2.887	51.401
Netherlands	6.966	1.651	3.413	39.252
Spain	2.621	1.455	2.273	8.668
			Total	114.1
			Average	28.525

Table 11: Metaphor coefficient in Euro news outside Euroland (November 1999-March 2000). Countries that were not willing to adopt the Euro at the time of the study

Countries	F x	I x	D=	C
Norway	2.382	1	3.636	8.661
Denmark	2.174	1.667	2.583	9.361
USA	5.048	1.982	3.355	33.567
			Total	51.589
			Average	17.196

Conclusions

The results show that countries that were willing to participate in the EMU at the time of the study have a higher metaphor coefficient than those outside the EMU. The frequency and intensity of metaphors indicate metaphor power in the news discourse. They were higher among the same countries (Sweden, Greece, the Netherlands and Spain in this sample), although content power was lower than in the non-Euro countries. As explained previously, reasons for these results suggest that the frequency (F) of the metaphor usage among EMU members' newspapers is higher. It may also be concluded that the Euroland countries tend to use metaphors with a higher intensity (I) variable, while non-Euroland countries use less intense metaphors. Non-Euro countries have greater content power (D), but that does not change the final outcome, that EMU countries have the highest metaphorical standards.

References

Beer, F. (accessed November 28, 2000). Publications of Francis A. Beer, http://socsci.colorado.edu/beerbal l/PAPERS/papers.htrnl.

Beer, F. and C. De Landtsheer (eds.) (2004). *Metaphorical World Politics: Rhetorics of Democracy, War and Globalization*. East Lansing MI: Michigan State University Press.

Beer, F. and C. De Landtsheer (eds.) (2004). "Metaphors, Politics and World Politics," pp. 10-66 in F. Beer and C. De Landtsheer (eds.) *Metaphorical World Politics: Rhetorics of Democracy, War and Globalization*. East Lansing Ml: Michigan State University Press.

Black, M. (1962). *Models and Metaphors: Studies in Language and Philosophy*. Ithaca, NY: Cornell University Press.

Boles, K., F. McDonald, and N. Healey (2002). "The Euro: A Future International Currency?," pp. 119-134 in M. Farell, S. Fella, and M. Newman (eds.) *European Integration in the 21st Century*. London, UK, Thousand Oaks, CA, and New Delhi, India: Sage.

Chilton, P. (1996). *Security Metaphors: Cold War Discourse from Containment to Common House*. New York, NY: Peter Lang Publishing.

De Landtsheer, C. (1987). *De Politieke Taal in de Vlaamse Media* (Political Language in Flemish Media). Antwerpen, Belgium: Wetenschappelijke Uitgeverij Kluwer.

De Landtsheer, C. (1988). "Een Theoretische Bijdrage tot de Studie van Taalgebruik in de Politiek" (A Theoretical Approach to Political Speech), pp. 151-167 in *Tijdschrift voor Sociale Wetenschappen*, Vol. 33, No. 2.

De Landtsheer, C. (1991). "Function and the Language of Politics: A Linguistic Uses and Gratifications Approach," pp. 299-344 in *Communication and Cognition*, Vol. 24, No. 3-4.

De Landtsheer, C. (1992a). "The Language of Unification: Specification of a Coding Process as a Basis for Observation," pp. 287-314 in A. Burkhardt and K. Fritzsche (eds.) *Sprache im Umbruch. Politischer Sprachwandel im zeichen von "Wende" und "Vereinigung"* (Language in Transition: Changes in the Political Speech of Change and Unification). Berlin, Germany and New York, NY: Walther de Gruyter.

De Landtsheer, C. (1992b). "Metafoor en Conjunctuur. Een historisch-semantische analyse van het politieke taalgebruik in Vlaamse media in de periode 1845-1914" (Metaphor and Conjuncture: A Historical Semantic Analysis of Political Speech in Flemish Media, 1845-1914), pp. 109-118 in H. Kleijer, A Knotter, and F. van Vree (eds.) *Tekens en Teksten. Cultuur, Communicatie en Maatschappelijke Veranderingen vanaf de Late Middeleeuwen* (Signs and Texts, Culture, Communication and Social Change from the Late Middle Ages). Amsterdam, the Netherlands: Amsterdam University Press.

De Landtsheer, C. (1994). "The Language of Prosperity and Crisis," pp. 63-85 in *Politics and the Individual*, Vol. 4, No. 2.

De Landtsheer, C. (1995). "Political Communication," pp. 1-20 in C. De Landtsheer (ed.) *Political Communication. Special Issue of Politics, Groups and the Individual*, Vol. 5.

De Landtsheer, C. (1998). "The Political Rhetoric of a Unified Europe," pp. 129-145 in O. Feldman and C. De Landtsheer (eds.) *Politically Speaking: A Worldwide Examination of Language Used in the Public Sphere*. Westport, CT: Praeger.

De Landtsheer, C. (2004). "Integrative Complexity, Metaphor Power and Modality in the Rhetoric of Dyab Abou Jahjah, Leader of the Arab European League (AEL)." Paper presented at the 27th Conference ISPP, London, UK, July 15-18, 2004.

De Landtsheer, C. and I. De Vrij (2004). "Talking about Srebrenica: Dutch Elites and Dutchbat. How Metaphors Change during Crisis," pp. 163-192 in F. Beer and C. De Landtsheer (eds.) *Metaphorical World Politics: Rhetorics of Democracy, War and Globalization*. East Lansing, MI: Michigan State University Press.

De Landtsheer, C. and I. De Vrij (1999). "Talking Srebrenica: Dutch Elites and Dutchbat. Broadening Integrative Complexity by Way of the Crisis Communication Combination (CCC) Hypothesis." Paper presented at the ISPP annual meeting, Amsterdam, the Netherlands.

De Landtsheer, C. and O. Feldman (eds.) (1998). *Politically Speaking: A Worldwide Examination of Language Used in the Public Sphere*. Westport, CT: Praeger.

De Landtsheer, C. and O. Feldman (eds.) (2000). *Beyond Public Speech and Symbols: Explorations in the Rhetoric of Politicians and the Media*. London, UK: Praeger.

De Landtsheer, C. and A. Recchi (July 4, 2000). "Soccer and the Mass Media Framing of National Identities: A Case Study for Italy." Paper presented to the 23rd Annual Scientific Meeting of the International Society of Political Psychology, Seattle, WA.

Dobrzynska, T. (1995). *Metafora a Spojnosc Tekstu* (Metaphor as a Text Unifier). Warsaw, Poland: Ossolineum.

Farell, M., S. Fella, and M. Newman (eds.) (2002). *European Integration in the 21st Century*. London, UK, Thousand Oaks, CA, and New Delhi, India: Sage.

Fella, S. (2002). "Introduction: Unity in Diversity - the Challenge for the EU," pp. 1-14 in M. Farell, S. Fella, and M. Newman (eds.) *European Integration in the 21st Century*. London, UK, Thousand Oaks, CA, and New Delhi, India: Sage.

Fowler, H. and F. Fowler (eds.) (1959). *The Concise Oxford Dictionary of Current English*, 4th Edition. Oxford, UK: Clarendon Press.

Gaus, H. (2001). *Why Yesterday Tells of Tomorrow. How the Long Waves of the Economy Help Us Determine Tomorrow's Trends*. Leuven, Apeldoom, Belgium: Garant.

Hahn, D. (1998). *Political Communication: Rhetoric, Government, and Citizens*. State College, PA: Strata Publishing. PA: Strata Publishing.

Kittay, E. (1987). *Metaphor: Its Cognitive Force and Linguistic Structure*. New York, NY: Oxford University Press.

Lakoff, G. and M. Johnson (1980). *Metaphors We Live By*. Chicago, IL: University of Chicago Press.

Luczak, H., J. Springer, M. Wolf, and S. Simon (1997). "The Role of Metaphors in Computer Supported Cooperative Work." http://www.human.wasda.ac.ip/wwdu97/PrcHP/941/index-.html. Date accessed: November 28, 2000.

Richards, I. (1936). *The Philosophy of Rhetoric*. London, UK: Routledge.

Richardson, M. (1994). Quoted in H. Luczak, J. Springer, M. Wolf, and S. Simon (1997). "The Role of Metaphors in Computer Supported Cooperative Work." http://www.human.was-da.ac.ip/wwdu 97/PrcHP/941/index.html. Date accessed: November 28, 2000.

Taran, S. (2000). "Mythical Thinking, Aristotelian Logic, and Metaphors in the Parliament of the Ukraine," pp. 120-145 in C. De Landtsheer and O. Feldman (eds.) *Beyond Public Speech and Symbols: Explorations in the Rhetoric of Politicians and the Media*. London, UK: Praeger.

Chapter 10
Press Reporting on the Euro

Marianne Law and Jerry Palmer

London Metropolitan University, London, UK

David Middleton

Open University, London, UK

Abstract

The current study aims to analyze certain trends in reporting about the European Monetary Union (EMU) in the press of four EU countries: France, Germany, the Netherlands, and the United Kingdom. It examines the profile that the new currency has acquired when it was launched and particularly, the extent to which the currency is profiled in press reporting as a matter of national versus transnational as well as economic versus political significance. The purpose of this type of analysis is to examine the "framing" of the EMU. This study follows a well-established tradition in which media output is analyzed to examine how cumulative reporting of an issue (or a series of linked issues) results in a more or less coherent profile of the issue in question.

Introduction

As is well known, the European single currency was launched on January 1, 1999. On the night of March 15-16, the entire European Commission resigned in the wake of allegations of fraud and financial mismanagement. This followed the resignation of Germany's Finance Minister Oskar Lafontaine on March 11, 1999. The exchange rate of the new currency scarcely faltered during March 16: it fell rapidly in the morning, but equally rapidly regained its strength in the afternoon (*Die Welt*, *Guardian*, *Frankfurter Algemeine Zeitung*, *Le Monde*, March 17, 1999). In early January, it traded at approximately $1.16 (US) and £0.7. During January and February, it fell gradually against these and other major currencies. In the days following Lafontaine's resignation, it rose against the pound sterling but fell against the dollar. During the week of March 10-17, 1999, it fell to $1.07, but rose again to $1.09 before the Commission's resignation (*Die Welt*, March 17, 1999). On the morning of March 16, it fell to $1.0814, but regained its value during the afternoon. It also fell from yen 127.37 to 128.62 (*Le Monde*, March 17, 1999) or 127.85 to 128.7 (*Die Welt*, March 17, 1999), but later regained its value. Its sterling value rose somewhat after the Commission resigned. Table 1 records its trading record against the pound sterling during these few days.

Table l: The Euro versus the pound sterling (March 10-17, 1999). 1 Euro = £ sterling. Trading information on the Euro taken from Dutch national bank statistics at www.dnb.nl

Date	Sterling exchange rate	Event
March 10	0.6746	
March 11	0.6694	Lafontaine resigns
March 12	0.6686	
March 15	0.6739	
March 16	0.6703	Commission resigns
March 17	0.6744	

It is legitimate to speculate what would have happened to a single nation's currency if its government had been forced to resign under such circumstances. No doubt, the currency would have suffered a very different fate. Of course, the European Commission is not a government, but neither is its relationship to the Euro entirely a matter of indifference. Also, had the crisis arisen closer to the launch of the Euro, things might have been different. Strasbourg could have provoked the crisis in January, but chose to appoint the commission of "wise men" instead; no doubt, the fate of the Euro was a major factor in the Parliament's deliberations (*Le Monde*, March 18, 1999). Searches of the newspapers (*Le Monde, Liberation, Daily Telegraph, Guardian, Bild, Sueddeutsche Zeitung*) in January 1999 produced no mentions of possible links between the conflicts that led to the Commission resignation and the value of the Euro. Indeed, the rapid fall of the Euro in the few hours following the resignation announcement indicates the possibility that things might have developed entirely differently. According to *Die Welt*, the slide of the Euro on March 16 was halted by a briefing from the European Central Bank (ECB) that stressed its constitutional independence from both the Commission and other political authorities. According to the *Daily Telegraph* and the *Guardian* (March 17, 1999), the briefing also hinted that interest rates would not be altered.

An online search through the archives of major newspapers in France, Germany, the Netherlands, and the UK using the terms "Commission," "resignation," "Santer," and "single currency" in varying combinations (plus relevant cognate terms and in translation as appropriate; dates searched were March 12-18, 1999, inclusive) produced few articles. Of course, searches using these terms separately produced many articles. The reason for the massive reduction of mentions in combination was soon apparent: the number of articles which actually analyzed the possibility of a link between the Commission's resignation and the exchange rate was very small. There was one article each in the *Guardian*, the *Daily Telegraph, Die Welt, Le Monde* (quoted above), the *Daily Mail*, and the *Sueddeutsche Zeitung*; two appeared in the *Frankfurter Algemeine Zeitung*. All these articles followed the event (i.e., were dated March 17, 1999 or later). Searches of *de Telegraaf* and *V'olkskrant* found no articles analyzing (or even mentioning) the possibility of a link between the two. While the online searches may have been fallible, it seems certain that the volume of reporting of the possibility of a link was extremely feeble and entirely retrospective. The consensus of all reports which did mention it was that currency markets were largely indifferent to the resignation; mentions of the resignations' possible impact on the stock market were even fewer.

In other words, in advance of the mass resignation, the possibility of a flight from the Euro was not part of any mass media agenda. In retrospect, the issue scarcely seemed worth mentioning. Media silences are difficult to account for unless alternative formation sources reveal that a silence was deliberately organized and .maintained by some mechanism or other (Palmer, 2000). Silence can always be dismissed as simple absence: nothing happened; therefore, there was silence. In a sense, this is what happened in this instance; however, the reason why "nothing happened" is clearly that there was sufficient confidence in the insulation of the new currency from Brussels politics to ensure that nothing happened. Such a position (and its public acceptance) has to be created and maintained as much in public opinion as in any other forum. While it is possible that sudden events .may have a rapid and dramatic impact on public opinion, in the circumstances in question, it would appear that trust in the ECB was a long-term matter, linked to its perceived independence from political pressure and its role as the trustee of a transnational currency. The relative silence about the link between the Commission resignation and the exchange rate is a mark of that trust and of the perceived independence of the currency from political pressures.

At first sight, this indicates that press agendas did not see EMU as primarily a political matter during the period in question. An earlier comparative analysis (Palmer, 1998) found that previous attention was primarily focused on the political dimension of EMU; the study referred mainly to Autumn 1995 (i.e., the period leading to the Madrid summit, where the name "Euro" was chosen and the nature of convergence criteria was high on public agendas). Studies analyzing the German press of the same period indicate that the political dimension of currency union was high on agendas (Settekorn, 1998; Loenneker, 1998). A study of the francophone Belgian press during the same period finds that, although political aspects of the currency union were indeed mentioned with some frequency, the matter had a low level of prominence and was not regarded as a controversial matter, except in one left-wing regional daily (Lits, 1999). A recent comparative study of television news coverage of EMU in Denmark, the Netherlands, and the UK finds that the introduction of the new currency was overwhelmingly reported in terms of its economic consequences at the moment when it was introduced (De Vreese, 1999). In combination, these studies may indicate that the profile of the new currency has shifted away from the political, toward the economic. However, an analysis of UK broadcast news coverage of European economic issues highlights the many ways in which the issue is presented in terms which emphasize opposition (Britain-and-Europe), rather than unity (Britain-in-Europe). The same study points to a dearth of analysis focusing on the relationship between media coverage and attitude formation in pan-European matters (Gavin, 2000).

The analysis of "frames" derives from the study of agenda-setting. In the words often quoted as the starting point of this tradition:

> The press may not be successful much of the time in telling people what to think, but it is stunningly successful in telling its readers what to think about (Cohen, 1963, p. 13).

This perception was confirmed by the original (1972) Chapel Hill agenda-setting study (McCombs and Bell, 1996). The agenda-setting function is operationalized as the parallel rank ordering of a set of nominated issues, both in the mass media and in public opinion, as shown by content analysis and opinion polling. Thus, what is measured in the two parallel survey instruments is comparative issue salience in a given body of media output and in a body of public opinion. Reviews of the now substantial body of research literature in this tradition point out that the majority of studies support the central hypothesis of a substantial correlation between the two agendas; reviewing 375 such studies, Dearing and Rogers (1996, pp. 10, 49-50) state that 65% support the central contention. Although correlation, alone, does not prove any causal link, further studies in this tradition demonstrated that the inference of causality (explicit in Cohen's statement) is legitimate (Dearing and Rogers, 1996, p. 92; McCombs and Bell, 1996, pp. 99-100). However, in later studies, the place of the agenda in the communication process as a whole has been foregrounded in a way that makes the simple attribution of linear causality dubious. The central question here is: Where does the media agenda come from? Dearing and Rogers' review of the concept of agenda-setting shows that agendas cannot realistically be analyzed without reference to some external agency. In particular, they stress the role of two entities: policy elites whose actions lead them to seek to dominate public agendas via the mass media and so-called "spectacular news events" (Dearing and Rogers, 1996, pp. 25-28, 34-35). The emphasis on the role of policy-making elites is broadly in line with a well-established research tradition into news sources which, in general, concludes that "Sources Make the News" (according to Sigal, 1973 and 1986; Gandy, 1982 and 1992). However, the central role of spectacular news events (also called "trigger events") is not entirely compatible with the stress on policy elites since it is unclear whether such events acquire their public profile as the result of initiatives by such news sources; indeed, the example they choose (the striking profile of the Ethiopian famine) is usually attributed to journalistic initiative (Philo, 1993). Some analysts conclude that a linear explanatory model is not useful and that a "multi-polar" model of meaning production, involving "multiple systems of meaning production" with multiple fora and interacting feedback processes is more useful (Hansen, 1991; Palmer, 2000).

The previous discussion is based on the presupposition that the focal point of any discussion of agenda-setting is issue salience. However, it has become central to debates about agenda-setting that "salience" may not be an adequate concept for the task it is allotted in two respects: 1) "salience" lacks any evaluative dimension and 2) perhaps as a result of the first, it is only a cognitive concept, entirely lacking a persuasive dimension.

The lack of an evaluative dimension clearly reduces its usefulness. For example, it would be easy to demonstrate that abortion is an issue with a high degree of salience in public agendas in the US in recent years; it would probably turn out that there was a high correlation with media agendas in this instance. However, there is a big difference between abortion having a high salience in the context of the pro-life argument and salience in the pro-choice argument. The traditional agenda-setting thesis explicitly rejects this distinction. However, if issue salience derives from the activities of policy elites, then we can be sure that (in this instance) media content will not be entirely separate from the attempts of the two (opposed) elites in question to define the issue. In this instance, we can clearly see the link to the second criticism, based on the absence of a persuasive dimension: attention to abortion considered as a question of issue salience tells us nothing about how this issue is publicly understood and the extent to which elite domination of news agendas is successful in producing shifts in public opinion.

Recognizing that this is a problem in agenda-setting studies, it is manifest in the argument by McCombs and Bell that there is now a "second generation" of agenda-setting studies. Here, it is no longer the salience of an "object" which is studied though correlations between two rank orderings of issues, but the salience of some "attribute" of that object (McCombs and Bell, 1996, pp. 101-102). In other words, it is no longer what is talked about that is the focus of analysis, but what is said about it. It is this "second generation" of agenda-setting studies to which the term "framing" is commonly applied.

Frames consist of patterns of "persistent selection, emphasis and exclusion" in reporting (Gitlin, 1980, p. 7). Entman defines them as a combination of four factors: selection and salience of issues; definitions of problems; diagnosis of the cause of the problem; and judgment about their nature. He finds that consistency of framing over a long period may amount to establishing an "agenda" in the public domain or something even more stable and fundamental: "culture is the stock of commonly invoked frames" (Entman, 1993, pp. 52-53). If an issue is analyzed not in terms simply of its most general outline (e.g., "abortion"), but in terms of how it is framed, then its capacity to dominate public understanding may be clearer. For example, Jasperson, et al. (1998, pp. 207-208) analyzed the role of the framing of the federal budget deficit in US news media during Winter 1995-1996. During this period, the salience of this long-running policy issue changed dramatically once it was publicly linked with the President's decision to shut down all federal offices because of political disagreements between the executive and the legislative branches of the government about the budget. Before the link was publicly made, the budget deficit was not a salient issue; once the link was made, it became salient.

In other words, the "framing" of the issue was responsible for its increased salience.

However, the status of framing, itself, is uncertain (Scheufele, 1999). The origin of the concept is in the "social construction of reality" tradition (Scheufele, 1999, p. 106; Pan and Kosicki, 1993, pp. 55-56); therefore, it refers as much to how audiences "decode" messages about the world as to how the messages are "encoded" in the moment preceding emission. Scheufele demonstrates that analyses using the concept of framing move between conceiving of the "frame" as a construct of the individual mind and a construct of media representations, as well as between conceiving of the frame as determined by some outside force or determining public understandings. He presents this as a 2 x 2 matrix (see Table 2).

Table 2: Framing variables

Frames seen as:	Dependent variables	Independent variables
Media	A	B
Individual	C	D

When frames are analyzed in the variety of ways that this schema suggests, we find that some studies present "frames" not as caused by media agendas, but as a resource used by audiences in their efforts to decode media messages and/or understand the world around them. Indeed, this resource may not even be the dominant one in this undertaking (Gamson, 1989). Thus, the move from "agenda-setting" in the original sense to its "second generation" version involve a reduced capacity to produce an attribution of causality.

Studies showing the existence of news frames are numerous. For example, the reporting of HIVIAIDS in the UK in the early 1980s eventually produced a "frame" in which this matter was defined as a public health issue, rather than an issue of personal morality (Miller and Williams, 1993); here (arguably), a long-term frame of reference was established. A more short-term example is the reporting of the confrontation between Shell and Greenpeace over the Brent Spar oil storage facility in 1995, which framed the issue as one of protest about environmental damage, rather than routine oil industry engineering procedures (Palmer, 2000). As Scheufele's schema implied, such studies may focus on "upstream" communications strategies by news sources as is the case in the last two mentioned plus many others (Weaver, 1994; Gandy, 1982 and 1992; Deacon and Golding, 1994). They may also focus on the downstream "impact" on the public or some defined segment of it (Capella and Jamieson 1996; Newman, 1986; Bruce, 1992, pp. 137-140). In the interest of terminological consistency in this chapter, "issues" refers to particular events or a linked series of events; "agenda" refers to some ranking of issues in a hierarchy of media attention; and "frame" refers to the way in which combining these two leads to establishing an overall profile of the entity or entities in question. Our analysis concentrates on the "persistent selection, emphasis and exclusion" that Gitlin uses as his definition of a frame; we make no inferences about the behavior of news sources nor of the frame's impact on public opinion. Establishing what the "frame" constitutes is a necessary preliminary to the analysis of either "upstream" strategies or "downstream" impacts. This approach is akin to the "tracking" studies used to evaluate the impact of communications strategies (Hampton, 1997).

While different studies use many different approaches to analyze news content, quantitative content analysis is frequently used on the grounds both of reliability and its capacity to handle large volumes of material. This is the method chosen for the current analysis. The choice of method was dictated partly by the sheer volume of potentially relevant material and partly by the need to develop a method that would be capable of handling material in different languages and referring to numerous discrete real-world referents. For example, any analysis of real-world individuals and institutions referred to in press reporting across national boundaries must deal with the fact that the empirical entities are individuated, yet functionally equivalent (e.g., heads of state, national banks, political decisions, economic reports, exchange rates, etc.). This requires creating an analytic device that is capable of recording the presence or absence of these entities in several national media spaces and allowing strict comparability. Content analysis is well suited to such a task.

Sample

The analysis is based on a sample of the national press systems (i.e., nationally circulating newspapers) of the UK, Germany, France, and the Netherlands. Regrettably, resources did not allow any analysis of broadcast coverage. The number and selection of nations was dictated by resources and the availability of relevant language skills. All coding was done by native speakers of the languages in question, with the exception of French; two of the researchers have adequate bilingual skills in this respect. It is important that the nation sample includes one "out" country. The basis of the equivalence is that the sample is approximately equally representative of the four national systems. It is partly dictated by the availability of online archive access. Table 3 shows the titles chosen to represent each national system. Horizontal alignment indicates approximate equivalence among titles based on a series of indicators: market sector, political allegiance, and level of business reporting.

The time frame of the sample was October 1, 1998 to March 31, 1999. All analysis of this sample is based on percentage distributions of the units of analysis within each national press system. This allows for the fact that each national system has very different quantities of coverage. The total number of articles located by online searches for "single currency," "economic and monetary union," and various cognate terms in relevant languages was approximately 10,000. The sample analyzed covers between 5% and 10% of articles in each national sample devoted to the single currency. It follows the levels of journalistic interest by taking every l0th or 20th article in the chronological sequence of articles. Therefore, the sample is not random and its stratification follows the logic of news agendas insofar as the agendas are indicated by numbers of reports.

Table 3: Nationally circulating newspapers of countries included in the sample

United Kingdom	Netherlands	France	Germany
Daily Mirror			*Bild*
Daily Mail	*De Telegraaf*		
Daily Telegraph		*Le Monde*	*Frankfurter Algemeine Zeitung*
Guardian	*Volkskrant*	*Liberation*	*Sueddeutsche Zeitung*

The Design of the Analysis

All sampled text was divided into units of meaning. All units of meaning are either agents or events. "Agents" are the persons, organizations, or institutions whose activities are reported. "Events" are all the sets of circumstances, actions, and contexts which are mentioned. Each "unit" is a mention (i.e., a piece of text of indeterminate length but with a single focus); typically, it is a word or phrase.

Both agents and events are assigned to one of the following categories: political, economic, or civil. The first two categories are used in their commonsense meaning, although the coding scheme has rules for their application to ensure consistency. For example, a minister of finance is considered a political agent, a central bank is an economic one; this usage reflects constitutional arrangements. "Civil" means everything that is not political or economic; basically, it refers to everything to do with public opinion, except actual elections. Thus, trade unions are economic agents when they take action (e.g., strike), but individual trades unionists or officials expressing an opinion count as civil agents.

In addition, both agents and events are categorized according to their location. If they are located inside the nation whose press system is being analyzed, they count as "national home." If they are located in one another country in the European Union, they count as "national foreign." If they are located in more than one EU country or belong to the EU as a whole, they count as "transnational." If they are located outside the EU, they count as "international."

Reliability was achieved iteratively. A significant percentage of the articles sampled were double-coded after preliminary individual coding; the resolution of any discrepancies that were revealed was then applied to the rest of the sample. For example, this sentence would be coded in the following manner:

> Europe's most powerful banker yesterday cast a shadow over the launch of the euro by delivering a humiliating snub to the French (*Daily Mail*, December 31, 1998).

- Agents: a) "Europe's most powerful banker" (identified in the following sentence as Wim Duisenberg, President-designate of the European Central Bank): Agent = Economic, Transnational; b) "the French" (French government, in this context): Agent = Political, National, Foreign.
- Events: a) "cast a shadow": Event = Economic, Transnational (this refers to his refusal to accept an abbreviated appointment); b) "over the launch of the Euro": Event = Economic, Transnational; c) "by delivering a humiliating snub to" (the French): Event = Economic, Transnational (because it involves a transnational entity, the ECB, in addition to a European country).

Each of these entities would be recorded as one mention of the appropriate category. Additionally, all agents are given an "authority" score that indicates how much objectivity and partisanship is involved in the reporting of their actions. Analysis of this feature of the study is not included in this chapter. However, at this point, it is important to realize that the relationship between "active" and "passive" mentions of agents as well as "positive/negative" reporting of their actions is encoded with authority scores, not mentions. One crucial element of the authority score is a numerical indicator of the fact that an agent is presented as responsible for the event being reported; in the previous example, Duisenberg would be the responsible agent.

The purpose of these devices is to let us see whether the EMU is presented as primarily a matter of politics, economics, or public opinion; and whether it is a matter of primarily internal/domestic or transnational concern. Therefore, these devices are the operationalization of our focus on the "framing" of the EMU issue. They are intended to locate elements of meaning that are relatively independent of the details of the ebb and flow of everyday events, in the sense that their presence/absence is unlikely to be directly event-sensitive. The size and stratification of the sample were dictated by this factor.

Given the nature of the subject under discussion, it is obvious that the distinction between "political" and "economic" is not always easy to establish with certainty. Two issues arise: validity and reliability. Where validity is concerned, we followed the constitutional separation between government and central banks in EU countries and the Union institutions, themselves. Where reliability is concerned, the iterative double coding (the basis of the reliability of the coding in general) produced consistent agreement about the assignation of agents and events across these two categories.

The Results

Agents by Domain of Activity

Table 4 shows the extent to which the national press systems give different levels of attention to political, economic, or civil agents. The differences in tables 4 and 5 are statistically significant at $p<0.001$, using chi square on the original Ns. This only records the fact that these agents were mentioned and the distribution of these mentions; it says nothing about what the agents said. It gives a preliminary indication of whether the EMU is considered primarily as an economic, political, or civil matter. The UK press is dominated by reporting the activities of political agents; the Dutch press gives approximately equal attention to political and economic agents. While it appears that the French and German press are similar in their emphasis on economic agents, in both cases, there is only a 12% to 13% difference in the reporting of economic and political agents. Although it is true that the reporting of the EMU is seen as primarily economic (in terms of agents), it is also viewed as having a large political dimension in these two countries. This is probably not to be explained by variations in the amount of business reporting in the press title sample because the UK and German press are close to equivalent in this respect. The same is true of the French and Dutch press; however, the French/Dutch press sample is different from the UK/German press in this respect since it is likely to reflect genuine differences in agendas.

Table 4: Percentages of all mentions of agents by domains of activity and nation

	United Kingdom	Netherlands	France	Germany
Political	54	43	36	39
Economic	34	45	49	51
Civil	12	12	15	10
Total %	100	100	100	100
N	799	957	1,298	1,475

In all four countries, attention to civil agents is relatively marginal. In general, public opinion on this matter is not much reported in any of these countries. No doubt, this is partly because events which are directly the product of civil activity (such as conferences and opinion polls) are relatively less frequent than the activities that figure here under "economic" and "political" headings. However, it also reflects the categories of people whose activities are seen as relevant; in other words, it is a clear indicator of framing. Lits (1999, pp. 123-124) also finds that in the Belgian press, civil sources (such as unions or associations of citizens) are rarely quoted. The marginalization of the representation of civil agents is a significant silence in the framing of the EMU in the international press. Further analysis is needed to establish what political or communication strategy was responsible for this marginalization.

Events by Domain of Activity

Table 5 shows the extent to which national press systems give different levels of attention to political, economic, or civil events. Here, we are looking no longer at the identity of the agents whose actions are being reported, but at what those actions are and the contexts in which journalists think they are being carried out. This is when agents' actions start to be interpreted since journalists exercise editorial choice over the actions or the context that they portray as significant in respect of any individual or organization. The UK press gives equal attention to economic and political events, whereas the other press systems are heavily dominated by the reporting of economic events where the EMU is concerned and, to a degree, that is relatively consistent across "Euroland" countries.

Table 5: Percentages of all mentions of events by domains of activity and nation

	United Kingdom	Netherlands	France	Germany
Political	47	19	22	17
Economic	47	79	75	81
Civil	6	2	3	2
Total %	100	100	100	100
N	2,705	1,770	4,044	4,183

Comparison of These Two Indicators

In Euroland countries, the two indicators tell roughly the same story. In France and Germany, both agents and events are markedly more economic than political, if by a different margin. Throughout Euroland, the difference between mentions of agents and events shows that many of the political agents are portrayed as acting in a context defined as economic, not political; this is scarcely surprising given the subject matter. In the Netherlands, the difference between the two indicators (agents/events) is striking. It is probably accounted for by the nature of the sample. A high percentage of the Dutch coverage comes from the tabloid *De Telegraaf*; in general, tabloid reporting features less description and analysis of the actions of each agent whose actions are reported than is usual in broadsheets. As the analysis of the German and French media (not to mention common sense) suggest, if political agents are acting in an economic context, then the pattern of tabloid reporting would produce a relative increase in the number of political agents and a relative decline in the number of economic events.

It is not possible to give a clear interpretation of this without reference to material from outside this analysis. In other words, it is only by looking at other details of the articles in question that it would be possible to see any further pattern of ascription of political agents' activities to one or the other domain of activity (e.g., any pattern of individual agents' ascription to a particular domain, a pattern of positive or negative mentions of such activity). If this pattern were visible, it would theoretically be possible to analyze the communication strategies of the various political actors to see if they were attempting to define events as either political or economic. To date, this analysis has not been done.

In the UK, the discrepancy between the two indicators also suggests that a significant percentage of politicians are seen as acting in a primarily economic context when their actions are related to the EMU. The difference between mentions of political and economic agents is both wider than in Euroland and shows the opposite emphasis (more political, rather than less), yet the margin between political and economic events is narrower (in fact, nonexistent). This suggests that a significant percentage of the UK political actors are being portrayed as dealing in economic matters and that this percentage is far greater than in Euroland. The implication is that everything is more politicized in the UK press than in the Euroland press. However, background knowledge of UK politics in this respect suggests that the Conservative Party (and the Conservative press) constantly seeks to make potential UK membership of the EMU into a directly political issue by bringing the question of sovereignty and national identity to the foreground. The Labour government seeks to define it as a pragmatic and economic matter. The figures in Tables 4 and 5 suggest that the Conservative Party is not succeeding in persuading journalists to see the EMU as primarily a political matter, but also that the Labour government has not succeeded in defining it in an entirely economic and pragmatic fashion. This point only holds good for the period analyzed, up to March 31, 1999; no evidence is available for the subsequent period. Also, these distributions include business page reporting. If the sample included only general news pages, the distributions might be very different. At a seminar at London Guildhall University in 1999, Bob Worcester (head of MORI opinion polls) pointed out that one difficulty for the English Conservative Party's policy of increasing opposition to the UK's membership in the EMU was the volume of favorable reporting of EMU in the business pages.

If we amalgamate the two indicators, Table 6 shows that for the UK press, monetary union is primarily political (subject to what was previously mentioned), whereas for the Euroland press, it is primarily an economic matter. The divergences between the three Euroland countries do not seem to indicate any significant difference. In other words, the lack of divergence may be taken to indicate a high degree of transnational press consensus on this matter.

Table 6: Percentages of all mentions of events and agents by domains of activity and nation

	United Kingdom	Netherlands	France	Germany
Political	50.5	31	29	28
Economic	40.5	62	62	66
Civil	9	7	9	6
Total %	100	100	100	100

We can also amalgamate the indicators to express the contrast between Euroland and the UK more directly in Table 7.

Table 7: Percentages of mentions of domains (events and agents): ins/outs

	United Kingdom	Ins
Political	50.5	29
Economic	40.5	64
Civil	9	7
Total %	100	100

Here, the "Ins" column shows the averages of the three Euroland press systems; the divergence between the UK and Euroland is striking. This table confirms what could have been deduced from the earlier evidence: the UK press is operating to a different set of news values than the Euroland press where the EMU is concerned. As a result, the framing of the issue is significantly different in the two cases. To avoid confusion, we are using news values in one of two possible senses. Possibility 1 is "universal" news values (such as timeliness, proximity, human interest, etc.); possibility 2 (used here) is the "local" features of particular events which are timely, proximate, interesting, etc. (Palmer, 2000).

Analysis of the Distribution of Meaning by Domain of Activity

Although it appears obvious that in Euroland, the single currency will be seen primarily as an economic matter (since the single currency now exists in Euroland), in reality, it is far from obvious. It means that those in Euroland who want to define national participation in the single currency as primarily an economic matter have succeeded in gaining the initiative where press agendas are concerned.

Location of Agents and Events

Is the EMU mainly a domestic or a transnational matter? Agents and events are coded according to their location as well as their domain of activity. Table 8 examines the distribution of agents according to whether they are located in the country whose press system is being analyzed or elsewhere in the world.

Table 8: Percentages of mentions of agents by nation: domestic/non-domestic

	United Kingdom	Netherlands	France	Germany
Domestic	53	24	39	43
Non-domestic	47	76	61	57

This indicator suggests that the UK press is preoccupied with internal UK agendas, whereas the Euroland press is dominated by transnational matters if by significantly different margins. If we turn to how the analysis of events informs the same question, we see essentially the same thing. Table 9 also shows that the UK is dominated by internal concerns, Euroland by transnational ones. Amalgamation of the two indicators in Table 10 tells the same story.

Table 9: Percentages of mentions of events by nation: domestic/non-domestic

	United Kingdom	Netherlands	France	Germany
Domestic	55	26	29	32
Non-domestic	45	74	71	68

Table 10: Percentages of events and agents by domestic/non-domestic

	United Kingdom	Netherlands	France	Germany
Domestic	54	25	34	37.5
Non-domestic	46	75	66	62.5

Inferences from these tables is subject to caution because the amalgamation of meaning objects into the categories "domestic" and "non-domestic" is likely to give more of the latter, since there are three ways of being non-domestic (refer to Possibility 2). However, this restriction does not invalidate inferences based on the differences of priority that separate the UK from the Euroland countries, nor those based on the differences between the margins of difference in the various countries. As can be seen from Table 10, the UK press is dominated by domestic matters (albeit by a relatively small margin), whereas the Euroland press systems are clearly dominated by non-domestic matters (albeit by different margins). The extraordinary imbalance between Dutch attention to domestic and non-domestic matters is no doubt due to geographical and cultural factors deriving from the size of the nation and the extent of its now-traditional orientation to the outside world; but the margin of difference in the French and German presses is also clearly significant.

Analysis of Distribution of Meaning by Location

In the UK press, the distribution between domestic/non-domestic agents and events is similar (Tables 8 and 9), suggesting that agents are dealing with matters that are dictated by their location. In the French and German press, there are more domestic agents than domestic events (and conversely for non-domestic), which implies that domestic agents are dealing with non-domestic matters in some greater proportion than in the UK. This is a further indicator of a difference in framing between the UK and Euroland. In the Dutch press, the balance between national and trans-national matters is unequivocal in every respect.

Again, it may appear obvious that inside Euroland, the EMU will be seen as a transnational matter. But it has been successfully defined as such and, at least during the period surveyed, domestic concerns are not above transnational ones in the press agendas in these Euroland countries.

Conclusions

News reporting is event-centered. Each event is presented in terms based on a judgment about which aspect or dimension of the event is considered significant, according to news criteria (Palmer, 2000). To use the terms discussed earlier in this chapter, each news story is about an "issue." In the case of "human interest" stories, the issue base may be less than obvious. (For a discussion of an example of sexual scandal, see Palmer, 2000.) Journalists' choices of which issues to report collectively constitute an agenda (which may or may not result in the "setting" of a wider public agenda). The combination of the two results in a "frame," in terms of which the issue(s) in question acquire a more or less defined profile. This profile may be the result of "upstream" activities by news sources, autonomous journalist decisions, or some mixture of the two. It may have some "downstream" impact on public opinion. Certainly, news sources make well-documented efforts to ensure the compatibility of event-profiling with their strategic intentions (Weaver, 1994; Miller and Williams, 1993; Palmer, 2000; Gandy, 1982; Sigal, 1986). The study reported here aims to show how two significant dimensions of the reporting on the EMU underlie the mass of reporting of individual events and issues in the press. These dimensions are the questions about the national/transnational and the political/economic/civil. A propos each of these dimensions, it is clear that the UK press "frames" the EMU distinctively differently from that adopted in the Euroland press systems studied. Whether this is the result of conscious "upstream" communications strategies cannot be established on the basis of this analysis; an analysis of the range of sources used would go some way to achieving this. Nor does this study allow any analysis of the actual impact on public opinion. However, it seems likely that the framing in question corresponds to some significant element of public opinion (upstream or downstream) in the countries in question.

References

Bruce, B. (1992). *Images of Power*. London, UK: Kogan Page.

Capella, J. and K. Jamieson (July 1996). "News Frames, Political Cynicism and Media Cynicism," pp. 71-84 in *Annals of the American Academy of Political and Social Science*, Vol. 546.

Cohen, B. (1963). *The Press and Foreign Policy*. Princeton, NJ: Princeton University Press.

Deacon, D. and P. Golding (1994). *Taxation and Representation*. London, UK: John Libbey.

De Vreese, C. (July 1999). "Framing the Euro in the News and in Public Opinion." Paper given at the meeting of the International Association for Mass Communication Research (IAMCR), Leipzig, Germany.

Dearing, J. and E. Rogers (1996). *Agenda-Setting*. London, UK: Sage, Communications Concepts series.

Entman, R. (1993). "Framing: Toward Clarification of a Fractured Paradigm," pp. 51-58 in *Journal of Communication*, Vol. 43.

Gamson, W. (1996). "Media Discourse as a Framing Resource," pp. 111-132 in A. Crigler (ed.) *The Psychology of Political Communication*. Ann Arbor, MI: University of Michigan Press.

Gandy, O. (1982). *Beyond Agenda Setting*. Norwood, NJ: Ablex.

Gandy, O. (1992). "Public Relations and Public Policy: The Structuration of Dominance in the Information Age," pp. 131-163 in E. Toth and R. Heath (eds.) *Rhetorical and Critical Approaches to Public Relations*. Hillsdale, NJ: Lawrence Erlbaum Associates.

Gavin, N. (2000) "Imagining Europe: Opinion Formation, Political Controversy and Media Coverage of Europe and the Economy," pp. 352-373 in *British Journal of Politics and International Relations*, Vol. 2, No. 3.

Gitlin, T. (1980). *The Whole World is Watching*. Berkeley, CA: University of California Press.

Hampton, F. (1997). "Integrating PR Monitoring into the Overall Corporate/Product Marketing Function," pp. 280-288 in *Journal of Communication Management*, Vol. 1, No. 3.

Hansen, A. (1991). "The Media and the Social Construction of the Environment," p. 4 in *Media. Culture and Society*, Vol. 13.

Jasperson, A., D. Shah, M. Watts, R. Faber, and D. Fan (1998). "Framing and the Public Agenda: Media Effects on the Importance of the Federal Budget Deficit, pp. 205-224 in *Political Communication*, Vol. 15, No. 2.

Lits, M. (1999). "Contes et décomptes de l'euro" (Calculations and Miscalculations About the Euro), pp. 121-130 in P. Marion (ed.) *L 'Année des Medias 1998* (Year of the Media 1998). Louvain-la Neuve, Belgium: Academic Brylant.

Loenneker, B. (1998). "L'Euro, l'Europe, les nations - et les stereotypes" (Euro, Europe, and Nations: The Stereotypes) in M. Lits, J. Palmer, and W. Settekorn (eds.) L'*Euro Médiatisé. La construction de la monnaie unique dans les médias européens* (The Construction of the Single Currency in the European Media). Louvain-la-Neuve, Belgium: Les Dossiers de L'ORM/COMU, Université Catholique de Louvain-la-Neuve.

McCombs, M. and T. Bell (1996). "The Agenda-setting Role of Mass Communications," pp. 93-110 in M. Salwen and D. Stacks (eds.) *An Integrated Approach to Communications Theory and Research*. Hillsdale, NJ: Lawrence Erlbaum Associates.

Miller, D. and K. Williams (1993). "Negotiating HIV/AIDS Information. Agendas, Media Strategies and the News," pp. 126-142 in *Glasgow University Media Group Getting the Message: News, Truth and Power*. London, UK: Routledge.

Newman, K. (1986). *The Selling of British Telecom*. New York, NY and London, UK: Holt, Rinehart and Winston.

Palmer, J. (1998). "L'Union monétaire dans la presse de cinq pays européens: quelques comparaisons quantitatives" (The Monetary Union in the Press of Five European Countries: Some Quantitative Comparisons), pp. 43-62 in M. Lits, J. Palmer, and W. Settekorn (eds.) *L'Euro Médiatisé. La construction de la monnaie unique dans les médias européens* (The Construction of the Single Currency in the European Media). Louvain-la-Neuve, Belgium: Les Dossiers de L'ORM/COMU, Université Catholique de Louvain-la-Neuve.

Palmer, J. (2000). *Spinning into Control. News Values and Source Strategies*. London, UK: Leicester University Press/Continuum.

Pan, Z. and G. Kosicki (1993). "Framing Analysis: An Approach to News Discourse," pp. 55-15 in *Political Communications*, Vol. 10, No. 1.

Philo, G. (1993). "From Buerk to Band Aid: the Media and the Ethiopian Famine," pp. 104-125 in D. Eldridge (ed.) *Getting the Message: News and Power*. London, UK: Routledge.

Scheufele, D. (1999). "Framing as a Theory of Media Effects," pp.103-118 in *Journal of Communication*, Vol. 49.

Settekorn, W. (1998). "L'Euro en Images ou l'Imagination de l'Imaginaire" (Images of the Enro or Imagining the Imagined), pp. 7-16 in M. Lits, J. Palmer, and W. Settekom (eds.) *L 'Euro Médiatisé. La construction de la monnaie unique dans les médias européens* (The Construction of the Single Currency in the European Media). Louvain-la-Neuve, Belgium: Les Dossiers de L'ORM/COMU, Université Catholique de Louvain-la-Neuve.

Sigal, L. (1973). *Reporters and Officials*. Lexington, MA: D.C Heath.

Sigal, L. (1986) "Sources Make the News," pp. 9-37in R. Manoff and M. Schudson (eds.) *Reading the News*. New York, NY: Pantheon Books.

Weaver, P. (1994). *News and the Culture of Lying*. New York, NY: Free Press.

Chapter 11
The Ukraine Media on the Orange Revolution

Natalya Krasnoboka and Christ'l De Landtsheer

University of Antwerp, Antwerp, Belgium

Abstract

This chapter is a part of a larger analysis of Ukrainian political transition. It reports the results of one case study. Based on the importance of media and their message in the country, we argue that media language helps us understand the process of political transition in a given society. Transition is inherently a political crisis. Thus, the language of transition is, by definition, a language of crisis. Crisis Communication Combination (CCC) theory is our major theoretical and methodological tool. CCC theory says that the language of crisis is less complex, more metaphorical, and directed toward the audience (demagogical). This lets us determine if the current language of Ukrainian transition can be qualified as a language of crisis. It helps us to register possible language diversity between different media outlets. It allows us not only to answer questions about language complexity, its metaphoric filling, and audience-directed modality use, but also to watch these trends evolve and compare them. The central questions of this chapter are: Does the language of Ukrainian media follow a crisis pattern? How does it change over time and between outlets? Our study confirms that the language of Ukrainian media follows a crisis pattern. This is particularly visible in less complex, more metaphorical language. As we expected, different media outlets showed different levels of crisis pattern.

Introduction

In November-December 2004, a peaceful Orange revolution occurred in Ukraine. Despite the real danger and threats, weapons were not used. Instead, Kyiv celebrated its biggest carnival. There were many oranges, dances, songs, costumes, and words: words that united people and some that separated them; words that celebrated victory and others that promised unrest and bloodshed. Ukrainians believed it was a real revolution, using words as weapons. Another weapon was a color. There was a clear distinction between the words and colors of both camps: "white-and-blue Russian" for the outgoing regime and "orange Ukrainian" for the opposition. These "colorful languages" became factors of success or failure. Undoubtedly, the combination of a color-word struggle resulted in a highly picturesque rhetoric that was very symbolic and expressive.

Ukrainians like to use expressive, vivid language. It is a part of their national culture. Soviet censorship contributed to the development of a language of "hidden meanings." Ever since its independence, Ukraine faced a period of transition, the critical nature of which only reinforces the use of expressive talk. The last years of Kuchma's regime reintroduced censorship practices, pushing people to refresh their skills in using "coded" language. The Orange revolution became the highest point of the post-Soviet crisis. Thus, it would be reasonable to suspect that the expressiveness of the language reached its heights as well.

This chapter reports the results of one case study. Based on the importance of media and their message in the country, we argue that a media language helps us understand the process of political transition. Crisis Communication Combination (CCC) theory was our major theoretical and methodological tool (De Landtsheer and De Vrij, 1999, 2004).

Theoretical Framework

Evaluating the importance of language in politics, Feldman (1998, pp. 195-196) claimed that "language becomes an important instrument of power, a means for winning political office, a tool for influencing policy, and a weapon for mobilizing the public's support." It helps people change or influence political reality. "As people assess their environment, language is created which structures, transforms, or destroys the environment. Language serves as the agent of social interaction; as the channel for the transmission of values; and as the glue that bounds people, ideas and society together" (Denton and Woodward, 1998, p. 45).

While language helps people explain reality, it is as polyphonic as reality itself. Within its polyphonic nature, language is political based on who and what kinds of meanings are chosen for the linguistic signs. We believe polyphonic language is very important for a transition period characterized by an intense struggle for the country's future directions, including future meanings of language signs. At the same time, within its social function, language "prescribes, constrains, socializes, reinforces, and conserves the status quo" (Corcoran, 1990, p. 70); when a society/regime strives for language stability (resulting from a group's victory), it has a certain vision of reality. With its victory, this vision will be "fixed" in language status quo till the next transition. "Society produces different techniques in order to stop the floating line of signifiers which are called to overcome the horror of meaning uncertainty of iconic signs" (Barthes, 1989, p. 305) to have "one nation, one people, one society [which is] often simply translated into 'ours' – 'our' industry, 'our' economy, 'our' nuclear deterrent, police force balance of payments, etc." (Hartley, 1982, p. 82).

Meadow (1980) finds several reasons to use symbolic discourse in political affairs: 1) symbols that contain a huge amount of information in a compressed form are adopted easily and get quicker responses from people than long messages; 2) symbols with many meanings can mobilize larger numbers of adherents; 3) even if there is always a danger of a symbol's response to a wrong object, the behaviors that follow such responses may be "uniform" (Meadow, 1980, pp. 34- 35). What is its aim? "To arose groups and individuals to action" (Cobb and Elder, 1972, p. 85) and to support political decision.

Crisis

Crisis heightens metaphoric use of a language (De Landtsheer, 1994, p. 77) and elevates the importance of symbolic discourse in real life (Kiew, 1998, p. 81). Pocheptsov (1997, p. 24) considers a function of the symbolic discourse during such times as a kind of psychotherapy "when society is in panic and trouble, it tries to find new ways out of crisis, it necessarily switches to the metaphoric language." Voloshinov (1930, p. 27) suggested that only periods of social crises and revolutionary changes could open the real multi-accentual nature of the signs.

Research into the language of prosperity and crisis (De Landtsbeer, 1994, p. 77) concludes that "political language becomes more ornamental, emotive, and less similar to everyday-life language as economic recession progresses." Kiew (1998, p. 81) sees the language of crisis as a terministic/dramatic screen, which "directs our attention and through which one sees reality." The selection of words, symbols, and terms may make people experience reality in a certain given way and not any other. At the same time, Kiew stresses the power of crisis to "unite people around a plot and a narrative" (Kiew, 1998, p. 81).

Transition

We believe that political transition is one of the most vivid examples of political crisis with all implications this may have for its language. We also argue that transitional crisis differs from critical patterns in more stable societies. Language use in stable societies seldom goes beyond the boundaries of the existing social and political order. So even when language and society are seriously shaken by revision and changes in the discourse, the entire political system and language signification does not collapse and a "new order" is not created. On the other hand, transition can be characterized by its "intermediary" position between two political systems as well as their differences in language. Transition is a combination of a previous political system and a new (declared, but still rather vague and unknown) one. This leads to a combination of at least two discourses: the previous system's and the new one's emerging discourse. Moreover, the nature of transition itself leaves a vivid mark on a current situation and discourse.

Symbolic language holds society together and bridges the gap (Meadow, 1980), but it is possible only when a symbolic discourse is understood and recognized (if not by all, at least by many). A period of transition is characterized not only by a struggle of various political and ideological possibilities but also by a variety of language and symbolic patterns, many of which are understood and recognized only by a certain social group. In this respect, we can talk about a double crisis (of transition): a critical situation needs to be explained via the critical use of language, which finds itself in a period of crisis.

The countries of the former Soviet Union provide good examples of society-language crisis. The rapid, unpredicted shift from totalitarianism toward democracy produced quick and rather unforeseen changes in the people's perception of reality. These countries are caught between the old and new myths (Pocheptsov, 1997, p. 40) of reality. The collapse of the Soviet Union came naturally, but too early for other alternatives to be ready to replace old system(s).

Post-communist dynamics cannot be explained by referring to the previous regime's universally shared social, economic, cultural, and institutional structures. Negative "inheritances of the past can be overcome, and that a more nuanced explanations should be constructed in order to determine which legacies will and which will not play a role in shaping the direction of change" (Kopecky and Mudde, 2000, p. 527).

Based on the political transformation of former Soviet republics, we may expect that their languages undergo similar dramatic transformations. We assume that the language of transition is, by definition, a language of crisis. For this reason, we believe that applying Crisis Communication Combination (CCC) theory to our case study will be beneficial in several aspects: 1) we can determine if the current language of Ukrainian transition can be qualified a language of crisis; 2) we can register possible language diversity between different groups; 3) the combination in one theory of the three important indicators of semantic and cognitive use of language will allow us not only to gain answers to the questions of language complexity, its metaphor filling, and audience-directed modality use, but also to see the evolution of all these trends in their unity and comparison.

CCC Theory and Method

Crisis Communication Combination (CCC) theory is our major theoretical and methodological tool (De Landtsheer, 1998, 2004). It lets us theoretically and empirically examine the crisis (non-crisis) pattern in political speech (text). It assumes that crisis language is simple, is easily accessible, appeals to emotion rather than cognition, and addresses the audience directly. Political communication during crises is increasingly persuasive and demagogic. The CCC index reflects the level of crisis in political discourse.

De Landtsheer's CCC theory was based on original methodology developed to study language complexity (Suedfeld and Bluck, 1988; Suedfeld and Tetlock, 1977; Baker-Brown, et al., 1992), metaphor power (De Landtsheer, 1994, 1998; Beer and De Landtsheer, 2004), and pragmatically ambiguous modals (Sweetser, 1990; Anderson, 1998). The final stage of analysis is the crisis communication combination index (CCC). It is measured in accordance with De Landtsheer's methods: multiplying a metaphor power index (C) by empathic modals index (E+) and dividing this result by the cognitive complexity index (CC) multiplied by the content modals index (E-): $CCC=(C*E+)/(CC*E-)$.

Language Complexity

The crisis pattern approach is based on assumptions and observations that language during periods of political, economic, or social crisis differs considerably from language in times of political or economic stability (Lasswell, 1949; De Sola Pool, 1956). Several studies on language complexity showed sometimes dramatic changes in complexity of politicians' speeches during periods of crisis (Suedfeld and Rank, 1976; Suedfeld, et al., 1977; Wallace and Suedfeld, 1988; Suedfeld, et al., 1993; Wallace, et al., 1993; Wallace, et al., 1996). According to the theory of integrative complexity, 1ow levels of complexity in public speech represent black-and-white thinking; intermediate levels represent increasing differentiation between points of view; and high levels point to integrative thinking and the ability to synthesize. Low complexity of political speech makes the speech simple and accessible to a broader audience. The lower the complexity of the speech, the more it resembles the impressive rhetoric by demagogues who are only interested in their audiences (Windt and Ingold, 1987, p. xix). We symbolize integrative complexity via the CCC index.

Integrative complexity is measured on a 7-point scale: 1 is undifferentiated perspectives or dimensions toward a topic; 3 is a clear differentiation between alternative perspectives or judgments; 4 and above indicates different degrees of perspectives and dimensions of integration. To find integrative complexity (CC), divide the sum of all scored paragraphs by the number of paragraphs.

Metaphor Power

"Metaphors are emotive components of language that are highly reassuring as they simplify reality. [T]hey, beside, add particular desired subjective connotations to the subject which is discussed, and can therefore also have a mobilizing effect" (De Landtsheer and De Vrij, 1999, p. 6). Metaphors can be seen as broadening (non)complexity in political rhetoric. In metaphor theory, innovative and original metaphors are more intense and persuasive than commonly used ones. Metaphors taken from the "vocabulary" of sports, crime, violence, or illness are more powerful than those from the everyday or nature "vocabulary." Based on these features, De Landtsheer's theory measures a metaphor's power index (of a text) as "a meter reader of anxiety in society" (De Landtsheer and De Vrij, 1999, p. 6). A period of crisis provokes an increasing use of metaphors; then, metaphors have stronger than usual expression and are linked to less everyday notions (e.g., crime, violence, game, disease, death). Trend studies for the European Parliament and the Belgian press confirmed that both political language during economic crisis and rhetoric by "extremist" politicians are more metaphorical than during periods of economic prosperity and speeches by "democratic" politicians (Landtsheer, 1994, 1998). To support these conclusions, one study of Ukrainian parliamentary rhetoric suggests a strong relation between metaphor use and mythical thinking. Extremist politicians use more metaphors and mythical thinking to criticize the present situation; they aim to destroy the logic of the present and its semantic discursive construction. Moderate politicians emphasize the merits of the actual situation, which they analyze logically (Taran, 2000). In a transitional political situation, the logic of the present and its discursive construction are continuously challenged. Metaphor relies on contrast, conflict, and a distorted perception of reality. With the past and present on fire, metaphor becomes any politician's weapon in the struggle for a new reality and its discursive construction. Metaphor power in political rhetoric is symbolized by C.

The metaphor power index (C) is measured by multiplying the frequency of metaphors per 100 words (F) with metaphorical intensity (I) and the content score (D): C=F*I*D. Frequency is the number of metaphors (m) per 100 words from a general number of words (w): F=(m* 100)/w. Intensity (I), measured on a 3-point scale, is the sum of weak (w, value 1), normal (n, value 2), and strong (s, value 3) metaphors, divided by the total number of metaphors (t): I= (1*w+2*n+3*s)/t. Content score, measured on a 6-point scale, is a sum of popular metaphors (p, value 1), nature metaphors (n, value 2), political/intellectual metaphors (po, value 3) disaster/violence metaphors (d, value 4), sports/games metaphors (sp, value 5), and medical/illness metaphors (m, value 6), divided by the total number of metaphors (t): D=(1 *p+2*n+3*po+4*d+5*sp+6*m)/t.

Modals

The content use of modals refers to the social or physical world a communicator experienced; the epistemic use of modals directs the audience's attention to the communicator's state of mind; the use of "speech act" modals aims at interaction with the audience. Anderson (1998) suggests that electoral politicians who try to collect support (to mobilize people) chose epistemic and speech act modals rather than content modals, contrary to totalitarian rulers for whom content use of modals is crucial. Applying these assumptions to the study of political speech in pre- and post-independent Russia, Anderson concludes that the Soviet Union's totalitarian regime used only content modals, while post-Soviet political discourse is characterized by using a combination of three types of modals.

Modals "inject possibility, necessity, or obligation into unmodified utterances" (Anderson, 1998, p. 65). Anderson based his research on Sweetser's (1990) concept of pragmatic ambiguity of modals. "Because some modals are pragmatically ambiguous, an audience encountering these parts of speech must think about, however momentarily, whether the speaker is communicating about the content of the message, the reasonableness of the speaker, or the relationship with the audience established by the utterance. Of course, resolution of the ambiguity goes unnoticed; the decision is overlearned and automatic. ... Nevertheless, this unnoticed decision controls the interpretation of the whole utterance. Control of the interpretation determines whether the audience attends to the event reported by the speaker, to the warrant for the speaker's belief about the event, or to the linguistic interaction between the speaker and the audience" (Anderson, 1998, pp. 67-68). In other words, the speaker can choose to seek direct contact with the audience through the speech act use of modals or let the audience share some of his own thoughts through the epistemic use of modals; in which case, we say that the speaker's use of modals is "empathic." To the extent that the use of modals gets more emphatic, the rhetoric becomes the "impressive" type favored by demagogues (Windt and Ingold, 1987, p. xix). We symbolize the empathic use of modals by the E+ index. E+ is calculated on the basis of the general number of epistemic and speech act modals (e) per 100 words from a general number of words (w): E+=(e*100)/w. If the speaker uses the "content" modals and does not interact with the audience, the speech resembles the "expressive" rhetoric of doctrinaires. We symbolize this nonempathic use of modals by the E- index. E- is calculated on the basis of content modals' use (c) per 100 words from a general number of words (w): E(c*100)/w.

Media

Can CCC theory be applied to study the media's language patterns? Nowadays, delivery of public speeches is mainly performed via the media. One study of media performance in international crisis suggests that democratic regimes use the mass media prior to a conflict to prepare public opinion for war.

Sorely (l998, p. 119) states that media "offer a linguistic rendering of events that is typically perceived as a proxy for an objective reality." He also claims: "Given that media productions are perceived as objective representations of reality, they attain a status that enhances their legitimacy and ascendancy over alternative accounts and allows them to become a 'material' for construction of opinions, norms, and judgments."

Based on the previous studies, we may argue that as well as the language of politicians, the language of media changes during politically and economically critical periods. We may expect that during such periods, a language of media is far removed from its everyday pattern (which in the case of media, means an unemotional, dry language of facts). We may also expect that in these periods, a language of media particularly highlights and emphasizes the issues and/or personalities most important and/or controversial for a current moment.

The importance and evolution of the media in the former Soviet Union lets us assume that media may be a major source of information for post-Soviet citizens on any issue. We assume that people seek answers in media outlets. Simultaneously, we realize that certain political and cultural groups (elites) successfully affect and manipulate media's message. Media cannot be considered "innocent" transmitters of impartial, unbiased information, particularly when sensitive issues of a country's identity and future are concerned.

Case Study: Orange Revolution

Ukrainian society's euphoria on gaining independence in 1991 was replaced by deep pessimism, apathy, and distrust of possible rapid changes, once citizens realized that the country was falling into a new type of oppressive regime. Soviet totalitarianism was replaced by the transitional authoritarianism of Leonid Kuchma (who stayed in power for almost 12 years as prime minister and, later, president). At that time, Ukraine lacked serious political opposition and a strong civil society movement. After 1999 (Kuchma's re-election for a second term), the independent media were stifled by the reintroduction of the Soviet practice of censorship. With very few exceptions, media outlets accepted practices of self-censorship and loyalty to the president. Those trying to resist were pushed to the "margins of information discourse" of the time: they moved online. The Internet paper *Ukrainska Pravda* has become the front post of media struggle for freedom of speech. In summer 2000, Internet media began to shape into the most visible and strongest civil opposition to the ruling regime. That was followed by the dramatic disappearance and murder of *Ukrainska Pravada's* chief editor, Georgy Gongadze. In November 2000, Olexandr Moroz (the leader of Ukrainian Socialist) publicly accused Kuchma of masterminding the killing of the journalist. Mass protests and the creation of an oppositional coalition followed. By the time of 2002 parliamentary elections, the country was divided between two political and information realities: the regime and the opposition. These were two parallel realities, where the regime's right hand was the opposition's left hand. Media were discussing similar issues, highlighting similar events, but applying opposing discourses. Slowly, the general rather vague but highly expressive division within the country emerged. On one side, the ruling regime was openly supported by Russia and other post-Soviet authoritarian rulers. It controlled traditional media by predominantly using Russian language and focusing on their stronghold in the country's east and south (where the majority of the ruling elite resided). On the other hand, the more or less united opposition was strongly supported by civil society groups and Internet media whose priority was European integration; their stronghold was in the country's center and west with its predominantly Ukrainian speaking population. That division was reinforced by a so-called Soviet identity among the supporters of the ruling regime and a new Ukrainian national identity as a part of a broader European identity among opposition supporters.

This division continued until the 2004 presidential elections, which everybody saw as the most decisive moment in the country's future evolution. According to the constitution, President Kuchma did not have any legal right to stay in power after 2004. By that time, the opposition had its national leader widely supported and praised around the country. Victor Yushchenko had an image not only of a democrat and a professional, but also of a highly moral and deeply religious person; these qualities were very important for Ukrainian voters. The ruling regime declared Victor Yanukovich as its candidate. In addition to his ruling class identity (Soviet type of manager, Russian-speaking, from the heart of Eastern Ukraine), Yanukovich was twice convicted and imprisoned during his youth. As a result of their respective backgrounds, the competition between Yushchenko and Yanukovich became a battle between good and evil, white and black. When Yushchenko was poisoned in the midst of the election campaign, it added yet another highly symbolic and emotional point to the struggle. Yushchenko won the first round of elections, but he did not get 51% of the vote; therefore, he and Yanukovich entered the second round of elections. When Yanukovich was announced the winner of the second round, the opposition called for mass mobilization of its supporters and mass protests. Millions of people went on the streets and did not leave them until the new re-vote was called and Yushchenko was proclaimed the new president of the country.

Media During and After the Orange Revolution

Ukrainian media is deeply divided; the 2004 presidential campaign and the Orange revolution reinforced these divisions. Although the Internet confirmed its position as the opposition's major information tool, television continued to serve as the ruling regime's major mouthpiece. Newspapers were more or less equally divided (quantitatively) between the opposition and the president.

Although it became rather obvious during the early stages of the presidential campaign that the opposition would not give up this time and in case of falsifications would call for civil mobilization and disobedience, the first days of the Orange revolution took the majority of the traditional media by surprise. They continued to obey the regime until occasionally individual journalists or small groups of journalists began to openly announce their support of the revolution. In contrast to the events of the 1991 collapse of the Soviet Union, journalists as a professional class and intellectual elite were no longer in the vanguard of the civil movement. However, that did not prevent the ability of separate media outlets and journalists to become front posts of the revolution. The Fifth Channel has been named "the channel of the honest news." On that channel, news was broadcasted non-stop on the huge TV screen on the Kyiv's Independent Square. Interestingly, the position of this channel and a few other outlets and journalists has been self-presented as a civil position of citizens in contrast to a professional position of journalists. The later meant subordination to the will of authorities. Needless to say, the Internet was totally "Orange." Internet journalists were doing their best to combine their civil and professional duties, to be on the Square, and to support the flow of information and news on their websites. As a marginal information medium of marginalized opposition yesterday, online media then became the major information tool and news source of the Orange revolution.

Post-revolutionary reality supplied (and continues to do so) media with another test of their civil position and professional standards. The new power proclaimed freedom of speech among its key priorities. Then, media proclaimed their independence from any political influence. What does it mean in practice? Both online and traditional media are struggling to find their ways. For online media, a major question is: Should we support the new authorities which we helped to bring to power by giving them time and an opportunity to evolve or should we "constructively oppose" any authority by definition because media belong to the civil society and ideally perform a watch-dog function? Traditional media ask: Should we believe that these authorities are qualitatively different and will not impose new controls over media, thus allowing media outlets to develop their own strategies or should we "change our color" and become mouthpieces of new authorities because no power would ever give up a chance to control media? Traditional media's dilemma is complicated by the fact that, financially, most of them still belong to the former ruling regime and the current opposition.

This problematic, multidimensional situation raises the questions: How do media behave in such conditions? Do these political changes and transformations have any impact on them? And if so, what exactly is this impact? One way to answer these questions is to look at the content of media messages in its dynamics in the period between the presidential election, the Orange revolution and the former opposition's rise to power, and its subsequent performance.

This study looks at the media's language use. The key questions are: Does the language of Ukrainian media during the period between the 2004 presidential election and the subsequent performance of the new government follow a crisis pattern? Does this crisis pattern differ between outlets and change across time periods? In this study, we test a set of hypotheses applied in a study of crisis and non-crisis language patterns in political speech by De Landtsheer and De Vrij (1999, 2004); these hypotheses are known as the CCC theory. In some ways, this study diverges from the theory's original application; in others, it stays intact with the original settings. Although it examines language patterns in the period of crisis (as well as shortly before and after it), this study applies CCC theory to a transitional society and compares patterns of language use between different media. Based on previously conducted content analysis of the 2002 parliamentary elections by different groups of Ukrainian media (Krasnoboka and Brants forthcoming), we concluded that "traditional media and most of the Internet provide a mirror reflection of each other in their reporting; but at the same time, this is a distorted reflection because different media highlight and ignore different parts of reality. In the most radical cases and situations, such differences between old and new media can result in the presentation of different political realities." Also the study of the media content during the first wave of the political crisis in Ukraine 2000-2001 has shown serious differences between online and traditional media in their coverage of the former regime and opposition activities (Krasnoboka and Semetko, forthcoming).

We studied the crisis language pattern during the 2002 parliamentary election (Krasnoboka and De Landtsheer, 2004), revealing significant differences in crisis language patterns between different outlets; the Internet had the highest levels of crisis language use. That was explained by the highly oppositional nature of the Internet toward the ruling regime. At that time, newspapers featured the middle position (between Internet media and television); we argued that the newspapers' position may make them more reliable and balanced sources of information for those who did not take any side. More interestingly, newspapers have chosen a position of the "country's interest" and evaluated any occurrences from such a "safe tower." In terms of metaphor use, the discourse of construction prevailed, reflecting precisely the situation in the country and job-to-be-done mentality. Another feature of that discourse was the "relocation" of the major "enemy" outside the country, positioning it more as an external threat. This external threat, according to the media discourse, might become a real challenge through the help of foreign satellites who "work" inside Ukraine and try to "sell" the country to the "overseas sellers of dog food" or to allow the "Russian tractor to plow our field." These conclusions from our previous studies allow us to make certain assumptions about more general language patterns of media reporting.

Hypotheses and Expectations

We believe that the Orange revolution in Ukraine is a clear example of political crisis. This allows us to assume that political discourse during the revolution follows a crisis language pattern. Since the election campaign occurred shortly before the Orange revolution and was a direct cause of the public unrest, we expect that the rhetoric during the election campaign also reflects the crisis. For two "ordinary" time periods in our analysis, we expect to see a reverse picture.

We expect that the crisis language pattern will differ between online and traditional media and that this difference will change while the political situation evolves. We expect that online media will follow the "original" pattern of crisis, which will reach its highest point during the time of the Orange revolution and, to a lesser degree, the election period and then, it will go down. At the same time, we expect to see lower levels of crisis pattern in the traditional media during the period of the Orange revolution and in the election campaign. Traditional media will try to downplay the crisis, applying (among other tools) less critical discourse to preserve the feeling of stability and control of the situation.

Based on these assumptions, we expect that the mass media rhetoric of the Orange revolution (and, to a lesser degree, the rhetoric of the 2004 presidential election) will show the crisis pattern (high CCC index), with a (subsequently) low level of integrative complexity (low CC index), high metaphor power (high index), low use of content modals (low E- index), and frequent use of empathic modals (high E+ index). The crisis pattern will show up as more outspoken in the online media than in the traditional media. During the two "ordinary" periods, we expect no crisis pattern (low CCC index), with a high level of language complexity (high CC index), low metaphor power (low C index), high use of content modals (high E-index), and low use of empathic modals (low E+ index).

Selection Criteria

We studied the language patterns of two media outlets: an online paper, *Ukrainska Pravda* (UP), and a traditional newspaper, *Den'*. We selected four weeks for the analysis: a week prior to the second round of elections (November 15-21), called "election week"; a week of political crisis (December 1-7, beginning on Wednesday), called "revolution week"; a week after the new government was formed (February 7-13, beginning on Monday), called "ordinary week 1"; and a week in May after the so-called "100 days" of the new power (May 16-22, beginning on Monday), called "ordinary week 2."

Quantitatively compared samples were composed from each outlet, which included only political news. We analyzed full articles for each outlet. As a result, a sample of the newspaper *Den'* contains 194,663 words; a sample of the online paper *Ukrainska Pravda* contains 136,180 words.

We do not apply any differentiation between news and editorials because Ukrainian media are still, as a rule, very opinionated and, in most cases, do not correspond with the formats of Western media (e.g., distinction between news, analysis, and comments sections). Although this can be seen as a big challenge in terms of general media performance, it fits well the end of our study: we can treat selected news items as entire and comparable texts. There are few unscorable paragraphs in the texts.

In this study, we tested two hypotheses. The first predicts that during the period of the Orange revolution, the media's language will follow the crisis language pattern. At a lower level, this pattern will also be preserved for the election week Two ordinary weeks will show lower (non-crisis) language patterns. Applicability of the CCC theory has been tested on each of its components, namely the metaphor index, use of modals, and language complexity, and on the general crisis communication pattern.

Metaphor Index

The highest score for the metaphor power index is 22.10 for the online paper *UP* during the "revolution week" and 25.22 for the traditional newspaper *Den'* during the "election week."

The metaphor power index of *UP* clearly follows the predicted pattern. It reaches its highest score during the "revolution week," decreases during the election week, and declines further during the two ordinary weeks. The pattern of the traditional *Den'* is different: its highest score is reached during the "election week" while the three other weeks (including "revolution week") have similar, relatively low scores. These metaphor power index differences mainly arise from high frequencies of metaphors in *Den'* (4.89) during the "election week" and high frequencies of metaphors in *UP* (4.18) during the "revolution week."

Average frequency of metaphors is 3.90 for *UP* and 4.12 for *Den'*. Average intensity scores are 1.66 for *UP* and 1.55 for *Den'*. Compared to *Den'*, *UP* has a greater percentage of normal (34.15%) and strong (16.35%) metaphors against 26.38% of normal and 14.35% strong metaphors found in *Den'*. Both outlets have the highest intensity score during the "election week" (1.72 for *UP* and 1.65 for *Den'*). Both outlets also have an equal average score (3.10) for the content of metaphors. Distribution of metaphors is also similar between different content categories. The category "society" has the highest percentage (33.25% for *UP* and 34.71% for *Den'*), followed by the "everyday" metaphors (24.23% for *UP* and 23.65% for *Den'*) and "sport" metaphors (16.94% for *UP* and 16.66% for *Den'*). In the case of metaphors' content, both outlets have their highest score during the "revolution week" (3.15 for *UP* and 3.16 for *Den'*).

Modals

In terms of modals' analysis, we see a clear decline of empathic modals and a definite rise of content models for the traditional newspaper *Den'* while the political situation changes from a crisis to more ordinary times. This pattern (but somewhat less clearly) can also be seen in the online newspaper *UP*.

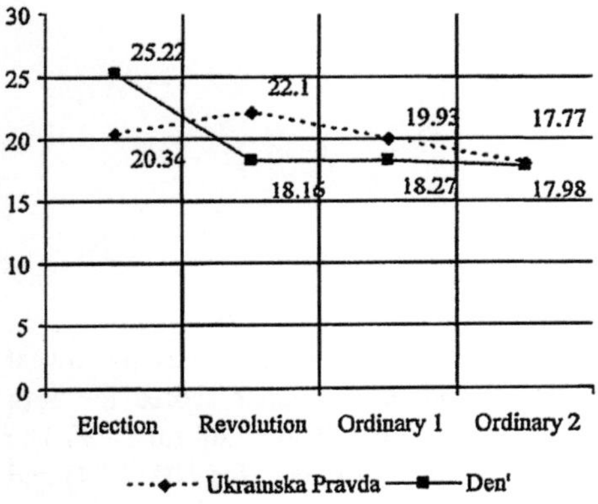

Figure 1: Metaphor index (c)

On average, *Den'* has higher frequencies of both content (0.38) and empathic modals (0.36). Most frequently, content modals appear in "ordinary week l" for *UP* (0.46) and in "ordinary week 2" for *Den'* (0.45). Empathic modals are most frequent during "election week" for *UP* (0.37) and equally frequent during "election week" and "revolution week" for *Den'* (0.39).

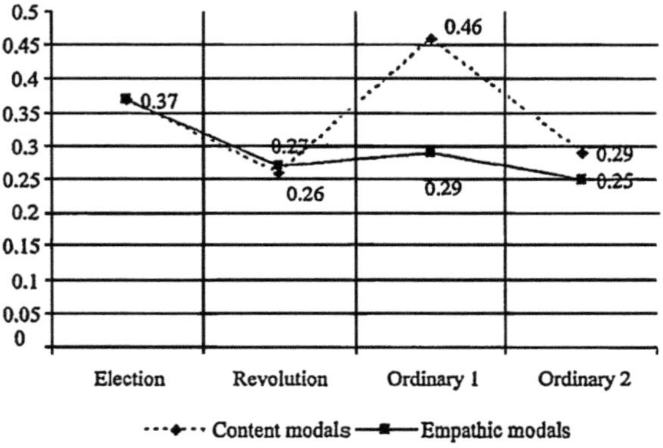

Figure 2: Modals - Ukrainska Pravda

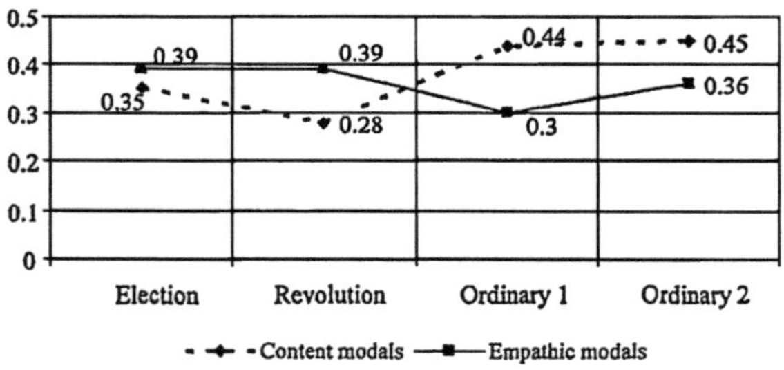

Figure 3: Modals -Den '

Language Complexity

Language complexity confirms our expectations in both cases: it has its lowest (almost equal) scores for both "crisis weeks" and much higher scores for both "ordinary weeks." Average language complexity is 2 for *UP* and 2.68 for *Den'*. The lowest language complexity is observed during "election week" for *UP* (1.84) and "revolution week" for *Den'* (2.20). The highest language complexity appears during "ordinary week l" for *Den'* (3.42) and during "ordinary week 2" for *UP* (2.24).

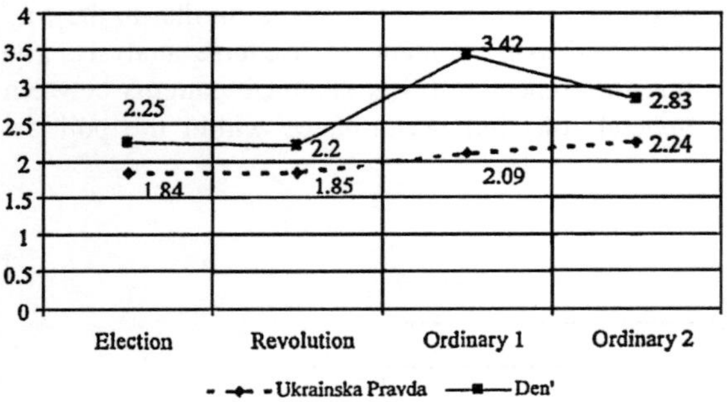

Figure 4: Language complexity (cc)

Crisis Style Pattern

The average CCC index is 9.13 for *UP* and 8.08 for *Den'*. It reaches its highest during "revolution week" for *UP* (12.38) and "election week" for *Den'* (12.30). "Ordinary week 1" has the lowest CCC index for both outlets (6.04 for *UP* and 3.65 for *Den'*).

Discussion

This study clearly shows that CCC theory can easily be applied to a transitional society. There were also no difficulties in applying this theory to media outlets.

Our CCC index in both cases shows clear differences between "crisis weeks" and "ordinary weeks." For *UP*, the difference between the highest CCC index during "revolution week" is twice as high as the lowest CCC index during "ordinary week 1." For *Den'*, the difference between the highest CCC index during "election week" is more than three times higher than the lowest CCC index during "ordinary week 1." Thus, the CCC index for *UP* completely confirmed our hypothesis about crisis language pattern during the Orange revolution. *Den'* similarly confirmed our hypothesis but in more general terms, namely it shows great difference in CCC indexes between the "crisis weeks" and the "ordinary weeks," but it has its highest CCC index during "election week," not "revolution week" as we might expect. However, such "behavior" of the CCC index for the traditional newspaper *Den'* confirms our second hypothesis which expects to find differences in language patterns of both outlets, particularly as far as the "revolution week" is concerned. Based on our previous studies of content and political/partisan differences between traditional and online media, we expected *Den'* (as a "representative" of more traditional media) to somewhat downplay the significance of the Orange revolution. In this respect, the result of this study indicates that the CCC theory can be used not only to investigate crisis language patterns, but also the general political performance of the media, similar to the way in which such behavior is investigated using content or discourse analysis. The question then is: How do we link differences in crisis language patterns between two outlets with their more general role and performance within the political context of the country?

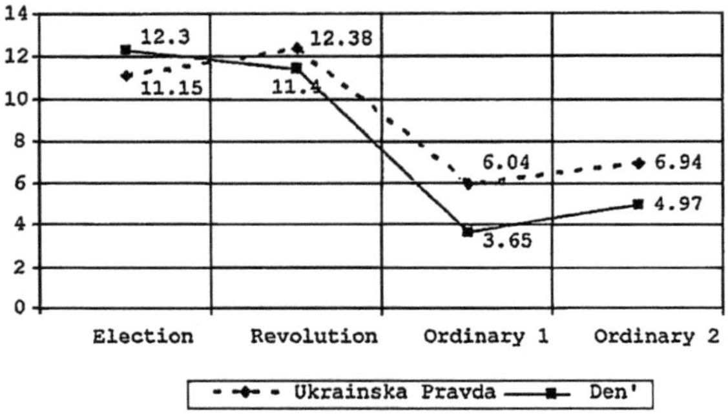

Figure 5: CCC index

The high CCC index of *Den'* during "election week" can be explained by the following political factors. It is known that *Den'* experiences two major political influences. One comes from the former head of the National Security Council, Evhen Marchyuk, who has not openly supported any candidate in the election race. However, neither has he expressed any concerns about obvious falsifications employed by the pro-presidential groups. The second influence comes from the members of the Social Democratic Party (united) who have been actively involved in the election campaign on the side of the pro-presidential candidate Yanukovich. These two influences may differ in their affiliation with the pro-presidential candidate, but in both cases, the possibility of any civil unrest or disagreement with the final results of the elections has been rejected. Therefore, "election week" was perceived and presented by the newspaper as the highest crisis moment in the recent political situation in the country.

Lower indexes of *Den'* during the week of the Orange revolution can have several explanations. In our opinion, they confirm the fact that traditional media have failed to be in the vanguard of the civil movement; they were unprepared and did not believe in the possibility of civil unrest and disobedience. As a result, their message during this week was one of confusion, inability to take any side. Another possible explanation is that, based on its previous experience of "survival" during a period of unrest (as in 2000-2001), *Den'* decided to downplay the importance of this protest as well. This approach can be most clearly seen in its metaphor indexes for "revolution week," which is almost equal to its metaphor index of "ordinary weeks." Hoping that this protest would not bring change in elites and that the ruling regime would ultimately regain control over the situation, the newspaper decided not to get at the frontline of protest but to safeguard its position as an "independent" witness. In this respect, discourse is similar to president Kuchma's and Evhen Marchyuk's (the political guardian of the newspaper), both of whom took a position "above the battle." During the Orange revolution, *Den'* did not openly and clearly support any of the two candidates, thus it followed in the footsteps of the persons to whom it remained loyal throughout all previous periods of contention.

On the contrary, *Ukrainska Pravda* has always been at the frontline of the civil opposition movement. Together with other civil groups and political opposition, it registered all violations of the pro-presidential candidate during the election campaign. From early on, this outlet supported the possibility of civil unrest and disobedience if the final results of the elections were falsified. Thus, it was not only prepared for the possibility of the Orange revolution, it prepared the very revolution. We suggest that the CCC index for the crisis language pattern of *UP* during "revolution week" would be even higher if its journalists and regular contributors had not become the most active participants of the revolution. They simply did not have enough time to write articles because they were spending days and nights on Independence Square in Kyiv or travelling through the regions. Their articles during this period are mainly short reports of the ongomg events which do not require a lot of thinking and beauty of style. However, even in such conditions, they managed to use highly crisis-like language.

Based on this analysis and more specifically the language complexity analysis, we noticed another interesting tendency in media performance: the online paper *Ukrainska Pravda* clearly serves a more partisan, but also more "watchdog," function. Its very low language complexity score demonstrates that it does not provide different alternatives (which may correspond with different opinions and points of view), at least not in the same paragraphs. The *UP* follows a more black-and-white or zero-sum approach than expected if it had followed the objective, nonbiased liberal model of media performance. In comparison, *Den'* shows higher levels of language complexity which are related not only to the presentation of different alternatives, but also to its attempts to find consensus between alternatives as well as to respect the position of non-involvement

In this respect, we would like to discuss the two "ordinary weeks" in our analysis. Indeed, very low CC indexes *Den'* had during these weeks may be interpreted as a sign that finally, with the change of power in the country, media outlets (which are now free from any political pressure) are making rapid attempts to follow the Western liberal model of objective, unbiased journalism. However, the real political situation in the country is far from being settled and resolved. Already in May ("ordinary week 2" in our analysis), only six months after the elections, the new government and the president were facing unpleasant complaints and allegations, which are only increasing with time. *Ukrainska Pravda* has clearly taken the position of the uncompromising critic of the new power holders. As such, its position is reflected in higher (and rising) CCC indexes than *Den'* for both ordinary weeks. Certainly, *Den'* follows the same pattern of the CCC index rising in the last analyzed week, although at the lower rate. Which of these two tendencies will become decisive in the further logic of traditional media performance? Will they preserve the tendency to react to the critical moments in the country's political life (as the rising CCC index suggests) or will they go back to the old practice of serving the man in power (as lower *Den'* CCC indexes during the last two weeks suggest)? The current political and media situation in Ukraine provides an excellent opportunity to follow these (and possibly other) tendencies, Next spring, the country faces new parliamentary elections as well as a possible change in its political system from a presidential to a parliamentary republic, which can bring more new and interesting data into the analysis. Moreover, further analysis should not neglect television, the country's most widespread and popular medium.

References

Anderson, R. (1998). "Pragmatic Ambiguity and Partisanship in Russia's Emerging Democracy," pp. 64-78 in O. Feldman and C. De Landtsbeer (eds.) *Politically Speaking: A Worldwide Examination of Language Used in the Public Sphere*. London, UK: Praeger.

Baker-Brown, G., E. Ballard, S. Bluck, B. de Vries, P. Suedfeld, and P. Tetlock (1992). *Coding Manual for Conceptual/Integrative Complexity* http://www.psych.ubc.ca/-psuedfeld/REST lab/Complexity.

Barthes, R. (1989). *lzbrannye Raboty. Semiotika. Poetika* (Selected Works. Semiotics. Poetics). Moskva, Russia: Nauka.

Beer, F. and C. De Landtsheer. (2004). Metaphorical World Politics: Rhetorics of Democracy, War and Globalization. East Lansing, MI: Michigan State University Press.

Cobb, R. and C. Elder (1972). "Individual Orientati.ons in the Study of Political Sybolism," pp. 83-86 in *Social Science Quarterly*, Vol. 53.

Conway, L., P. Suedfeld, and S. Clements (2003). "Integrative Complexity of Middle Eastern Leaders During the 9/11 Crisis." Paper presented at the ISPP annual meeting, Boston, MA.

Corcoran, P. (1990). "Language and Politics," pp. 51-85 in D. Swanson and D. Nimmo (eds.) *New Directions in Political Communication: A Resource Book*. London, UK: Sage.

De Landtsheer, C. (2004). "Integrative Complexity, Metaphor Power and Modality in the Rhetoric of Dyab Abou Jahjah, Leader of the Arab European League (AEL)." Paper presented at the 27th Conference ISPP, London, UK, July 15-18, 2004.

De Landtsheer, C. (1998). "The Political Rhetoric of a Unified Europe," pp. 129-145 in O. Feldman and C. De Landtsheer (eds.) *Politically Speaking: A Worldwide Examination of Language Used in the Public Sphere*. London, UK: Praeger.

De Landtsheer, C. (1994). "The Language of Prosperity and Crisis: A Case Study in Political Semantics," pp. 63-85 in *Politics, Groups and the Individual*, Vol. 4.

De Landtsheer, C. and I. De Vrij (2004). "Talking about Srebrenica: Dutch Elites and Dutchbat. How Metaphors Change during Crisis," pp. 163-192 in F. Beer and C. De Landtsheer (eds.) *Metaphorical World Politics: Rhetorics of Democracy, War and Globalization*. East Lansing, MI: Michigan State University Press.

De Landtsheer, C. and I. De Vrij (1999). "Talking Srebrenica: Dutch Elites and Dutchbat. Broadening Integrative Complexity by Way of the Crisis Communication Combination (CCC) Hypothesis." Paper presented at the ISPP annual meeting, Amsterdam, the Netherlands.

De Sola Pool, I. (1956). "Variety and Repetition in Political Language," pp. 217-231 in E. Eulau (ed.) *Political Behavior: A Reader in Theory and Research*. Glencoe, IL: The Free Press.

Denton, R. and G. Woodward (1998). *Political Communication in America*. London, UK: Praeger.

Feldman, O. (1998). "Epilogue: Where Do We Stand?," pp. 195-204 in O. Feldman and C. De Landtsheer (eds.) *Politically Speaking: A Worldwide Examination of Language Used in the Public Sphere*. London, UK: Praeger.

Hartley, J. (1982). *Understanding News*. London, UK: Routledge.

Kiew, A. (1998). "The Crisis Tool in American Political Discourse," pp. 79-90 in O. Feldman and C. De Landtsheer (eds.) *Politically Speaking: A Worldwide Examination of Language Used in the Public Sphere*. London, UK: Praeger.

Kopecky, P. and C. Mudde (2000). "What Has Eastern Europe Taught Us About the Democratisation Literature and Visa Versa)?," pp. 517-539 in *European Journal of Political Research*, Vol. 37.

Krasnoboka, N. and K. Brants (forthcoming). "Old and New Media, Old and New Politics? On- and Offline Reporting in the 2002 Ukrainian Election Campaign." Accepted for the special edited volume of the ECPR workshop presentations.

Krasnoboka, N. and C. De Landtsheer (2004). "Transitional Identity: Language Patterns in Media (Re)construction of Ukrainian Transition." Paper presented at the 27th Conference ISPP, London, UK, July 15-18, 2004.

Krasnoboka, N. and H. Semetko (forthcoming). "Murder, Journalism, and the Web: How the Gongadze Case Launched the Internet News Era in Ukraine." Accepted for the special edited volume of the ECPR workshop presentations.

Lasswell, H. (1949). "The Language of Power" in H. Laswell and N. Leites (eds.) *Language of Politics: Studies in Quantitative Semantics*. New York, NY: George W. Stewart Publisher, Inc.

Meadow, R. (1980). *Politics as Communication*. New Jersey: Ablex.

Pocheptsov, G. (1997). *Imidzh I Vybory. lmidzh Politika, Partii, Prezidenta* (Image and Elections. Image of a Politician, Party, President). Kiev, Russia: Adef.

Sorely, M. (1998). "The Media, the Markets and the Crash: A Consideration of Financial Press Narratives," pp. 117-128 in 0.Feldman and C. De Landtsheer (eds.) *Politically Speaking: A Worldwide Examination of Language Used in the Public Sphere*. London, UK: Praeger.

Suedfeld, P. and S. Bluck (1988). "Changes in Integrative Complexity Prior to Surprise Attacks," pp. 626-635 in *Journal of Conflict Resolution*, Vol. 32.

Suedfeld, P. and D. Rank (1976). "Revolutionary Leaders: Long-Term Success as a Function of Changes in Conceptual Complexity," pp. 169-178 in *Journal of Personality and Social Psychology*, Vol. 34, No. 2.

Suedfeld, P. and P. Tetlock (1977). "Integrative Complexity of Communications in International Crises," pp. 169-184 in *Journal of Conflict Resolution*, Vol. 21.

Suedfeld, P., P. Tetlock. and C. Ramirez (1977). "War, Peace, and Integrative Complexity," pp. 427-442 in *Journal of Conflict Resolution*, Vol. 21, No. 3.

Suedfeld, P., M. Wallace, and K. Thachuk (1993). "Changes in Integrative Complexity Among Middle East Leaders During the Persian Gulf Crisis," pp. 183-199 in *Journal of Social Issues*, Vol. 4.

Sweetser, E. (1990). *From Etymology to Pragmatics: Metaphorical and Cultural Aspects of Semantic Structure*. New York. NY: Cambridge University Press.

Taran, S. (2000). "Mythical Thinking, Arestotelian Logic, and Metaphors in the Parliament of Ukraine," pp. 120-143 in *Beyond Public Speech and Symbols. Explorations in the Rhetoric of Politicians and the Media*. Westport, CT: Praeger.

Voloshinov, V. (1930). *Marksizm I Philisophiya Yazyka* (Marxism and Philosophy of Language). Leningrad, Russia.

Wallace, M. and P. Suedfeld (1988). "Leadership Performance in Crisis: the Longevity-Complexity Link," pp. 139-151 in *International Studies Quarterly*, Vol. 1.

Wallace, M., P. Suedfeld, and K. Thachuk (1993). "Political Rhetoric of Leaders Under Stress in the Gulf Crisis," pp. 94-107 in *Journal of Conflict Resolution*, Vol. 37, No. 1.

Wallace, M., P. Suedfeld and K. Thachuk (1996). "Failed Leader or Successful Peacemaker? Crisis, Behavior, and the Cognitive Processes of Michail Sergeyevitch Gorbachev," pp. 453-472 in *Political Psychology*, Vol. 17, No. 3.

Windt, T. and B. Ingold (1987). *Essays in Presidential Rhetoric*. Dubuque, IA: Kendall/Hunt Publishing Company.

Chapter 12
Post-Communist Media in Russia

Vitaly F. Konzhukov

Abstract

The disintegration of the Soviet Union in December 1991, coupled with the full-scale collapse of communism in East/Central Europe, brought expectations of Russia's quick transformation into a democracy. Russia's President Boris Yeltsin repeatedly expressed his commitment to democratic processes and launched an ambitious program of changes to reform the country, making it a truly open and economically stable society.

One of the major tasks of such a transition, creating free and independent media, has proven quite difficult. This chapter overviews Russian media (both print and electronic) and concentrates mainly on the economic challenges they faced during the early years of the country's post-communist history. In addition, it reviews the Russian government's attempts to control the press and television.

Introduction

Since 1917, when the Bolsheviks seized power and realized the importance of controlling access to information, the media have been an intricate part of Soviet politics. According to doctrine prevailing then:

> . . . propaganda and agitation have general and permanent roles to spread the ideas of Marxism-Leninism, to explain to the masses the policy of the party, and to influence them emotionally to support this policy actively (Buzek, 1964, p. 17).

For over 70 years, the Soviet media served as one of the most important tools of official propaganda supervised by the Communist Party and several censorship agencies, including the KGB. On many occasions, the latter also forced journalists to perform intelligence or counterintelligence duties or sent its own agents abroad as "foreign correspondents" of different Soviet news organizations (Vachnadze, 1992, Chapters 2 and 10). Often, the KGB resorted to quite underhanded tactics. For instance, in 1990-91, many Russian publications ran a series of articles exposing the agency's clandestine operations. But according to Yasmann, one source of those exposures was orchestrated to "pit younger security officers against 'democrats' and vice versa, as well as to prevent officers from joining Yeltsin's camp" (Yasmann, 1993, p. 19).

A major change in Soviet media began in 1985. Then, Mikhail Gorbachev initiated his perestroika (restructuring) campaign. He apparently considered a liberated media instrumental to his reforms, but was reluctant to loosen control over them, so he set certain limits on media glasnost (openness). While he almost never criticized the more conservative publications, he often lashed out against those that were the most persistent and vigorous supporters/critics of his policies, such as *Argumenty i Fakty* and *Moscow News*.

But Gorbachev had released the media genie from the communist bottle. The limits of media freedom were continually expanded until the Soviet Union collapsed in December 1991. The post-Soviet media faced the challenges of economic chaos and political instability in Russia. Their managers and journalistic staffs had to deal with numerous and unprecedented problems of transition, including continuing governmental control without enough financial support from advertisers.

Newspapers and Readership

Much as in the Soviet past, newspaper reading remained a major leisure activity in democratization (Rhodes, 1993a, p. 39). Russian polling companies conducted a series of surveys in 1993 and produced some important statistics on the country's readership then (Rhodes, 1993a, pp. 39-42). For example, in 1993, 36% of adults in European Russia living outside Moscow read a newspaper almost daily. More than half those respondents (58%) claimed to do so at least three days a week; 78% at least once a week (Rhodes, 1993a, p. 40).

According to this survey, Muscovites were more avid newspaper readers than other Russians, with 50% of the city's adult population reading one daily. Only 16% of adult Muscovites did not read newspapers at all or had not read one within the three months prior to the poll, compared with the 20% in the rest of European Russia. When asked whether they read more or less than they did a year before, 15% of Moscow residents said they were reading more; 45% claimed to be reading less. Approximately 39% of those questioned did not notice any changes in their reading patterns (Rhodes, 1993a, p. 40).

The local press had a larger regular readership throughout the country than did the national press. Such publications combined political articles with coverage of social problems, sports, and popular culture. Also, readers' interests varied substantially, depending on their demographic characteristics. Moscow men tended to be more interested in sports, while readers under 25 years old looked for information about music and concerts. Younger readers leaned toward many of the new papers which presented a more popular format and more liberal views; women and older Muscovites preferred the more established press.

Women were the primary readers of many papers. Apart from sports publications, only two newspapers (*Kuranty* and *Kommersant*) had a predominantly male readership in Moscow (53% and 68%, respectively) (Rhodes, 1993a, p. 41). Moscow readers named local news and listings of television programs as the topics which interested them most. National and international politics also ranked in the top ten popular issues. At the same time, most other interests on the list related to local problems, practical information, and entertainment.

Television and Its Audience

Television has been an important medium in Russia since the late 1960s when TV sets became common in most households. As in the Soviet past, television networks were still overwhelmingly state-owned and subsidized from the country's budget. In the early 1990s, a series of attempts were made to create independent TV, such as the Moscow-based Sixth Channel and NTV. The former was started in 1992 as a joint venture with CNN; the latter went on the air in October 1993. However, the viewing audience for programs on both stations was limited because their broadcasts could not be received outside Moscow (Wishnevsky, 1994, pp. 11-12). The number of available channels in the country varied from place to place, but nowhere did it exceed six. The two major state-owned national channels attracted the largest audiences. Cable TV was relatively new to Russia. Its presence was substantial in large metropolitan areas (e.g., 35% of Moscow households) (Rhodes, 1993b, p. 5).

A number of surveys of European Russia in the early 1990s showed that 96% of all households had TV sets (94% ownership in rural areas; 96% in urban centers). Approximately 40% of urban households had two or more sets; about three-quarters of the households had a color TV.

Prime time viewing throughout the week was between 8:00 p.m. and 11:00 p.m. Most Russians watched TV daily. About 60% of urban respondents did so every weekday and 50% on weekends. Rural residents watched slightly less frequently. Men spent more time in front of their TV screens than did women. People under 25 and over 54 were the most frequent viewers.

In 1991-93 the two most popular programs in the country were the newscasts "Vesti" at 8:00 p.m. and "Novosti" at 9:00 p.m., with 40% and 50% of all Russian households watching each, respectively. Television remained the most important source of domestic and international news for both rural and urban Russians. At the same time, the majority of people still regarded TV as an entertainment medium (Rhodes, 1993, pp. 54-56).

Economic Challenges and Struggle for Survival

As soon as Yeltsin started his economic reforms and lifted government price controls on January 2, 1992, all of the Russian media found themselves on the verge of bankruptcy. Under the former Soviet system, the print media belonged to the state (i.e., the Communist Party). They were financed from its budget and were centrally distributed. Since all media were part of the propaganda machine, nobody was really concerned about their cost. The nationwide system of delivery (Soyuz-pechat) was centralized. Most print media did not make a profit; the state covered all the deficits. After the USSR disintegrated, newsprint and ink prices skyrocketed. While in 1991, newsprint could be purchased at 33 rubles a ton, by January 1992, it cost 240 rubles a ton, and by July 1992, it rose to 21,000 rubles (Daniloff, 1993, p. 44).

By early 1992, Soyuzpechat split into a number of national systems in the newly independent states. Each was given its own media monopoly. Few new privatized alternative delivery services could compete with Rospechat (the successor). Distribution prices also skyrocketed.

Soaring publishing and distribution costs, aggravated by inflation, sent subscription and newsstand prices sky high. As a result, newspaper and magazine circulations decreased dramatically. In 1991, the Soviet press lost about one-third of its 1990 subscribers, even though numerous new publications were started. In 1992 and 1993, this trend continued. According to the subscription rates for 1993, *Izvestia* kept 25% of its 1992 subscribers (800,000 compared to 3,200,000), *Komsomol'skaya Pravda* 15% (1,831,000 of 12,941,000), *Nezavisimaya Gazeta* 39% (27,000 of 70,000), and the weekly *Argumenty i fakty* 35% (8,873,000 of 25,693,000) (Androunas, 1993, p. 15). In their struggle for survival, newspapers and magazines attempted to increase advertising revenues and sought (with varying degrees of success) to diversify their activities by publishing supplements and setting up joint ventures with domestic and foreign firms.

The audiovisual media were not immune to economic problems either. Unlike the bulk of newspapers and magazines, which by 1993 had already been privatized, the overwhelming majority of TV and most radio stations were still state-owned. In the early 1990s, a major change in the electronic media was the disappearance of what used to be Gosteleradio (Soviet State Television and Radio Company). Control shifted to the former Soviet republics. But each of them, including Russia, continued with its own state TV and radio broadcasting.

In the previous Soviet model, the major expense for TV broadcasting was not programming, but transmission costs. Since the Ministry of Communications was responsible for the entire transmission system, a part of the national TV budget was appropriated for it. In the post-Soviet era, in addition to these expenses, Russian TV had to pay producers for movies it showed, which it never did before. The payment situation with sports events and entertainment was the same. At the same time, expansion of commercials and joint ventures on TV went faster than in the press because larger investments were made. Nevertheless, economic hardships forced TV organizations to fight for their survival.

State Subsidies and Political Pressures

In the Soviet system, the state both controlled and supported the press. But with the disappearance of the communist regime, financial support for the media faded away, too. Interestingly enough, finding themselves in dire straits, many "privatized" editors and journalists appealed to the government for help. Apparently, they failed to realize that they were putting themselves in a very vulnerable position and risking their newly won independence. The financial situation became critical in February 1992.

When a few large newspapers did not appear for several days, President Yeltsin signed an executive order "About additional measures for legal and economic defense of periodical press and state book publishing" (*Nezavisimaya Gazeta*, February 22, 1992, p. 1). This order restored fixed prices (lower than production costs) for 70% of the newsprint and other kinds of paper for printing and publishing in the country. It guaranteed supplies for state book publishing and "newspapers and magazines published according to programs approved by the Ministry of Press and Mass Information of the Russian Federation" (Androunas, 1993, p. 61). Government-sponsored publications were not only guaranteed supplies, but also exempt from paying taxes on their hard currency revenues. Special funds to reimburse them for distribution and delivery expenses were also provided "within the framework of subscription circulation" (*Nezavisimaya Gazeta*, February 22, 1992, p. 1). Not unexpectedly, there were also a number of cases in which the government tried to make its financial support conditional on a newspaper's agreement to refrain from publishing an article which criticized the government (Tolz, 1993, p. 3).

Since government-owned TV and radio fell under Yeltsin's strict control, it adhered to the "party line." During Yeltsin's confrontation with the Russian parliament and the subsequent October 1993 armed reprisals in Moscow, TV played an important role as the main source for pro-government propaganda.

In January 1992, Yeltsin authorized the merger of the country's biggest news organization, TASS, with the Russian Information Agency "Novosti" (RIAN), thus creating a huge media structure under the auspices of the government. Officially, this move was explained as a solution for budget problems, but critics raised the issue of Yeltsin's desire to monopolize information sources. (Interestingly enough, by the end of 1991, TASS had actually begun to show a small profit.) It is reasonable to assume that the government chose to subsidize the agency to prevent it from becoming independent (Androunas, 1993). At the same time, RIAN also aggravated Yeltsin by running a series of articles critical of his economic policies.

To strengthen presidential control over the state-run media even further, Yeltsin in late 1992 set up a Federal Information Center to supervise both television and radio and the TASS-RIAN conglomerate. He put one of his close associates Mikhail Poltoranin, in charge of the Center.

From 1991-93, when executive and legislative members waged a full-scaled political war, most of the country's media joined one or the other side which explains obvious pro- or anti-government biases of different media outlets at the time. The government, in turn, also paid close attention to what journalists had to say. In the aftermath of the October 1993 mutiny, the president reinstated censorship and imposed a ban on 13 newspapers and one TV show (*The New York Times*, October 15, 1993, p. A7).

The Law on the Press

In the communist past, the media were regulated by the "Law on the Press and Other Mass Media," adopted by the Soviet legislature in June 1990. In fact, this was the only legal document of its kind in the entire Soviet history.

After the USSR ceased to exist, all Soviet laws were declared invalid. But the new "Russian Federation Law on the Mass Media" was passed in December 1991. According to one observer, the Law on the Press reveals many compromises to accommodate the conservatives and their penchant for suppression. The 30-page law has none of the simplicity and ambiguity of the First Amendment to the US Constitution (Daniloff, 1993, p. 40). The document proclaimed prior censorship "inadmissible" (Article 3) (all articles are quoted from *European Broadcast Statutes*, Vol. 11 , No. 2, pp. 625-656); however, it required media organizations to register with the Ministry of Press and Information (Articles 8-15). Registration was not just a formality since it could be denied (Article 13). The media bore "criminal, administrative, disciplinary, or other responsibilities" for various violations and could be silenced (Articles 4 and 59). Journalists had certain rights (Article 47) and responsibilities (Article 49). Retail sales of erotic publications required discreet packaging (Article 37); calls for a "seizure of power," racial violence, propaganda, or war were prohibited (Article 4).

Despite the existence of numerous restrictions and regulations, the press was able to operate quite freely much of the time. For instance, the pornography boom that started in the late 1980s continued into the 1990s. By 1991, pornographic publications became available virtually everywhere in Russia. As one expert notes, "the pornography issue pits conservatives against liberals, with the former wanting complete suppression and the latter urging civilized ways of control." In another example, some Moscow newspapers also embarked on aggressive anti-Semitic campaigns (Daniloff, 1993, p. 40).

A lack of any professional standards and a passion for sensationalism resulted in many libel suits against media outlets. The Russian media in this period were "much more opinionated and less fact-based than their American counterparts" (Daniloff, 1993, p. 41). To some extent, this can be explained by the historical lack of access to information in a Soviet closed society. They saw themselves as heroes, crusaders, and independent journalists who had something to say, just like their Western European counterparts:

> . . . common in Europe is the concept of the active or participant journalist, the journalist who sees himself as someone who wants to influence politics and audiences according to his own political beliefs (Horvat, 1991, p. 196).

Finally, harsh economic conditions and political chaos in Russia took their toll on the media, making journalists vulnerable to the influence of special-interest groups. Bribery became common for many news organizations (Daniloff, 1993, p.

41; Androunas, 1993). In 1991, Yegor Yakovlev, then head of Russian national TV, publicly admitted that "the level of corruption around advertising, including information programs, is difficult to describe" (*Kommersant*, No. 44, 1991, p. 11). For example, on numerous occasions, different private businesses paid for commercials illegally and directly to the TV crew, which subsequently stole the money. Similarly, newspaper journalists were involved in what was called "hidden advertising" (interviews or reports that were actually advertising but not identified as such) (Androunas, 1993).

Conclusions

The transformation of Russia's media, which started in the mid-l 980s, continued into the early 1990s. The freedom of expression which Soviet journalists had first experienced under Gorbachev was expanded even further after 1991. Substantial progress was also achieved in privatizing Russia's press.

Yeltsin and subsequent economic hardships affected the media, leaving them struggling. In addition, the new Russian government was quick to use a new (not ideological, but rather economic) means of media control. It subsidized the "loyal" publications and gave them tax breaks as well as special deals on newsprint, ink, and publishing expenses. The result was that "economic pressure has, at times, become political pressure for the media in terms of . . . government subsidies or lack thereof" (Wilson, 1995, p. 113).

In its attempts to restrain the media, the government also employed some of the tactics of its communist predecessors, such as the reinstatement of censorship and trumped-up criminal prosecutions. It also consolidated its control over the state-owned press and created a superficial media watchdog agency: the Federal Information Center. The government refused to privatize TV and radio so that the most influential remained under state ownership. Because of the chaotic conditions in the country, the government frequently failed to enforce its own new laws regarding the press (e.g., regulating pornography and advocating racial violence prohibitions).

Generally, the situation in the Russian media by the mid-1990s reflected the situation in the country as a whole: a painful transition from the old authoritarian communist system (with no comparable experience from previous history) to an uncertain future which may (or may not) be based on democracy and the market. (For an update on this topic, see Fossato and Kachkaeva, August 1999.)

References

Androunas, E. (1993). *Soviet Media In Transition*. London, UK: Praeger.

Buzek, A. (1964). *How The Communist Press Works*. London, UK: Pall Mall Press.

Daniloff, N. (Winter 1993). "Will Russian Media Survive" in *The Fletcher Forum*.

European Broadcast Statutes (1993). "Russian Federation Law on Mass Media (1991)," pp. 225-256, Vol. 11, No. 2.

Fossato, F. and A. Kachkaeva (August 1999). "Russian Media Empires V." Found at http://www.-rferl.org/nca/special/rumedia5/index.html.

Horvat, J. (1991). "The East European Journalist," pp. 191-200 in *Journal of International Affairs*, Vol. 45.

Kommersant, No. 44 (1991). "Borovoy Nakonets-to Otsenil Televidenie. A Kupit ne Smog" (Borovoy Has Finally Started to Value Television. But He Cannot Buy It), p. 11.

New York Times (October 15, 1993). "Permanent Ban for 13 Russian Newspapers," p. A7.

Nezavisimaya Gazeta (February 22, 1992). "O Dopolnitel'nyh Merah Po Pravovomu I Ekonomicheskomu Obespecheniu Periodicheskih Izdaniy I Gosudarstvennogo Knigoizdania" (About Additional Measures for Legal and Economic Defense of Periodical Press and State Book Publishing), p. 1.

Rhodes, M. (1993a). "The Newspaper in Russia Today," pp. 39-42 in *RFE/RL Research Report*, Vol. 2, No. 45.

Rhodes, M. (1993b). "Russians and Television," pp. 54-56 in *RFE/RL Research Report*, Vol. 2, No. 39.

Tolz, V. (1993). "The Media in the Countries of the Former Soviet Union," pp. 1-5 in *RFE/RL Research Report*, Vol. 2, No. 27.

Vachnadze, G. (1992). *Secrets of Journalism in Russia*. Commack, NY: Nova Science Publishers.

Valery, R. (November 17, 1992). "Uchenyi, 'Prodavshiy Rodinu,' Nakonets Poluchil Advodata" (Scientist Who "Sold Out the Motherland" Finally Gets a Defense Lawyer), p. 2 in *Izvestia*.

Wilson, L. (1995). "Communication and Russia: Evolving Media in a Changing Society," pp. 109-119 in *The Social Science Journal*, Vol. 32, No. 1.

Wishnevsky, J. (1994). "The Role of the Media in the Parliamentary Election Campaign," pp. 8-12 in *RFE/RL Research Report*, Vol. 2, No. 46.

Yasmann, V. (1993). "Where Has the KGB Gone?," pp. 17-20 in *RFE/RL Research Report*, Vol. 2, No. 8.

Part 4
Critiques of the Emerging Virtual/Media World

Chapter 13
Media and Terrorists

Russell F. Farnen

Professor (Emeritus) of Political Science, University of Connecticut, Storrs, Connecticut, USA

Abstract

The public role of the mass media in most Western industrialized societies is (in addition to making a profit) to inform and educate citizens in the ways of democracy. By contrast, the goal of organized terrorists groups is to upset these orderly processes and to achieve private usually unpopular, political and informational goals. Along the way, these violent groups use and abuse the media and the state. Thy, in turn, are reciprocally used and abused in the process.

Both terrorism's and media's roles, techniques, and expectations are explained and the media-terrorist interactive system described. A case study of the Italian Red Brigades' (Brigate Rosse or BR) 1978 kidnapping and murder of Aldo Moro is presented for illustrative purposes. Some conclusions and suggestions for changing the cycle-of-violence system through media, governmental, diplomatic, and rhetorical reforms are also offered for consideration in the context of future public/media policymaking and publicizing terrorism for informational, rather than exploitative, purposes.

Introduction

In addition to making a profit, the public role of the mass media in most Western industrialized societies is to inform and educate citizens in the ways of democracy. By contrast, the goal of organized terrorist groups is to upset these orderly processes and to achieve private, usually unpopular, political and informational goals. Along the way, these violent groups use and abuse the media and the state, and they are reciprocally used and abused. Media become witting and unwitting winners and losers in this process, which shares elements of both a game and a drama. In order to perform their controlling and socially reinforcing role in the communications processes, media must regularly capture the public's attention (i.e., they must force the public to digest important news and consumer information). Therefore, media seduce consumers with sports, comics, human-interest stories, crime, scare headlines, and enticingly violent leads.

Although *Accuracy in the Media*, *The Moral Majority*, *Conservative Digest*, *Media Monitor*, and the *New Right Report* regularly attack the alleged liberalism of the three major networks, the Public Broadcasting System (PBS), National Public Radio (NPR), and major newspapers (e.g., the *Washington Post* and the *New York Times*), this so-called liberal slant is illusory. NPR may be unique in more severely criticizing Republican rather than Democratic presidents from 1974 to 1983, but most major newspapers and all of the networks are more noteworthy for their uniform criticism of all presidents, regardless of party stripe, their quest of middle-of-the-road positions on partisan political questions, and their avoidance of entanglement in current public policy disputes (Larson, Spring 1989). The mass media in America are mainstream in ideology and strongly establishment-oriented, as are other large American corporations. For example, during the conservative resurgence from 1972 to 1984, between 42% and 71% of the major American newspapers (which controlled between 49% and 77% of total newspaper circulation) endorsed the more-conservative Republican presidential candidate. This is in contrast to the 5-12% that endorsed the less-conservative Democratic presidential candidate and the 23-42% that remained uncommitted during this same 12-year period (Stanley and Niemi, 1988).

Above all, media (using Ben Bagdikian's term) employ the so-called twin sovereigns to get attention: sex and violence (Bagdikian, 1987). They stress murders, rapes, robberies, and other deviant, unusual, and "abnormal" events, each unique in its own way. Since the media have an unquenchable thirst for unsavory violence and "man bites dog" stories, militant groups find them easy targets for manipulation. But the reverse is also true. While television, newspapers, magazines, and radio could exist without as much violence in their daily diets, the products, appeal, and nature of the mass media would change and their effects would probably be minimized.

Terrorism could not exist in its present form without a mass audience. Without widespread popular exposure, the very nature of the terrorist phenomenon would radically change. Indeed, what we know as terrorism is actually a media creation; mass media define, delimit, delegitimize, and discredit events that we have not actually seen, but that we all instantly recognize as terrorist acts.

The influence of television, within its mass media setting, can be approached through a variety of theoretical constructs. These theories help to explain why people pay attention to and use new media. Harold Lasswell's post-1945 model of the communications process maintained that the more personal the communication, the greater the effect. Therefore, personal communication is more effective than television, which (in turn) is more effective than film, radio, or print media. Klapper's (1960, pp. 8, 55, 92-97) subsequent work recognized the fact that previous exposure to issues was a significant intervening variable. He also described selective information processing and the conversion process. Those media seeking to promote change had a direct effect, were reinforced positively, or were neutralized by other mediating factors, which produced change in different directions.

Later, in the same decade, uses and gratification theory stressed the recipient of the messages and his/her selective exposure, which created cognitive dissonance or consonance in the communications process. In the 1970s, the "gatekeeping" and "agenda-setting" functions of the press were explored as was the "need for orientation" theory. The latter states that people must relate to their environments through issues; media are used to satisfy personal needs, thus influencing individual agenda setting (Freedman and Sears, 1965). Along the way, the role of personal interactions among opinion influencers or news elites and the two-step flow of communications also came into the literature.

The gatekeeping and agenda-setting functions of the media are most relevant to the subject of terrorist news. Knowledge and information, the media's tools, are used to ensure system maintenance through feedback and distribution control. In complex pluralistic and interdependent societies, the print and broadcast journalists serve as arbiters of conflict management. Journalists also perform watchdog or surveillance functions. These functions allow social stress or subsystem dysfunctions to be resolved or handled without resort to civil strife and resultant social chaos. News broadcasts and stories serve to keep the flow of information moving so that tension and ultimate release (resolution) follow the very crisis that the media and political spokespersons jointly created. The media provide discrete knowledge of an issue or event rather than in-depth knowledge about a controversy or public policy. Media often avoid the latter, since those dangerous topics may require delving into causes and proposed solutions, both of which may be extremely divisive. Instead, the media selectively combine sights, sounds, images, and symbols into a meta-reality. These not only depict reality, but actually create, recreate, replace, or displace it. This media function is well documented in postmodern semiotic, humanistic, and cultural studies of the news genre (Graber, 1980, pp. 117-154; Agee, et al, 1982, pp. 17-33, Robinson, 1984, pp. 199-221).

Of course, violent bombings, kidnappings, or robberies actually involve very few perpetrators and relatively few victims. Any small war or state military action, such as the Grenada invasion or "police action" in Libya (which some label "state terrorism"), are far more elaborate in both the number of killers and killed, as are the weekly totals of gun-related deaths or highway mayhem on American roads. So the relative scale of militant violence or the extent of public risk of physical injury is relatively small. In fact, the number of actual terrorist incidents was only 127 out of 258 reports in the *Los Angeles Times*, *Washington Post*, and *New York Times* in the 1980-1985 period; that is, an average of about 25 per year (Picard and Adams, March 1988, p. 1). In the United States, a person is more likely to die as a victim of an asthma attack than as a victim of a terrorist attack.

If we examine the statistics from a conflicting perspective, we see the number of international terrorist incidents reported in 1985 was 812 (a 36% increase over 1984), with 177 involving US targets. Domestically, there were only seven actual incidents that same year (with 23 thwarted attempts, according to FBI reports). Of course, certain highly visible incidents caught media and the public attention. Among these were the TWA 847, Achille Lauro, and Rome and Vienna airport assaults in which American nationals were also victimized (Picard and Adams, March 1988). Despite relatively small numbers, what we remember is the residue of psychological threats, diminution of national pride, and challenges to sacred morals, precious symbols, and hallowed myths. These have longer lasting and more qualitative significance to the citizenry and its leaders. This is why the most proficient terrorists seek to strike at the heart of the state and the core of the establishment; they aim to destroy those elements that represent the highest symbolic and media values: American tourists, flagship carriers, embassies, or military personnel.

As with studies of crime, mugging, alcoholism, and other social ills, statistics are used to buttress the rationality of this phenomenon, which, as a UMI publication and Yonah Alexander say, "affects every person in the global community and inspires fear in many" (UMI Research Collections Information Service, 1989). Ambassador at Large for Counter-Terrorism L. Paul Bremer's (March 1987, pp. 1-4) official US definition of terrorism allows his assertion that there were 600 such incidents in 1984; 780 in 1985; 800 in 1986; and 2000 so-called casualties in 1987. Other statistics from the RAND Corporation in 1987 claim that anti-US terrorism peaked in 1977 with 99 cases. In 194, there were 68 cases; in 1985, 27; and in 1986, only 11. In the latter year, the US share was only 3% of the 400 deaths attributable to international terrorism as a whole (Dobkin, November 1989, p. 17).

By defining terrorism, any administration can control and own the problem itself, particularly if the media repeat the unquestioned assertions and afford them legitimacy as larger-than-life social drama with a huge public audience. Although terrorism is more dramatic than everyday crime news, both serve a moral, socially solidifying, and ideological function. In addition to accepting administration labels, the media help to brand terrorism as a foreign, strange, and evil occurrence – an abnormality that has no social context and that is irrational by Western standards. As Said (1988, pp. 149-158) says, the "wall-to-wall nonsense about terrorism can inflict grave damage . . . because it consolidates the immense, unrestrained, pseudo-patriotic narcissism we are nourishing." This obsession with terrorism has not only led to irresponsible acts, but, as Secretary of State George Shultz said in 1985, has also bordered on considering a declaration of war against Libya. The deliberately concocted scenarios of mortal danger and threat to America's vital national interests are responsible for popular approval of warlike acts and repressive measures such as the air raid on Libya in 1986. The buildup of tension after the administration's erroneous attribution to Libya of responsibility for the Berlin disco bombing inevitably led to the bombing of Tripoli.

With the international state system no longer under the hegemonic control of either Western or Eastern powers, counterterrorism efforts are directed at restoring international principles of legitimacy and order. The popular panic engendered by media and administration rhetoric is used not only to justify a deadly answering force, but also to quash forever any hope of ascertaining if a legitimate basis for the terrorist grievance exists (Bruck, Winter 1989). The misuse of the terrorist threat also allows an administration based on "peace through strength" and a $3 trillion military buildup to rationalize the use of weaponry so that Americans can once again "stand tall" regardless of its effect on the longer range issues of world order and a lasting peace. As Der Derian says of the "national security culture" in the United States:

> Much of what we do know of terrorism displays a superficiality of reasoning and a corruption of language which effects truths about terrorism without any sense of how these truths are produced by and help to sustain official discourses of international relations (Der Derian, 1989, p. 234).

Obviously, there is more at stake here than normally meets the popular or journalistic eye (Palmerton, 1988; Dobkin, November 1989; Bruck, Winter 1989). Bruck's review of critical theory, ideological closure, and hegemonic analysis of the communications media (e.g., Todd Gitlin, 1980, pp. 25-26, 284) indicates that there may be hope for a revised journalistic perspective on terrorism reporting and coverage, as has happened in recent years with the peace movement. As he said:

> Against a depiction of the media as a relatively seamlessly reproducing apparatus consistently serving the entrenched powers, I want to argue that the media show discursive openings, inconsistencies, and contradictions. They can provide the basis for developing strategic politics by alternative groups and movements (Bruck, Winter 1989, p. 113).

Although his study is based on a Canadian daily newspaper's coverage of peace, disarmament and security issues, Bruck's discussion of media systems is equally applicable to the United States. Consequently, there is some room for optimism about breaking down the terrorist act/media response/government definition/popular panic nexus in such violent international dramatic events.

The interactions between mass media and violent terrorism are akin to host (media) and parasite (violent terrorism). This symbiotic relationship requires the media to use violence to sell magazines or newspapers and gain viewers and listeners. They seek to increase their readership and audience share to sell billions of dollars of advertising. This increases everyone's profitability, with the possible exception of the terrorists. In Eastern or Western state-controlled mass media societies (whose numbers in the West decrease daily), publicly owned media regularly give high visibility to terrorist violence. Why? Because the news canon requires them to report all major events to ensure their continued legitimacy and credibility as a truthful or free press. With numerous and increasing external sources of news via satellite and radio, any international news event spreads like wildfire through technological societies. This occurs even without benefit of normal media contexts despite the state's mechanisms for communications control. Even the Eastern socialist press covered terrorist events in order to maintain credibility as to benefit from invidious comparisons between the "wild West" and the "orderly East," where peace and quiet reign supreme.

This situation highlights the need to examine a series of interrelationships between the media and terrorism. Among others, two of the most interesting questions are:

- Do the media actually help or hinder terrorism despite their societal role as cheerleader in support of basic antiviolent norms? (This is the contagion or epidemic theory regarding the spread of the terrorist virus or infection.)
- Do media/publicity-starved terrorist groups not only recognize this media dependence on violence, but also structure their campaigns to insure maximum media coverage and involvement for their own purposes?

In the process of answering these two queries, both terrorism's and media's roles, techniques, and expectations will be explained and the media/terrorist interactive system will be described. A case study of the Italian Red Brigade's (Brigate Rosse or BR) 1978 kidnapping and murder of Aldo Moro is presented for illustrative purposes. Some conclusions and suggestions for changing the cycle of violence system are also offered for consideration in the context of future public/media policymaking.

Common Roles, Expectations, Techniques: Mass Media and Terrorism

A description of the unique and common roles of mass media and terrorism as international phenomena may help to show that these seemingly disparate transnational entities have certain mutually reinforcing qualities. Each is, therefore, the captive or the victim, the friend or the foe, of the other. However, role reversals are not unusual during the course of terrorist incidents.

International Terrorism Defined and Described

The terrorist is considered the "ultimate criminal." With the sudden demise of post-Gorbachev communism as the main enemy, terrorism has become "public enemy number one" in American public discourse (Said, 1988, p. 149). Both the media and the political establishment share responsibility for so framing and defining in domestic terms this mainly international problem. Therefore, it has high salience value in the public's mind. The power to name, label, and define terrorism is especially relevant to this discussion since terrorism is so distant and beyond the average person's experience. It is a case (as in much international discourse) where the media wield exceptional power over popular conceptions of reality. The media usually accept the official or institutionalized definitions of abstract, foreign, or new events. This is especially true when there is an established party line in the government regarding abstruse or unfamiliar events.

Although there was some difference in the Reagan administration's earlier definitions of terrorism, a clear party line emerged by 1984. In 1983, a US Army journal defined the international targets of terrorism as a case where

> The calculated use of violence or the threat of violence to attain goals political, religious, or ideological in nature . . . done through intimidation, coercion, and involving fear . . . it involves a criminal act that is often symbolic in nature and intended to influence an audience beyond the immediate victim (Dobkin, November 1989, p. 15).

The next year, a State Department definition called it "premeditated, politically motivated violence perpetrated against noncombatant targets by subnational groups or clandestine state agents (Dobkin, November 1989, p. 15). The US Ambassador at Large for Counter-Terrorism, L. Paul Bremer (March 1987, p. 1), added to the official definition in 1987, when he said, "Terrorism's most significant characteristic is that it despises and seeks to destroy the fundamentals of Western democracy – respect for individual life and the rule of law." That same year, John Whitehead, a deputy secretary of state, said that terrorism is the new enemy for it is no longer "the random, senseless act of a few crazed individuals" but is now "a new pattern of low-technology and an inexpensive warfare" and "a strategy and a tool of those who reject the norms and values of civilized people everywhere" (Dobkin, November 1989, p. 16). Yonah Alexander (an academic spokesman close to the Reagan and Bush administrations' vies) is directing a University of Michigan (UMI) international resource file on terrorism and has edited this journal for the last decade. The UMI view on modern terrorism is summed up in the following way:

> Modern-day terrorism is a challenge to every society. It is an issue which somehow affects every person in the global community and inspires fear in many. Through the increased use of victimization, psychological warfare and munitions technology, terrorists have ushered in a New Age Terrorism sometimes termed "Low Intensity Conflict" – a new form of warfare in which soldiers are indistinguishable from civilians. Yet, some say "one man's terrorist is another man's freedom-fighter." The terrorist may be viewed as a criminal by some and heroic by others. Politics, propaganda and patriotism cloud the issue, and the public remains confused or overwhelmed. Experts debate on the most effective means to eliminate the ever-present danger of terrorist incidents. It is a controversial subject – one not yet fully understood – and the questions and concerns surrounding the topic have fueled an enormous amount of documentation and scholarly research in the past twenty-five years (UMI, 1989, p. 2).

Whole nations can be held hostage. A small band of unified and dedicated, seemingly irrational, instantly important, and ultimately threatening men and women (usually young) may, supposedly, do violence to us all. Terrorists, though relatively impotent, recognize these fears. Consequently, they plan and control the calculated use of violence, mayhem, and death. Their aim is to provoke and inspire extreme fear and dread among individuals, groups, nations, and international agencies and institutions.

During the 1980s, we had the dubious advantage of more than 100 opperative definitions of terrorism. One expert on the subject, Martha Crenshaw (1987, pp. 4-8), defines terrorism as "a strategy any political actor can use." She also says that it requires few resources (i.e., it is cheap); it involves "violent coercion" in order "to intimidate an opponent"; and "it is intended to compel a change in an enemy's behavior by affecting his will, not to destroy the enemy physically" (Crenshaw, 1987). Terrorism also relies on suspense and "psychological reactions of shock, outrage, and sometimes, enthusiasm" (Crenshaw, 1987). Moreover, terrorism usually occurs in times of peace rather than war. Noncombatants are the usual objects; the targets or victims have symbolic value, being representatives of a class, nation, or a cause. Crenshaw concludes: "Terrorism is fundamentally a strategy of demoralization, directed against the entire population of a nation rather than its armed forces, as would be the case in traditional warfare" (Crenshaw, 1987).

In her writings, Crenshaw tries, as she says, to avoid a "normative judgment" about terrorism. However, Walter Laqueur (not known for the neutrality of his views on the subject) says that "there is no such thing as pure, unalloyed, unchanging terrorism, but there are many forms of terrorism. In the circumstances, a case may be made for broader and, of necessity, vaguer definitions" (Laqueur, 1987, p. 145). More typical of such definitions was that of the US Task Force on Disorders and Terrorism (1976), which defined terrorism as "violent criminal behavior designed primarily to generate fear in the community . . . for political purposes" (U.S. Department of Justice, 1976). Other definitions of terrorism describe individual hijackings of commercial transport vehicles or state terrorism, which involves training and deploying assassins and paramilitary guerrilla bands to invade another land. In terms of objectives, terrorists may be grouped into those seeking financial reward (criminals), those seeking personal glory and fame (crazies), and those using violence for political goals (crusaders) (Hacker, 1976).

Terrorist groups may also be categorized across the political spectrum as extremists of the right (e.g., neo-Fascist, KKK, racist); leftist (e.g., anarchist, Maoists); national liberation (e.g., IRA, PLO); or religious evangelists (e.g., Hanafi Muslims and Islamic Jihad). Terrorists themselves advertise their political goals, preferring to be called freedom fighters, revolutionaries, liberators, soldiers or nationalists. These defensive terms are meant to combat the pejorative abuse uniformly heaped upon them in most mass media. Occasionally, however, extremist or marginal newspapers (like certain government-controlled media) have used similar favorable terms to describe those militant bands with whose violent motives or politics they agree. Simply put, terrorism may be red, brown, or black; uniformed or dressed in ethnic regalia; or otherwise decked out to communicate and symbolize their "just" cause against a powerful and evil enemy, the state.

In more technologically primitive days, terrorists frequently demanded media interviews, press releases, printing of demands, statements, or photographs, and the like. More recently, however, terrorist (or quasi-terrorist) groups have produced videotaped reports on the condition of hostages, used hostages as spokespersons, spoken directly to television audiences, or even compiled a documentary record for publication of their exploits (as the Animal Liberation Front did in 1985 after a California laboratory break-in). Their increasing use of new video technology is evidence of the parallel development between terrorism and the media. As Laqueur says, "the media are the terrorists' best friends" (Laqueur, March 1976). He also maintains that "the terrorists' act by itself is nothing; publicity is all." So close is this connection that one Associated Press correspondent recently claimed that terrorists are so media-wise that they now play journalists "like a violin" (Livingstone, 1987, p. 220). Of course, the most severe critics of media's role in publicizing terrorist exploits would like to enroll media as a front-line soldier in fighting back or winning the war against terrorism, labeled a "hydra of carnage," in "low-intensity operations." Also of note is the use of this military jargon for a small war (Livingstone and Arnold, 1987; Ra'anan, et al., 1986).

Picard and Adams (March 1988) point out that both media and actual witnesses to acts of political violence use more neutral nominal language (such as shooting and attacker) to delineate events, whereas government officials use more highly charged, descriptive words (such as criminals, terrorists, and murderers). The latter are more judgmental, inflammatory, and sensationalistic. In these stories, the primary media characterizations were of their own making. Media seldom quoted primary sources. This occurred only 6% of the time in relevant *Los Angeles Times*, *New York Times*, and *Washington Post* stories from 1980 to 1985.

Complaining that US and Soviet journalists also have no real understanding of the other's conceptions of either freedom or of terrorism, Cooper further defines the problem in this way:

> The sum total of people categorized as terrorists do not fit a pat, unchanging stereotype. In-depth interviews with those depicted as terrorists in many countries do not reveal a uniform pattern of deranged, hostile, illiterate, macho, psychotic madmen. Although such people exist, much, if not all, of our monolithic image of terrorists is presented to us, not by people who call themselves terrorists, but by mass media (Cooper, July 1988, p. 5).

Since few, if any, of us have seen, spoken to, or met a terrorist (or are likely to), we are at some disadvantage. The same unfamiliarity applies when we appraise the worth of foreign news personalities such as Arafat and Qaddafi. Much the same ignorance also prevails among those strangers who label Americans as "state terrorists." Actually, we may each share the undesirable attributes we assign to one another: a low estimation of human life; lack of mutual respect; projection of power orientations; demonstrated rigidity; and espousal of a self-serving ideology.

Although the Nixon administration had its domestic enemies list, a high priority of the Reagan administration was the production of an international enemies list. Those so listed at various times included the USSR (branded the "focus of evil" or the "evil empire") or the so-called outlaw Qaddafi regime in

Libya whose leader is regularly called a madman. Increasingly, the public idiom leads the citizenry to automatically equate many of these enemies with terrorism so that the words enemy and terrorist have virtually become so synonymous and interchangeable that the resultant need to declare war on international terrorism becomes self-evident. In 1989, much the same sequence of events led to a renewed war on drugs when "narcoterrorists" in Colombia were declared US public enemies, fully deserving the complete attention of the president, his "drug czar," William Bennett, the Department of State, and the US military, if need be.

In the drug war, all alternatives are considered save legalization and public control of drugs – considered an immoral choice. Alcohol regulation had a similar history in that it has been banned and legalized, taxed and allowed duty free, plus used medicinally and declared the nation's most dangerous drug. In popular and official perception, alcohol abuse has variously been deemed immoral, showing a lack of willpower, illegal, a disease, and now (by the Veterans Administration and the federal courts) a self-inflicted, preventable illness, which does not deserve veteran's health benefits. These various public and social definitions of disease (as with AIDS) and definitions of and responses to terrorism are critical in the identification and solution of a public problem.

Noam Chomsky's radical critique of "the culture of terrorism" assumes American responsibility for what it gets back internationally because of what he calls "the fifth freedom" that is, America's "freedom to rob, to exploit, and to dominate, to undertake any course of action to ensure that existing privilege is protected and advanced" (Chomsky, 1986 and 1988). Chomsky documents America's role in Latin-American, African, and Asian repression and provides evidence of US state terrorism and clandestine terrorism activities throughout the world now and in the recent past. He also assails the Reagan administration's conservative "right turn" politics and decries that administration's establishment of thought-control programs and agencies, such as Operation Truth and the Office of Public Diplomacy. These activities are "wholesale terrorism" in Chomsky's vernacular, whereas what passes for terrorism on the evening news is merely "retail terrorism" by individuals and groups. In sum, Chomsky's view of the media-supported official terrorist line is summed up in his quotation from Henry David Thoreau, who wrote in his Journal over a century ago:

> There is no need of a law to check the license of the press. It is law enough, and more than enough, to itself. Virtually, the community have come together and agreed what things shall be uttered, have agreed on a platform and to excommunicate him who departs from it, and not one in a thousand dares utter anything else (Chomsky, 1986, p. 37).

Worse yet is Chomsky's fear that the people will not lack courage to express themselves, but rather that they will not have the capacity to think since they are products of the "engineers of democratic consent."

America's violent films, political assassinations, racial conflicts, violent strikes, use and threat of military force and massive retaliation, drug wars among urban guerrillas, and hundreds of thousands of annual highway injuries and deaths seem to validate the description of America as a violent society. By comparison, Arafat, the George Washington/Charles DeGaulle of the PLO, claims to be just a freedom fighter, resisting the appellation state terrorist of the Israelis and their American allies. But all of this PLO "terrorism," American "Ramboism," Qaddafi "irrationality," and like creations are products of the mass media, bearing only some, if little, resemblance to reality.

Terrorist groups are frequently foreign or exotic, unknown or inexplicable, or religious based; they also produce disinformation and thrive on military secrecy, group bonds, or a blood pact. When mass media approach such groups, they are bound to fail in their comprehension, story telling, or reporting since their perceptions are seldom realistic, often adversarial, and always distorted. They are also at times self-serving, biased, or ethnocentric, and they are frequently rigid, ideological, purposeful, and negative. While terrorism is at best unpleasant, it deserves the benefit of a realistic treatment. By denying it such treatment, we not only are dishonest to ourselves, but we also infuriate and heighten the animosity of these supposed adversaries both today and tomorrow (Cooper, July 1988, p. 5).

Media Defined and Described

Large, syndicated, multinational corporations and governments have dominant control over newspapers and television throughout the world. Ownership and control are increasingly centralized. The major purpose of the media is not, as the *New York Times* masthead claims, to publish "all the news that's fit to print," but rather just that news it takes to achieve high readership (or ratings in the case of radio and television). Consequently, a newspaper today (though less so in Europe) is merely a bundle of advertisements wrapped in a tissue of news, features, and photographs. Since the corporate spirit runs high in Western capitalist economies, even Andy Warhol said, "Good business is good art." So the twin arts of journalism and terrorism have negotiated a mutually beneficial contract: One is rewarded with dollars and the other with instant fame and publicity.

As on television (the pictorial headline news), what sells the particular communications medium is the bizarre, the investigative report, the exposé, the heinous crime, the sexy, or the spectacular. The average viewer or reader spends very little time using the educational or informational components of the mass media. For example, readers spend an average of 16 minutes with a US newspaper, concentrating mainly on sports, features, advertising, and "soft" news. By contrast, opinion leaders spend more time with a variety of media and are better informed. However, the average viewer prefers entertainment to education and the "cool" television to the "hot" printed message. ABC's Sander Vanocur discounts the "enlightenment or education business" functions of mass media as well as "the people's right-to-know" argument for a free press. He says that media:

> . . . are in a business, the business of information. Whatever anyone else may claim for us, that is what we are supposed to do – pass on information, as best we can, as quickly as we can (Ra'anan, et al., 1986, p. 259).

In maintaining this position, Vanocur must necessarily forget the longstanding US custom and tradition (codified in the Federal Communications Act of 1934), which links an informed and educated public to the existence of a free government. Without this social objective, there is no need for the First Amendment's guarantee of a free and unfettered press. He must also necessarily ignore the Federal Communications Act, FCC regulations, and federal law, which have regulated radio, cable, and television broadcasts in the public interest for the last 50 years. For most of this time, laws and regulations required documentary evidence of public-service broadcasting for approval of a station's license renewal application. Of course, these public-service standards were minimal, shabby, and perfunctorily enforced.

A free and responsible press in the US precludes prior restraint, but public responsibility under law also makes the media subject to prosecution under laws governing libel and slander. By 1989, television's equal time doctrine (under congressional mandate) alone survived the onslaught of the Reagan "deregulation revolution." This policy abolished restrictions, limits, or requirements for fairness, children's news, and public affairs programming, programming logs, and advertising time. That was a decided swing away from previous FCC rules, dating from the 1960s. However, the FCC pendulum may still swing the other way. Congress may also involve itself more directly in legislative oversight of communications. The free market may yet abuse the public interest too severely by adhering to the communications-as-business philosophy, the result of a privatization obsession led from the Reagan and Bush White Houses.

Instead of defining the media as information or news agencies, perhaps it is useful and more accurate to accept some of Vanocur's argument. We may agree that the media (particularly radio and television) are mainly in the profitable entertainment business – sexual and violent entertainment at that. Mass media operate on providing minimum context, supplying broad and quick coverage, and giving the reader or viewer what he or she wants. At best, the context for news is the standard journalistic litany of answering the who, what, when, where, how, and occasionally, why questions learned in Journalism 101 classes. Seldom do the media provide their readers or viewers with the background, context, or parallel information needed to follow a story over time or to understand a topic in depth. It is a small wonder that readers and views cannot internalize, assimilate, and conceptualize a story into their highly valuative, cognitive maps and perceptual frames of reference. The texts of news stories and television scripts are often more "writerly" than "readerly." In the absence of regular coverage, with context, for an important continuing story or recurrent social theme (such as work hazards, defense, or violence toward others), the reader cannot realistically understand the news. When Bhopal, defense corruption, or the latest terrorist story catapult on the screen or front page week after week, they remain unique, inexplicable, strange, and forever inassimilable and meaningless.

Certain basic requirements are necessary for the news genre's existence. That is, news must be timely (critical, crisis, recent); unique (new, fresh); entertaining (drama, pathos); adventurous (dangerous, a horse race, unfolding, risky, a life-or-death battle); and it must relate to the reality of the viewer (human identification, everyday life, innocent victims) (Alexander and Finger, 1977). To this list can be added two other news criteria: authenticity (validity) and credibility (trust), features which both news and terrorist acts share in kind. The predominant journalistic values require news to be about unexpected, sensational, and conflictual events. Violent groups are more than willing to supply an ample measure of each ingredient required to make their story newsworthy.

As a case in point of media crisis coverage of violent domestic disturbances, Graber (1989, p. 306) describes the clash over "self-preservation" issues between the media and government. The media's "responsibility to serve public needs" is in direct conflict with the government's desire "to control, direct, and even manipulate the flow of news for public purposes." Graber finds that crisis coverage typically runs through three stages. First, when background information on the crisis is announced, basic details fo who, what, when, where and how are revealed and a kind of ordered panic or chaos prevails while news (frequently distorted and inaccurate) is spread throughout a "wired" society. At this stage, media messages also tend to be calming and convey the message: "Don't worry. Everything's okay." Stage two finds the media trying to provide context for the crisis and to supply rational and coherent explanations for the event. The final interpretive stage takes a coping posture and a longer range view. Its goals are tension relief, morale building, panic prevention, and reinforcing the viewpoint of "everything's under control" in this unique situation.

Throughout these stages, the media depend on government sources for their information and practice self-censorship to allay fears and to prevent panic. The picture portrayed of competent government officials ("doing something") is reassuring and calming to the media's viewer, listeners, or readers. As a crisis matures, however, the media may develop a feeding frenzy in their lust for news. For example, crisis coverage of the Detroit riots in 1967, the Three Mile Island disaster in 1979, the Tylenol poisonings in 1982, the TWA hijacking in 1985, and the stock market crash in 1987 all produced unexpected and unanticipated results.

Reportage on the Detroit riots produced a multiplier effect by encouraging new rioters; similarly, a rash of "copycat" crimes followed the 1982 cyanide deaths. The stock market panic in 1987 was also inflamed when media pointed out its parallel with 1929. The deployment of an antiterrorist strike force against the TWA hijackers was curtailed after widespread media reports eliminated the vital element of surprise (Graber, 1989, pp. 316-317).

Despite preexistent and widespread media plans for crisis coverage of natural disasters and civil disorders, the complacency engendered from years of rosy reports on nuclear power plant safety took its toll in 1979. Previous problems at Three Mile Island had been so well hidden, minimized, or ignored that a 3-day delay resulted before a central communications center was established there. This center essentially performed a centralized media censorship and control function for official and corporate press releases. It kept the lid on the crisis through "balanced" new releases. However, other unedited reports from the scene were contradictory, exaggerated, speculative, and frightening to area residents (Graber, 1989, pp. 312, 314, 318).

Crisis coverage planning, although widespread, is probably more successful in planning a scenario for covering the event post hoc than it is in either preventing or predicting the crisis. Media personnel regularly assume that widespread panic and contagion will result if the extent of rioting or civil disorder is fully and accurately reported. While relevant social science data do not support this view, media decisionmakers believe violence will beget violence. Therefore, they act accordingly. For example, in the 1967 Winston-Salem riots, the *Winston-Salem Journal* had a roughly prearranged game plan for reporting on racial violence and cooperation with the police and local officials in order to calm racial tensions and to curb violence (Paletz and Entman, 1981, pp. 114-117). The Journal's reporting guidelines were designed to limit the news, convey tranquility, blame "thugs" and "hoodlums" for the riots, reduce exaggeration, avoid basic grievances, ignore rumors, and underplay the extent of violence. The guiding maxim was, "when in doubt, leave out." As the story developed over four days, there were 200 arrests, 100 injuries, extensive property damage, but no deaths. On the first night of rioting, a news blackout was imposed. Thereafter, the story was reported almost exclusively from the viewpoint of the police and local officials, and concentrated on portrayals of blacks who supported the local elite's game plan.

The *Journal's* white establishment, reporters, and editors covered events as they would any important crime story where violence threatened legitimate authority. No coverage of minority grievances, underlying social problems, or statements from the black leadership or citizenry was provided to readers. In this way, not only were black demands (e.g., that police brutality against one of their number be investigated and handled) crushed but also:

> The coverage probably reduced the political power of already inefficacious poor people. Simultaneously, it may have enhanced the prestige of the police department – at least among whites (Paletz and Entman, 1981 p. 117).

Graber's viewpoint on the Winston-Salem case is that the official/police/National Guard/media concurrence could be credited with reducing the level of violence and its harmful effects:

> In the short run this helped keep the situation under control, but the long-run effects of carefully limited coverage are more troubling. In terrorist incidents or prison riots, failure to air the grievances of terrorists and prison inmates deprives them of a public forum for voicing their grievances. Their bottled up anger may lead to more violent explosions. Needed reforms may be aborted (Graber, 1989, p. 322).

Graber also discusses the contrary positions of those who would prefer to allow the violent confrontation or reaction and complete media coverage to run their course versus those who would mute, censor, and black out overly violent incidents. The former claim that shocking the public conscience is a likely outcome of extensive and accurate reporting, whereas the latter maintain that more restrained coverage will reduce conflict and hatred while allowing reasoned reform after the fact. Although the media and public leadership have usually chosen the news suppression option, Graber observes:

> The true test of genuine freedom does not come in times of calm. It comes in times of crisis when the costs of freedom may be dear, tempting government and media alike to impose silence. If a free press is a paramount value, the die must be cast in favor of unrestrained crisis coverage, moderated only by the sense of responsibility of individual journalists (Graber, 1989, p. 322).

Media and Terrorism: Symbiotic Relationships

> Terrorism is different, dramatic, and potentially violent. It frequently develops over a period of time, occurs in exotic locations, offers a clear confrontation, involves bizarre characters, and is politically noteworthy. Finally, it is of concern to the public (Hoge, 1982, p. 91).

Since terrorism so clearly fills the bill as a major news event, media fiercely compete for coverage, scoops, and live footage or photographs that can be labeled "exclusives." This drive to win, as Jody Powell says, is a direct product of the competition "for ratings and circulation between newspapers and networks and for personal advancement within a given news organization" (Livingstone, 1987, p. 219). Media coverage of the TWA flight 847 hijacking in June 1985 effectively destroyed certain flimsy, self-imposed media guidelines established for such coverage. Some major print and broadcast agencies developed these standards for coverage as a result of the 1985 Hanafi Muslim's siege staged in the nation's capital. Back then, a media orgy saturated the television screens with live stories and terrorist interviews from the scene. Reporters and radio hosts tied up telephone lines, and the lives of undetected building occupants were endangered they nearly missed an opportunity to escape.

Even while recognizing the importance of their roles as virtual abettors of such violence and terrorist's objectives, many reporters later opposed all guidelines for covering terrorism. Their position was anticensorship, pro-free speech and press, anti-prior restraint, and advocacy of a general "right to know." During the TWA hijacking, the media actually broadcast events live. They interacted with the terrorists, experts, victims and their relatives, and the pilot, thus becoming an integral part in expanding the problem. Perhaps it was the earlier Iran hostage debacle which set the standard. The latter was so exhaustively and regularly covered (with, for example, a daily countdown of the number of days of hostage captivity) that in a 1981 *Washington Journalism Review* article, David Altheide concluded that "more media attention was given to the hostages in Iran than any single event in history, including the Vietnam War" (Livingstone, 1987, p. 223).

The history of media coverage of terrorism has also provided the validity of Daniel Schorr's observation that "many people have found that the royal road to identity is to do something violent" (Anzovin, 1986, p. 101). For example, the Palestinian terrorists who attacked the Israeli Olympic team in Munich in 1972 instantly found themselves in the living rooms of over 800 million people. By creating a climate of fear in an attack on (or even killing of) unknown victims, the relatively and comparatively powerless terrorists hope to compel far more powerful state or media officials to comply with their wishes. Since terrorists are so much weaker than the establishment they are challenging, they must use guerilla hit-and-run tactics to create the psychological state of mind needed to ensure public and official compliance with, or acceptance of, certain aggressive goals.

The motor of the BR: "Strike one to educate one hundred" is worth noting here as is its similarity to Lenin's revolutionary slogan: "Kill one, frighten a hundred." After the BR struck violently, the media ended up educating the public, while the BR served as a principal accomplice in the media war which followed. Indeed, the BR had earlier targeted the media and prominent journalists as potential victims in its war against the multinationals and the "imperialist state." By 1977, journalists, editors, and members of the Italian press had been branded "servants of the imperialist apparatus of repression." After several journalists were brutally "kneecapped" or shot dead in quick succession, the popular and press reaction to these violent incidents was equivalent to that following an invasion from outer space.

The BR later switched its attention to "armed propaganda" for political recognition and attacks "at the heart of the state" to prove to all that revolution was "within . . . reach." Media were transformed from objects of attack to useful instruments of war. The BR deliberately focused in attacks on "the heart of the state" and enlisted the media as its publicists in the kidnapping of Christian Democrat Party President Aldo Moro in 1978. (Moro previously had been prime minister and foreign minister of Italy for six year.) After Moro's assassination (in which the government actually exploited the media, as did the terrorists and everyone involved, save Moro himself), the BR kidnapping of a prominent judge (Giovanni D'Urso) in 1980 also allowed them to use media for their purposes before releasing their prisoner. A year later, however, the BR shot a hostage after their demand for media time was rejected. But the kneecappings of journalists and media brutality of the 1970s were not reinstituted in the 1980s. Instead, the BR created its own media research and coordination group for public relations, which they called their "psychological front."

As Daniel Schorr observes, television has a "love affair with drama and a love affair with violence" (Anzovin, 1986, p. 101). Ted Koppel, ABC's Nightline host, is of a like mind:

> Without television, terrorism becomes rather like the philosopher's hypothetical tree falling in the forest: no one hears it fall and therefore it has no reason for being. And television, without terrorism, while not deprived of all interesting things in the world, is nonetheless deprived of one of the most interesting (Anzovin, 1986, p. 97).

Mass media's coverage of the news is mainly focused on politicians, corporate leaders, criminals, athletes, and other public and entertainment figures who have "star quality." Terrorist leaders also recognize the importance of mass media just as New Left advocate Jerry Rubin did. He rebuked his revolutionary brothers for being "too puritanical" in mass media use, perhaps because "Karl Marx never watched television." "You can't be a revolutionary today without a television set," he wrote, "It's as important as a gun" (Rubin, 1970, p. 108).

And use the media they do. Terrorists use dozens of sophisticated media techniques, such as direct public communication of their grievances, demands, and requirements for compliance. They also seek to form public opinion by disinformation, "confessions" from hostages, criticisms of the government, direct broadcasts over open network channels, and appeals for help. These groups often directly attack the media by using violence against journalists or by using journalists as negotiators. They also bomb or occupy broadcast facilities. Through the media, they can also advertise their cause, incurring favorable attention through releasing hostages, thus seeking Robin Hood status. Such groups also use the media as watchdogs against police perfidy to learn about hostage identities, possible police reprisals, and current public opinion; to communicate with allies; and to identify targets or enemies to be dealt with in the future (Schmid and de Graaf, 1982, pp. 53-54).

Even a spokesman for the PLO recognized the importance of media in its quest for United Nations observer status and legitimacy saying: "the first hijackings aroused the consciousness of the world and awakened the media and world opinion much more – and more efficiently – than 20 years of pleading at the United Nations" (Hickey, 1976, p. 10). As Paul Lazarsfeld and Robert K. Merton recognized in 1948, the media also provide a "status-conferral" function (i.e., by singling out terrorism for the mass audience, these behaviors and opinions are seen as significant enough to deserve public notice) for terrorists (Lazarsfeld and Merton, 1971, pp. 554-578). Moreover, media coverage not only provides free publicity for the terrorists, but also may establish them as role models for others.

There also may be a spiraling cycle of violence (i.e., and interactive effect between the quantity of media coverage and the scale of terrorist violence). However, which factor (media or violent incident) causes this or what else causes both is often unclear. Media coverage affects the public and combative groups alike. Regardless of their motives, as terrorists upscale their violence, they are reinforced and rewarded with more media coverage. In turn, as media coverage increases, terrorists are encouraged to top their last execution, threat, or demand (Weimann, 1983; Tan, 1987, p. 151). This view of terrorism as an epidemic that news media spread (though believed by the public, press, and some experts) is not supported in the social science literature as other than a contributing cause. Some of the associated allegations which remain unsubstantiated include beliefs that new groups are formed, new actions are incited, public support is generated, the level of violence is escalated, and media control is forfeited to the terrorists.

There is little proof that the press is so powerful as either potential censors or terrorist groups may imagine. Nevertheless, in 1985, Prime Minister Margaret Thatcher called for press controls which would deny terrorists and hijackers of the "oxygen of publicity" needed to fuel the resultant flames of their violence. Edwin Diamond of New York University's News Study Group claimed in a *TV Guide* article that once the television put a human face on the TWA flight 847 passengers and crew and charged the incident with "everyday emotions," then "all military options were dead" (*TV Guide*, July 31, 1976). CBS's Lesley Stahl said of the press, "We are an instrument for the hostages. We force the administration to put their lives above policy" (Davies, October 1985, p. 4). Consequently, these events become "institutionalized crises" which crowd out all other news (Picard, July 1988, p. 1). And Michael J. Davies, former editor and publisher of the *Hartford Courant*, typified news personnel's attitudes when he said:

> Publicity is the lifeblood of terrorism. Without it, these abominable acts against the innocent would wither quickly away. Yet few responsible critics would suggest that the media enter into a conspiracy of silence that would ignore all acts of international terrorism (Davies, October 1985, p. 5).

By and large, the media-as-contagion theory depends on transferring the findings of televised violence and aggression to the terrorism arena. However, widespread public perceptions also support this relationship. The popularity of this view among law enforcement officials has helped gain support from some experts (such as M. C. Bassiouni, who said that, except for the "ideologically motivated," there is a certain "intuitive reasonableness" to the contagion theory. Schmid and de Graaf (1988, p. 2), two Dutch experts, also claimed that media reports helped to "reduce inhibitions" and offered "models," "know-how," and motivations to potential terrorists.

In response, others (such as Brian Jenkins of the RAND Corporation) reply that "the news media are responsible for terrorism to about the same extent that commercial aviation is responsible for the airline hijackings" (i.e., the media are just "another vulnerability" in a highly vulnerable technological and free society) (Schmid and de Graaf, 1988, p. 31). Other related studies have shed some light on this phenomenon. For example, hierarchy was used in one study by Midlarsky, Crenshaw, and Yoshida (June 1980) as a theory to explain the spread of terrorism "from the least powerful" and "from the weak states to the strong" (i.e., from Latin America to Western Europe). European terrorist groups borrow ideology, rhetoric, and methods from the Third World, as well as techniques of bombing, which transfer quite easily. Through intergroup cooperation, they move across boundaries to new locations that provide a suitable site for the proposed act. The careful planning and specialized technical knowledge that some groups display could not have been learned from television or in newspapers. Diffusion of these ideas is more likely based on interpersonal channels of communications. The media's role in furthering the awareness aspect of the process (if not in the evaluation, acceptance, and adaptation parts of the same process) may reinforce, if not cause, such diffusion. At any rate, diffusion theory probably offers a better line of research than does the imitative effect of "copycat" violent acts, scenes, and situations.

Since media engage in sensationalism, can interfere with law enforcement, may endanger lives and help spread irrational fears, they have become closely associated with terrorism, though they still have not become its primary cause. Moreover, if terrorism really seeks the media publicity it gets through violence, why should potential terrorists not receive appropriate media coverage for their grievances before they resort to violence? Not only can the media adopt a responsible, reasoned, and measured approach to terrorism, once begun, but they can also regularly provide ample outlets for expressions of relevant public and group concerns, thereby addressing or reducing grievances, while evaluating current controversial public policies. Such a modified response to terrorism would actually require more, although very different, coverage of terrorist violence. This could be done without glamorizing the perpetrators. New media formats could provide useful and valid information, consider consequences of past or hypothetical acts, improve the public's capacity to deal with large crises, aim to reduce attendant public fears, and increase the public's understanding. These new formats could provide continual context while they perhaps help to reduce the general level of violence in the society (US Department of Justice, 1976, p. 65; Picard, July 1988, pp. 4-6).

As the terrorist sideshow unfolds, the public is usually mesmerized. Viewers see the black-and-white spectacle of heroes and villains fighting it out, not on the set of Miami Vice, but in a real scene with real guns, bullets, bombs, hostages, and murders. They are eyewitnesses to a human morality play, with its real winners and losers. In a way, this portrayal even becomes the "theater of the obscene" in that the television screen (reinforced in radio, newspaper, and magazine features) displays a huge international "snuff film," rivaling execution scenes from World War II and Vietnam documentary footage. These real-life scenarios are left to the viewer to interpret. The media seldom report the social, economic, or political objectives or rationales for these unpaid terrorist "actors" who play starring roles even though they are not members of Actors' Equity (Paletz, Ayanian, and Fozzard, 1982, p. 166).

Indeed, the media's message, though antiviolent, may have other appeals to different audiences. Media effects reveal that the public may use their sense of a "just world" for evaluative purposes. Here, even the victims may be held responsible for their own suffering, the terrorists may be absolved of guilt, or the terrorist grievance, redress, or cause against the government may be supported. On this point, Schmid and de Graaf conclude:

> Through the way the media present terroristic news, through selection of some facts out of the multitude of potentially relevant facts, through the associations they lay between the terroristic act and the social context, the media can have a profound influence that can create public hysteria, witchhunts, fatalism, and all sorts of other reactions that serve certain political interests – and not only those of the terrorists (Schmid and de Graaf, 1982, p. 98).

Dobkin (1989 and November 1989) recently described the terrorism and media connection as one in which the American government has not only manufactured the problem and dominated both its definition and public importance, and, therefore, its "public ownership" and "responsibility" for the problem, but has also turned the issue into "an instrument of US foreign policy." In contrast to traditional research, which stresses the interdependence of terrorism and media coverage ("media determinism"), Dobkin emphasizes the power inherent in the national security state not only to engineer popular consent, but also to enlist public support for state-sponsored, official repression. Creating a so-called public crisis cuts off nonmilitary responses. The increasing level of panic and cycle of violence challenge international order. It requires the government to act in a lethal way while either muzzling the media or so dominating the terms of discourse that alternatives to military action (e.g., redress of any legitimate grievances) cannot easily be considered (Dobkin, November 1989, pp. 1, 21).

Similarly, America's 40-year dependence on deterrence theory and mutual assured destruction (MAD) also has its impact on terrorism, as does classic just war theory's emphasis on proportionality in meeting an armed attack. Since the public and its leaders believe that deterrence has kept the peace, we are at a loss to explain why a group of terrorist Lilliputians can so effectively cripple the powerful American Gulliver. "Why does deterrence not work?" we ask, never recognizing that this idea is actually irrelevant to the type of low-intensity, civil-war, or guerilla conflict to which terrorism is similar.

The Brigate Rosse and the Moro Case

Two interesting pieces of research apply to the question of what terrorists get from the media. The first from Italy is a January 10, 1982 opinion poll published in *L'Espresso*. It indicated that whereas 31% of the Italian public believed that the BR were "dangerous murderers" (negative), over 30% believed that the BR "aims at achieving a just goal by using the wrong means" (positive), and 10% believed that they led the "fight for a better society" (mixed, positive). Certainly, the media's coverage of terrorism was not expected to produce such results. The violent nature of Italian society, a preference for spectacle politics, longstanding divisive and fractious party activity, higher frequency of regime change, and cops-and-robbers of "Keystone Kops" approaches to resolving domestic violence may be contributing factors to this totally unexpected, unintended, and often hidden aspect of the problem (Payerhin, 1988, p. 14).

Why this happens may in part be explained through an interesting, but small-scale, American research project Gabriel Weimann queried students about their reactions to reading stories about two obscure terrorist groups in the context of total group attitudes and opinions about terrorism. Those reading about these South Moluccan and Croatian groups remained generally negative toward terrorism. However, after exposure to these news articles, between 43% and 51% of the exposed group labeled the problem "important," in need of greater public knowledge, and a subject of interest to them. The control group's responses to similar questions was significantly lower (16%, 14%, and 33%, respectively). In other words, there may be an unintended media enhancement of terrorist activity, which is either promoted and/or obscured through media treatment of "terrorism as a spectacle" (Weimann, 1983, p. 43).

What do the newspapers and television get out of this coverage of political extremism? And what does the political regime have to gain from this process? The government clearly dominates most news sources and official reports during most terrorist crises. Moreover, since many European countries (FRG, UK, France, etc.) have terrorist/media guidelines, public officials can limit media excesses that "glorify" terrorists. Since the media take the law-and-order, social control theme to heart during such a crisis, the government gets its favorite tune played in the terrorist saga. During such episodes, the competence of the regime is displayed since the officials orchestrating the state response look powerful, competent, in control, popular, and act in the public interest. Since the government actually wins nearly all these "battles" in the long run (if not today, then tomorrow), these terrorist "Davids" have little chance against the state "Goliaths."

Palmerton has examined CBS news coverage during the first days of the 1979 Iranian hostage crisis. Although of limited scope, her study concludes that news coverage reinforced the terrorist strategy by focusing the cause (or blame) for the crisis on US governmental institutions and by suggesting that military action was necessary to reestablish institutional control. Furthermore, she finds that the "rhetorical impact of terrorism" is mainly a function of others' responses (particularly the media) to terrorist activity. A peincipal problem of regions under terrorist attack is how to maintain both control and one's status as a victim of terrorism. Indeed, as she says, "the primary threat to governmental institutions is not the lives lost in terrorist acts, but the questioning of governmental institutions" (Palmerton, 1988, p. 105). Lack of realistic and proportional perspective about the terrorist danger or threat in media reports on terrorism helps to construct "a variety of meanings about terrorist events" and "those meanings may well serve the terrorist cause" (Palmerton, 1988, p. 117).

As for the mass media's gains from terrorism, besides the "hot" news akin to a continuing soap opera/criminal film, what else does the publisher or broadcaster gain? Because the crime beat and reports of violence are part of the daily diet of all media, it is no surprise that terrorism, hijacking, armed siege, political violence, assassinations, and like crimes against the state and people are given widespread publicity. In the case of terrorism, media have a virtual gold mine of news which never dries up or pans out – it has universal appeal and a built-in demand for more coverage up to and beyond the saturation point.

An interesting case in point is the Italian media's treatment, coverage, and involvement with the state, the hostage, and the BR during the kidnapping and murder of Aldo Moro and five of his bodyguards in 1978. Since the Moro crisis lasted nearly two months during the spring of 1978, the roles of all prominent forces and actors in this bloody drama had a chance to be played out with the predictability of an ancient Roman coliseum scene. The saga was complete with "Christians" (Moro and his martyred bodyguards), BR "lions," state "Caesars," media "tribunes," and the anxious Italian public, ever eager for more bread, circuses, and carnivals. Wagner-Pacifica (1987) has described the "Moro morality play" as a form of "social drama."

Ignoring for the moment the complex state, corporate, and party links of the Italian press and broadcast media, Italians' media usage differs appreciably from that of northern European and other Western European publics. For example, regular newspaper purchases are among the lowest in Europe, particularly in the southern parts of the country. The media in Italy are also strong on debate, rhetoric, conflict, journalistic competition, and sordid exhibitions, particularly reports on widespread crime and violence. There is a minimum level of confirmed sources, careful investigation, analysis of causes, background context, and socially productive reporting. One fact is clear, however: the public's attention to the media skyrocketed once the Moro case hit the streets and airwaves. For example, all of the five principal newspapers increased sales dramatically (between 56% and 89%) after the Moro kidnapping (Lumley and Schlesinger, 1982, pl. 603).

In addition to this obvious effect, the symbiotic relationship between the print and nonprint media on the one hand and militant groups on the other warrants further analysis. With respect to the Moro case, what is the evidence that the establishment-oriented Italian press unwittingly contributed to the BR's success? To what extent was the BR media-wise in handling the Italian communications media in order to present their cause in a favorable light, thus pressuring governmental decision makers?

In the 1970s, the BR conceived of the press as an "instrument of war," discounting media and party claims that they and other "red terrorists" were neo-Fascist creations. They threatened: "To the psychological war we shall respond with psychological war and retaliation." Spokesmen for the BR also said their main aims in the Moro kidnapping were "prisoner exchange" and political recognition through the use of "armed propaganda." Their objective was to prove that the day of proletarian deliverance was near at hand. To accomplish these aims, the BR had to follow the news canons previously described (i.e., conflict, timeliness, symbolism, recognition, maximum effect, escalation, and drama). The BR strategy was clearly dramatic in its initial use of violence and death and symbolic in its choice of a famous statesman and party leader, Aldo Moro. They attacked the state itself since Moro, the former prime minister, was expected to be the new president of Italy before year's end. They maximized the goal of social and political recognition since, under Moro's leadership, a historic and unifying compromise between the Christian Democratic, Socialist, and Communist parties seemed at hand. Timeliness was also achieved since this "attack at the heart of the state" was in conflict with the new national solidarity cabinet which was t be announced on the very day of the kidnapping. They also drastically challenged the entire democratic system's ability to handle its 38th postwar governmental crisis, thus achieving maximum effect (Caserta, 1978, p. 101; Rosso, 1976, p. 282; Bocca, 1985, pp. 206, 219; Payerhin, 1988, p. 61).

The BR was well known to the Italian media and readily recognized by the public. They fulfilled the black/white or good/bad values. Their past, present, and future credibility (regarding the use of violence as a political instrument) was well established and maintained as the crisis escalated with additional shootings and murders. The BR regularly supplied enough news so that the Moro case remained an international media event for nearly two months. Through their selection of a prime target (Moro) in a prominent place (Rome), with a well-planned, bloody, and efficient initial event (kidnap and murder), the BR effectively achieved maximum effect and set the news agenda in Italy for 55 days. Even in their choice of site, the BR wanted to avoid civilian casualties so that, as a spokesperson said, "we absolutely did not want the action to present any terrorist characteristics; we wanted to be clear that it was a military action directed against the state and its high representative" (Bocca, 1985, p. 208; Payerhin, 1988, p. 67). Even the choice of killing on the spot or abducting Moro had its intended media impact, since a political martyr was worth far less press coverage than a captive hero pleading for his life.

The technique of regularly issuing communiques and letters from Moro to the press through intermediaries kept the event on the public agenda every day. Secrecy about the captive's location also added to the mystery, as did the media being called to retrieve secret documents hidden in seven major Italian cities. Most of the releases were announced simultaneously the day before prime news days. Since the messages were long, the papers had no choice but to print only "hot" news, leaving analysis until later. This split-second timing and planned releases of Moro's messages also served to heighten conflict and to break the society wide open. This escalation increased even more when Moro realized that the party and the press intended not to deal with the BR. This ensured both his eventual death and subsequent martyrdom. His trial and conviction in a BR kangaroo court, photographs holding a newspaper to prove his vitality, and even the symbolic placement of his dead body in the center of Rome, on a street linking the two major party headquarters, all had mediagenic and symbolic meaning to the BR and the public. All of these events were carefully planned and implemented to achieve maximum effect on the media, public, and government.

Throughout the Moro crisis, the BR continued to gain standing and legitimacy through the media from a variety of quarters, including the Vatican and the United Nations. Pope Paul VI personally begged the BR to release Moro. Kurt Waldheim, then United Nations secretary general, referred to the BR "cause," a term which infuriated the Italian government and required Waldheim to issue an apology for a "translation error" (Sciascia, 1978, p. 144; Payerhin, 1988, p. 75). The BR held the entire Italian Republic hostage through its media campaign and psychological warfare. During this debacle, they influenced public opinion through their managed news releases, interactions with the media, and other techniques and strategies which gained them adherents, followers, and supporters, while neutralizing much of their opposition. They accomplished these feats with the mass media's and the state's unwilling assistance.

For its part, Italian media coverage of the Moro tragedy followed its familiar formats (i.e., publishing accounts from various sources in a hurried fashion without the benefit of context or analysis). For example, the media offered the public neither explanations for these violent acts nor any theories about terrorism, its meaning, sources, objectives, or variants (Lumley and Schlesinger, 1982, pp. 607, 624). The Moro affair was treated much like an inexplicable natural disaster or an act of God – much like a volcanic eruption, an earthquake, or a sudden, violent storm (Silj, 1978, p. 215; Payerhin, 1988, p. 75). The media treated the Moro event like a two-month soccer game in which each of the two teams (the press/state versus the BR) used different rulebooks, though they shared the same playing field. Immediacy, undigested news, daily coverage, and inflamed rhetoric were the order of the day. As one critic noted, the tendency was to report "immediately and with the most details possible, even if fabricated . . . just to exhibit their own professionalism" (Bechelloni, 1978, p. 225; Payerhin, 1988, p. 78).

Though little state pressure and no prior restraint were exerted from Rome, the media practiced self-censorship. From the start, the common position of the government and the Christian Democrats was maintained. Only this perspective, one of "no negotiations," was maintained without any consideration of alternatives. The attack was denounced and the other victims' funerals covered, but the fate of Moro remained the true focus of attention. Paper after paper wrote of preserving his life, were it not for the overriding needs to resist "blackmail," to respect the "law," and to avoid making deals with terrorists.

While Moro was made a hero even before his death, the press tried to prepare the public for the inevitable. They actually began a public mourning period for him while he was still alive. Even the validity of Moro's pathetic letters was debated, since according to Prime Minister Giulio Andreotti, the views expressed were not morally ascribable to him. Appeals for Moro's life, his family's pleas for negotiations, and other cries for mercy went largely unheard. The media stood steadfast behind the government's hard line of no negotiating. The news media published whatever the government distributed, without criticism or qualification, just as it did with BR demands and reports. The story line that emerged linked the future of Italian democracy with maintaining law and order through governmental intransigence. Workers' strikes and demonstrations in the factories were taken as symbols of popular support for the government, though management was behind some of them. Newspapers also took this opportunity to attack one another with accusations of support or sympathy for the BR cause. False interviews were also published to support such allegations. Other themes of unity, stability, public support, consensus, and maintaining democracy were also used symbolically throughout the period (Silj, 1978, pp. 45, 50, 65, 80, 93, 97, 117, 211, 231; Lumley and Schlesinger, 1982, pp. 609, 613, 619; Payerhin, 1988, p. 75).

Front page coverage, banner headlines, photographs, and large amounts of space were devoted to the continuing coverage of the Moro incident. In three papers, the entire front page was regularly used for this purpose. Practically all other political, cultural, and foreign news was blacked out. On selected days, from one-quarter to one-half the news (average 37%) was devoted to this story. This emphasis was so great and so unusual that it, too, became a general subject of concern in media debates. This situation produced a curious logical impasse. That is, the media regularly assured its readers the BR could not paralyze the state, yet the media coverage seemed to convince the public that all other public business was at a standstill (Silj, 1978, p. 49; Payerhin, 1988, p. 86).

Foreign media treatment of the Moro case was a microcosm of Italian press coverage. Themes in the foreign press denounced the "terrorists"' the small number of "criminals" responsible; and the "ruthless" band of "psychopaths," "professional killers" and "murders," "fanatics," and "savages." They were also branded as

"Marxist urban guerrillas" and "Marxist revolutionaries," seeking to throw the country into a civil war (Davies and Walton, 1983, p. 40). These opinions were primarily based on official government sources, had few terrorist sources, and did not mention any public support or underlying causes for the BR actions. The use of quotation marks surrounding the name Red Brigades and phrases such as so-called of self-styled BR appeared frequently, particularly early on in the drama. The international media (excluding *Pravda*) also gave the story regular, prominent, and front page coverage. The treatment of the BR in US, Western and Eastern news media (e.g., *New York Times*, *Washington Post*, *Manchester Guardian*, *Tribuna Ludu* [Warsaw, Poland], CBS, NBC, BBC, ZDF, ARD, etc.) never analyzed the complexities of international, revolutionary violence. The media preferred to reduce the story to an irrational act – without meaning, cause, ore explanation. Davies and Walton's analysis noted:

> . . . a pattern of description which is not simply biased in favor of parliamentary democracy as one would expect, but which strongly prefers certain parties, positions and ideologies over others which legitimately inhabit the legislative sphere both in and outside the parliament.
>
> The visual and verbal content of the Moro news story tells more about the maintenance of an ideologically safe version of consensus by media demarcation than it does about the "events" which constitute the news (Davies and Walton, 1983, p. 48).

The Moro kidnapping has also been analyzed from a mythical perspective. Moro's martyrdom achieved social consensus. This event symbolized an end to social division through the historic compromise (Davies and Walton, 1983, p. 8). This sort of dramatic analysis can also be applied to other violent incidents such as the October 1985 Achille Lauro hijacking when the sole victim, his wife, and family were eulogized for two weeks in the New York Times until he became a hero and a symbol of all that was good in America. This later justified the US diversion (hijacking) of the four terrorists on an Egyptian airliner to a NATO landing strip in Italy. The following year, the US responded to the Berlin disco bombing, in which several US military personnel were killed and injured, by bombing Libya to punish Qaddafi for his allege involvement. This "take a life, bomb a city" response completely lacked proportionality. However, the press and public voiced little opposition to this raid which the UK assisted and France rejected, in terms of permission to overfly sovereign territory (Lule, 1988, pp. 1-15).

The Systemic Relationship Between Terrorism and the Media

All forms of terrorism cannot be defined or described simply, nor can their relationships to different news media and governments be generalized. Nevertheless, it is possible to capture some of their essential relationships using a schematic diagram. Figure 1 lays out some of the key elements in this dynamic interactive relationship among terrorist groups, the media, terrorism, public opinion, and public policy decisions. A democratic political system, in which a relatively free and unfettered press normally functions, is hypothesized. The key terms used in the diagram are as follows:

1. Terrorist Groups have various objectives and take different actions, all involving violence of the threat of violence. Most objectives are global, vague, changing, and ideologically rooted.
2. Mass Media include national and international radio, television, newspapers, magazines, and other print and nonprint news media which set the public's agenda. Media coverage may be exhaustive or minimal, firsthand or secondary, dramatic, and violence-prone, with no attempt to analyze underlying group motives or social causes. Media magnify, distort, and oversimplify through use of value-laden, establishment-based stereotypes, usually obtained from governmental sources.
3. Terrorism is a larger-than-life product of media treatment. The result is a concept, affect, and throughput, which bears little resemblance to the much smaller, insignificant group which initiated the threatened violence.
4. Public Opinion is the national and international set of values, opinions, attitudes, feelings, and concepts/cognitions on which the public bases its supports and demands for given public policies or preferred state action.
5. State Action and Public Policies in part rely on media information, public opinions (usually vague and uninformed), establishment goals, and independent information. All terrorist activity is automatically branded unlawful, unjust, and nonnegotiable. But the response thereto varies with the importance of victims, the options available, and the accessibility of the terrorist group for the imposition of sanctions. Negotiations, as a first step, and use of violent interdiction as a last step in the process, are more routine today than in the early 1970s. The public policy on media coverage, laws nationalizing the media (as in a military alert), or regulations governing allowable media activity are made under the umbrellas of "national security" or ensuring "law and order." There is an underlying supposition that the normally establishment-oriented media are difficult to control, predict, or manage in such situations. Therefore, media are potentially more threatening to regime maintenance, perhaps even more so than the terrorist activity itself.
6. Political Environment consists of the political culture and history, the normal level of order, violence, press freedom, or democracy in the society. Also of the influence are other governments and international organizations, as well as the international media network.

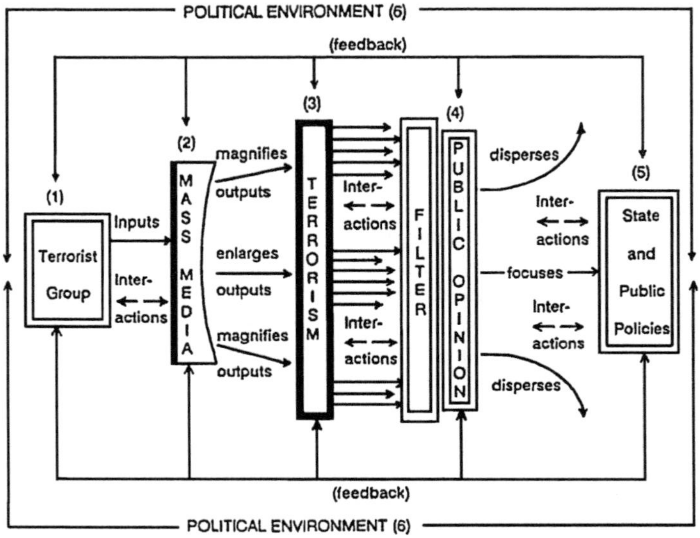

Figure 1: Terrorism and the mass media: an interactive system

A useful construct for the analysis of the relationship between terrorism and mass media is deviance amplification. This process, as it applied to drug use, was described in the work of Leslie Wilkins and Jock Young in 1965 and 1973, respectively. Their work depicts a "deviancy amplification spiral," whereby society defines a group as deviant and isolates their members. The ensuing group alienation results in increased deviancy and increased social reaction resulting in more deviancy, more isolation, and further escalation of the initial so-called abnormality. The dynamics of the interactions between the agencies of social control and the deviant group are also influenced through information provided by the mass media. This information is on drug uses, the police, the extent of public indignation, possible societal responses, and statistics on drug abuses. The whole "fantasy stereotype" of the drug taker is a media fabrication which, while untrue early in the process, assumes greater reality as the self-fulfilling prophecy about the drug culture increases. The result is increased isolation, more secrecy, ossification of values, greater group cohesion, more professional distribution of drugs, and increased public demands for solutions and social control (Cohen and Young, 1973, p. 350).

Much the same process occurs with respect to the interaction between media and terrorist groups in the nature of terrorism has been greatly changed with the help of the mass media (see Figure 1). Reports from a given terrorist group with its peculiar or unique aims and style of violence are picked up as news by the ever-watchful media after coverage of a violent incident or release of a group's claim of responsibility for an act. The mass media lens or filter then starts the magnification process, using terms and negative imagery, such as disorder, violence, threat, irrationality, secret society, ruthless criminals, fanatics, etc., which produces a new and larger social phenomenon labeled terrorism.

The term terrorism has certain encoded meanings, for example, civil war, guerrilla actions, widespread violence, crisis, proletarian uprising, Marxist revolutionaries, irrationality, siege, rebellion, and extremism, with highly negative valence. Terrorism then has an impact on public opinion about the terrorist group, its motives, its causes or objectives, government's alternatives, media reports, treatment of terrorists, victims, handling of new threats and demands, negotiations process, and surrender.

But the public does not take the raw news as gospel. Instead, people filter, compress, and interpret the news through the two step flow of communications/"opinion influencers" and conceptual frames of reference (filters). This is the sum total of previous memories, information, and attitudes about such political events as terrorist attacks, governmental corruption, trust and cynicism, and good and bad politicians. Some of the resulting impressions are either neutralized and inhibited or blocked, while others are scattered or dispersed, like light through a prism. Still others become more closely focused on political decision makers in terms of supports or demands, much as light passes through a convex lens.

The process finally results in official short- and long-term actions or public policies. These include meeting demands, mounting rescue operations, antiterrorists/media controls of guidelines for coverage, negotiation, stonewalling, news releases, etc. These are the result of information, media reports, public opinion, input from other governments, and previous public policy positions on terrorism.

These events can occur over long or short periods of time, the Moro and Iran cases being examples of long duration events, and the Achille Lauro, Munich Olympics, and TWA Flight 847, short. They also occur within a political environment which has its own levels of order, violence, or limits on legally permissible behavior. For example, the level of normal or acceptable violence may vary from that seen in relatively more violent societies, such as the US, Lebanon, and Italy, or on the high seas, where international law carries the threat of certain moral sanctions. In other settings, where an international band of terrorists may victimize the nations of one country on the soil of a third, neutral, biased, or friendly country, the legal restrictions, governing laws, or permissible level of violence also condition the environmental context in which the event occurs or is played out.

The political climate or culture of a country may help to explain public policies taken to resolve a given terrorist incident. For example, in Italy in 1978, violence in the streets challenged the political system on a daily basis. Italy was also about to witness the "historic compromise" of a parliamentary alliance among Progressive

Christian Democrats, Socialists, and the Italian Communist party. Worker protests, high unemployment, and youth demonstrations also reflected or promoted anti-governmental cynicism and popular alienation. Within this political culture, Prime Minister Giulio Andreotti voiced the intransigent government position of no negotiations and no concessions to BR terrorists, under any conditions. The Italian and international press maintained and supported the government's stand. It naturally and inevitably resulted in doom for Aldo Moro, Italy's own state of civil disorder and parliamentary chaos on the eve of the "historic compromise" was a critical factor in shaping the way in which the government and the news media handled the Moro crisis, the terrorists, and the story over a 55-day period. Within this political environment (characterized by the terrorist/news media/government/public opinion nexus), elements of the system interacted and fed back to one another in a dynamic fashion. That is, the BR carefully orchestrated its violence and its press releases. The government remained adamant, while selectively releasing inflammatory and self-serving news to the press. The news media repeatedly played up the themes of law and order, democracy hanging in the balance, no compromise, and the willing sacrifice of Moro for the public good against the BR's unfounded and irrational demands, which were not to be met under any circumstances.

The press, however, had an unexpected effect on public opinion. The news audience soon realized just how feeble a threat the BR posed to the supposedly unstable and fragile political system. The public also began to identify with the BR cause against the corrupt, unstable, and unpopular Roman regime. The news media, unexpectedly and purposely, helped to bring about this viewpoint. They convinced the people of the BR's public importance, and thereby helped to legitimize their claims and antigovernment posturing, if not their violent methods. By upholding the official party line and by not examining the underlying societal links and causes of the BR phenomenon, the news analysts failed in their task to inform the public. The media were satisfied with entertaining the masses with one new spectacular event after another. Though they tried to delegitimize the BR (along with all terrorists), the media did not succeed in their mission. Preventing this were deeply rooted social divisions endemic to the Italian political system, culture, and environment. Though the establishment line was harshly antiterrorist, the stereotyped and sensationalist treatment of the BR did not endure in the public's consciousness. Instead, the BR was transformed into an Italian Robin Hood band, an impression which no amount of negative press could dispel.

This result should give pause to those considering the effects on public opinion of news coverage of terrorism. It seems that strongly held preexistent views provide a barrier against media penetration. When the public has a negative view of the political system, the regime, and its power brokers, any news story may not easily be able to change these perspectives. This amounts to the public having a news cosmology or ideology that it also uses a filter (or concave lens) through which citizens can reduce an exaggerated account into more simple pro- or anti-government, regime, or system evaluations. This exists at a much more simplified, basic, or gut level, based on preexistent political predispositions, perceptions, feelings, attitudes, and cognitions. Therefore, the desire of the government or media for public support of a predetermined public policy stance may not be forthcoming in the face of a solidified, unified, and clear expression of popular opinion. This situation, which sometimes may allow the government to carry out an unpopular policy without public hindrance or objection, may not always be transferrable to another, later, or similar incident. It may not result in renewed public support for the regime, system, or office holders. What a different governmental or mass media approach would yield remains to be seen. There is seldom, in any country (with the possible exception of Great Britain), a concern for an in-depth media analysis of causes, motives, social conditions, or alternative contexts (or lenses, in this illustration) for interpreting news about terrorist acts. Meanwhile, the public remains mystified about the roots, manifestations, and solutions to terrorism (e.g., is more or less democracy necessary?) and puts such incidents in the category of the "wrath of nature," much like an act of God or a freak of nature – here today, gone tomorrow – lacking any rhyme or reason.

Statistics on both international and US domestic terrorism indicate a decided decline during the 1980s as compared with the number of incidents in the 1970s. In 1978, for example, out of 2725 international incidents reported, 60 were attributed to the BR, with 16 deaths in Italy. During this decade, the total number of such incidents has varied from 600 to 800 per year, with about 150 aimed at US nationals or American targets. Domestically, in 1985, for example, there were only ten actual incidents (as contrasted with 112 in 1977) due to a changed political climate, better airport security, counterterrorist activities, and more frequently thwarted attempts (e.g., 23 preventions in 1985). Though fewer in number, there is also a commensurate increase in the symbolic significance afforded attacks, such as the execution of Col. W. R. Higgins, the Terry Anderson kidnapping, the Achille Lauro/Klinghoffer incident, the TWA 847 hijacking, and the Berlin disco and TWA Lockerbee bombings. Each such incident has been associated with real or imagined American links to Israel, the West Bank and the Gaza Strip, Lebanon, or other Middle Eastern problems (Genovese, 1988, p. 143).

In Gerbner's (March 1988, p. 1; July 1988, p. 1) discussion of symbolism, violence, and terror, he maintains that such "symbolic uses benefit those who control them: they are usually states and media establishments, not small-scale or isolated actors or insurgents." Gerbner also observes:

> . . . though perpetrators of small-scale acts of violence and terror may occasionally force media attention and . . . seem to advance their cause, . . . such a challenge seems to enhance media credibility . . . and is used to mobilize support for repression often in the form of wholesale state violence and terror or military action, presented as justified by provocation (Gerbner, July 1988, p. 1).

Prime television is also a man's world where the power wielders control the symbols and victimize vulnerable women, the young, old, and minorities. The regular and disproportionate appearance of criminals, law enforcers, the violent, and murders bears little relationship to everyday reality; yet it accustoms us to the symbolic structures of social power. Gerbner believes such media violence "cultivates a differential sense of vulnerability and stigmatization, placing heavier burdens on selected minorities and nationalities" (Gerbner, July 1988, p. 1).

John Newhouse's recent article on intelligence gathering and terrorism is an excellent summary of the international state of the art (or the lack thereof), in meeting terrorist threats, and in solving past mysteries about responsibility for violent and unexplained aircraft disasters. A fine piece of detective reporting, the article also lays out the human technological problems associated with curbing terrorist attacks against civilian aircraft. As Newhouse sees it, the problem is much larger than either the human or technological solutions proposed. For example, JFK airport issued 47,000 passes and Heathrow in London issued 38,000 passes onto the tarmac. The new thermal neutron analysis (TNA) machine for detecting plastic explosives is not only very expensive, bulky, and as yet unavailable, but also is not very fast. For example, it would take at least two hours to screen a fully loaded 747 jumbo jet. Since Pan Am alone has over 30 scheduled departures each day and 400 trans-Atlantic crossings per week, screening all luggage is unthinkable. With false alarms sure to slow down the system and with the inevitable resort to selective screening based on secret potential terrorist profiles, the increased measure of psychological security resulting from a new system will only last until a piece of lethal luggage slips by the underpaid and often harried airline employees (Newhouse, 1989, p. 71). What is more interesting is that at the end of his account, Newhouse reverts to a larger policy point by saying:

> Terrorism feeds on the bitterness and frustration of people for whom the future seems to offer nothing, and in the attention paid to acts of violence by more of us who feel threatened by them. Another dynamic – such as a credible peace process in the Middle East – might upstage and gradually neutralize terrorism (Newhouse, 1989, p. 82).

It is interesting to note that other than passenger inconvenience, Newhouse saw no problems with the technological and human solutions proposed by airline and government officials. The reality is that one intrusive technological fix will undoubtedly lead to another, each more invasive of privacy than the last. Indeed, the real threat of terrorism is that its control will lead to a variety of new, repressive measures. This becomes more likely as research findings increasingly point to the success of repressive regimes in reducing terrorism in contrast to the fewer successes of open, democratic societies.

There are also international proposals to combat terrorism. For example, in December 1985, a UN General Assembly resolution appealed to member states to join existing international conventions on terrorism. The UN also asked members to act domestically against the problem, to work cooperatively with other member states and the International Civil Aviation Organization to establish new measures for law enforcement, and to take collective action against political terrorists killing innocent civilians, and taking them hostage. While recognizing that some terrorist groups are part of liberation or freedom fighting movements, General I. J. Rikhye of the International Peace Academy says others engage in sheer violence, seemingly for publicity or just for its own sake. Rikhye acknowledges that the complexities of the problem lead to simultaneous branding and counternaming pro- and anti-PLO and Israeli groups in the media as terrorists and linking states (such as Libya, Iraq, and Syria) to alleged sponsorship of violent groups they have harbored in the past. He also believes that both terrorism and military action against terrorism are equally ineffective, citing international publicity as the only gain of the first and the example of Egyptian commandos in Malta as illustrative of the second (Rikhye, 1989).

While maintaining these views, Rikhye once again proposes the need for more military cooperation to combat terrorism, namely, "an elite international peacekeeping unit, highly skilled in hostage rescue, to undertake this responsibility." He also proposes extension of the US-USSR 1985 informal agreement which ensures shared information on chemical and nuclear terrorist activities. An agency along the lines of the UN Disaster Relieve Organization could also be established to pool information on potential terrorist activities and arrests for international security purposes. Once again, however, these approaches are reactive, post hoc, and treat the symptom, not the causes of terrorism as a public phenomenon and problem (Rikhye, 1989, pp. 20-22). Although information sharing and concerted diplomatic responses may help to resolve a terrorist incident, it is unlikely that any kind of international "SWAT" team would be able to accomplish much since the character of international terrorism changes daily.

The issue of using military force to free hostages or to retaliate against state sponsors of terrorism was widely debated in the mid-1980s. Two different views were then expressed by the former Israeli ambassador to the UN, Benjamin Netanyahu and Martha Crenshaw, professor of government at Wesleyan University. Both agreed on the fact that US nationals had increasingly been the focus of international terrorist attacks from 1968 to 1985, providing one-third of these victims during a time which saw a rise from 125 to 782 in the total annual numbers of international terrorist incidents. Each was also concerned with the role of the media in a terrorist crisis (Netanyahu, 1986; Crenshaw, 1986).

Netanyahu's position is that modern terrorism is both state-sponsored and media-inspired. He maintains that unilateral military action (regardless of state sovereignty claims) can deter terrorism, as Israel's example has proven since the dramatic Entebbe raid in 1976. The West fails in the war against terrorism because of greed, political cowardice, and both moral and intellectual confusion about terrorists and terrorism, he says. Instead, a combination of political and military courage, and the will to take risks and to speak the truth (however painful) to valorous citizen-soldiers (who must be willing to sacrifice to ensure clarity of social purpose), are the civic virtues that will overcome the fear upon which terrorism depends.

In response, Crenshaw believes that the nature of the terrorist threat changed in the 1980s. An action-reaction-escalation spiral changed the natures of the game. Terrorists now use safe harbor states, split up hostages, and practice suicide bombings. Against these acts, elite strike force teams are ineffective. Moreover, preventive and retaliatory measures must be practical and discriminate. We cannot randomly kill innocent civilians.

But will deterrence work? Will the terrorists value calculus be influenced? Crenshaw believes not. We do not understand terrorists, their frames of reference, their motivations, or how they calculate risks. While states may be deterred, terrorist groups may not. As she says, in terrorist incidents, "the glare of publicity isolates and magnifies the consequences of miscalculation and accident." Terrorism is time-, space-, and incident-bound; it is so differentiated that it will not respond uniformly to countervailing forces.

Media must teach "the lesson of terrorism." Ta]hat is that "even the most powerful states cannot hope to control their environments." Since terrorism is so crisis-oriented, the media do not focus on the terrorist threat as part of the normal course of events in a disorderly world. The media hype accompanying an incident is followed inevitably by neglect and unpreparedness. This is "a pattern encouraged by the fickleness of media (especially television) attention," which induces "complacency and a false sense of security." Media attention not only distorts, but also glorifies violence; it fails to signify terrorism as a strategy not of warring armies, but of the weak. If this persists, it will result in the "most impressive achievement modern terrorism has claimed." The final risk is that our response to terrorism will "transform it into the grand spectacle the terrorists sought all along and raise its practitioners to the status of mythic heroes or villains" (Crenshaw, 1986). Perhaps even more risky than such symbolic warfare are the prospects for the use of Israeli-styled repression against our own nationals and foreigners on airplanes, at the borders, and in the society at large. Violation of another nation's sovereignty is an act of war and a serious legal lapse for a major world power. Violating citizens' basic rights is not an acceptable alternative for the lead country in the Western alliance, priding itself on its moral, ethical, and humane values.

Two researchers have interpreted the results of their elaborate empirical and statistical cross-national study of intracountry terrorism and the contagion effect in 16 countries from 1968 to 1978 as follows:

> Democratic, affluent, and well-educated states seem to have a particular difficulty in reversing terrorism, whereas autocratic, poor, and uneducated countries do not.

> . . . Our findings reinforce warning[s] that citizens and governments of open societies must respond very carefully to terrorism in order to avoid cures that are either ineffective, or worse than the disease (Hamilton and Hamilton, 1983, p. 52).

While Newhouse sees some hope in ameliorating the terrorist threat through technological and human solutions, Morrison (1986, p. 4) has little faith in a "technocratic consciousness" that would use information technology, replete with abundant "noise," or an ABM/SDI defense mode, frequently plagued by "misses" and "false alarms," to solve problems which stem from human aggression, conflict, disputes, and grievances. In the end, such human surveillance fixes may be used in an Orwellian fashion to solve the terrorist problem should even a few climactic incidents validate the need. When repression and invasion of privacy arrive, in addition to finding the few guilty criminal conspirators, human error will surely take its toll on the many innocent bystanders. Major US airlines are already collecting travelers' passport numbers months in advance of overseas flights so they can run them through for computer checks.

Alternatively, Morrison sees that many of the world's most pressing problems (e.g., species destruction, nuclear weapons, resource rape, and poverty) require nontechnical and human analysis and solutions if they are to be ameliorated. We ignore at our peril the human causes of war, environmental destruction, and starvation. The Third World hungers not from a lack of land, seed, or contraception but rather from historical and continued "Western exploitation, intervention, and manipulation" (Morrison, 1986, p. 15). Technological solutions to these crises or the problem of terrorism will not work, but human efforts just might. As Morrison said, "Nevertheless, while human efforts (compromise, negotiation, intermediaries, etc.) may indeed fail, they offer the real possibility of providing solutions." And, he continued:

> The possibility remains therefore that components of the terrorist problem are resolvable through continuing human efforts at resolution. But based on the evidence that has been presented, the success of such efforts is compromised by the dominant technocratic consciousness and its reflexive reaching for familiar off-the-shelf solutions (Morrison, 1986, p. 14).

Jimmy Carter's credentials as one such mediator are longstanding and philosophically based. They were substantiated in 1979 with agreement on the Camp David accords. They last to the present day in that he arranged for an Ethiopian peace conference at his Presidential Center in Atlanta in September 1989. During his administration, the Iran crisis proved to be nonnegotiable. In part, this was because the political goal of the hostage release was timed to embarrass Carter and benefit Ronald Reagan at the start of his presidency. This might even be one of the compelling reasons why Reagan later chose to do what he pledged never to do: trade arms from the "Great Satan" nation for US hostages.

In Carter's case, every solution for the Iran crisis was considered (as was his usual style), including an ill-fated rescue attempt and an eleventh-hour proposal for a military invasion to save his presidency. The daily pressure CBS News anchorman Walter Cronkite, who repeated the countdown on the length of captivity each day, placed on the administration delivered Carter's presidency into the hands of two elements: the Iranians and the American people. Both groups believed in Carter's media-created impotence; each was determined to prove this self-fulfilling prophecy by retaining the hostages until Reagan's inauguration day and by turning him out of office, respectively. The passion for diplomacy which Carter evidenced at Camp David and in the Panama Treaty accords did not always bear fruit, as his Salt II Treaty failure proved. However, the US news media, as much as the Iranian mullahs, were behaving irresponsibly when they depicted Carter as a failed leader. Their demands for action in this media-generated crisis, when no action save a bloody war was possible in the face of an intractable Iranian theocracy, cannot be termed responsible, however much it was "good television" of a "good story." Despite Carter's failure Martin and Walcott (1988) correctly conclude that a combination of diplomacy and law enforcement can best contain international terrorism.

The imposition of an idealistic or pluralistic model of communications on the terrorism/government/media interrelationship will not yield a panacea. More public discourse or improved news reporting formats will not solve the problem of terrorism either as an issue, an event, or a policy question. Terrorism as a media event (along with drugs, alcohol, crime, or drunken driving) is related to the larger question of establishing proportionate media perspectives on national and international problems. One related issue is the media's role in social control and the allocation of power, which Der Derian (1989, p. 158) calls "part of the hegemonic domination of given societies." Another issue is the need for national security-obsessed states to begin using international diplomacy and new social programs to address root causes of terrorism, rather than resorting to knee-jerk military responses as the first – rather than the last – solution.

Media self-censorship or governmental cooptation of the media are not reasonable policy alternatives in democratic societies. However, the belief in media determination as the root cause of the terrorist "theater of terror" assists central governments in their regular attempts at social control. But this is an inherently undemocratic, unnecessary, and ineffective policy. Since both media and governmental representatives control the language of rhetoric and discourse surrounding terrorism, an attempt on the part of both to differentiate between criminal and ideological terrorist acts would be a proper starting point. Each could clearly focus on the media-dominated objectives of terrorists; for example, as providing the context for explaining terrorists' communication objectives to their fellow terrorists, the media, governments, public opinion, and others. The manipulation of the media through terrorist activities is also a topic that media and governmental officials can elucidate during a crisis since the mass audiences become willing victims of terrorist propagandists, whose efforts usually succeed in enhancing their status and their cause (Weimann, 1983, pp. 38-45).

Since presidents and prime ministers (as national spokespersons) help to frame the terrorist event, they can help to reduce panic, define the crisis, clarify roles (as victim or perpetrator), signify competence, and present nonmilitary options. When an administration and the media treat terrorism as high drama, the mythmaking ability of the press is enhanced and military intervention, which is seldom actually used, is legitimated in a cops-and-robbers, good-guy or bad-guy scenario. Strangely enough, government and media leaders do not understand that, as Palmerton (1988, p. 107) says, "[i]t is the response which becomes the primary persuasive vehicle for the terrorist." The terrorist, in other words, seeks the status of a victim, and therefore, encourages repressive responses. Terrorists' challenges to state authority encourage public support for subsequent state repression, violence, terror, or military action. The media assist in legitimizing this state-sponsored counter-violence, and such justifications allow more authoritarian rule to secure a firmer hold over the domestic society as well (Gerbner, 1988, p. 3). The process of consent building, in which the media play a vital role, may produce a public which is not only amenable to suppression of terrorism at any cost, but is also willing to accept self-repression (Dobkin, November 1989, pp. 4, 10).

The media create reality and, through their interpretive frames and social conventions, teach readers and viewers not just what to think, but what to think about. Media decision makers (publishers, editors, and directors) not only share the dominant elite views toward public policy but also shape their reports in this context for public consumption.

Democracy, pluralism, nationalism, social responsibility, and order are key themes which describe these "media frames" of reference. Such conventions have so distorted terrorism reportage on the networks that Middle Eastern terrorism is exaggerated, Latin American and anticorporate terrorism is minimized, and government victimization is espoused. According to one study of the 1969-1980 period,the actual pattern of world terrorism is different from that portrayed on the networks. When news broadcasts and stories are produced within these institutionalized modes, they serve to create the so-called public character of events, a function shared with political officials and celebrities, who also share responsibility for this agenda setting role. Since politicians rely on journalists and vice versa for information, this symbiotic relationship is especially critical during a terrorist crisis when news may be managed and state power is no longer veiled. As a vital part of this process of norm encoding and image creation, politicians also label "good" and "bad" terrorists ans "enemies" or "freedom fighters" to produce public support for national policies. When applied to terrorists, these labels short circuit popular thinking and reduce the community's opportunity to think about causes of injustice (Gerbner and Gerbner, July 1988, p. 1).

David Altheide's (1987, pp. 161, 174) US and UK cross-national analysis of television coverage of an IRA terrorist incident in 1982 indicates that the format of a news show also has an impact on the message an audience receives. That is, event-type formats focus on visuals and tactics, whereas topic-type formats (with interviews and documentaries) better deal with the purposes, goals, and basis for terrorism incidents. In other words, visuals are more restrictive than are contextual and documentary formats, which increase the chance for elite and audience reflection. Consequently, one clear signal of impending government repression is the higher likelihood of restriction of the latter format, which Britain has done with respect to IRA and the US with respect to Canadian and USSR documentaries. Government leaders prefer to use "one-liners" and event formats to inform the public, engineer consent, label, depersonalize, and delegitimize the "enemy," and curry favor for governmental positions, however untenable. The increasingly common pictorial news headline format, which is "just good television," helps to achieve these purposes.

Cross-national surveys at the end of the 1970s indicated that most West Germans, British, and Americans believed terrorism was a very serious problem. Respondents wanted the death penalty for terrorists, sanctioned use of "special forces," and accepted police state or extraordinary measures against them. They also accepted news embargoes and monitored conversations with lawyers during a terrorist crisis. Also of concern was being careful not to appear pro-terrorist. This meant opposing the death penalty, supporting legal aid, feeling pity, or believing some of the terrorist's criticisms were unjustified (Gerbner and Gerbner, July 1988, p. 3). Despite these popular fears, Gerbner maintains the greatest threat is "collective, official, organized and legitimized violence." Television violence and small-scale terrorist attacks are not as dangerous to social stability as are "illicit commerce, wars, unemployment, and other social trends that allow the wielders of power "to depersonalize enemies, to cultivate vulnerability and dependence in subordinates, to achieve instant support for swift and tough measures at home and abroad in what is presented as an exceedingly mean and scary world" (Gerbner and Gerbner, July 1988, p. 3).

The government is one of the prime sources of emotional and pejorative descriptions of anti-state activities. Nevertheless, it is strange, indeed, that the FBI and State Department are often the prime movers behind media and public policies designed to ensure self-control or to mandate guidelines for media's coverage after each such violent frenzy. Terrorists are such an embarrassment to the US State and Defense Departments that Secretaries George Shultz and Caspar Weinberger wanted nothing to do with the Iran-contra arms deal, which Poindexter and North managed out of the Reagan White House. In 1988, Shultz banned Arafat from attending the United Nations meeting in New York, forcing the General Assembly to meet in Geneva. His rationale was based on the PLO's alleged terrorist links and nonrenunciation of terrorism. Arafat subsequently renounced terrorism, terrorist organizations, and terrorist links to the eventual satisfaction of the Reagan administration. Although the significance of these pronouncements in terms of public policy decisions involving the US, the PLO, and Israel (e.g., on resolving the future of the West Bank) remains clouded, the fact that Bush administration diplomats have met with PLO representatives and that the PLO has lately agreed to become part of the antiterrorist network holds promise for more agreements in the future.

Official party lines in approved articles from US military personnel also speak of controlling the media to control terrorism. For example, a Quantico-based Marine Corps provost marshal has joined the call for a "war" against terrorism, with the media conscripted to play a vital part in the process (Wilber, 1985, pp.20-23). He says that "something more than peacenik campouts around our European missile installations ought to be considered in our terrorist planning." This officer was very much in favor of professional media guidelines along ethical lines in contrast to those based on "event-oriented sensationalism" or "mundane commercialism." Unless the media clean up their act, the colonel said, "assertions of national interest may ultimately take priority over the public's historic rights to be informed." Guidelines need to be "mutually acceptable, realistic, and workable" and "applied by both sides during terrorist incidents," but so done that they "do not foster the idea of 'sides'" (Wilber, 1985, p. 21). For example, USIA proposals for a blue ribbon panel on media self-regulation and guidelines were also endorsed as topics for media and law enforcement discussions, after socializing in ice-breaker sessions. These sessions could relieve media paranoia and lead to soul-searching recognition by the media that they are part of both the problem and the solution.

The media themselves must resist manipulation, dissuade imitators, and use proportionality, balance, objectivity, context, and minimum intrusiveness in their terrorist coverage. These principles require the use of pools, less obtrusive lighting, limits on interviews primary reliance on officially designated spokesmen as sources of information, and avoidance of tactical questioning. They should also delay inflammatory reporting, suppress information on incident locations, obscure tactical information, balance information from participants with official sources, use predisclosure verification of facts, and avoid the spectacular. These are basic and commonsense, workable, and palatable media guidelines, according to the provost marshal. "The right of a hostage to survive and the right of a society to self-preservation are also important rights, too important to be left to the media" (Wilber, 1985, p. 23). To ensure reasonable accommodation, the media and its academic allies must accede to these simple rules of operation. Zemel versus Rusk (1965) was quoted approvingly to the effect that "[t]he right to speak and publish does not carry with it the unrestrained right to gather information" (Rusk, 1965, pp. 16-17).

Just why the US government should be seeking self-restraint or prior restraints on media's – and especially television's – coverage of terrorism or should be enlisting the media as an ally in the "war" against terrorism is not easily explained. With such limitations in place, the media establishment's quasi-adversarial role vis á vis the government would be further compromised through another form of governmental cooptation. When the concept of a "war on terrorism" comes into being, the media partners risk becoming tools or voices for the state, much as they did with managed news events during the Grenada invasion, the Libyan air strike, and other military operations against Libyan aircraft and the Achille Lauro hijackers.

Press treatment of incidents such as the TWA 847 case is usually rather bland, pro-government biased, and hostage oriented. Atwater's (1988, pp. 1-8) study of network news coverage of the TWA flight 847 hijacking indicated that there was massive television coverage of this event, with 12 hours of coverage devoted to it over the June 14-30, 1985 period. Although Laqueur (1977) and Alexander (1978) maintain that publicity is the key to terrorism's success and that establishment media wittingly or unwittingly are tools of terrorist strategy, this did not prove true in the TWA case study.

Atwater found that most reports came from Washington or New York and few from the actual site. Over half of the stories were on hostage conditions and US government reactions. Far fewer focused on terrorist demands, acts, Islam, or Lebanese internal or external difficulties. While the coverage was "dramatic, reactive, and extensive," the Iranian crisis mode of reporting was used. It had great detail, but no interpretation or education useful to the viewers, this finding was similar to that noted in the Paletz, et al. (1982, pp. 146-165) study of the IRA, FALN, and Red Brigades coverage in network news. The networks treated these groups evenly, covering the same events with a similar portrayal. There was not legitimacy afforded the groups. Their causes were not defined as just. No explanation was given of the causes or objectives behind the acts of violence, and most stories did not even mention the organization or its supporters. In a follow-up study of network news coverage of terrorism (see Milburn, et al., reported in Gerbner and Gerbner, 1988), not only were such causes ignored, but severe mental instability was also ascribed to both terrorists and their leaders. This line, of course, implies that no negotiations are possible with "crazy people."

Since governments have, or ought to have, control of the scene of a crisis or crime, they can limit media access as they would in any war, crisis, or emergency zone. Publishing and reporting terrorist events, however, are responsibilities of the press, not the government. As *Dallas Morning News* Executive Editor Ralph Langer (Genovese, 1988, p. 151) said, "the basic cause of terrorism is not news coverage. . . . Terrorism comes from real or perceived disputes and problems that aren't resolved." Should media ignore terrorism, terrorists may well escalate the level of violence. Further, the credibility of the press will be questioned across the board if terrorism is squelched in the news. As *Chicago Tribune* Editor James Squires maintains:

> No policy other than a policy balancing hostages with national security and readers' interests is all that can be hoped for in a free and responsible press environment. . . . We don't want to be used and manipulated by anyone. So we try to be as skeptical and as cautious about being compromised in the interest of some special cause or group of people as we are on a day-to-day basis when we deal with government (Genovese, 1988, pp. 151-152).

Should such guidelines be negotiated or legislated, they would likely be unenforceable. The press would also be made to suffer for any alleged violations. When the government seeks involuntary guidelines and prior restraint, the classic case of the sovereign blaming the messenger who brought the bad news comes to mind. Should the press be forced to surrender its historic role as the fourth estate's check on governmental power as a specious palliative to quiet minimalist terrorism? The government and the terrorists may each share an interest in controlling the press, but the public's interest is certainly not thereby served.

In this regard, R. J. Rummel's (1988, p. 60) studies of the relationships among political systems, violence, and war are worth noting. Rummel's empirical research indicated that the more democratic a political system, the less likely the incidence of internal violence against its people and the less likely the event of war with other states, particularly democratic states. The reverse is true for totalitarian states. Internal violence in the 20th century has been three times as bloody as that from all the wars in this time period. Rummel concluded that, "[i]n a nutshell, democratic freedom promotes nonviolence" To "minimize collective violence" and elements of war, ". . . one must embrace and foster democratic institutions, civil liberties, and political rights here and abroad" (Rummel, 1988, p. 60). This proactive democratic stance toward preventing internal and external violence may also be applicable as a tool in the real campaign against terrorism at home and abroad.

Other advocates of proactive media roles for conflict resolution hope to reduce group grievances, frustration, and despair by using forums and encouraging free expression. These vehicles would afford a hearing, provide legitimacy when appropriate, and lend credibility to the unnecessary use of violence in a media-rich society. Present media modes reward terrorists for using violence; new modes could reward the sensible discussion of nonviolent alternatives to past aggression, fearsome reports, coerced coverage, and lengthy media-prolonged violence. Though these alternatives, like the diffusion theory (as an alternative to the contagion theory), are worthy of consideration, the, like allege media-exacerbating behavior, are als based on informed judgments or suppositions. That is, although they are hypotheses, they are still sound ideas worthy of testing. The provision of a UNO office to the PLO; extensive Western media coverage of Arafat, Gaza, and West Bank Palestinian uprisings; PLO acceptance of Israel and rejection of terrorism; and US diplomatic initiatives toward the PLO are all recent and relevant developments. They indicate that what Secretary of State Shultz as recently as 1988 called a "terrorist group" (thus refusing Arafat a US visa to speak at the United

Nations) may eventually enjoy UN observer status, as does Switzerland. And the US moral stature cannot be increased through an erratic policy which one day declares a group anathema and the next day offers it a seat at the bargaining table.

Of course, post hoc interviews with those responsible for prior violent acts, such as the IRA, PLF, Red Army, or Animal Liberationists, also make some sense. The group's motives, grievances, plans, and demands can be safely revealed in these "media therapy" sessions, which provide a safety valve and a legitimate platform for dissenting views. Causes, policies, alternatives, shared selection of and control over topics, propaganda encounters, and deep and informed questioning would be necessary parts of such formats. Replies to critics who are sure to label them as "meet your friendly neighborhood terrorist" shows must also be considered. But unless the national government is supportive of, and participates in, such programs, they are likely to fail. Even the recent Columbia School of Journalism Media Studies Center series, which focused on the media and terrorism, failed to have any "guests of dishonor" at the event. No PLO, IRA, PQ, Basque, or Puerto Rican Nationalist advocates or spokespersons were present. Trying terrorism in absentia in such forms, which specialize in exchanging the conventional wisdom about media guidelines (voluntary or imposed) versus press freedom, will do little to prevent forthcoming violence in which media are sure to be major actors. Since 1982, the British government has actually used the threat of IRA terrorism to restrict English press freedom and, more recently, to circumscribe the right of witnesses against self-incrimination – a 300-year-old procedural due process rule which applies to all citizens, terrorists and nonterrorists alike. Similarly, the US State Department strenuously opposed an NBC news interview of 3.5 minutes duration in May 1986 with a PLF leader involved in the Achille Lauro hijacking. A spokesperson claimed that "terrorism thrives on this kind of publicity," and it "encourages" that which we are seeking to "deter" (Picard, July 1988, p. 6).

Healthy debates about the broader causes of violence (e.g., publicity seeking, easy transport, cheap weapons and explosives, private and governmental funding, and media and governmental intransigence) may be more useful contexts for media-based discussions of the terrorism dilemma (Picard, July 1988, p. 5). Rather than seeking a single cause for this seemingly irrational and antistatist form of protest (which has existed for thousands of year), terrorism must be placed in the context of typical violent reactions to the existence of normally violent societies. Moreover, the realities of modern technology have promoted the state's monopoly on the use of force. World arms sales annually total in the hundreds of billions. A puny group of terrorists is nothing compared with the thousands of preventable highway, drug, and job-related deaths every year or a 3-million person US military establishment, with annual budgets approaching $300 billion per year. This is just another necessary part of the context needed for understanding terrorism in the late 20th century.

Recent events such as the Pan Am flight 103 bombing in December 1988 and the poisoned Chilean grapes incident in March 1989 indicate that terrorism has transformed itself in a variety of ways. No group claims responsibility for the crimes, the incidents are at the miniature or micro levels (a transistor radio bomb or hypodermic syringe filled with poison), and the protagonists and antagonists operate at the highest symbolic level of abstraction (i.e., symbols of a whole country are randomly threatened and/or attacked). These recent events also portend the likely continuance of this micro-level violence. It, perhaps, may take on still newer forms, such as the use of chemical-biological weapons rather than nuclear suitcase-size devices. These will have total, surgical, quick, and limited geographical effects on a specific population group, such as a city. Biological-chemical terrorists would not run the risk of unexpected, collateral, and universally unpopular results which would follow even the smallest nuclear explosion.

When handling these recent events, the Western media mainly showed the carnage, ascribed blame to the British and American governments for inadequate forewarning, and provided emotional coverage of victims' families. The grape incident was handled in a fashion that played up public fears, intensified the danger, and illustrated governmental (FDA) competence in protecting the public's health and safety. Without a clear sense of a victim, victimizer, demand, goal, or continuing dramatic process in the Pan Am 103 bombing, the media were forced to improvise in their reporting formats. While they met the standard criteria for news, these bizarre occurrences failed to meet the typical standards for a terrorist drama. Once again, however, the media greatly magnified these events as threats to us all as well as incidences of sudden and unexpected violence. Yet they continually failed to provide any context (other than governmental competence of blundering) for the public to interpret these new features of the changing face of international terrorism.

The political environment or symbolic context for terrorism also relates to the centrality of the pledge of allegiance debate in the 1988 presidential elections. National pride and personal loyalty were introduced as campaign issues, just as they previously had been in the Klinghoffer case, the Achille Lauro hijacking, and the TWA 847 incident, in which a living symbol of America's military was denigrated, brutalized, and murdered. When national emotions are allowed to exaggerate what is essentially a police matter into an international incident which provokes (as did the bombing of the Berlin disco) a military assault on Libya and the US counterhijacking of an Egyptian ally's plane as responses to terrorism, more sensible options must surely be available. This is merely "knee-jerk" patriotism, which invites even further provocation and combative retaliation down the line.

As a case in point, on January 8, 1988, Ted Koppel, host of ABC's *Nightline*, had Yassir Arafat as his guest. Arafat maintained that the US and Israel were united in "state terrorism" against Palestinian, Libyan, and other peoples. Though Koppel pressed him, Arafat held his ground. Moreover, the abundant international media coverage which Arafat received in 1988 (during the UNO Geneva meetings and as a result of the US-PLO diplomatic rapprochement) failed to inspire a rash of terrorist incidents or proterrorist sentiment in the US or elsewhere. Though Arafat received widespread media coverage, the state-directed antiterrorist system has not collapsed. Censoring him or other advocates of unpopular, antiestablishment positions in the US makes no sense in a democratic society.

Short-term solutions to the terrorist-media interaction often focus on media self-censorship, responsibility, and restraint. For example, the *Hartford Courant's* editor and publisher, Michael Davis, recently endorsed media self-censorship in the recent Lt. Dol. William Higgins murder and the Joseph J. Cicippio videotapes widely broadcast on network television. Davies applauded ABC and Peter Jennings, the ABC News superstar anchorman, for refusing to be "used as a vehicle by terrorists" and labeling the event "a characteristic tactic to put pressure on the US and Israel via the American public" (Davies, 1989, p. 83). Charles Glass, and ABC correspondent and former videotaped hostage also joined in support of the ABC position by claiming that such broadcasts "hurt the hostages' position because it was doing exactly what the captors wanted." Davies applauded the ABC position and said this was a far cry from the TWA flight 847 hijacking days when the networks were used "as a megaphone for terrorists" because their job was to report the news, competition demanded it, and the consequences were irrelevant. Despite their "lack of restraint," ABC News and Jennings, said Davies, "are blazing new tails for television without leaving the American public uninformed." He added, "Hooray for them. When will the other networks catch up?" In addition to providing a fine example of the prevailing view on prior self-restrint, it is also interesting to contrast Davies' earlier views on the media's need to avoid "a conspiracy of silence" in terrorist reporting (Davies, 1985).

Before the business of government becomes regulation of the news in the name of national security and symbolism, the free press needs to inform the public about policy alternatives and just what is at stake. This may mean antagonizing the old or new power brokers, who would have the media promote even more of their private financial, oligopolic, and corporate interests, which deregulation has only encouraged. Mass media news coverage is tame, bland, and establishment-oriented as it is. To promote further restrictions would not only be redundant, it would also serve to erode our shrinking press freedom even further.

Discussion and Conclusions

The foregoing analysis of the terrorism/media/government/public opinion/policy-making connection is mainly useful for a general analysis of the topic. It helps, perhaps, to explain how the media have interacted with the US cultural milieu to affect American norms, values, attitudes, interests, and perceptions about terrorism as a recurrent crisis event and its perception as an enduring public problem. The broadcasting industry is but one part of a broader institutional framework for the identification, definition, salience estimation, evaluation, policy formulation, and assessment of terrorism as a public issue.

The focus of this chapter has been on those aspects of the terrorist phenomenon in which the media play a critical role. This is mainly in determining the definition, ownership, context, agenda, importance, proportionality, selection of alternatives, technological ramifications, power relationships, and evaluative aspects of the issue. These are all important parts of the terrorism question. They are also ones to which media are closely linked – as are the terrorists, the US government, other governments, and public spectators. The latter also serve as cheerleaders, critics, consumers, judges, and juries in evaluating and assessing media and official policies and countermeasures.

The communication aspects of this political, economic, and social problem are vital parts of the eventual solution used to resolve or ameliorate terrorism as a problem or crisis. Be they active military or countercrimianal (i.e., forcible) options, active negotiations, or passive acceptance or forbearance of that which is intractable (hostages in captivity), the media are as much partners in the event as are the other major dramatic actors. Resolution of this problem, with its international dimensions, would require looking at the phenomenon from other important vantage points of the policy process. These include careful examination of hidden and preexistent causes of the multidimensional problem, nonmilitary policy options that have proved successful in the past, media techniques for context development, and continual search for a favorable climate to encourage international, diplomatic, and law enforcement solutions to such incidents, each of which has both unique and generic features.

In both its international and domestic forms, terrorism has many guises and multiple causes. It is not a monolith any more than world communism has ever been. Simplistic solutions, such as using strike teams, demanding media self-censorship, threatening military invasion, bombing terrorist training camps, declaring war, or otherwise violating international law, will only create much larger problems (the dimensions of which are beyond speculation) for Americans. The policy implications of US options seriously considered in past international conflicts (e.g., carrying the ground war in Vietnam to the north; using force to break the Berlin blockade' invading Cuba, Iran, or Libya; placing large numbers of American military "advisers" in Afghanistan or Nicaragua, etc.) are too horrific to contemplate. Each of these untried options would have been costly, deadly, and disastrous in the long and short run. No pax Americana or pax Sovietica against world terrorism has been or will be possible in our lifetimes, nor is this a necessary, desirable, or practical hope. Terrorism as a public phenomenon is intimately and intricately connected to America's cold war mentality, which maintained a national security state to the tune of more than $300 billion per year. American taxpayers and consumers expected more for their money than keeping the peace through deterrence. They wanted the security of a star wars umbrella, secure transportation technology, and a peaceful world, dominated by American national, social, economic, and political values. They distrusted the Russians, the Arabs, the mainland Chinese, the Japanese, and most of the other peoples living on what was increasingly considered to be a very scary planet.

The United States has had a long and bloody history. We have been at war (both declared and undeclared) about one-third of the time since our baptism by fire as a new nation. This violent past continues to the present day and is symbolized by comments such as that of the 1960s black radical H. "Rap" Brown (1969), who said that "violence is as American as cherry pie." The recent Time magazine report in July 1989 on just one week of US gun-related deaths indicated that the large majority of the victims died at their own hands, were the objects of someone known to them, or were just accidents. This was a far more common cause of death than the criminal use of weapons. The number of "underclass" Americans who were victims of these weapons was conspicuous in these statistics. While standing behind our nuclear deterrents, we seldom negotiate weapons reductions, except for the recent INF and CFE treaties. The US (with the USSR) has been a principal arms merchant for the world. We commit highway mayhem daily and practice domestic violence at home with a vengeance. It extends everywhere. Knee-jerk militarism is publicly supported at every turn. For example, in August 1989, a majority of Americans wanted to send US troops into Colombia to fight narcoterrorism, and only one-third of respondents objected (based on a *Newsweek* poll reported on National Public Radio on August 28, 1989). Middle East Muslim spokespersons decry the use of Christian bombs dropped by Israeli aircraft against Arab noncombatants. The cycle of violence in which international terrorism is enmeshed must be broken if the US mass media are to become more civilized and humane.

The mass media have played an essential role in the construction of a national paranoia about foreign peoples and governments, into which ethnocentric schema terrorists all too easily fit. The detachment of terrorism from America's symbolic conflict with the rest of the world (in which our national ego is improperly enmeshed beyond mere ethnocentricism) is the responsibility not only of the broadcasting industry, but also of responsible educators, clerics, politicians, opinion leaders, and world figures who regularly influence what we hold close as "our own" facts and opinions. It is these real, peace-oriented counterterrorists who can focus attention on the pressing problems of the day; hunger, homelessness, disease, drugs, authoritarianism, racism, environmental and species destruction, militarism, and so forth – from which terrorism springs and by which terrorism pales in comparison. If national and international priorities are misplaced, the mass media can help to reorient them, but this cannot be done single-handedly. The US mass media have been particularly susceptible to elite control and influence from the corporate board rooms of networks and advertisers, from the publisher and producers, or from network superstars or editors. The news we get, how much, and what type is prescreened and filtered through these elite few who act as gatekeepers and agenda setters. These circles of power are subject to governmental, organizational, and public pressures that can also exert influence. For example, interest groups, such as Action for Children's Television or Ralph Nader's Public Interest Lobby, have had some impact on televised violence or public interest reporting. There are now enough of these groups sharing a common interest in breaking the cycle of media-reinforced violence that some countervailing power against gratuitous violence can be exercised within First Amendment limits. Terrorism, crime reporting, police show, war news, and other public celebrations or unexplained violence feed on one another in a systemic and symbiotic fashion. A more careful analysis of these interrelationships, connected with efforts to break the actual cycle of domestic and international violence in which the US participates, might help produce both a less scary and less violent society against which many international terrorists now strive measure for measure.

Blaming the media for our ills (in effect, threatening to imprison the bearer of bad news) will be short-sighted and ineffective as a solution to world terrorism. The media's responsibility in this public problem is to rethink its role along fundamental lines of analysis. Essential guidelines for the reanalysis include adopting certain overlapping maxims for a sound reassessment. These include, for example, 1) expressing unwillingness to be used exploitatively by terrorists or official spokespersons; 2) independently redefining terrorism as a public problem; 3) setting contexts for terrorist incidents in a responsible way; 4) seeking alternative nonmilitary solutions to violent domestic or international incidents; 5) developing independent sources for information on such incidents from foreign news reports and observers; 6) keeping abreast of terrorist groups through network and wire service research files and newspaper "morgues"; 7) providing regular contextual treatment in stories, broadcasts, documentaries, interviews, and discussion formats of terrorism groups, goals, countermeasures, leaders, arms, techniques, and uses of technology; 8) freely interviewing terrorist spokespersons in news segments and group discussion formats; 9) deinstitutionalizing terrorism, and recontextualizing, humanizing, and personalizing the phenomenon; 10) using the many communications levers at hand to provide terrorism with a human face; 11) providing air time to radical critics (such as Noam Chomsky) who make a case for US involvement in state terrorism and the excesses of our allies (e.g., against the oppressed Palestinians in Israeli-occupied territories); 12) developing game plans for reporting on domestic and international violence and terrorism that explore no forcible solutions until the bitter end, despite daily pressures to do otherwise; 13) developing "white papers," television journals, television specials, and other in-depth programs on terrorism that have a life beyond the dramatic moments of their broadcasts in journalism, politics, psychology, and sociology classes and public educational forums, such as the Kettering Foundation's National Public Issues Forums annual nationwide town meetings of citizen discussion groups and study circles; and 14) redefining the news canon so that terrorism can be divided into its component manifestations (i.e., domestic and international; political and economic; significant or insignificant; state-sponsored, -supported, or -aided; or private, unique or patterned; well-documented or vague – in terms of causes or perpetrators; low- or high-level symbolic; grievance-based or irrational; and like categories).

The media's responsibility in leading such an analysis of terrorism would have wide-ranging significance for our communications proficiency and media competence. The range of significant social issues (going beyond terrorists as outcast barbarians and enemies) which could be discussed in such an approach would immeasurable contribute to our social and intellectual enlightenment as intelligent media consumers. Therefore, while we can accept media's important role in the definition and amplification of world terrorism, one cannot blame or hold solely responsible the messenger for the message. We can, however, hold the broadcast industry responsible for helping to educate all of us on what to think about and how to respond to tomorrow's or next year's terrorist event, for it will surely come and in a new wrapping – conceivably chemical, biological, or even nuclear.

Current conflicts in South Africa and Northern Ireland, like the former civil war in Algeria, exhibit the elements of civil strife rather than terrorist activity. This is also true of Nicaragua, Cuba, El Salvador, Burundi, Cambodia, Chile, Angola, and other conflicts in which individual terrorist acts or wholesale mass murder took place. Media's role is to help us sort out each type of violence, relating the facts to resistance against tyranny, wholesale slaughter, or something in between. Media must also tell us when these unheard trees fall in distant political forests, since our own government has no interest in doing so unless our official interests are threatened.

In 1946, UNESCO declared that, since wars begin in the minds of men, it is there that the defenses of peace should be constructed. Much the same is true of terrorism. The media can be frontline forces in this permanent and larger battle to wage peace and to ensure justice and popular sovereignty at home and abroad.

The course of international terrorism continues to run along well-established but increasingly meandering lines. Recent developments, all heralded in the international mass media, indicate that terrorism as a media subject still excites public interest and concern. Daily news reports, new books and articles, and television programs depict motorboat assaults on Israeli beaches, the cessation of US diplomatic initiatives toward the PLO, and the latest flaws in TNA, and surveillance techniques designed to promote airline safety. The drama of terrorism as an indigenous national problem (as with the Basques and the IRA) or as a state-supported international movement (as in the case of sanctuary for Red Brigade leaders in the German Democratic Republic along with safe passage for other notables, such as the infamous "Carlos," in Eastern Europe) continues to interest scholars, journalists, and media consumers alike. Members of the Arafat family, such as Yasir and his brother, are now featured in Washington Post and Times (London) articles in conjunction with lengthy biographical specials of the "this Is Your Life" variety, which only tangentially relate to the essential features of the terrorism dialog and debate. With all this, the saga of terrorism seems to provoke either explanations, answers, or solutions (as in the debates over freedom fighter versus terrorist, national versus international responses, and national versus international causes and solutions). However, with the passage of time, the proponents of international approaches to solve such problems seem to have the edge in terms of the weight of their arguments and applicability to a changing world situation. New considerations of the multiple causes of terrorism, its varieties, similarities, and uniqueness, and like analyses point toward the utility of removing or ameliorating the causes of terrorism and increasing the use of East-West and North-South cooperation to promote information exchange, to provide extradition when warranted, and to monitor cross-national activities of potential perpetrators of violence against innocent civilians.

In this respect, the May 1990 presidential report from the Aviation Security and Terrorism Commission (which, naturally, made instant news headlines) is an anomaly, out of synch with the passage of events. This report might have been more properly titled "The Lockerbie Report" since it was a necessary political response to the tragic deaths of 270 people in December 1988. Some of the commission's proposals (such as improving airport security procedures) are self-evident and reflect current policy anyway. However, it would have been nice if the details about TNA machine failures had not been so explicit since this might have provided a measure of comfort to travelers as well as a deterrent to some would-be bombers. Some of the commission's other proposals (for example, appointing a new "terrorist czar" in the State Department and improving their emergency notification procedures, and allowing the CIA to do covert investigations) may or may not accomplish much. Only time will tell if these measures will have any specific (since they are unlikely to have any general) effects on terrorist activities.

To certain of the commission's proposals, it is possible to make serious objection. For example, the Lockerbie disaster may have been linked to the July 1988 deaths of 290 Iranians from a US warship's missiles. If so, the idea of sanctioning preventive strikes will only initiate and invite further retaliation and escalation.

The commission's report (which fulfills a media dream) is also obviously linked to our emerging concept of low-intensity warfare, replacing the rationale for US military might now that the Soviet threat is in decline. In this fashion, the media have helped to reconvince taxpayers that they must support the defense budget to pacify a mean and scary world. It is a wonder that nowhere in the commission's 60 recommendations does the report endorse or highlight ideas such as researching the causes of terrorism, using diplomacy, resolving conflicts, negotiating, determining peace settlements, or removing the causes of violent discontent while encouraging the spread of economic freedom, social justice, and political democracy. With the course of international rapprochement running so smoothly (if surprisingly) these days, it can only be hoped that the commission report has served its purposes, revived interest in the topic, and allowed us to accept its best motives as our own. It is necessary, however, to improve media channels of communication with governments, publics, and potential terrorist groups to improve our knowledge about causes, solutions, and the mass media's future role in terrorism as a systemic symbiotic, and symbolic set of phenomena.

References

Agee, W., et al. (1982). *Perspectives on Mass Communications*. New York, NY: Harper & Row.

Alexander, Y. (Spring/Summer 1978). "Terrorism, the Media, and the Police" in *Journal of International Affairs*, No. 32.

Alexander, Y. and S. Finger (eds.) (1977). *Terrorism*. New York, NY: John Jay.

Altheide, D. (June 1987). "Format and Symbols in TV Coverage of Terrorism in the United States and Great Britain" in *International Studies Quarterly*, No. 31.

Anzovin, S. (ed.) (1986). *Terrorism*. New York, NY: H. W. Wilson Co.

Atwater, T. (March 1988). *Network Evening News Coverage of the TWA Hostage Crisis*. Boston, MA: Terrorism and the News Media Research Project, Emerson College.

Bagdikian, B. (1987). *The Media Monopoly*. Boston, MA: Beacon Press.

Bechelloni, G. (1978). "Il colpa di stato in diretta" in A. Silj (ed.) *Brigate Rosse-Stato*. Florence, Italy: Valecchi.

Bocca, G. (1985). *Noi Terroristi*. Milan, Italy: Garzanti.

Bremer III, L. (March 1987). "Practical Measures for Dealing with Terrorism," pp. 104 in *Department of State Bulletin*.

Brown, H. (1969). *Die, Nigger, Die*. New York, NY: Dial Press.

Bruck, P. (Winter 1989). "Strategies for Peace, Strategies for News Research," pp. 111-113 in *Journal of Communication*, Vol. 39, No. 1.

Caserta, J. (1978). *The Red Brigades*. New York, NY: Manor Books.

Chomsky, N. (1988). *The Culture of Terorism*. Boston, MA: South End Press.

Chomsky, N. (1986). *Pirates and Emperors: International Terrorism in the Real World*. Brattleboro, VT: Amana Books.

Cohen, S. and J. Young (1973). *The Manufacture of News*. Beverly Hills, CA: Sage.

Cooper, T. (July 1988). *Terrorism and Perspectivist Philosophy*. Boston, MA: Terrorism and the News Media Research Project, Emerson College.

Crenshaw, M. (1986). "Terrorism: What Shall We Do?" in S. Anzovin (ed.) *Terrorism*. Bronx, NY: H. W. Wilson.

Crenshaw, M. (1987). "The International Consequences of Terrorism," pp. 4-8 in *The Sovereign Citizen*, Vol. 2, No. 1.

Davies, H. and P. Walton (1983). "Death of a Premier," p. 40 in H. Davies and P. Walton (eds.) *Language, Image, Media*. New York, NY: St. Martin's.

Davies, M. (August 20, 1989). "Self-Restraint on Hostage News," p. 83 in *The Hartford Courant*.

Davies, M. (October 1985). "Mass Media and Televsion." Speech to Associated Press, San Francisco, CA.

Der Derian, J. (1989). "The Importance of Shredding in Earnest: Reading the National Security Culture and Terrorism" in I. Angus and S. Jhally (eds.) *Cultural Politics in Contemporary America*. New York: NY: Routledge.

Dobkin, B. (1989). "Rhetorical Depiction of Terrorism as an Instrument of U.S. Foreign Policy" in *Speech Communication Annual*, Vol. 3.

Dobkin, B. (November 1989). "Terrorism and Media Research: Perspective on the Creation of a Public Problem: Perspectives on the Creation of a Public Problem." Paper prepared for the Speech Communication Association Annual Convention, San Francisco, CA.

Freedman, J. and D. Sears (1965). "Selective Exposure," pp. 58-97 in *Advances in Experimental Social Psychology*, No. 2.

Genovese, M. (1988). "Terrorism," p. 143 in R. Heibert and G. Reuss (eds.) *Impact of Mass Media*. New York, NY: Longmans.

Gerbner, G. (March 1988). "Violence and Terror in the Mass Media" in *Reports and Papers in Mass Communications*. Paris, France: Unesco.

Gerbner, I. and G. Gerbner (July 1988). *Symbolic Functions of Violence and Terror*. Boston, MA: Terrorism and the News Media Research Project, Emerson College.

Gitlin, T. (1980). *The Whole World is Watching: Media in the Making and Unmaking of the New Left*. Berkeley, CA: University of California Press.

Graber, D. (1989). *Mass Media and American Politics* (Third ed., rev.). Washington, DC: Congressional Quarterly Press.

Graber, D. (1980). *Mass Media and American Politics* (First ed.). Washington, DC: Congressional Quarterly Press.

Hacker, F. (1976). *Crusaders, Criminals, Crazies*. New York, NY: W. W. Norton.

Hamilton, L. and J. Hamilton (March 1983). "Dynamics of Terrorism" in *International Studies Quarterly*, No. 27.

Hickey, N. (July 31 and August 7, 1976). "Terorism and Television," p. 10 in *T.V. Guide*.

Hoge, J. (1982). "The Media and Terrorism," p. 91 in A. Miller (ed.) *Terrorism and the Law*. Dobbs Ferry, NY: Transnational Publishers.

Klapper, J. (1960). *The Effects of Mass Communications*. Glencoe, IL: The Free Press.

Laqueur, W. (1987). *The Age of Terrorism*. Boston, MA: Little, Brown.

Laqueur, W. (1977). *Terrorism*. Boston, MA: Little, Brown.

Laqueur, W. (March 1976). "The Futility of Terrorism" in *Harpers*.

Larson, M. (Spring 1989). "Presidential News Coverage and 'All Things Considered:' National Public Radio and News Bias," p. 351 in *Presidential Studies Quarterly*, No. 29.

Lazarsfeld, P. and R. Merton (1971). "Mass Communication, Popular Taste, and Organized Social Actions," pp. 554-578 in W. Schramm and D. Roberts (eds.) *The Process and Effects of Mass Communications*. Urbana, IL: University of Illinois Press.

Livingstone, N. and T. Arnold (eds.) (1987). *Fighting Back*. Lexington, MA: D. C. Heath.

Livingstone, W. (1987). "Terrorism and the Media Revolution" in N. Livingstone and T. Arnold (eds.) *Fighting Back*. Lexington, MA: D. C. Heath.

Lule, J. (March 1988). *The Myth of My Widow*. Boston, MA: Terrorism and News Media Research Project, Emerson College.

Lumley, B. and P. Schlesinger (1982). "The Press, The State, and Its Enemies" in *American Sociological Review*, No. 30.

Netanyahu, B. (ed.) (1986). *Terrorism: How the West Can Win*. New York, NY: Farrar, Straus & Giroux.

Newhouse, J. (July 10, 1989). "Annals of Intelligence (Terrorism)," p. 71 in *The New Yorker*.

Martin, D. and J. Walcott (1988). *Best Laid Plans: America's War Against Terrorism*. New York, NY: Harper & Row.
Midlarsky, M., M. Crenshaw, and F. Yoshida (June 1980). "Why Violence Spreads: The Contagion of International Terrorism" in *International Studies Quarterly*, No. 276.
Morrison, P. (1986). "Limits to Technocratic Consciousness: Information Technology and Terrorism as Example" in *Science: Technology and Human Values*, No. 11.
Paletz, D., J. Ayanian, and P. Fozzard (1982). "The IRA, The Red Brigades, and the FALN" in *New York Times Journal of Communication*, No. 2.
Paletz, D. and R. Entman (1981). *Media Power Politics*. New York, NY: The Free Press/MacMillan.
Palmerton, P. (1988). "The Rhetoric of Terorism and Media Response to the 'Crisis in Iran,'" pp. 52, 105-121 in *Western Journal of Speech Communication*, Vol. 52.
Payerhin, M. (1988). "Terrorism and the News Media: The Case of Moro." Unpublished Master Thesis, Department of Political Science, University of Connecticut, Storrs, CT.
Picard, R. (July 1988). *News Coverage as the Contagion of Terrorism*. Boston, MA: Terrorism and the News Media Research Project, Emerson College.
Picard, R. and P. Adams (March 1988). *Characterizations of Acts and Perpetrators of Political Violence in Three Elite US Daily Newspapers*. Boston, MA: Terrorism and the News Media Research Project, Emerson College.
Ra'anan, U., et al. (1986). *Hydra of Carnage*. Lexington, MA: D. C. Heath.
Rikhye, I. (1989). *The Future of Peacekeeping*. New York, NY: International Peace Academy.
Robinson, G. (1984). "Television News and the Claim to Facticity," pp. 199-221 in W. Roland and B. Watkins (eds.) *Interpreting Television*. Beverly Hills, CA: Sage.
Rosso, S. (1976). *Brigate Rosse*. Milan, Italy: Feltrinelli.
Rubin, J. (1970). *Do It*. New York, NY: Ballantine.
Rummel, R. (September 1988). "Political Systems, Violence, and War" in *USIP Journal*, Vol. 1, No. 4.
Rusk, Z. (1965). *381 US 1*. Washington, DC: United States Supreme Court.
Said, E. (1988). "The Essential Terrorist," pp. 149-158 in E. Said and C. Hutchins (eds.) *Blaming the Victims*. New York, NY: Verso.
Schmid, A. and J. de Graaf (1982). *Violence as Communication*. Beverly Hills, CA: Sage.
Sciascia, L. (1978). *L'Affaire Moro*. Palermo, Italy: Sellorio.
Silj, A. (ed.) (1978). *Brigate Rosse-Stato*. Florence, Italy: Valecchi.
Stanley, H. and R. Niemi (1988). *Vital Statistics on American Politics*. Washington, DC: Congressional Quarterly Press.
Tan, Z. (1987). "Mass Media and Insurgent Terrorism." Ph.D. dissertation. Ann Arbor, MI: University of Michigan.
T.V. Guide (July 31, 1976).
UMI Research Collections Information Service (1989). *Terrorism: An International Resource File Brochure*. Ann Arbor, MI: University of Michigan Press.
US Department of Justice (1976). *Task Force on Disorders and Terrorism*. Washington, DC: GPO.
Wagner-Pacifica, R. (1987). *The Moro Mortality Play: Terrorism as Social Drama*. Chicago, IL: University of Chicago Press.
Weimann, G. (1983). "Theater of Terror" in *Journal of Communication*, No. 43.
Wilber, H. (April 1985). "The Role of the Media During a Terrorist Incident," pp. 20-23 in *FBI Law Enforcement Bulletin*.

Chapter 14
Democracy and Virtual Politics

Andy Koch

Appalachian State University, Boone, North Carolina, USA

Abstract

This chapter examines the impact of digital technologies on the construction of political subjectivity. We examine three models of political agency: the passive agent, the rational actor, and the sovereign subject. Using the 2000 German Green Party convention in Baden-Württemberg, the thesis will challenge the notion that information technologies can create a sovereign subject. Based on Jean Baudrillard's writings, we will argue that information technologies will do little more than create a simulation of democracy.

Introduction

Considerable debate has emerged recently over the role and impact of new information technologies for political life. Attitudes range from glowing predictions of the new technology's ability to open public space for open discourse and a reinvigoration of democratic life to various pessimistic appraisals of the new technologies as the harbinger of a technological police state. In the middle, one finds claims suggesting that information technologies are not likely to change very much in the political culture since they will adapt to the existing structures of society rather than alter them in any wholesale fashion (Resnick, 1998, p. 49). In fact, evidence can be put forward to support each of these claims.

These discussions often overlook the impact of digitization on the subject as political agent. The digitized communications media is usually discussed as if it can transmit a full spectrum of information in any context of communications. Technical limitations are not usually discussed. In fact, where it is discussed at all, the technology is usually applauded as a liberating potential. As stated by Anna Sampaio and Janis Aragon, cyberspace is a place of anonymity, where traditional markers of hierarchy (e.g., age, sex, and race) no longer are tagged to human subjectivity (Sampaio and Aragon, 1998, p. 153). One is free to enter a chat room and take on any identity one wishes.

Without hierarchy and the symbolic tags of human identity, cyberspace is a place where reason can have its domain. It is a place of democratic potential, a public sphere designed for interactivity and participation. As Juliet Roper (1998, p. 69) describes it, cyberspace can provide the Habermasian space for communicative action, free from the influences of domination and subordination.

This chapter explores another aspect of information technology's impact on political subjectivity. To the extent that the technology is use for organizational/informational purposes, it is a medium of one-way communications. In this regard, it is little different from television or radio, apart from some additional selectivity afforded by the technology. The subject is still a passive agent. However the optimist's argument regarding the new technologies is predicated on the idea that it is also used as a means of interactive discourse in which a subject can log onto chat rooms and websites in which there is two-way communication. This interactive process provides not only the chance for political organizing and mobilizing like-minded participants, but also developing ideas and on-going discourse and discussion. In this form, information technologies reinforce the model of the Cartesian rational actor in the world, seeking information to engage in the pursuit of rationally conceived ends. Finally, carried to its political conclusions, the new technologies available via the web have the potential to provide an arena of sovereign interaction. In this use, continuing within Cartesian logic, the subject is assumed to be an autonomous actor capable of making transcendentally arrived at conclusions in a public arena that will direct the exercise of collective power.

This chapter examines the 2000 political convention of Baden-Württemberg's Green Party as a step toward implementing the sovereign actor model of subjectivity. While still not at the level of state sovereignty, participants in the party meeting were able to vote and make decisions that were binding on the party. After describing some details surrounding this meeting, we analyze the nature of sovereign subjectivity in cyberspace. Lurking in the background of the rational actor view of human subjectivity are concerns regarding the extent to which such a view applies in the post-Cartesian, post-industrial, and postmodern world. Using the insights of the French postmodern thinker Jean Baudrillard, we will argue that the medium is at least partly responsible for shaping the actors engaged in political activity. Baudrillard claims that our social world has lost its connection to a transcendentally grounded notion of reality. What we call reality is an increasingly simulated experience of the world. The digitized politics of the Green Party meeting in Baden-Württemberg was simply a step further toward simulated politics and, more specifically, simulated democracy.

Organization of the Green Party Convention in Baden-Württemberg

The Virtual Party Convention of the Greens took place between November 24 and December 3, 2000. This party convention opened up a new phase of the use of Internet technology by parties and political organizations. For the first time (at least in Germany), a party convention was completely organized using electronic networks. Members, party delegates, and the executive committee of the party made decisions in cyberspace. These decisions were then binding for the entire party within Baden-Württemberg. The party convention debated two issues: shop opening hours and, appropriately, electronic democracy. The online discussions were based on these two topics, with different motions on the two topics being introduced in the course of the discussions. The process of discussing the issues, changing the wording of motions, and making decisions about these changes, as well as the final party statements, were done via the Internet.

Regarding the organization structure of the meeting, the organizers hoped to mirror the structures and characteristics of a real party convention as completely as possible. This was also necessary to guarantee the legitimacy of the convention and to protect against charges that somehow the results were not consistent with democratic procedures. Access to the activities of the convention was organized on three different levels. 1) Spectators to the party activities. This was essentially open to any interested person with an Internet connection. To gain access; one only had to log onto www.virtueller-parteitag.de. Anyone could listen in to the discussions and learn about the results of the voting process. 2) Green Party members acting as participants. When these members notified the Green Party's administrative office that they intended to participate, they were sent a password via regular mail. The password enabled this group of participants to enter into the discussions, formulate amendments to the motions, and support amendments of other participants. In this regard, they were able to participate as "rational actors" but not sovereign ones. 3) Green Party delegates. Just as in a traditional party convention, voting was restricted to the party delegates. This group included officially elected party delegates and the members of the executive committee.

The virtual space found at the website was subdivided into various rooms and functional spaces. In the virtual convention office, visitors could gain information about the organization and the highlights of the convention as well as actual news. In the Convention Hall the discussion forums took place using a content-management system for the automatic administration of the participant's statements and amendments. Finally, there was the voting space with an electronic voting booth that could be accessed by the party delegates. By encrypting the data and the authentication of digital votes via a trust center, a high degree of data security was achieved. The data security issue was dealt with by the company BROKAT, which is a technology leader in this field.

The Participants and Their Experience

The Greens in Baden-Württemberg claim 7,500 members. Only 303 members participated at the party convention. Out of this group, 113 were voting members, as either officially elected delegates or as executive committee members. The other 190 participants were interested party members, who took part in the discussions and wanted to explore the new Internet experiments. Surveys (conducted by the Institute for Technology Assessment in Stuttgart) of the participants indicated, with very few exceptions, that participants had already been very politically active. Most said they had participated in previous party conventions. They were also very computer-literate and were regular Internet users. The participants were further distinguished by their high educational levels. Up to 90% had passed the abitur and

70% had completed a university degree or were studying at a university. Only one participant had a basic school degree.

Since non-voting party members could participate in the discussions, compared to regular party conventions, a bigger group of simple party members participated. Furthermore, there was a record number of discussion statements: 792. Close to every second official participant made some contribution to the discussion, so participation levels were high. In the end, 62.7% of participants either endorsed or supported an amendment, indicating intense participation.

From this data, it is clear that the obstacles to direct participation were much lower then at a real party convention. Many more people voiced opinions and did so repeatedly. There was no need to stand up in a huge auditorium where people instantly reacted to one's opinion. The participants also believed that a real party convention would take much more of their time and did not fit as neatly into their daily routines. This made it much easier to combine work, family, and politics.

The data gathered from the delegates indicated two problem areas. Generally, the participants were satisfied with the content of the debate, but not the structure. Many participants had problems with the often unstructured and unmoderated discussions. The party convention had 20 discussion forums running; if one moved about the various forums or disconnected for a period of time, it became difficult to follow the flow of the arguments. The various forums were unsorted and unmoderated and postings were listed only based on temporal criteria. This was a conscious decision on the part of the party to avoid the perception that the executive committee was trying to intervene and manipulate the outcome. In the end, this contributed to an impression by a large number of delegates that the virtual convention was complex and, at times, difficult to follow.

The greatest problem participants cited was lack of personal contacts. One-to-one communication was hardly possible and the informal talks that usually take place at a party convention did not occur at the virtual convention. Because participants were to post their comments to public and semi-public spaces, it was impossible to communicate synchronically or confidentially with specific groups or a single person. The participants were not able to see who was online at the same time they were. At the end, many participants missed the atmosphere of a "real" party convention; the majority claimed that real conventions are much more fun. They missed the emotions, the high-flying speeches, the back room maneuvering, and the opportunity to get to know new people not just as postings on a screen, but as real, complex, multi-dimensional, human beings.

In the end, the data gathered showed that only one person indicated that the virtual convention should replace the real party convention in the future. The virtual meetings were seen as a means to augment the party in its organizing activity or for special issues that arose, but that they should not be a wholesale substitute.

The questions surrounding the data on the party convention are not the facts themselves, but what interpretive framework should be used to analyze the data. In the following sections, different characterizations of human agency will be developed. The focus will be on the relationship between the use of information technology and the model of human agency enhanced by the use of the technology. A detailed discussion of Jean Baudrillard's take on information technology and human beings will follow. We will then return to this data for some analysis.

Three Models of Human Agency and the New Information Technology

Optimists regarding the use of the new technology claim that it can expand democratic participation in the Western democracies. From this perspective, the Internet constitutes a new public space in which the citizenry can become informed and organized for rational political activity. Pessimists claim that the Internet is equally compatible with hierarchical rule (Schmidtke, 1998, p. 65). From this perspective, no automatic expansion of democracy should be expected from the new technology. Impossible as it may be to adopt either wholesale optimism or pessimism about the impact of information technology on political life, it is possible to make observations about some of the impacts of this technology.

However, to fully understand these changes, it is necessary to make one assumption: human nature is not static. In the contact with the various forms of information technology, the behavior, norms, and self-understanding of human subjectivity become altered. Following the claims of Marshall McLuhan (1962) (and a position adopted by Jean Baudrillard), we will assert that the human subject is altered by the conditions of communications technology. The new information technologies cannot be seen as simply being adapted to a static conception of subjectivity but are, themselves, part of a cultural milieu that, in turn, shapes the parameters of thought and the expectations of collective action. McLuhan claims that as print caused the alteration of our conception of self, so the information technologies of today are reconstructing our means of thinking about ourselves in a social and political context. Subjectivity is shaped and reoriented based on this new technology. In this context, distance is overcome by speed. Today, scarcity of information is replaced by what Baudrillard refers to as an "obscenity" of information, as information overload. Therefore, no uniform outcome can be expected from the new technology. Outcomes will be reflective of the way in which the subject interacts with the technology itself. Three such models of interaction can be identified: passive agent, rational actor, and sovereign actor.

Passive Agent

To the extent that human interaction with information technology constitutes a one-way flow of information from a person, group, or commercial interest to the viewer of web material, the passive agent model of subjectivity is being reinforced. In this usage, the viewer may be seeking information or be solicited by the person or organization possessing the viewed material. In either case, the viewer is engaged with the material as a passive agent, not interacting or engaging in any discourse with the material, beyond possibly clicking from one subsection to another. In this role, the Internet simply has the character of any other mechanism for mass communications. It hosts the display of prepackaged material, without the possibility of active engagement on the part of the web viewer.

This model has predominated in the commercialization of the web, but it has also been adopted by organized political groups, activist organizations, political parties, and government entities. In this usage, the Internet takes on the character of a sophisticated billboard for advertising purposes. In political terms, this usage has been undertaken by political parties in most of the industrial democracies as well as by government, itself. Examples of government's use of this model can be found in American cities (e.g., Glendale, Passadena, and Santa Monica in California). However, this model is not what Habermas had in mind as expanding the public sphere. As Oliver Schmidtke (1998, p. 67) puts it, the Internet provides the perfect public relations tool for government because it can disseminate information to rationalize all of its policies. In terms of usage, this model is the most consistent with top-down hierarchical control; it has the effect of reinforcing group identity, without regard for bottom-up political influence.

Rational Actor

If the passive agent model can be said to raise concerns about the continuation of hierarchy and control, optimists point to the rational actor model as carrying the potential for a new form of civil democracy. Here, the idea of a newsgroup (in which there is an ongoing question-and-answer format) replaces the Internet as a medium of passive consumption. Individuals can seek special information or organize chat rooms, interest groups, or e-mail lists, all at a very low cost (Resnick, 1998, p. 64). In this usage, the net resembles a pluralistic civil society, egalitarian in terms of each participant's voice having the same potential, where only the stronger argument will prevail. For this reason, Douglas Kellner (1998, p. 173) stresses the importance of resistance groups to mobilize via the web to counteract the organized economic interests seeking to subjugate the populous.

This raises an interesting question with regard to the web and its content. On this level; the web lends itself equally well to agents of change on both the left and the right of the political spectrum. It is a medium of discourse for both anarchists and fascists. Therefore, regarding political ideology and the Internet, it is necessary to conclude that the web contains no implicit normative bias toward democracy. It contains potential as both a medium of control and a means to encourage more democratic participation. Either potential can be realized.

What can be claimed is that the Internet used in this mode has a conditioning influence on subjectivity. Here, the Internet reinforces the Cartesian idea of an individual rational subject seeking to grasp the objective environment as part of his/her life experience. As Tim Jordon (1999, p. 96) puts it, from this perspective cyberspace is a "place where individuals can finally wrest control of their being from institutions, governments, corporations, and oppressions." However, since the Internet contains no necessary normative claims with regard to community and since it reinforces an individualistic conception of subjectivity, some scholars have concluded that the political outcome of the web's influence on human subjectivity will be one of political fragmentation (Schmidtke, 1998, p. 61).

Sovereign Actor

The sovereign actor model, in its ideal form, seeks to carry the rational actor model to its political conclusion. As a sovereign actor, the individual approaches the Internet both as a medium of information and a venue for participating in binding collective decisions for some administrative unit. In this model, the web is a place to conduct direct or plebiscite democracy. Some see this as the means to overcome the apathy and cynicism increasingly found in Western democracies.

While yet to be implemented in this form, various experiments tilted in this direction. In Athens, the Pericles project was launched in 1992 (Tsagarousianou, 1998). Started by a group of intellectuals and scientists, "Network Pericles" set up a terminal in Athens so citizens could raise issues, gather information, and express opinions by voting. While the results are not binding and constitute more of an ongoing public poll, the framework could be used as a model for expressing collective decisions. Experiments are taking place in other European cities such as Amsterdam, Manchester, and Bologna. In the US 2000 presidential primaries, citizens of Arizona were able to cast their votes online. The party meeting of the Greens in Baden-Württemberg also moves in that direction. Delegates were able to raise issues, exchange ideas, and then cast binding votes for the party.

Critics of the sovereign actor model generally raise the issue of access. Will this be democratic if all people do not have an Internet connection? But on the level of the political impact of the web on human subjectivity, a more complex paradox emerges. Even if one adopts the Cartesian model of the rational subject, it would seem that two features of the Internet operate to inhibit the realization of the online revitalization of community and democracy. As discussed in the previous section, the specialized information that can be provided on the web does not require allegiance to the local institutional authority. Because the web has no territoriality and no boundaries, all notions of geographic boundaries are not generally reinforced as part of socialization on the web. All exists as a simultaneous presence. In other words, there is no necessary reason to engage in a relegitimation of the nation-state. The extra-territorial nature of the Internet does not reinforce the normative components of territorial administration. From this perspective, the nation-state is nothing but nostalgic fiction (Angell, 1996; Ohmae, 1995). As Kenichi Ohmae (1995, p. 64) describes it, the nation-state is reduced to a protection racket designed to protect the biggest racketeers.

Debate regarding the political role of the Internet generally falls into one of these three categories. But is this all that can be said about the significance of the web for social and political life? In the next section, we will explore the work of Jean Baudrillard. He shifts the focus away from the liberating potential of the Internet and raises questions about how the technology also serves as a system of epistemological constraints on communications. As a result, serious questions are raised about information technologies' liberating potential.

Baudrillard's Developmental History and Rise of Simulated Politics

French philosopher Jean Baudrillard has written extensively on the topics of technology, media, and culture, among other interests. His writings represent a synthesis of Marshall McLuhan's work on media, Max Weber's concerns about Enlightenment rationality, leftist politics, and postmodern epistemology. To put it mildly, Baudrillard is pessimistic about how the new information technologies are used. In the context of different models discussed previously, optimism regarding the use of these new technologies requires a belief that they will enhance the rational actor or sovereign actor models of political life. Baudrillard does not view the technology that way. For him, the use of information technology reinforces the passive agent model of human subjectivity; thus, it is not a mechanism for political liberation, but a new medium for domination and control.

For Baudrillard, information technology represents a medium that diminishes the value of human subjectivity itself. Meaning is lost within the network of communications. Thought is replaced by stimulation. Deliberation is replaced by immediacy. The real is being "murdered" by the process of rationalization and the virtual world (Baudrillard, 2000, p. 164).

In this context, political life is not just altered; it is destroyed. Political life (which was characterized by the drama of subjects struggling against the alienating components of economic and political repression) now disappears in a digitized universe. In contrast to McLuhan, the medium does not create the global village, but the isolated and alienated subject, a subject now cut off from the public space needed for real political interaction. In its place is a simulation of politics. Using the Internet as a medium of politics furthers the process of estrangement in social life and neutralizes the potentials of political interaction.

Baudrillard and Poststructuralist Epistemology

While at times criticizing other poststructuralists and denying his part in the postmodern movement, Baudrillard's epistemology clearly aligns him with poststructuralists. Generally, poststructuralism can be said to incorporate three elements: the rejection of reason's transcendental character, the historical nature of truth, and the claim that power relations are the basis of social and political life.

To poststructuralists in general, Western philosophy since Plato has been engaged in a misguided enterprise. It sought to create a body of knowledge that can claim to have the status of an ahistorical truth that can survive the vicissitudes of material being. A column of truth is to be erected around which social and political life can be ordered (Derrida, 1981). To do this, some form of dualistic philosophy is necessary in which the faculty of "reason" is said to ascend to this universal form of "knowledge." For Plato, this is accomplished via the dialectic and the fixed nature of the forms. In Descartes, Kant, and others, a similar process (called "reason") uncovers the universals that transcend historical change.

Influenced by Friedrich Nietzsche's claims, Baudrillard and other post-structuralists assert that all claims to knowledge are historical. Knowledge is created to serve human needs that are historical and material in nature. When identities are assigned to objects and hypotheses are constructed to explain the interaction of those objects, the results are always hypothetical and probabilistic in character. Ethics are constructed to meet immediate human social problems and should not be assigned any universal or transcendent character. Baudrillard (1983, p. 86) assigns the notion of natural law to the medieval period in Western history.

In epistemological terms, "knowledge" reflects the conditions of its own generation. That is, the production of knowledge is circular. What we term knowledge always reflects and reinforces the assumptions of the context out of which it was created. Out of need, we construct a model of the real. We then make the world conform to the model (Baudrillard, 1983, pp. 1-3). The knowledge contained in the model is a simulation of the world, but the simulation is reinforced as if it is real via its own enactment and dissemination. This is not unlike Niklas Luhmann's (1990) notion of "self-referencing systems."

If the logocentric tradition in the West is rejected by Baudrillard and the poststructuralists, so too is the Cartesian model of the human subject. There can be no "rational actor" making autonomous decisions about his/her life if the conditions for transcendent choice are not present. For Baudrillard, information technologies are not vehicles for liberation but new sets of constraints in which communications takes place. In contrast to the rational actor model, the new technologies require a further refinement and filtering of the means of communications, thus constraining the character of communications.

Rejecting the model of the rational actor also eliminates the possibility of sovereign actors and the idea that information technologies can enhance democratic practice. In the absence of universal truth around which to organize social and political practice, the idea of democracy itself takes on a historical character. Political life is a struggle for the domination of models and metaphors. Therefore, the real question regarding the new information technologies will be the effect they have on altering the metaphors and the models to which humans must conform. Baudrillard's conclusion can best be understood in the context of his claims regarding simulation and what he terms the three orders of appearance.

The Three Orders of Appearance

The central concept in Baudrillard's middle and later work is simulation. Simulation (which represents the current means of constructing the symbolic order) is actually the third form by which value is generated since the Renaissance. In the simulated order, Baudrillard contends we have lost the ability to distinguish the real from the fabrication. In place of the real are operational models in which the real is replaced by organizations of signs and symbolic reference points that point to other signs within the operational model. All that is not explained by the model must be either ignored or destroyed. Baudrillard claims that in today's political realm, participation increasingly takes on the character of a simulation

The first "order of appearance" Baudrillard calls the counterfeit. The counterfeit emerges as a reaction to the rigid structure of status represented by the feudal order. The emergence of the Renaissance (with the belief in human equality, transcendent reason, and natural law) required a new distribution of social signs and a new mechanism for generating the signs of value. In order for all classes to use the signs equally, a new mechanism for the production of value was required. Still grounded in a notion of the real, the symbolic value of the real could be copied and distributed to the masses in the system of exchange that characterized the development of the bourgeois order (Baudrillard, 1983, p. 86).

The second order of appearance emerges with the industrial revolution. In what Baudrillard (1983, p. 96) refers to as the "industrial simulacrum," symbolic value is manufactured on a massive scale. While the counterfeit retained a certain individuality in its reproduction of the real, the development of industrial production was organized to generate a series of identical products. Baudrillard's interest is not just in the technological aspects of this transformation, but in its cultural impact. The significance of the process is rooted in the fact that organizational principles replace those of representation (Baudrillard, 1983, pp. 93-95). As a result, human beings are subordinated to the machine in the process of production. Natural law is replaced by mercantile value and the calculation of force (Baudrillard 1983, p. 9). It is through the ability to mass produce that money, value, and signs are distributed in the society (Baudrillard, 1983, p. 97).

In political terms, the production of value as a series not only subordinates human beings to the machine and the operational necessities of the production process, it also creates a cultural standard of value. The political order is characterized by conformity, as a series that is also mass-produced. Baudrillard makes it clear that the emergence of industrial production sets up a logic of operations that cause the "liquidation of the real" (Baudrillard, 1983, p. 95). However, it is with the emergence of simulation proper that this process reaches its fruition.

To Baudrillard, our contemporary age is characterized by simulation. Simulation represents the generation of the "real" without reference to an origin. In other words, the project is to make the real conform to a simulation (Baudrillard, 1983, p. 2). Simulation represents a condition in which the measure of truth, meaning, and value are validated by their correspondence to the prevailing model in which they are constructed (Baudrillard, 1983, p. 32). Today, we live in a hallucination of the real (Baudrillard, 1983, p. 148). Discourse on the metaphysics of being has given way to the metaphysics of the "code," a projection of an "objective" form of knowledge. As Baudrillard describes this process, the Jesuit drive for unity and certainty has returned to us in the postmodern era in the form of mapping DNA, a task designed to remove any ambiguity about human nature.

To understand the significance of what Baudrillard means by simulation, remember that to the poststructuralists in general, truth, value, and meaning are historical constructions. Therefore, technology and communications play a significant part in the construction and significance of the sign. This means that the mechanisms employed m the process of transmitting signs, value, and meaning circumscribe the limits of what can and cannot be transmitted. Quoting McLuhan, Baudri1lard repeats that the "medium is the message" (Baudrillard, 1983, p. 124).

The medium today is electronic communication, particularly the Internet. The Intenet is a digitized medium, characterized by binary code. Baudrillard's claim is that there is a parallel process taking place on a cultural level in which the entire realm of social interaction is entering a phase in which the computer's binary code is being replicated within the forms of human interaction. Today, we have the "mystic elegance of the binary system, of the zero and the one from which all being proceeds" (Baudrillard, 1983, p. 106). Human contact is being replaced by a digitized realm where only that which can lend itself to digitization can be considered as the proper content of communications. This means that political interaction increasingly takes the form of a choice among binary opposites.

Technology, Politics, and the "Code"

Baudrillard (2000, p. 64) asserts that today, the real has been murdered by the process of rationalization and the virtual world. The significance of this notion for politics cannot be overstated. While Baudrillard views all three orders of appearance as means of control, he focuses most on the plight of freedom within the process of simulation. Baudrillard saw the political process within the Enlightenment as dominated by a particular drama, as the masses struggled against forces that sought to alienate or oppress them. The Enlightenment conception of reason was the tool of liberation, as reason was to enlighten a superstitious mass to the understanding that their acquiescence is what allowed despots to live (Baudrillard, 1988, p. 217). Today, we are no longer subject or object, alienated, or free. This is so because now, man's alienation by man is a thing of the past (Baudrillard, 1993, pp. 58-59). Now, we are alienated by machines and the code.

The "telecomputer man" of the contemporary age is not aware of the condition of his own servitude (Baudrillard, 1993, p. 59). We have been integrated into the machines of communications (Baudrillard, 1993, p. 58). This "prosthesis" displays the spectacle of thought, but is incapable of displaying thought itself (Baudrillard, 1993, pp. 51-52). Freedom is manifested as freedom for virtual interaction rather than real social and political action (Baudrillard, 1994a, p. 30).

The result of this digitized interaction of screens rather than people is that real political interaction is dead (Baudrillard, 1993, p. 41). Today, the value of a political message is not in its meaning, but in its circulation. The idea of human agency (of subjects acting in the world) is replaced by a new metaphor. Human beings now become sending and receiving "satellites" connected in webs of networks, in which being connected and transmitting information becomes an ontological end in itself, a new means of gratification (Baudrillard, 1988b).

This new means of gratification is satisfied by an orgy of superfluous information. Baudrillard calls this the new form of obscenity (Baudrillard, 1988b, p. 24). Within this context, the idea of meaningful public space is disappearing. All is transparent, but all is on the surface. There is no depth and no meaning (Baudrillard, 1988b, p. 12). The use of binary coding for the transmission of information alters the content to fit the technology. With binary coding, the symbolic dimension of language is lost (Baudrillard, 2000, p. 69). Politics (as a struggle to overcome the condition of alienation and oppression) takes on the character of a simulation. Virtual liberation masks the continued expansion of the instruments of oppression. The transpolitical replaces the political and the political game in the world becomes that of seduction (Baudrillard, 1988b, p. 59).

The simulation of politics is coupled with a de-ideologicalization of the masses (Baudrillard, 1993, p. 41). Baudrillard does not view this as a positive development because of the process that has come to replace that of an ideological commitment. In the place of ideology, Baudrillard sees the public opinion poll. The process of opinion polling sits at the nexus of several of Baudrillard's comments about the political. The opinion poll is part of the orgy of information that obfuscates the struggle against oppression. It covers up the real structure of oppression because the public does not really form independent or transcendent positions anyway. Baudrillard believes that the opinions of the masses are responses shaped by cues received from the political class and from a prepackaged corporate media structure that does not allow space to construct an independently formed opinion (Baudrillard, 1993, p. 41). The real effect of the concept of "public opinion" is to neutralize class antagonisms. It seeks to substitute the idea of a single outcome, a united path, among competing and antagonistic groups.

The de-ideologized mass now becomes "prey to probability theory" (Baudrillard, 1993, p. 41). Opinion polls and statistical analysis now produce "truths" for simulated politics. There can be no rational dissention because "objective data," probability theory, rational choice ontology, and expanding consumer consumption now establish the singular path to the future. The unity of humankind is established. All are the same. The power of seduction is such that to think otherwise is to be irrational.

From this perspective, introducing the Internet into the political realm does not open up new areas of public space. Baudrillard's contention is that public space is disappearing because the virtual space of the web is not real public space (Baudrillard, 1988b, p. 19). Within this framework, the politics on the web is part of the erosion of the political. Political parties represent the compulsion of the game, organizations designed to extend the influence of power. This process requires more than one party since debate between two subgoups of the political class can create the illusion of legitimacy. Therefore, claims Baudrillard (1983, p. 132), political parties position themselves to render a 50/50 split in the voters so election results are simply the product of chance. Election results do not lead to major changes anyway since both political factions tend to represent the conditioning of the corporate interests and the political class as reflected in the media. The Internet is just one more medium for organizing and controlling the masses.

For Baudrillard to draw this type of conclusion, he must reject the idea that media, in general, are mechanisms that further the notions of either rational or sovereign actors. The masses are simply passive agents of manipulation, mesmerized and seduced by the illusion of political choices that appear to them on voting day, whether that voting is to take place in a booth at a fixed location or via the web in cyberspace. Whether represented by the Greens in Baden-Württemberg, the Pericles project in Athens, or the Arizona primary, all extend the conformity of the dominant ontological model of consumption and expansion.

Party in the Simulacrum

Within the framework for analysis suggested by Baudrillard, the virtual party convention in Baden-Württemberg must be seen as reflecting a number of problematic and even contradictory elements. On the one hand, virtual politics has the ability to take the democratic ethos of the Enlightenment project and expand it with the use of the new technology. On the other hand, with virtual interaction replacing human contact, using the web to enhance political sovereignty only produces a simulation of democratic political practice.

Claims about the strength of the technology focus on the level and quality of participation by the delegates. Using the web has the potential to produce high levels of participation. In theory, this is qualitatively different participation than passively watching the event on the screen, the type promoted by TV or other one-way media. Participants can respond, raise questions, and vote via the web. All of these can be seen as having the potential to expand democratic practice.

However, such optimism masks several problems relating directly to the constraints imposed by the technology. Baudrillard, in particular, seems to raise important questions about using information technology, anticipating a number of the reactions by the participants in the party convention. The data suggest that high levels of participation were exhibited among the participants. But the high amount of participation came at a price. It appears that there was a type of information overload (a more suitable term than "orgy"). Participants in the virtual convention claimed to have too many issues to follow, too much information to digest, too many forums in which to participate. The virtual convention represents a microcosm of what Baudrillard said about the cultural impact of information technologies themselves. The result is a paradox with regard to democracy. The party hierarchy correctly noted the problem that imposing a structure would present for the goal of promoting grass-roots democracy. However, the lack of structure makes it difficult for anything coherent to emerge from the discussion.

As a result, one casualty of the increased numbers and the level of participation is depth in the discourse that occurs. This problem is conveyed in participants' concern for the lack of personal contact at the meeting. One reason for this is contained in the technology, itself; using binary code removes the depth and subtlety from communication. Human contact can convey the emotion of speech, whether one-to-one or to a large crowd. Web politics removes that dimension from political discourse. It gives preeminence to the march of reason in the world, but at the cost of human contact and a reduction in the value of human emotions as part of social and political life. Charisma (which people like Max Weber saw as the essence of political life) is diminished by binary transmission.

In the end, one could imagine a political arena in which everyone has access, everyone could speak, and no one would care. All is bland. No one wants to participate because no one has any interest. This is the political life of Nietzsche's "last man." This is the danger that Baudrillard sees the web posing for political life because the vitality and emotion of real politics is displaced by its simulation. More people can participate, but the reason to care will disappear along with the idea of ideological commitment.

Cut off from the real, the virtual becomes our reality. In that regard, the web constitutes another aspect of the march of reason in the world. The Internet will not become the means to overcome the alienation of human beings but become one more, and very powerful, source of that condition. All that can be digitized will become our reality; all that cannot be digitized will be discarded.

Conclusion

To say that Baudrillard aligns himself with the pessimist on the role of technology would be a gross understatement. He admits that he could be considered a type of nihilist (Baudrillard, 1994a), but only in the sense that he is interested in the disappearance of the real. As he describes it, today's nihilism is not from destruction but from transparency and simulation. Meaning disappears in a world saturated with stimuli, with an orgy of information.

Virtual politics is not the answer to a public that is increasingly disenfranchised, cynical, and alienated from real political engagement. In the end, virtual politics will heighten such feelings. It will produce a world in which a technical structure will oversee artificially contrived choices for a public whose opinion has already been shaped by the conditions of their own oppression. This is the nature of simulated politics. Information technologies are not the solution, but the cause of this condition. The Internet simply extends and furthers the conditions already present in the media age that extends back to the 1930s.

Baudrillard rejects positive claims of the rational and sovereign actor models. All are receivers, not actors. The simulation of the political constitutes a system of control. Using information technology to further advance the message of interest groups, political parties, and the state simply enhances a system of domination already in place. Today, it is no longer a question of maintaining the social contract. The contest today is between a totalitarian system of self-reference on the one hand and an infantile mass on the other (Baudrillard, 1993, p. 78). Within this framework, the state feels justified in brutalizing its own populations.

Like other poststructuralist writers, Baudrillard conveys a strong element of philosophic anarchism. One can either accept these assumptions or not, but they cannot be ignored. It has long been recognized that the Internet has a Western bias, owing to both economic factors that limit access and the fact that the ASCII code used on the web is a Western script. What has been less recognized is that technology, itself, constitutes a bias that promotes and extends a particular form of life. We live in an age in which technology has sold itself with promises that it cannot possibly fulfill. The result is a world (of which human beings are a part) that must be reshaped in order to convince us of its own success. That leaves us with a simple truth. Today, we are born to serve the technology.

References

Angell, I. (1996). "Winners and Losers in the Information Age" in *Culture and Society*, Vol. 34, No. 1.

Baudrillard, J. (1983). *Simulations*. New York, NY: Semiotext.

Baudrillard, J. (1988a). *Selected Writings*. Edited by M. Poster. Stanford, CA: Stanford University Press.

Baudrillard, J. (1988b). *The Ecstasy of Communication*. New York, NY: Semiotext.

Buadrillard, J. (1993). *The Transparency of Evil*. London, UK: Verso Press.

Baudrillard, J. (1994a). *The Illusion of the End*. Stanford, CA: Stanford University Press.

Baudrillard, J. (1994b). *Simulacra and Simulation*. Ann Arbor, MI: University of Michigan Press.

Baudrillard, J. (2000). *The Vital Illusion*. New York, NY: Columbia University Press.

Davis, R. (1999). *The Web of Politics*. Oxford, UK: Oxford University Press.

Derrida, J. (1981). *Dissemination*. Chicago, IL: University of Chicago Press.

Jordon, T. (1999). *Cyberpower*. London, UK: Routledge.

Kellner, D. (1998). "Intellctuals, the New Public Sphere, and Technopolitics," p. 173 in C. Toulouse and T. Luke (eds.) *The Politics of Cyberspace*. New York, NY: Routledge.

Luhmann, N. (1990). *Essays on Self-Reference*. New York, NY: Columbia University Press.

McLuhan, M. (1962). *The Gutenberg Galaxy: The Making of Typographical Man*. Toronto, Canada: University of Toronto Press.

Ohmae, K. (1995). *The End of the Nation State: The Rise of Regional Economics*. New York, NY: Free Press.

Resnick, D. (1998). "Politics on the Internet: The Normalization of Cyberspace," p. 49 in C. Toulouse and T. Luke (eds.) *The Politics of Cyberspace*. New York, NY: Routledge.

Roper, J. (1998). "New Zealand's Political Parties Online," p. 69 in C. Toulouse and T. Luke (eds.) *The Politics of Cyberspace*. New York, NY: Routledge:

Sarnpaio, A. and J. Aragon (1998). "To Boldly Go Where No Man Has Gone Before: Women and Politics in Cyberspace," p. 153 in C. Toulouse and T. Luke (eds.) *The Politics of Cyberspace*. New York, NY: Routledge.

Schmidtke, O. (1998). "Berlin in the Net," p. 65 in R. Tsagarousianou, D. Tambini, and C. Bryan (eds.) *Cyberdemocracy: Technology, Cities, and Civic Networks*. London, UK: Routledge.

Tsagarousianou, R. (1998). "Back to the Future of Democracy" in R. Tsagarousianou, D. Tambini, and C. Bryan (eds.) *Cyberdemocracy: Technology, Cities, and Civic Networks*. London, UK: Routledge.

Chapter 15
The Electronic Media Deficit

Mary A. Hepburn

Professor Emeritus, Vinson Institute of Government, The University of Georgia, Athens, Georgia, USA

Abstract

In 1998, the National Commission on Civic Renewal in the United States declared that television has become a "destructive force" in society because it entices people to spend many hours in front of the TV screen, away from civic activities and social relations in their communities. Two decades earlier, American professor Neil Postman (1979) warned that television was developing into a learning system that competes with the schools and predicted that TV would eventually dominate. Entreating educators to pay attention to the dramatic changes taking place in the communication of news and entertainment, Postman urged them to teach students about television's effects, biases, and relationship to learning. Few educators were concerned. The public generally considered television a promising, convenient conveyor of news and family entertainment to their homes. Educators in schools and colleges saw videotape as a handy replacement for bothersome 16mm-film projectors. At home, educators (like most of the American public) viewed for short periods the evening news, short dramas, or variety shows. In the 1970s and early 1980s, there seemed to be little awareness or discussion among civic/political educators of the growing power of television to socialize and instruct (Hepburn, 1990).

In the 1970s, courses for political educators taught about "socializing agents" that supported "regime norms." In civics courses, textbooks and teachers conveyed to students a view of the several "agents" that shaped them politically: family, school, peers, church and other social groups, and the media. These agents were not considered of equal importance in the civic development of young people. Family was considered most influential, exerting particularly strong sway on political identification and partisanship (Jennings and Niemi, 1974). The school's influence was considered minimal, based mainly on a study of high school students (Langton and Jennings, 1968), which later was challenged by educational researchers for the lack of measurement validity and reliability (Hepburn, 1980). Meanwhile, Torney, Oppenheim, and Farnen (1975) showed that classroom experiences do affect civic understanding. Social and church groups were considered to significantly influence civic attitudes and behavior in that early literature (Easton and Dennis, 1965; Sigel, 1965). But there was little discussion of the mass media. Social conditions received some attention. Some studies examined how Blacks experienced a duality in the US political culture (Marvick, 1965; Greenberg, 1970). Societal conditions were often extraneous to the "agents" model. Moreover, the influence of each agent was likely to be examined independently, providing a somewhat disconnected picture of the process.

The sources and use of media have changed political learning. The interaction of the electronic media with family and social factors affected the process. Political educators and political socialization researchers now consider electronic media's extensively direct effects on youth and its indirect effects on all other who interact with young people. Mass media shape perceptions of the young and mature population as well. The electronic lifestyle of the majority of Americans (a change that now affects much of the world) must be considered when theorizing about or studying how political learning takes place.

Pervasiveness of Electronic Mass Media

In the US, television is now the main source of both news and entertainment. About 99% of US households have at least one television set and 74% have several sets (Nielsen, 1998). Family viewing has declined and separate viewing by children and adults has increased as the number of TV sets in the household increased. Cable programming is found in 74% of households, greatly expanding the number of networks and independent stations that can be accessed. About 54% of children have a television set in their bedrooms; 87% of households have a VCR; and about $10 billion is spent annually on video rentals, double the amount spent at movie theaters (*Meidascope*, 1997).

In American households, average weekly viewing time has increased annually from 43 hours in the early 1970s to about 51 hours in the mid-1990s. Weekly viewing is highest (59.4 hours) in homes with four or more children, which is more than 8 hours per day! Children aged 2-11 spend an average of 22 hours a week watching TV (Nielsen, 1993, 1998). During prime time (7 to 11 p.m.), about 7 million teenagers and 9 to 10 million pre-teens are watching TV (Media Dynamics, 1996).

TV lifestyle appears to be related to social-economic conditions. People with low incomes watch more TV than those with higher incomes. People with more formal education watch fewer hours of TV than those with less education. The heaviest viewers are older people, especially retirees, some of whom watch 40 or more hours a week (*Mediascope*, 1997). Nielsen (1993) reports ethnic differences as well. African American children aged 2-11 view about 55% more TV than same-aged children in all other households. African American men (18 and older) watch 90% more daytime TV than their counterparts in other households. In Hispanic households, while adults viewed less television than Americans generally, teens and children watched more TV (Nielsen, 1998).

The Content and Effects of the Electronic Media

Communication by television is based on visual effects combined with sound. Television programming is usually vivid, fast-paced, and accompanied with voices and music, evoking emotional responses. Advertising is injected every few minutes into all types of programs on commercial TV in the US. Television news shows feature several short, dramatic, fast-paced reports of unconnected and sometimes insignificant events. The format for news seldom informs viewers about significant public issues, especially for the majority who admit that TV is their only source of news. One detailed analysis of TV news broadcasts and audience understanding concluded that news delivery failed to inform Americans about important issues and events (Davis and Robinson, 1989). The researchers determined that broadcast companies show little concern about the quality of news; they are mainly concerned about increasing the size of the audience. One analyst of American media observed that TV news operates on "borrowed time" in a commercial entertainment-oriented media system (Neumann, 1987).

News items are immersed in advertising, so the thoughts of viewers must shift from world events to soft drinks, automobiles, or laxatives; from Congressional decisions to running shoes, cosmetics, and headache pills (all products treated in colorful, dramatic, emotional presentations). The Internet now allows people to get more news in more detail by searching for it and printing it, but Internet news reports are also surrounded by flashing, colorful advertising to divert attention to products for sale. In 1998, only about 28% of Americans used the Internet (Nielsen, 1998).

The great majority of Americans rely on TV news and place a high level of confidence on television coverage. Close to 60% are inclined to believe television over newspaper, radio, and magazines (Stanley and Niemi, 1993). Apparently, people do not consider how easily video cameras can mislead and few evaluate the selection and presentation of news on most TV channels. Years of electronic news consumption, received in quick, brief visuals and sound bites of speech, produced a shorter attention span for news and less understanding of public affairs, especially for those who have little background knowledge (Adatto, 1993).

In a ploy to make news programs more engaging, hard news and light entertainment are subtly mingled. Vignettes of one individual's personal tragedy or gain are used to present a public issue. (For example, if the state builds a highway across this land, it will cut off "his" grandfather's farm; should this highway be extended? Or, the murder of "her" son took place in a district without a police station; should more police stations be built?) News presented this way offers little or no aggregate data related to a public issue, but leaves strong images of a single dramatic case. A political issue is presented as one person's problem; research show that these narrow personal narratives have a negative effect on viewers' cognition. In this way, TV news oversimplifies complex public issues, ignores implications for the community or the whole society, and suppresses thinking about possible public solutions (Iyengar, 1991). Such news coverage actually decreases the recall of information about public issues or a political event (Milburn and McGrail, 1992).

Another content problem in US television is the preponderance of violence in programming. Psychological, sociological, and medical researchers find that violent action attracts a lot of viewers, including children. Consequently, the producers and directors of television dramas (both fiction and non-fiction) trying to attract large audiences often include fast action and vivid violent scenes in the programs. Large national studies of the content of television programming clarify the degree, quantity, and the various contexts within which network shows, movies, and cable programs present acts of violence for viewers (UCLA Center for Communication Policy, 1995; National Television Violence Study, 1996, 1998). The majority of programs (57% in 1996, 60% in 1998) were found to contain violence and often included numerous violent acts. Much of the gratuitous violence is produced by Hollywood in movies that end up on TV. Not only are researchers concerned about the magnitude of violence on TV programs, the public also is worried. A national survey by the Pew Research Center (1997) reported that 75% of Americans say there is too much violence in non-news programs. But are people affected by it? Does heavy viewing of violence contribute to incivility and violent behavior?

Research teams from several leading universities found that most entertainment programs and TV movies include overt, vivid depictions of physical force, harm, and killing (National Television Violence Study, 1996). The American Psychological Association (1993) and the American Medical Association (Walsh, Goldman, and Brown, 1996) gathered research evidence of effects on young children, especially those who are heavy viewers and particularly those who experience no moderating influence by concerned adults. They tend to learn from TV that aggressive or violent behavior is appropriate in given life situations. They act out the violence they see in their play and in family life (Minow and LaMay, 1995). As these same children mature, they are also more aggressive and violent as teenagers; for some, it carries on into adulthood. Prolonged viewing of violence often has a desensitizing effect, leading to callous acceptance of violent behavior. For some young people, the daily scenes of killings, rapes, and beatings create fears (fear of being in dark areas, of being in school, of violence). There are signs that aggressive and even violent expression is increasing in American society. Incivility is widely reported in government, business organizations, and social groups. Fear also has civic implications. People are less likely to be out and about in their communities if they harbor fears of becoming victims.

Newspapers are changing their content in reaction to the popularity of television. An interesting example of the influence of one news medium on another is evident in research sponsored by newspaper editors (ASNE, 1996) who examined the media habits of young people aged 16 to 30. In the US, this group is referred to as "Generation X" (the first to be fully "raised" on television). Editors who sponsored this study of media tastes wanted to find out what newspapers can do to attract young adults to read papers. The survey showed that they enjoy night-time comedies; adventure-dramas about cops, crime, and emergencies; and daytime talk shows. Their favorite cable channel is MTV, but they also like sports and recent movies on cable networks. They claim to find role models in the TV shows; these shows were also their main sources for fashion ideas and public information. TV is ingrained in their lives. "For these young people, television served as a baby sitter, entertainer, educator, and a form of company for latchkey kids" (ASNE, 1996).

The newspaper editors group concluded that "we've got a good chance to connect with most of them if we make our papers more relevant to people in their teens and 20s" (ASNE, 1996, p. 7). Specifics are laid out in the report, challenging newspapers to cover the leisure pursuits of these young people ("fitness, cyberspace, career opportunities, budget dating, news on renting apartment"). Other statements from the report: "Put more resources into sports." "Do features on where to take dates, new and trendy restaurants, clubs and entertainers." The report advised that stories about rock stars be placed on the front page. Many Americans have seen this change in local print news. TV and the Internet are changing the content, style, and aims of print news. Consequently, the quality of print news about public issues and politics is declining, making it more difficult for the ordinary citizen to know what is happening in the public political arena.

Even when away from a TV set or computer, Americans are seldom far from electronic broadcast influences. An old media, radio, is enjoying a new popularity and use. Radio broadcasts accompany Americans on the jogging trail, on buses and planes, and while seated in their cars (commuting or trapped in traffic jams). Many stations that used to broadcast music and short news summaries now send out national or regional talk shows voicing the opinions of the hosts and the call-in audience. Shows discuss every aspect of life: medical advice, social and marital advice, car repair, legal matters, and viewpoints on politics. People seem to enjoy having "a say." But, similar to the Internet, there is seldom a check on the authenticity or accuracy of what is said. Talk radio shows tripled between 1989 and 1994; some of these shows are credited with contributing to a kind of populist negativism toward government and civic affairs.

Implications: Need for a Socialization Model for the Electronic Age

While television is currently most pervasive, all forms of electronic communication exert subtle influences on the social-political-economic thinking of users and ultimately affect behavior. The Internet changed the speed and form of written communication. It also is making TV and radio more interactive since broadcast stations encourage users to communicate via e-mail. Because the Internet is a more interactive mode of communication, some consider it more democratic. Nevertheless, in democratic societies, the public should view all forms of the media analytically and critically. Democracies shun censorships and rely on informing citizens so they can evaluate and make choices. How do we embed a critical perspective in political education? How can we assure that it is understood by professors who educate civics and political science teachers who, in turn, are responsible for the civic education of students in school. One step forward is to look for a more timely model of the socialization process.

Civic educators and socialization researchers must be cognizant of the significance of electronic media for political learning, especially in the lives of young people. Although the old model is still found in textbooks and teaching plans, it is clearly outdated. Agents of socialization are often discussed as contributors to the formation of public opinion with little examination of how the mass media interact with each of these other influencing factors in the context of societal conditions.

Among the textbooks used to train civics and government teachers, few examine the power of the media in shaping perceptions and political attitudes of young people. Consequently, there is a lack of critical discussion of mass media.

This omission in civic/political education in the US seems related partly to the fact that neither "media literacy" nor "critical viewing education" has been integrated into civic education. In the 1970s, there were several education projects in the US designed to raise students' critical consciousness of television (Brown, 1991), but these instructional research projects died during the 1980s and their materials are now unavailable. In Australia, Canada, and many other countries of Europe and Latin America, media literacy education and research have developed and remained remarkably strong across the disciplines, including political science education. Today, students in every democratic nation need systematic studies of the media in school. Media studies should include research on content and delivery as well as analysis of subtle psychological influence. In every civics class, students should examine and discuss media effects on politics, public opinion, and civility in the society (Hepburn, 1995).

The outmoded perception of the socialization process probably was reinforced by the lack of professional exchange beyond the traditional history and social sciences. Civics educators were quite isolated from psychological theory and research. Few may be aware of recent questions about the relative influence of parents and peers and the proposition that parents have less long-term influence on socialization than was assumed (Harris, 1995). Meanwhile, medical research and mass communications studies provided evidence of electronic mass media effects. Clearly, cross-disciplinary sharing benefits political socialization research and instruction.

To more accurately conceptualize political influences in today's electronically charged society requires an examination of interrelated forces that influence the socialization of young people. Let me suggest one approach. Drawing on the Lewinian field theory, it is instructive to depict students in their psychological "field" or the psychological world within which they learn. The concept of cognitive-field is useful for analyzing how young people perceive and respond to their psychological environment. It encourages thinking in terms of several interdependent factors that motivate learning and behavior. The field includes political, social, and economic conditions that affect youths' awareness as well as the school environment in which they operate each day. The field includes their social, cultural, and religious experiences plus specific conveyers (or "agents") of electronic media, which young people see and hear many hours daily and which not only affect them directly, but also indirectly by influencing the other factors in their social-psychological environment. Listening, reading, watching, and thinking about those media experiences shape attitudes and behavior.

Conclusions

There is adequate research to make us aware that the electronic media are now intricately involved in socialization from the early years. Political news and political imagery is immersed in vibrant, flashy ads, lively colorful animations, violent fearful crimes, shocking explosions, and hours of programming on various pop culture celebrities. Neil Postman (1990) foresaw that television would become "the command center of our culture." There are signs that the Internet is also gradually assuming that kind of powerful role. Yet within this environment of high-speed and colorful communication, the American public shows less interest in politics and public issues. For example, college freshmen express the lowest level of interest in politics in 30 years (Sax, et al., 1998). Patterson (1987) finds that the American public, which is increasingly indifferent to politics, has fewer psychological defenses. Patterson (1987, p. 53) said, "Once we have an uncommitted and uninvolved electorate, we also have an electorate vulnerable to the media's image of politics." Clearly, we need more research on media and civic learning; we also need an appropriate model for conceptualizing who youths gain political awareness from and learn the attitudes that shape their thinking about political life. Both educators and researchers are likely to benefit from greater insight into the media-barraged psychological field where political learning accumulates. The new model presented here is an effort to emphasize media interconnections of socializing agents and the interaction with social background factors in a psychological field charged with electronic images and sounds. It also implies the importance of political education that teaches students to critically analyze and evaluate the media messages around them. Perhaps these perspectives on political socialization will motivate rethinking about the complexities of the field and what it can contribute to the understanding of civic life in an age of seductive electronic communication.

References

Adatto, K. (1993). *Picture Perfect: The Art and Artifice of Public Image Making*. New York, NY: Basic Books.

American Psychological Association (1993). *Violence and Youth: Psychology's Response*. Washington, DC: American Psychological Assoc.

American Society of Newspaper Editors (1996). *What's Important to Generation X*. Reston, VA: ASNE Foundation.

Brown, J. (1991). *Television: "Critical Viewing Skills" Education*. Hillsdale, NJ: Lawrence Erlbaum Associates Publishers.

Davis, D. and J. Robinson (1989). "News Flow and Democratic Society in an Age of Electronic Media" in G. Comstock (ed.) *Public Communication and Behavior*, Vol. 2. San Diego, CA: Academic Press.

Easton, D. and J. Dennis (1965). "The Child's Image of Government," pp. 1-3 in *The Annals of the American Academy of Political and Social Sciences*, Vol. 361.

Greenberg, E. (1970). "The Political Socialization of Black Children" in E. Greenberg (ed.) *Political Socialization*. New York, NY: Atherton Press.

Harris, J. (1995). "Where is the Child's Environment – A Group Socialization Theory of Development," pp. 458-489 in *Psychological Review*, Vol. 102, No. 3.

Hepburn, M. (1980). "How Do We Know What They Know? Testing the Impact of the School Curriculum on the Political Knowledge of Students," pp. 425-438 in *Teaching Political Science*, Vol. 7, No. 4.

Hepburn, M. (1990). "Americans Glued to the Tube: Mass Media, Information, and Social Studies," pp. 233-236 in *Social Education*, Vol. 54, No. 4.

Hepburn, M. (1995). "TV Violence: Myth and Reality," pp. 309-311 in *Social Education*, Vol. 59, No. 7.

Iyengar, S. (1991). *Is Anyone Responsible? How Television News Frames Political Issues*. Chicago, IL: University of Chicago Press.

Jennings, M. and R. Niemi (1974). *The Political Character of Adolescence: The Influence of Families and Schools*. Princeton, NJ: Princeton University Press.

Langton, K. and M. Jennings (1968). "Political Socialization and the High School Curriculum," pp. 852-867 in *American Political Science Review*, Vol. 62.

Marvick, D. (1965). "The Political Socialization and the American Negro," pp. 112-127 in *The Annals of the American Academy of Political and Social Sciences*, Vol. 361.

Media Dynamics (1996). *TV Dimensions 1996*. New York, NY: Media Dynamics.

Mediascope (1997). Information from website at http://www.igc.apc.org/mediascope.

Milburn, M. and A. McGrail (1992). "The Dramatic Presentation of News and Its Effects on Cognitive Complexity," pp. 613-632 in *Political Psychology*, Vol. 13, No. 4.

Minow, N. and C. LaMay (1995). *Abandoned in the Wasteland: Children, Television and the First Amendment*. New York, NY: Hill and Wang.

National Commission on Civic Renewal (1998). *A Nation of Spectators: How Civic Disengagement Weakens America . . .Final report*. College Park, MD.

National Television Violence Study Council (1996). *Executive Summary 1994-1995*. Studio City, CA: Mediascope, Inc.

Neumann, W. (Winter 1987). "Knowledge and Opinion in the American Electorate," pp. 56-64 in *Kettering Review*.

Nielsen Media Research (1993). *1992-1993 Report on Television*. New York, NY: A.C. Nielsen Co.

Nielsen Media Research (1998). *1998 Report on Television*. New York, NY: Nielsen Media Research.

Patterson, T. (Winter 1987). "Television and the Decline of Politics," pp. 49-55 in *Kettering Review*.

Pew Research Center for People and the Press (1997). "Optimism About TV Ratings" from the January 1997 News Interest Index: Other Findings web page at http://www.people-press.org-/jan97mor.htm.

Postman, N. (1979). "The First Curriculum: Comparing School and Television," pp. 158-163 in *Phi Delta Kappan*, Vol. 61, No. 3 (November).

Postman, N. (1990). "Television and the Decline of Public Discourse" (an interview), pp. 4-6 in *The Civic Arts Review*, Vol. 3, No. 1.

Sax, L., A. Astin, W. Korn, and K. Mahoney (1998). *The American Freshman: National Norms for Fall 1997*. Los Angeles, CA: Higher Education Research Institute, UCLA.

Sigel, R. (1965). "Assumptions about the Learning of Political Values," pp. 41-57 in *The Annals of the American Academy of Political and Social Sciences*, Vol. 361.

Stanley, H. and R. Niemi (1993). *Vital Statistics on American Politics*. Washington, DC: CQ Press.

Torney, J., A. Oppenheim, and R. Farnen (1975). *Civic Education in Ten Countries: An Empirical Study*. New York, NY: John Wiley and Sons.

UCLA Center for Communication Policy (1995). *UCLA Monitoring Report 1994-95*. Los Angeles, CA: UCLA.

Walsh, D,. L. Goldman, and R. Brown (1996). *Physician Guide to Media Violence*. Chicago, IL: American Medical Association.

Chapter 16
Does the Media Reduce Political Participation?

Daniel B. German and Dragan Stefanovic

Appalachian State University, Boone, North Carolina, USA

Abstract

M. Kent Jennings and Richard Niemi examine the period effect theory on continuity and change in political orientations in the US. Period effects through political socialization can change a generation or an entire society. These authors refer to wars, depression, and similar major events as affecting entire populations. We hypothesized that September 11, 2001 (9/11) would have the effect of renewing American's interest in politics. The predicted specific effect would be a heightened consumption of news and participation in the 2002 off-presidential elections. The hypothesis was rejected because voter turnout was about 39%, pretty much in line with recent off-year presidential elections. News consumption patterns remain about the same as in pre-9/11 days, with increased attention to international affairs among past news consumer elites. Despite this low turnout, 9/11 appears to have had an effect on the Republican electorate. They increased their interest and turnout in the 2002 election, resulting in a Republican victory. In the 2004 national elections, turnout increased substantially bringing into question the reasons given for the lower 2002 turnout. A new hypothesis might be that a time lag exists between an event and its impact on turnout and/or that turnout for presidential elections is more susceptible to these types of events.

Background

September 11, 2001 was a major disaster for the US, comparable to the shock generated by the Japanese attack on Pearl Harbor in 1941. In political socialization theory, an event of this magnitude is considered sufficient to produce a period effect. In the midst of continuity and change over time, a period effect would favor change (even dramatic) in political orientations and behavior affecting an entire population. In a longitudinal study between 1965 and 1973, Jennings and Niemi (1975, p. 329) found that the civil rights movement, Watergate scandal, and Vietnam War appeared to move the entire population, but particularly the youth generation, to exhibit a growing cynicism toward the political system. They cited strong socialization effects resulting from events such as the Great Depression, the civil rights movement, and similar highly salient occurrences.

A close examination of two significant events in American history (the 1861 to 1865 Civil War and the Great Depression) illustrates the effects of a period event. There was a major shift in the elections of 1860 (pre-Civil War), 1864, and 1868 (post-Civil War) from Democrats dominating presidential elections to the dawning of a period of Republican hegemony in American politics that lasted until the Depression election of 1932. Political participation also increased during the Civil War. In 1860, voter turnout was 4,685,561; in 1868 it was 5,122,440 (with Mississippi, Texas, and Virginia not participating and Florida's legislature casting their electoral votes) (Diamond, 1976, pp. 271-273). The Depression also produced a shift in party fortunes and an increase in participation. In the 1928 election (pre-Depression), voter turnout was 36,790,364; in 1932, it rose to 39,749,382. Franklin D. Roosevelt (Democrat) was elected to four terms as President. Voter turnout rose from 48.9% in 1924 to 58.8% in 1940 (Diamond, 1976, pp. 288-289; Center for Voting and Democracy, 2003).

Prior to the 2002 election, the authors hypothesized that 9/11 would change the trend in the typically low voter turnout in previous elections and produce an increase. Often, the voter turnout was below 40% in recent off-presidential election years. The authors did not hypothesize a shift in party allegiance, although the possibility of this development was examined. The authors obtained the 2002 Final Midterm Pre-Election Poll conducted by the George Gallup organization to examine the demographics of potential turnout. The Gallup survey, conducted from October 31 to November 3, 2002, clearly predicted the Republican gains in the Senate and House. To examine the actual voter turnout and vote patterns, the 2002 American National Election Study was used.

Immediate and Long-Term 9/11 Effects

Immediately after 9/11, polls showed that Americans seemed to be re-evaluating the political system and their involvement in it. Prior to 9/11, approval ratings of Congress hovered below 50%, ranging from the low to high 40s. Following 9/11, Congressional approval ratings went as high as 84%. However, these figures quickly began slipping and by mid-year 2002, they fell into the 40s again.

The American public's view of the media went through a somewhat similar transformation. In early September 2001 (prior to 9/11), 35% of respondents in a Pew Center Research for People and the Press survey stated that they felt media reported with accuracy. This rose to 46% in November 2001 but by July 2002, it fell to 35%. In early September, 54% felt the media was professional. This rose to 73% in November, but went down to 49% in July 2002. In early September, 43% surveyed thought the media stood up for America. This skyrocketed to 69% in November, but fell to 49% by July 2002 (Pew Center for People and the Press, 2003) as the media shifted focus by Spring and Summer of 2002 to cover scandals surrounding the Enron and WorldCom accounting debacles.

However, it appears that American news consumption habits changed in following international news in 2002 compared to 1998. Table 1 shows an increase by 5% among the "Very Closely" group, but a drop for "Somewhat Closely" of 2%, indicating a gain of only 3% in the combined categories. Moreover, most of the gains occurred among a small highly-educated segment of the population, including higher income, college graduates, and senior citizens.

Table 1: Following international news: 1998 and 2002 compared

	Follows	
Year	Very Closely	Somewhat Closely
2002	21%	44%
1998	16%	46%

The rating of the president remained high after 9/11. Prior to 9/11, President George W. Bush's popularity was in the low 50th percentile. This was low, given the honeymoon effect which is supposed to accompany a new president's first months in office (Bill Clinton's ratings were also low). After 9/11, President Bush's popularity went as high as 87%. Although Congressional and media approval/support ratings fell considerably, Bush's approval remained close to or above 60% until March 2003.

There are several possible explanations for this trend. First, the President, as Chief of State, generally is central to the American people's attitude toward the US political system. Perhaps 9/11 had deeply affected the US citizenry to the point where they gave a large good-will (rally-around-the-flag) support for the Presidency. Second, President Bush may have had something to do with the support level because he did go to war with Afghanistan, indicating to many Americans that he was acting against terrorism. If the President had done nothing, Neville Chamberlain style, his popularity may have dropped regardless of 9/11.

The 2002 Election

The turnout in the 2002 elections was 39 3%. While this figure is 2.9% higher than 1998, it is only 0.5% higher than in 1990 and is less than the 39.8% of turnout in 1982. Voter turnout in 2002 was not noticeably higher than the general trend for about two decades. The 2004 election may reveal that the trend of a slight increase in turnout that began in 2002 may continue. For presidential elections, the voting pattern in recent years has been around a 50% turnout. If the turnout is much higher than this figure in 2004, we may be witnessing a period effect. (This data was drawn from Federal Election Commission, http://www.fec.gov, Congressional Research Service, Election Data Service Inc., and State Election Offices, 2003.)

With regard to a shift in electoral preferences, the Republicans did gain seats in 2002. They gained five seats in the 435-member House and two in the 100-member Senate. This is atypical of an off-presidential election year in which the incumbent president's party usually loses seats. In House seats, this type of loss occurred in 32 of 33 midterm elections between 1866 and 1994 (Campbell, 2003, p. 203). The Republican gain in 2002 is an interesting development; however, their net gains were small and we will have to await the 2004 elections to examine whether a shift is coming in terms of electoral allegiance. In the midterm elections from 1994 to 2002, 1994 is the only election which saw a party gain or loss of more than 10 seats in the House. Consequently, a small number of gains in the House and the Senate for the Republicans in 2002 is not out of line with most election results occurring for several decades (Campbell, 2003, p. 203).

A close examination of a right-before-the-election Gallup survey in 2002 suggests that 9/11 did affect voters both in terms of issues and voter turnout, albeit not very much, but in a distinct trend.

The 2002 Gallup Survey Results

During the period October 31 to November 3, 2002, the Gallup Organization conducted telephone surveys of 1,221 adults age 18 and over. The following analysis is based on our examination of a sub-sample of the survey provided by Gallup of 715 voters who were most likely to vote. Since this sub-sample focuses on the probable voters, it is the most reliable source of voter information on the 2002 election. Based on the survey results, the dynamics of the narrow Republican win (two Senate seats and five House seats) are easy to identify. The 2004 election may reveal the dynamics of a small shift, but the evidence is that the Republican support in 2002 was demographically similar to the support for George W. Bush in 2000 which constituted a victory in electoral votes, but a loss of popular vote. It is clear that Republican Party demographics held sway. Conservatives led liberals as being more enthusiastic by 65% to 60%. Males outdistanced females 57% to 52%. Higher incomes (except in the $50,000-$74,900 category) led lower income groups. Republicans led Democrats 64% to 51%. The South led other regions along with suburban and rural America. The only major variable running counter to a Republican win was education, high school or less leading all other categories as being more enthusiastic. In sum, this outcome reflects that the most likely non-Republican voters were liberal or moderate, with an income between $50,000 and $74,900, independent, from the east, from urban America, and with some college education. The most likely Republican voter was conservative, male, with an income between $30,000 and $49,900, from the south, rural America, and with a high school degree.

Table 2: Final 2002 midterm pre-election poll results – more enthusiastic demographics and issues

Ideology					
N	Conservative	Moderate	Liberal		
232	118 (65%)	69 (42%)	45 (60%)		
Sex					
N	Male	Female			
234	124 (57%)	110 (52%)			
Income					
N	>$75K	$50K-$74.9	$30K-$49.9	$20K-$29.9	<$20K
215	67 (58%)	41 (49%)	57 (61%)	23 (50%)	27 (51%)
Party ID					
N	Republican	Independent	Democrat		
232	114 (64%)	43 (44%)	75 (51%)		
Bush Job Approval					
N	Approve	Disapprove			
229	159 (58%)	70 (58%)			
Region					
N	East	Midwest	South	West	
234	42 (45%)	59 (54%)	86 (61%)	47 (56%)	
Type of Community					
N	Urban	Suburban	Rural		
233	53 (46%)	128 (57%)	52 (59%)		
Education					
N	Post-Graduate	College Graduate Only	Some College	High School	
233	40 (50%)	41 (59%)	66 (47%)	86 (63%)	
*The % given indicates the number of those who were enthusiastic (e.g., Conservatives at 65%, compared to liberals at 60%) (Gallup Organization, 2002).					

On issue evaluations, it is clear that voters favored Republicans (Table 3). The Republican Party was picked as better to control Congress. Particularly in Table 3, Iraq led as the most important issue with 61% reference. Terrorism as an issue also led over the economy. The latter issue was a negative for the Republicans since the economy is fairly flat in growth terms.

The 2002 National Election Study (NES) provided several interesting facts. For example, of all the voter education levels, the only one that did not provide the Republican candidates for the Senate and House of Representatives was the high school graduate (44.6% Senate and 50.0% House of Representatives). The most glaring exception to normally expected trends was the higher female vote for a Republican Congress (Table 4). This result can be tentatively interpreted as a vote for "security" on the part of the female voter; that is, the Republican Party is perceived to be better able to handle terrorism and Iraq.

Table 3:Final 2002 midterm pre-election poll results: party and presidential sup- port among the more enthusiastic voters

Better Party to Control Congress			
N	Republicans	Democrats	No Difference
224	105 (64%)	64 (52%)	55 (43%)
Satisfaction with the US			
N	Satisfied	Dissatisfied	
221	123 (60%)	98 (49%)	
Economic Conditions			
N	Excellent/Good	Only Fair	Poor
231	81 (56%)	93 (52%)	57 (56%)
Economic Momentum (Are you more enthusiastic			
N	Getting Better	Getting Worse	
213	112 (63%)	101 (51%)	
Most Important Issue to Vote			
N	Economic Conditions	Healthcare	Iraq
126 (54%)	66 (54%)	14 (40%)	46 (61%)
Most Important Issue to Vote			
Social Security	Terrorism	Education	
32 (56%)	33 (56%)	32 (56%)	
*The % given indicates the number of those who were enthusiastic (e.g., Republicans at 64% compared to Democrats at 52%) (Gallup Organization, 2002).			

Table 4: Vote for US Senate and House of Representatives in the 2002 national election

% Voted Republican		
Demographic Characteristics	Senate	House
Female	52.1	52.2
Male	50.0	51.1
South	63.5	60.8
Nonsouth	42.2	48.6
White	55.1	55.8
Black	7.3	12.7
Grade School Education	71.4	61.5
College Education or Advanced Degree	56.5	54.5
Protestant	58.2	57.2
Catholic	43.3	53.1
Jewish	00.0	19.2
Other and None	38.2	34.1
Source: American National Election Study (2002) N = 1,511		

Table 5: Reasons for not following international news for respondents with moderate/low interest

	Yes	No	Total
Lack of background	65%	35%	100%
Nothing ever changes	51%	49%	100%
Events don't affect me	45%	54%	100%
Too much war/violence	42%	58%	100%
Source: The Pew Research Center for the People and the Press (2002)			

Finally, we address the general problem of low media consumption and voter turnout in the US. Much is written about the decline of social capital in the US. The Pew Research Center for the People and the Press concludes that the reason people do not follow international affairs is their lack of background information in this area (Table 5).

Clearly, the main reason for not following international news is a matter of lack of knowledge for the largest number of respondents. The younger generation has more access to information through the Internet than older generations. Yet the Pew data show that they have lower levels of news consumption.

Previous generations at a similar stage in the life cycle followed the same pattern (Pew, 2002). Youth today tend to get their news online, but consumption of particularly network news as well as newspaper readership has declined. When push comes to shove, American citizens simply are not motivated to consume more international news. If it takes an incident as significant as 9/11 to motivate people to be more interested in worldwide politics, it is clear that short of war or other major incidents, very little can incite citizens to become better informed. However, they did take more interest during the Cold War when the prospect of war between the US and the Soviet Union seemed imminent. It is obvious that nothing since the Cold War has moved America to get more interested in international affairs. Moreover, they do not seem very interested in voting.

Our best answer as to why this is the case is the overall normalcy of politics and related events in America. People tend to be crisis-oriented and have mainly reacted to a war, civil war, economic depression, or other extraordinary major events that dramatically affected them. There is no reason to expect much change now, even though academicians might wish for more interest and involvement. Economically, Americans are near the top of the world's PPP (purchasing power parity) per capita scale. This is a primary reason why we are a satisfied and perhaps complacent population, not prone to become actually involved in politics.

The 2002 Election Re-examined

We hypothesized prior to the 2002 election that 9/11 would positively affect voter turnout. Low voter turnout in American elections has been a hallmark of the process in recent decades. We felt that 9/11 would produce what in political socialization theory is referred to as a "period effect." Period effects have been examined by using the US Civil War and the Great Depression as causal agents. Both of these events produced an increase in electoral participation and a shift in party alignment. While we did not hypothesize a party alignment shift, the possibility was considered prior to the 2002 election.

The 39% voter turnout in the 2002 midterm election was not seen as indicating an increase in participation. This figure is roughly in line with recent off-presidential-year elections. Also, the narrow 2-seat Senate gain and 5-seat House gain were not considered to indicate a party alignment shift in the electorate. While it is unusual for a party holding the White House to gain seats in a midterm election, the Republican gains were not really sufficient to declare a period of significant shift in electorate inclinations.

Explaining why 9/11 did not have a significant effect on the 2002 election participation is not easy. It seems that 9/11 affected the economy; particularly obvious is the decline in air travel and tourism. Americans appear to have been temporarily affected by 9/11 as evidenced by the dramatic increase in support of Congress. However, the underlying cynicism which began in the 1960s and 1970s has returned to dampen the spirit of participation. The general public is back to its mixed evaluation of Congress, an occurrence undoubtedly fueled by widespread knowledge of high interest group and personal contributions to political candidates and because of the media's continuous coverage of scandals.

The 2004 election may show a higher participation rate and a shift to Republican Party support. Such a trend will probably come from the same demographics as the 2002 Republican victory: male, conservative ideology, higher income, religious, suburban/rural America, higher education, white, and southern region.

We propose that the period effect theory needs to be accompanied by one or two attendant factors. Without one or both of these additional factors, it appears that change will not occur. 1) The period events must have a direct impact on a large number of people. The US Civil War had one of the highest casualty rates per number of participants compared to other wars in history. Many sons and husbands never returned home. During the Great Depression, 25% of the work force was unemployed and many others stood at the brink of unemployment. But 9/11 did not leave homes nationwide with dead members or result in a nationwide loss of income. 2) For the event to have an effect independent of direct impact, it must somehow be communicated in a high-impact way. When the civil rights movement affected many people, it may very well have been due to the newness of television. When citizens used this new medium to see people being beaten with billy clubs in America, they reacted with shock. Today, the American people have seen so much violence on TV that they seldom react with sufficient sustained shock for it to have any real impact. They have viewed a war live, seen students shooting up a school, etc., to the point where, it seems, they have perhaps an initial reaction to a particularly big event, but it wears off in the absence of a direct personal impact. In short, people are so used to seeing violent events on TV that they are immune to any long-term impact. There is no new medium in the US today that has the initial emotional appeal as TV once did.

*Table 6: Vote for US President (2000 and 2004)**

Demographic Characteristics	% Voted for Bush		% Change
	2000	2004	
Female	43	48	+5
Male	53	55	+2
White	54	58	+4
Black	9	11	+2
Hispanic	35	44	+9
Asian	41	44	+3
18-29 years old	N/A	45	N/A
30-44 years old	49	53	+4
60 and over	41	54	+7
*Grade School Education	40	49	+9
High School Education	49	52	+3
College Education	49	52	+3
Advanced Degree	44	44	+0
Protestant	58	59	+3
Catholic	47	52	+5
Jewish	19	25	+6
Other	28	23	-5
*Attend church more than weekly	N/A	64	N/A
Weekly	N/A	58	N/A
Monthly	N/A	50	N/A
A Few Times a Year	N/A	45	N/A
Never	N/A	36	N/A
South	55	58	+3
Northeast	39	43	+3
Midwest	49	51	+2
West	46	49	+3
Urban	26	39	+13
Smaller Cities	40	49	+9
Suburbs	49	52	+3
Small Towns	41	50	+9
Rural	59	59	+0
*Results of exit polls N = 13,660; Source: www.cnn.com/ELECTION/2004/pages/results/states/US/P/00/e polls.0			

2004 Election Resnlts

In 2004, the minor trends seen in 2002 expanded into the highest voter turnout (an estimated 59.5%) since 1968 (60.8%). The "enthusiastic" demographics of 2002 brought a very small shift to a substantial increase in certain voter categories for George W. Bush. A close look at the initial results indicates that the percentage of voters voting for George W. Bush increased in almost every demographic category except religious "other" and advanced degree (Table 6).

The regular church-going, grade-school-educated segment of the population probably increased their support for Bush in 2004 compared to 2000. These voters (combined with the higher support particularly from female, Hispanic, older, Catholic, Jewish, and urban voters who typically vote Democrat) gave Bush the popular vote he needed to become a clear victor in 2004, compared to 2000. The percentage of the backbone of the Republican Party, the college-educated Protestant, white, and southern voters who voted for George W. Bush also increased.

Voter Turnout - 2004

Possibly the most interesting aspect of the 2004 national elections was the increase in overall voter turnout. The 2004 turnout in the United States more closely resembled the 1968 election than the voter turnout for presidential elections since the Richard Nixon versus Hubert Humphrey race (Mellnick and Pitzer, 2004).

Political/social specialists give various reasons why voter turnout interest in politics and in political news has dropped in recent years. Bennett, et al. (2004) account for the drop in political news consumption, which is related to a lack of voter turnout, to:

1. Fall of the Berlin Wall in 1989
2. Media "feeding frenzies," "media circuses," "drive-by-journalism," and "attack journalism"
3. Over-attention to scandal
4. Negative campaigns (which "shrink the electorate and contribute to lessened interest in politics") (Benett, et al., 2004, p. 94).

The spin-off of the above leads to lowered levels of attentiveness, knowledge, and participation (Bennett, et al., 2004, 94).

It could also be that voters simply were not interested in the issues. The top issues in the 2004 elections were foreign affairs (terrorism 19% and Iraq 19%), moral values (22%), and the economy (20%). It could be that 9/11, the war in Iraq, combined with moral issues (such as gay marriage, gay clergy, and gay adoption) plus the question of economic recovery re-invigorated the electorate. Certainly, the media's general style of coverage apparently has not changed. Perhaps the reasons given by Bennett, et al. (2004) really do not necessarily apply to a public that experiences periods of relative inattention and participation in politics due to lack of issue interest.

References

American National Election Study (ANES), University of Michigan (2002).

Benett, S., S. Rhine, and R. Flickinger (2004). "The Things They Cared About: Change and Continuity in American's Attention to Different News Stories, 1989-2002," pp. 75-99 in *Press/Politics*, Winter.

Campbell, J. (2003). "The 2002 Midterm Election: A Typical or an Atypical Midterm?," pp. 203-207 in *PS Political Science & Politics*, Vol. 36, No. 2.

Center for Voting and Democracy (2003). Presidential Election Voter Turnout, April 28. http://-www.fairvote.org/turnout/preturn.htm

"CNN Election Results" cnn.com/ELECTION/2004/pages/results/states/US/P/00/epolls.0.

Diamond, R. (ed.) (1976). *Congressional Quarterly's Guide to US Elections*. Washington, DC: Congressional Quarterly, Inc.

Elections.gmu.edu/turnout_rates_graph.htm

Jennings, M. and R. Niemi (1975). "Continuity and Change in Political Orientations: A Longitudinal Study of Two Generations," pp. 1316-1335 in *The American Political Science Review*, Vol. 69.

Mellnick, T. and W. Pitzer (November 7, 2004). "How America Voted," p. 69 in *The Charlotte Observer*.

Pew Center for People and the Press (June 9, 2002). "Public's News Habits Little Changed by September 11."

Pew Center for People and the Press (March 28, 2003), "News Media's Improved Image Short-Lived." http://www.people-press .org/reports/print.php3.ReportID=56.htm

The Gallup Organization, Inc. (November 3, 2002). "CNN/USA Today/Gallup Final Mid-term Pre-Election Poll."

Note

The data which provide the basis for this analysis were furnished to the authors by The Gallup Organization, Inc. The authors' conclusions do not necessarily reflect the views of The Gallup Organization.

Chapter 17
Implications for E-Media, the Press, Government, and Politics in China

Song Yingfa

Associate Professor, Director, Institute of Higher Education, China University of Mining and Technology, Xuzhou, People's Republic of China

Miao Hongna

Assistant Professor, School of Government, Nanjing University, Nanjing, People's Republic of China

Abstract

In 1994, China adopted the international Internet TCP/IP protocol and became the 71st country with Internet access. Since then, the number of Chinese who logged onto the Internet expanded dramatically, from 0 in 1994 to 538 million in 2012. China is on the "information superhighway." The accelerating advance of information technology is changing the lives of common citizens; it is also the governing model of the state, catalyzing the transformation of Chinese society and politics.

This discusses the development of information and communication technology (ICT) and its impact as a new communication media on Chinese politics. The anticipated promise of the Internet as a revolutionary vehicle for Chinese politics prompted both ecstasy and consternation. The increased use of the Internet in heightened citizens' interest in and capacity for political participation, broadened the channel of civil participation, improved government efficiency, enhanced communication between government and citizens, and advanced the transparency of the government's functional departments. Meanwhile, the Internet has broken the pyramid structure of traditional Chinese society, but at the same time, it has formed a new bureaucracy and digital divide. The irrationality of electronic participation, the fragmentation of the legislative system, the disorganization of Internet use, and the government's strict control of the Internet's content are all barriers to Chinese cyber democracy.

China Enters the Internet Era

Since Chinese people accessed the Internet in 1994, the population of Chinese "netizens" expanded dramatically and the Internet penetration rate increased significantly. According to the 30th Chinese Internet Development Statistics Report from the China Internet Network Information Center (CNNIC), by the end of June 2012, China had netizens 538 million netizens, with 39.9% Internet users (Figure 1).

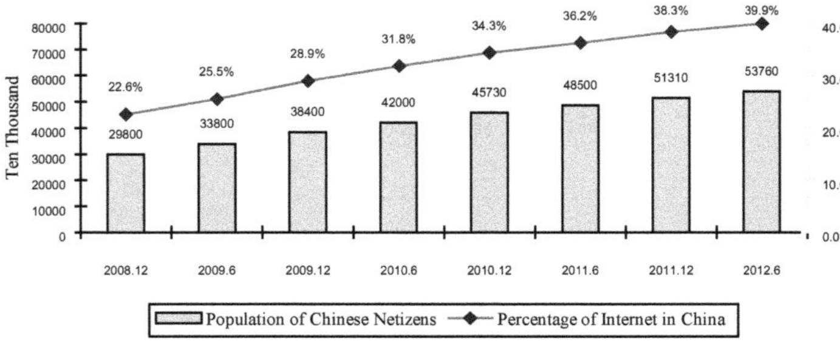

Figure 1: Population of Chinese netizens and percentage of Internet in China (Source: The Thirtieth CNNIC Statistics Report on Chinese Internet Development in June 2012)

The CNNIC is China's first Internet research institution and issues statistical reports each June and December since 1997. The data from the December 2008 CNNIC report showed that the population of netizens, netizens with broadband connectivity, and registrations of CN domain names all surpassed other countries. Moreover, the regional distribution, age structure, and demographic structure of Chinese netizens has been optimized. The popularity of the Internet among people who live in developed areas with easy accessibility is high; but it is gaining converts among people with little education and those who live in undeveloped areas. By the end of June 2012, the number of netizens in rural China had reached 146 million, an increase of 14.64 million since the end of 2011, and 27.1% of total netizens (Figure 2).

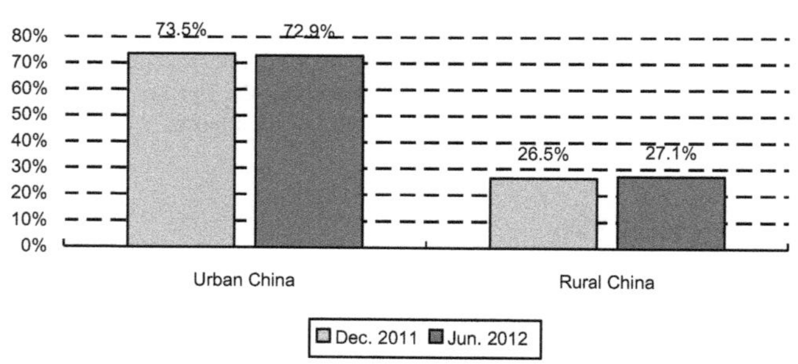

Figure 2: Urban and rural structure for Chinese netizens (Source: The Thirtieth CNNIC Statistics Report on Chinese Internet Development in June 2012)

In addition, the Internet infrastructure furnished access gradually, the Internet technology developed quickly, and the Internet performance improved continuously. By the end of June 2012, the number of IPv4 addresses approached 330 million, there were 8.73 million domain names, and there were 3.98 million CN domain names. The total number of websites increased to 2.5 million (see Table 1).

Table 1: The contrast in Chinese Internet infrastructure resources between December 2011 and June 2012 (Source: The Thirtieth CNNIC Statistics Report on Chinese Internet Development in June 2012)

	December 2011	June 2012	Amount of growth for the six months	Growth rate for the six months
IPv4 (N)	330,439,936	330,468,352	28,416	0.0%
Domain Name (N)	7,748,459	8,731,083	982,624	12.7%
Domain Name under .CN (N)	3,528,511	3.984,188	455,677	12.9%
Website (N)	2,295,562	2,503,533	207,991	9.1%
Website under .CN (N)	951,609	975,217	23,608	2.5%
International Export bandwidth (Mbps)	1,389,529	1,548,811	159,282	11.5%

The Chinese government also realized the Information Communication Technology had great significance for national political, economic, and social development, so the government actively promoted the Internet. People's Daily Online (opened on January 1, 1999) became the first important news website of the Central Committee of the Communist Party of China (CPC), which is achieving its web propaganda strategic goals via mainstream media. The 1999 launch of the "Government Online Project" was envisioned as a public relations showcase in the Internet era; it provided convenience for online service and government-public communication. Currently, Chinese e-government employs the top-to-bottom, crisscross patterned architecture, including "one station, two nets, four databases, and twelve operation systems." (One station means one government portal website; two nets include the government intranet and the government network; four databases are the databases for population, corporate units, spatial geography and natural resources, and macro economy; twelve operation systems provide information about the government's main business areas.) This e-government communicated with the central, provincial, municipal, county (or district), and town governments. 2008 was called "the first year of an era in Governance Online." Chinese chairman Hu Jintao communicated with netizens online for 22 minutes through the Forum of Powerful Nation (the forum's name comes from the BBS of People's Daily Online), which set the new precedent of online communication between China's highest leader and common netizens. Wen Jiabao, the premier of the State Council, first used text and video to communicate with the netizens all over the world through China Internet Information Center and Xinhuanet.com on February 28, 2009. During those two hours, there were hundreds of postings, and tens of thousands of feedback messages from mobile phone users.

Based on the rapid increase of micro-blog users, the government micro-blog appeared in 2010. The sense of Internet governance by Chinese government departments strengthened unceasingly; the mechanism of Internet governance was built up gradually.

The Internet developed quickly in China, but prosperity created problems: 1) the unbalanced development of the Internet existed among different regions in China, as well as between China and developed countries; and 2) Internet information security could not be guaranteed. These problems included lack of security measures, improper management, offline technical difficulties (partly unintentional because of technical glitches and system defects), and many serious security incidents concerning disclosure of sensitive information due to tampering, being attacked, and exploiting vulnerability. According to the Blue Paper, the Development and Research of New Digital Media in China 2012, with the development of mobile technology in new digital media, the threshold of information transmission will be greatly reduced; therefore, the problems of ideology security and information security will be prominent. This blue paper was an investigative research report about new media. The Development and Research of New Digital Media in China 2012 is the third volume of the blue paper system. The book includes the general report as well as reports on hot spots, the Internet media, plus mobile and electronic media.

Because of these problems, China began building the government-dominated nationwide strict Internet administration system in 1995. Various administrative departments that relied on a series of laws and regulations concerning Internet administration adopted multiple measures to set up the "Chinese National Firewall," which became the Internet with Chinese characteristics (Hartford, 2000). The administrative departments of Internet in China include: the State Council Information Office, the Ministry of Information Industry, the Ministry of Culture, the Ministry of Public Security, the Press and Publication Administration, the Ministry of Education, the Ministry of Public Health, and other departments. Similar Along with the huge number of administrative departments, China has had many laws and regulations concerning Internet administration since 1994, including Decision of the National People's Congress Standing Committee on Guarding Internet Security, Law of the People's Republic of China on Electronic Signatures, Regulations on Telecommunications of the People's Republic of China, Measures on the Administration of Internet Information Services, Regulations on the Protection of Computer Information System Security of the People's Republic of China, Regulations on the Protection of the Right to Online Dissemination of Information, Provisions on the Administration of Foreign-funded Telecommunications Enterprises, Measures on the Administration of Security Protection of the International Networking of Computer Information Networks, Provisions on the Administration of Internet News Information Services, Provisions on the Administration of Electronic Bulletin Services via the Internet, and so on. Relevant provisions of the Criminal Law of the People's Republic of China, General Principles of the Civil Law of the People's Republic of China, Copyright Law of the People's Republic of China, Law of the People's Republic of China on the Protection of Minors, Law of the People's Republic of China on Punishments in Public Order and Security Administration are all applied in the case of Internet administration. There are over 80 laws and regulations concerning Internet administration. Besides the laws and regulations, government still employs informal ways to administrate the Internet, such as instant text messages, mobile phones, e-mails, and informal discussions. The government directly regulates Internet content and indirectly controls it by restricting the users' access to the Internet (Wang and Hong, 2010).

Professor Li Yonggang of Nanjing University pointed out that in the last decade, the Chinese government's supervision of Internet content has changed. Because of the large-scale mobilization and high-investment equipment modifications, the Chinese government has taken the initiative and has remodeled the core belief of the whole ruling system. (Li, 2007)

In conclusion, the Internet's development in contemporary China exhibited two features: 1) the increase of netizens and the wide gap between the country's rich and poor coexist; 2) the government closely watched both the active use and the strict regulation of the Internet.

The Internet as the New Political Communication Media

The rapid spread of the Internet in China is based on its characteristics as a new media, such as activity, immediacy, extensiveness, openness, and richness. These are combined with the characteristics of information transmission in unidirectional mass media and bi-directional interpersonal communication. Chinese netizens use Internet applications to acquire information and to take advantage of e-commerce, communication, and online entertainment (see Table 2).

The Internet information (using video, audio, and other multimedia techniques) combined the multiple applications with splendid content and provided users with strong sensory stimuli that heightened their desire for interactive participation. This interaction was very attractive to Internet audiences and was unmatched by any other single technology form. The BBS (bulletin board system) provided netizens with a public place to express their opinions on any topic at any time. The anonymity of online discussion was considered a key attraction of BBS and gave netizens an opportunity to speak freely.

Table 2: Internet applications of Chinese netizens from December 2011 to June 2012 (Source: The Thirtieth CNNIC Statistics Report on Chinese Internet Development in June 2012)

Applications		June 2012		December 2011		growth rate for the six months
		number of users (ten thousand)	usage of netizens (%)	number of users (ten thousand)	usage of netizens (%)	
information acquisition	search engine	42860.5	79.7%	40740.1	79.4%	5.2%
	online news	39231.7	73.0%	36686.7	71.5%	6.9%
e-commerce	online shopping	20982.2	39%	19395.2	37.8%	8.2%
	group buying	6181.4	11.5%	6465.1	12.6%	-4.4%
	e-payment	18722.2	34.8%	16675.8	32.5%	12.3%
	trip reservation	4257.5	7.9%	4207.4	8.2%	1.2%
	e-bank	19077.2	35.5%	16624.4	32.4%	14.8%
	online stock trading	3780.6	7.0%	4002.2	7.8%	-5.5%
communication	instant messaging	44514.9	82.8%	41509.8	80.9%	7.2%
	blog/my space	35331.3	65.7%	31863.5	62.1%	10.9%
	micro-blog	27364.5	50.9%	24988.0	48.7%	9.5%
	social network	25051.0	46.6%	24423.6	47.6%	2.6%
	e-mail	25842.8	48.1%	24577.5	47.9%	5.1%
	forum/BBS	15586.0	29.0%	14469.4%	28.2%	7.7%
online entertainment	online gaming	33105.3	61.6%	32427.9	63.2%	2.1%
	online literature	19457.4	36.2%	20267.5	39.5%	-4.0%
	online video	34999.5	65.1%	32530.5	63.4%	7.6%
	online music	41060.0	76.4%	38585.1	75.2%	6.4%

The Internet's interactive communication capability (and its apparent power to foster inclusiveness and mobilization) possessed the characteristics of democracy and freedom, which the traditional media lacked. For this reason, many major presses, newspapers and other traditional media in China began using the Internet (such as Xinhuanet.com, People's Daily Online, CCTV.com, and STAR Group) to disseminate news. The news agencies as well as radio and television stations in China have used the Internet to develop their resources and brand advantages and to develop an open forum, bulletin board, and comment section to meet the people's need for communication.

In the political area, the rapid expansion and wide use of the Internet in China accelerated the remodeling of the Chinese political communication system. The traditional political communication modes (newspapers, broadcasts, and television) had difficulty satisfying the Chinese government's policymaking and implementation requirements; they also failed to cater to the public's appeal for political participation, discussion, and supervision. Thus, China's government readily opted for political communication via the Internet.

The Office of Publicity of Government Affairs of Liao Nin Province publicized the Government Work Report of all counties and districts in its jurisdiction online and appealed to the general public for comments for the first time in China on March 15, 2009. This indicated that the public was encouraged to discuss the Government Work Report, instead of relying on the deputy to relay their comment to the National People's Congress during its sessions. Consequently, the online comments gave the Chinese government a way to quickly learn about the people's opinions and recommendations and to accept the public's supervision.

The Internet has encouraged people to express their opinions and has facilitated political participation from the grassroots. The annual meeting of the National People's Conference (NPC) and the Chinese People's Political Consultative Conference (CPPCC) were vividly compared to a "yearly inspection" of government work and civic awareness. Since 2009, People's Daily Online has not only continued to conduct the traditional interactive columns (such as "NPC and CPPCC investigation," "Questions for Prime Minister," and "Words online"), but also promoted some new ones based on the interactive idea and information and communication technology (ICT). These include "the Netizens Hall," "E-NPC & CPPCC of Powerful Nation," "Bills and Proposals online," "Questions for Spokespeople." This allows millions of netizens to indulge their passion for political participation and gives them the opportunity to offer advice. In the "Netizen Hall" column, netizens could discuss various topics, express their opinions, and make recommendations and solutions to their representatives and deputies. In "Bills and Proposals online," NPC deputies and CPPCC members communicate with netizens and seek their advice. Both of these columns allow free discussion and thus motivate netizens' participation. "E-NPC & CPPCC of Powerful Nation" (a large-scale interactive column) combined the netizens' advice, voting recommendations, comments, and criticisms with interactive polls; thus, it became the netizens first choice for following NPC and CPPCC activities and for communicating their advice and opinions. Less than two days after those columns opened, almost 10,000 netizens registered for "E-NPC & CPPCC" membership, and posted hundreds of different proposals.

From "Participating in government and public affair via blog" to "E-NPC & CPPCC," netizens have offered advice and made proposals on economy and people's livelihood through People's Daily Online, Xinhuanet.com, CCTV.com, which merged into "the tide of reasonable proposals" in the era of the Internet. Citizens' concerns about and participation in NPC and CPPCC indicated their great interest in advancing Chinese democracy, the growth of citizens' consciousness, and the strengthening of belief, rationality, and responsibility.

Accordingly, almost all local governments have actively promoted building the infrastructure for online participation and enhanced interaction with the public. On

June 29, 2009, the general office of Guangdong provincial party committee held a meeting to solve the common problems posted by netizens for the first time in China; they assigned 17 issues on 5 topics to the departments concerned. On November 1, 2009, the first "Guangdong Netizen Forum" started at Guangdong Science Center. Thus, 150 famous netizens within and outside of Guangdong province and 50 government officials and experts from non-governmental think tanks got together to debate about the "financial crisis." The netizen forum was China's largest at that time.

In the past, Government Online was "speaking" with netizens online and "listening" to CPC committee and government offline. Instead of using reliable mechanisms to restrain and regulate participation, the online governance mechanisms focused on temporary ones (such as online e-mails, calls, and reports). The task-based meeting to solve common problems posted by netizens was convened to explore a consistent effective mechanism for interactive communication between government and netizens and to implement "online hearing" to promote "Governance Online." On the one hand during this process, government emphasized the importance of online public opinions, built platforms, and created opportunities for effective government-public communication. On the other hand, there was an upsurge of enthusiastic netizens' political participation; posting and criticism thus became the norm. The task-based meeting indicated the transition of Governance Online from "online hearing" to building a mechanism for expressing public opinions online. It heralded a commitment to foster interactive communication between the government and the public.

Microblogging on government and government affairs has become the new model and is an important platform for publicizing government affairs, serving the people, getting to know public opinions, and communicating interactively between government and citizens. Since its inception in 2011, microblogs about government first opened in Beijing, followed by Shanghai, Guangzhou, Hubei and other provinces. The microblog on government and government affairs has covered central and eastern China (Du and Zhang, 2012). The public sphere and public life has been affected and involved. According to the Assessment Report of Microblog on Chinese Government and Public Affairs 2011, by December10, 2011, there were 32,358 microblogs of CPC and government departments authenticated in Sina.com, Tencent.com, people.com.cn and xinhuanet.com; the CPC and government cadres had 18,203. The assessment report drew 1,000 samples from the microblogs of CPC and government departments and those of CPC and government cadres respectively. The statistics showed that in the microblogs of CPC and government departments, the proportion of city government and its subsidiary bodies was largest (58%), provincial government and its subsidiary bodies was next (22%). The microblogs of public security organizations accounted for 47% (the biggest one in CPC and government departments); next was the tourism department

(8%). The proportion of cadres' microblogs in public security organs ranked first (42%) in the CPC and government cadres, the next was in CPC departments (16%).

The dramatic expansion of microblogs on government and government affairs indicated that people-oriented, service-first ideals have driven the Chinese government to publicize its affairs ceaselessly. This resulted in strengthening the service from the street level, elevating the utility of governance resource and the performance of service via the Internet, and improving the government website from content-oriented to service-oriented. The government's striving for interactive communication with the public improved political communication and helped democratize the policymaking process.

The appearance of the netizen forum, online spokespeople, task-based meetings to solve common problems posted by netizens, microblogs on government and government affairs, and so on somehow initiated a new communication flow between officials and people. The interaction of government and the public via the Internet has built bidirectional communication and feedback models. This direct contact between the government and the public has elevated the administrative efficiency and governing capabilities and has rationalized the social governance structure. The cadres of government at all levels have noticed how the Internet makes it easier to seek advice from people, and have realized that getting to know the people's wishes, to use their wisdom, and to help them were essential aspects for improving the government's effectiveness and policymaking.

The Process of Internet Combination with Chinese Politics

Government Online (1999-2003)

The construction of Chinese governmental informationization began with the Government Online Project in 1999 and the Leading Group of National Informationization Work that same year.

Government Online means that governments can function well via the Internet, including controlling their image, relating governmental structures and procedures, disseminating information about related policies and industry, and providing proprietary governmental information. The first meeting of Government Online Project held on January 22, 1999, brought together the Chinese Telecommunication, State Economic and Trade Commission and 40 other ministries and institutions. Their goal was to bring more than 60% of state organizations and all governmental levels online in 1999 and to increase that by more than 80% in 2000. Thus the Government Online Project was formally launched and the informationization of Chinese governments entered a new era based on the international Internet infrastructure. Therefore, 1999 was called "the Year of Government Online."

The Circular of the General Office of the State Council Concerning the Establishment of the Leading Group of National Informationization Work, issued by the

General Office of the State Council of P.R.C on December 23, 1999, announced that the Leading Group of National Informationization Work (chaired by then Chinese vice premier Wu Bangguo) would be in charge of organizing and coordinating the research and development of important information across departments and industries and solving the problems concerned with the informationization project.

Half a year after the start of the Government Online Project, the number of domain names under gov.cn registered by Chinese governments at all levels reached 1,663, which was over three times more than the 561 registered in1998. Among others, over 720 governments set up their websites, as well as 63 central organizations, 174 provincial governments, and 467 prefectural governments. The telecommunication departments opened 198 special broadband lines to serve users. By June 2012, the number of domain names under gov.cn registered by Chinese governments at all levels reached 54,808, 33 times that of 1999. (The 1998 data is from the Second CNNIC Statistics Report on Chinese Internet Development in July 1998; the1999 data is from the Fourth CNNIC Statistics Report on Chinese Internet Development in July 1999; the 2012 data comes from the Thirtieth CNNIC Statistics Report on Chinese Internet Development in July 2012.) In addition, a batch of excellent provincial, municipal, and county government websites sprang up. The cornucopia of typical online application projects has been established, including databases of laws and regulations, databases of cities and counties, governments' dynamic news, leaders' email address, real-time traffic monitoring, online declaration and anti-smuggling, electronic taxing, and government online biding. During this period, the application of e-government grew both in form and content and began to rely on the international Internet's great coverage and powerful interactive capabilities. The e-government project in China has been used to offer convenient service and to elevate the performance of government organizations. It has become the indispensable means for the construction of a service-oriented government.

Service Online (2003-2008)

In July 2003, Wen Jiabao (then head of the Leading Group of National Informationization Work) pointed out that promoting the informationization vigorously is the important decision of the central committee of CPC. Complying with the trend of progress and the development of the world is the inevitable choice for Chinese industrialization and modernization; is the crucial link in promoting the leaping development of productivity, strengthening comprehensive national power and international competitiveness, and safeguarding national security; and is the strategic initiative in modernization construction. Governments should combine the informationization with improving government administration and transforming government functions. This speech heralded the transition of the e-government target from massive infrastructure construction to resource integration, application deepening, government transformation, and public service.

The Law of the People's Republic of China on Electronic Signatures, promulgated on August 28, 2004, was the first-ever formal informationalization legislation in China. This was considered an historical breakthrough in the legal environment of China's e-government.

The portal site of the central governmental of P. R. China (www.gov.cn) officially opened on January 1, 2006, which ranked number 2 in the popularity index of national government websites around the world, second only to the Canadian federal government's website. The portal site put the scattered governmental websites of all levels together, became the "joint portal site" of a batch of government websites, and had an important demonstrative effect for other government websites at the same time. The setup of the portal site was regarded as the innovation of Chinese administration and a significant step in the construction of a service-oriented government.

In the October 2007 Report of 17th National Party Congress, General Secretary Hu Jintao recommended that the Chinese government improve its responsibility system and the public service system to promote e-government and to strengthen social management and public service. For the first time, he defined the function of "e-government" as "the urgent means to accelerate the reform of the administrative system and to build a service-oriented government."

The Regulations of the People's Republic of China on the Disclosure of Government Information were promulgated and put into force on May 1, 2008. This stipulated that government agencies should take the initiative to reveal government information "on the basis of disclosure, and the exception of not disclosure." The regulations aimed to safeguard the rights of citizens, corporations, and other organizations to obtain governmental information in accordance with the law and to improve the transparency of government.

In May 2009, the first anniversary of the implementation of the Regulations of the People's Republic of China on the Disclosure of Government Information, the service platform for Chinese governmental information integration (http://gov-info.nlc.gov.cn) officially opened. It was the first Chinese service portal for the publicity of governmental information built by the national library. The platform was developed to provide a public consulting service and to become a convenient service portal for governmental information.

Governments at all levels kept on opening new ways to communicate with the public in the electronic platform, such as fax, e-mail, BBS, and microblog. Some local governments gradually promoted the level of online social security service, tried to use the intelligent card as the mode of identification authentication, and advocated making the social service and management functions (such as social insurance, employment, civil affairs, medical and health care, housing accumulation fund system, household registration management information, etc.) more accessible via the Internet. Some government websites provided public channels for online consulting and complaining; others used communication vehicles (such as the Call Center and the telephone) with high penetration rates to eliminate the difficulties for people who had no Internet connections and thus no access to government service. The Call Center offers people most online public services such as information, consultation, complaints, help, and feedback. The "Government Service Hotline" opened in some cities are the specific application of the Call Center.

During the period of "service online," the construction of e-government entered the complete implementation stage. With "one station, two nets, four databases, and twelve operating systems," the main content of e-government started. The fields related to e-government (such as information security, electronic signature, the development and utility of information resources) developed vigorously. In these five years, the construction of e-government in most Chinese areas (especially the economically developed regions) has benefitted from the investment in constructing the massive infrastructure and acquiring the necessary hardware. Now the focus shifts to the "application" stage, characterized by interconnection and resource-sharing.

Governance Online (2008-)

General Secretary of CPC Central Committee Hu Jintao communicated with netizens online and listened to public opinions through the Forum of Powerful Nation in People's Daily Online on June 20, 2008. Hu pointed out that the Internet is an important medium to do things, to make decisions, to get to know the condition of people, and to pool the people's wisdom. And Hu himself has paid close attention to netizens' advice and opinions (Tang, 2008). Governors used the Internet as the distribution center for ideological and cultural information and as the amplifier of public opinion, thereby promoting the transition of governing ideas effectively, the main value of Governance Online.

The rapid development of Governance Online in China benefited from the tremendous power of online public opinion offered via the online community, blogs, News posts, BBS, and online signature. (Now, the important BBSes in China are the Forum of Powerful Nation in People's Daily Online, the Forum of Development in Xinhuanet, and other forums in Sina, Sohu, and other portal websites.) In addition, plenty of senior leaders, deputies to NPC, and members of CPPCC were invited to be guests on the Internet so they could exchange ideas and discuss issues of public concern.

One important aspect of Governance Online is online supervision. China faced major problems in 2008 (such as the snowstorm in January, the Tibet riots in March, the earthquakes that hit Wenchuan in Sichuan Province and Yushu in Qinghai Province in May, the Weng'an event in June, the Beijing Olympic Games in August, the tainted milk scandal in September and the Longnan incident in

Gansu Province in November). The Internet played a vital role in delivering information and supervising government. A great number of corrupt and degenerate officials were reported through the Internet; therefore, 2008 was named The Year of Internet Supervision. The Chinese government attached great importance to the Internet's role in supervision and actively created conditions for the citizens to supervise the government. CPC Central Commission for Discipline Inspection and the Ministry of Supervision set up the informant websites as a new channel of reporting (www.12388.gov.cn) on October 28, 2009. The website also is used to receive reports from the public about and accusations of CPC members, CPC organs, and those who violated Party and government discipline. The website also seeks opinions and suggestions about party conduct and anti-corruption efforts. A series of episodes concerned with online anticorruption fully reflect the strengthening of "online civic consciousness." Chinese netizens used the Internet to safeguard their rights, to supervise and participate in the public issues, and to express their demands and needs. The social survey center of China Youth Daily conducted an online survey via www.minyi.net.com and www.qq.com. There were 1,983 respondents, including 75.5% who chose to take part in anticorruption via "exposure online" (which touched a much bigger proportion than other channels) by reports, exposure by traditional mass media, information disclosure, letters and calls, and audits (Huang, 2009).

The 2009 report of Analysis on Internet Public Opinion in China conducted by Internet Public Opinion Monitoring Room of People's Daily Online analyzed 77 influential social events; the result showed that 23 of the 77 events were exposed by netizens via Internet. That is, one-third of the public opinions were spread by the Internet, which has become one of the independent sources of news and public opinion. The 77 events involved the safeguard of civil rights, supervision of public power, maintenance of public order, and the upholding of public morality. Furthermore, along with the swift expansion of mobile media (especially mobile phone), the combination of the Internet with wireless terminals (mobile phones) has become an emerging mighty force. Mobile phones have facilitated information dissemination since the mobile media not only disseminate words, but also upload the pictures and videos on location and send a "live broadcast" for any emergency event. Governments were under great pressure to respond in a timely fashion and to maintain legitimacy.

The result of the big sample survey about "Governance Online" conducted by People's Daily Online, China National School of Administration, and Renmin University of China has showed that, among the 48,591 survey respondents, almost 70% of netizens were looking forward to "Governance Online" and 69% of respondents considered "Governance Online" as an effective way for CPC and government officials to gage public opinions. The replies of officials to netizens' messages and online posts were the most popular ways citizens use "Governance Online." According to 74% of netizens, the Internet could become a new way to prevent corruption. All these data prove that "Governance Online" had become an important feature of Chinese democratic politics in 2009 and would gradually increase. Although people have attached more importance to Governance Online and some local governments have used it as an index of official evaluations, not all officials approved of this experience; some officials saw it as a way to pretend that there was progress, others only went through the motions of using Governance Online and to quickly respond to netizens' opinions. Some Chinese officials saw Governance Online as something they were "not willing to use, not dare to use and not capable to use." At present, Governance Online in China limits netizens' communications from bottom to top, but does not allow government's affirmative actions from above to below.

Since the inception of e-government by the Government Online Project in 1999, the combination of the Internet with Chinese politics has improved China's administrative capacity and its ability to make decisions more efficiently, respond to public service demands, and deal with emergency events of central and local governments and party committees. It has had a positive impact on improving administrative efficiency, promoting information disclosure, transforming government functions, and raising the government's image. Despite these great achievements of e-government, it still has imperfections, such as "isolated islands of information," lack of service, and incomplete performance evaluation mechanisms which directly affect the low overall level of e-government. An obvious example is the UN E-government Survey 2012 released by the UN Department of Economic and Social Affair (UNDESA) and Division for Public Economics and Public Administration. In this survey, Chinese e-government ranks 78th in the world, drops 6 places in the ranking from the previous year, and appears overall as a downward trend (see Table3).

Table 3: Development index and ranking of Chinese E-government in the world

Year	Average Development Index of E-government in the world	Development Index of Chinese E-government	Ranking of Chinese E-government in the world
2004	0.4127	0.4356	67
2005	0.4267	0.5078	57
2008	0.4514	0.5017	65
2010	0.4406	0.4700	72
2012	0.4882	0.5359	78

The Internet's Impact on Chinese Politics

The Perspective of Western Scholars

Since the first Internet node opened in China in 1994, Western scholars have turned to the new technology. The relevant research topics covered the course of Chinese informationization, the government's supervision of the Internet, and the impacts of the Internet on Chinese politics. Western scholars are especially interested in the influence of the Internet on the liberalization and democratization of Chinese politics from the perspective of the relationship between state and society.

Because of the characteristics of the Internet, the advent of the technology has excited a core of democratization transformation advocates, who connected the expansion of the "free technology" (Sussman, 1989; Tobey, 1996) with Chinese political democratization. Lots of scholars convinced people that the development of the Internet had a direct impact on and implications for political institutions and ruling techniques and the Internet and democracy were symbiotic entities. Other researchers asserted that government could not control the Internet just like they control traditional mass media. The Internet broke the government's information monopoly and brought about a huge transformation in the press (Damm and Simona, 2006). In the Internet era, everybody became an information collector and informant, which virtually freed citizens from the bonds of hierarchy and undermined the government's authority. Chinese government used the Internet to obtain economic and political benefits and controlled the technology to minimize its political risk at the same time, but this was of no avail. On the contrary, the government itself might be transformed during the process (Chang, 2001). Furthermore, the Chinese government would not overly curb the Internet because any containment policy would not only impede foreign investment, but also hinder the full application of the Internet (Bi, 2001; Taubman, 1998). For optimists, the development of the Internet in China thus would be an inexorable catalyst of social and political transition.

With the growing evidence that China could control the Internet successfully and continue its opening policy, the belief that the Internet would inevitably promote Chinese political transition had aroused more suspicion. The Chinese democratization brought by the Internet seemed to be just a rosy picture painted by technocrats, but it was not a realistic portrayal (Pan, 2011). With the popularity of the Internet, little individual freedom and political progress might arise, but a more likely scenario is the consolidation of CPC's leadership and expansion of nationalism. Quite a few scholars concluded that CPC had taken advantage of the Internet functions in commercial activities and at the same time effectively controlled the negative political influence by multiple means (Banerjee, 2003; Harwit and Clark, 2001; Qiu, 2000; Shie, 2004). Even though the Chinese government is unlikely to prevent harmful information totally, it still could deter violations and irregularities by punishing those who visit illegal websites (Yin,

2009). The expansion of the Internet contributed to CPC's weakening control of information, but fundamentally the promise by optimists was a fiasco. CPC held back the trial of political transition promoted by the Internet by using the high-tech Internet Control System known as the "Chinese National Firewall." With the Chinese National Firewall, the Chinese government can use more developed technology than individuals and NGOs. Those who expected to use the Internet to advance China's political transition have to deal with both the information censorship as well as this technological obstruction. Basically, the Internet will not fundamentally transform Chinese politics, but it might support China's gradual transition to increasing diversity and accepting the fledgling democratization (Chase and Mulvenon, 2002).

Most Western scholars who do research on Chinese Internet politics recognize that the Internet contents are under strict censorship in China's authoritarian political system (K. Yang, 2007; Hong and Li, 2005; Lau, et al., 2011; Fairbrother, 2011). In their opinion, China's efforts to regulate the Internet echoed their traditional ideological methods, which considered the mass media as the "CPC's mouthpiece." By strictly regulating the Internet's contents, CPC made the Internet an effective vehicle for social control.

Consequently, the Chinese government is not opposed to the Internet. It constructed the Internet infrastructure to develop their e-government and used the Internet to improve its transparency and responsibility, to boost economic growth, to accelerate the construction of New Countryside, (Ting and Yi, 2012) and to consolidate CPC's leadership (Kalathil and Boas, 2003; Kluver and Qiu, 2003; Shie, 2004; Zheng and Wu, 2005; Bertot, et al. 2010). As far as social structure is concerned, the demographic "digital divide" (between rural and urban China and among regions) reduced the possibility of e-democracy and might exacerbate existing social conflict (Hartford, 2000). All in all, the Internet facilitated citizens' political expression, but it is not the determining factor in Chinese political democratization.

For a long time, the assertions of Western researchers about the Chinese Internet differed essentially from the opinions of Chinese scholars. The Internet's potential for democratization depends on how we understand "democracy." If we cannot clarify the meaning of "democracy," it is hard to say whether the Internet is getting closer to it or not. As Barber (1998) said, the existence and development of democracy don't rely on the quality and characteristics of technology, but the quality of the institution and the characteristics of citizens. Technology can't determine everything. The Internet can speed up the process of democratization and can maintain the non-democratic system. How the technology is used and in what kind of environment the technology exists has an effect on readiness for e-government (Khalil, 2011).

The Perspective of Chinese Scholars

Compared to the research of Western scholars, the studies of Chinese academia on the political issues influenced by the Internet are gradually becoming more comprehensive. On the basis of the literature review about Chinese Internet politics, the studies of cyber politics in China have been divided into three stages (Chen and Luo, 2011). During the initial stage (1994-1998), displaying both curiousity and caution, Chinese scholars mainly introduced and reviewed the construction of Internet abroad. In the growth stage (1999-2005), when the government online project began, the research focused on two aspects: the introduction of e-government and Internet security. The former included the environment, the basic models, current difficulties, and the social impact of e-government construction; the latter focused on the increasing number of Internet hackers, online fraud, and cyber infringement. At the same time, because of the need to maintain order on the Internet, the emphasis of both government and researchers switched to ideological education and Internet regulation. With the development of the idea of service-oriented government construction, Chinese scholars paid more attention on the exterior functions, including service online and interactive communication. With the "Governance Online" stage, most studies dealt with online public opinion, online supervision, online civil society, and so on. The researchers primarily focused on online political participation in the development stage (after 2006).

Chinese scholars had two different attitudes toward the emerging information and communication technology (ICT) and the Internet. Some upheld the concept of "instrumentalism" and insisted that (compared to the direct impact of historical traditions, development logistics, and institutional changes to the efficiency, service, and democratization of government activities) the impact of the Internet and ICT on the three aspects of government activities is only functional and indirect. Others considered ICT a "revolutionary" power and claimed that (compared to the traditional bureaucratic system) e-government was not only an innovative administrative tool, but would also bring about a brand new governance pattern. For them, the essence of e-government is how the government transforms and reengineers itself in the face of the ICT challenge and thus builds a new pattern of government that meets the needs of the information society and achieves good governance. Professor Yang Fengchun (2007) from Peking University said: "the arrival of the inevitable Internet era, will not the disaster of existent politics system, but the fortune for the people and government."

The Impact of the Internet on Politics: Gift or Curse?

Some scholars and politicians regard the Internet as a gift for China's political development because they think it can improve the Chinese political system by:

- Expanding civic participation. In China, the Internet is called the "Direct Train for Public Opinion." It alleviates the problems of traditional civic participation such as blocked participation channels, incomplete related laws and regulations, and limited willingness and ways to express political opinions.
- Promoting democratic policy-making. The Internet can change the traditional government-dominated "policy agenda-media agenda-public agenda" to "online public opinion- government policymaking." It also changes the passive subordinate status of the public and media in traditional society and helps them to actively influence the government's agenda.
- Boosting political transparency. This is viewed as a new effective democratic supervision pattern. On the one hand, the Internet expands the scope and depth of supervision. Via the Internet, some social issues can be raised and debated between government departments and the public. On the other hand, online supervision makes the Internet a multi-dimensional open platform for government information disclosure. The daily administrative activities (such as making and implementing policies) can be presented to the public via the Internet.
- Evolving the level of democratic service. Cyber politics affects democratic politics and services. The Internet environment increases citizens' awareness of all possible services in the areas of policies, society, economy, culture, education and healthcare. The public can access relevant government documents or deliver relevant information, demands, and appeals to the government via the Internet. Meanwhile, government can exchange opinions with the public at any time to discuss social issues and eventually reach a unanimous decision.
- Speeding up the process of political socialization. The Internet has become the important medium of political socialization. It plays a crucial role in influencing political culture, educating citizens, shaping political beliefs and political consciousness, and consolidating political rulings. Online political participation upgrades Chinese citizens' political knowledge and skills and develops more mature and stable political personalities (Xiong, 2008; Du and Zhang, 2012).

Some see the Internet as a political disaster because of its negative effects on the political life of China:

- Corroding political stability. The concealment, decentralization, openness, and immediacy of online political participation influences political stability negatively. For example, it is easy to spread false information from persons or organizations with ulterior motives via the Internet; this could confuse people's judgments and may lead to social unrest (Zheng and Wu 2005). From the civil rights perspective, the irrational and non-institutionalized cyber political participation may trigger group polarization which could threaten social stability, infringe on citizens' legitimate rights and interests, and seriously affect people's daily life (for example, the phenomenon of Internet Mass Hunting).

- Challenging government administration. The Internet differs from the authoritative mass media which is top-down style and dominated by centralized government. It poses a tough test for the traditional bureaucratic administrative pattern.
- Widening the digital gap. China's digital gap limits the information provided to people who do not have Internet access. This results in unbalanced political participation. The Internet's regional (urban versus rural) and personal (education, socio-economic, and age differences) imbalances limit online participation and cannot guarantee that all classes are heard. While cyber democracy provides various political participation channels and the gaps will undoubtedly narrow, Internet usage gives more access to the well-to-do, highly educated, and the more ideologically driven people.
- Jeopardizing state security. Online terrorism heavily undermines the authority of the government. Computer hackers target the national information center of political, economic, and military departments. This jeopardizes state security and violates civil rights and democratic institutions.

Statistics supplied by the National Computer Virus Emergency Response Center show that 72.16% of respondents had Internet security incidents in 2012. These incidents included maliciously tampering with the web page (75.08%), spam (73.65%), and Internet theft and phishing (64.87%). Moreover, the monitoring data from the National Computer Network Emergency Response Technical Team Coordination Center of China (CNCERT) showed that the overall evaluation of Internet security was medium in June 2011 when 8.15 million (76% higher than the previous month) Chinese computers were infected by viruses; 3,164 websites were tampered with, including 333 government websites. China National Vulnerability Database (CNVD) collected 447 system vulnerabilities, including 250 high-risk ones and 406 which could be attacked long distance. The software/hardware manufacturers affected were Adobe, Apple, Cisco, Google, IBM, Linux, Microsoft, Mozilla, Novell, and so on. The Chinese Internet security system is still weak in its ability to predict, respond to, prevent, and recover from threats. During China's social transition different factions used the Internet to further their values and political demands and to jockey for dominance. If the mainstream ideology cannot control the Internet, revolution could occur.

The Future of Cyber-politics in China

Enhance the Performance of E-government

E-government is called a "top leadership project" because the government plays a leading role in its planning and implementation. Chinese e-government aims to reshape the government structure, to make the government process transparent, and to develop an innovative administrative pattern. However, it is restricted by the bureaucracy's lack of commitment to live by the rule of law. There is also redundancy within the government's functional division, ingrained hierarchical control habits, and entrenched civil service policies that hinders the e-government's administration and discourages its growth. Therefore, to help e-government transform administrative patterns, the Chinese government must improve the bureaucratic structure, lower hardware restrictions, raise the level of bureaucratic software, and move it forward. To promote e-government's performance requires reforming the administrative system to meet citizens' basic requirements, making a commitment to complete every project, and expanding successful applications.

Expand Orderly Civil Online Participation

The Internet has become the new channel for Chinese citizens' political participation. One netizen of People's Daily Online insisted that every ordinary netizen can express their opinions and offer suggestions for CPC and government via posting and blogging. And a netizen from Xinhuanet.com left the message that the directness, interactive features, and immediacy of the Internet is a great convenience for Chinese citizens who want to express their views online. Much like a double-edged sword, online participation has both a positive and negative effect. The Internet also allows for disorderly, imbalanced, and emotional participation that negatively affects the evolution of Chinese cyber democracy. Since the Internet does not possess judgment skills, Chinese leaders need to standardize online behavior, to encourage rational and civil online participation, and to promote a harmonious and stable political order.

Establish E-governance for Social Harmony

Different from e-government, e-governance attaches importance to government informationization and the construction of a service platform; it pays more attention to informational interaction between the subject and object of public administration and the related virtual political and social structure and its interrelationship. To improve the performance and service orientation of e-government requires interaction among government, citizens, and NGOs. The traditional bureaucratic system stresses the top-down hierarchical management style, while e-governance (a new governance pattern in the information society) emphasizes people-centering, civic participation, information transparency and disclosure, interaction between the government and the public, and collaboration between government and NGOs. E-governance monitors the process of government administration, uplifts administrative efficiency, and increases transparency to build a clean and honest administration. Although currently e-governance in China is confined to supplementary functions of traditional government administration, it aims to become an online consulting service and offer innovations to encourage civic participation and eventually to construct the e-government.

Conclusion

Since the mid 1990s, especially as the technology has advanced, e-government is progressing in China. The emergence of cyber politics gives citizens convenient and cheap paths to participate in government and to benefit from its services. Cyber politics enhances citizens' ability to communicate and participate in the political process, improves political socialization, and shapes political beliefs and consciousness. But it also balances the power structure between state and society, strengthening the power of Chinese civil society. The positive influences of the rise of cyber politics on the development of Chinese politics are multifaceted. The Chinese government needs to take the initiative to adopt this trend and make cyber politics a new form of socialist democratic politics with Chinese characteristics. Of course, there are also negative effects. The inequality of online participation, the disorderly online participation process, the manipulation of online public opinion all constitute obstacles to Chinese political development in this period. Therefore, the Internet era is not the curse for existing politics, but rather a gift for the people and the government. The Internet expands the scope of orderly civic participation. E-governance is based on the active participation of netizens' and their ideological education and regard for the laws of China.

References

Banerjee, I. (2003). "Internet and Democracy in Asia: A Critical Explanatory Journey," pp. 1-25 in I. Banerjee (ed.) *Rhetoric and Reality: The Internet Challenge for Democracy in Asia*. St. Davids, PA: Eastern Universities Press.

Barber, B. (1998). *Which Technology and Which Democracy?* http://web.mit.edu/mit/articles-/barber.html

Bertot, J., P. Jaeger and J. Grimes (2010). "Using ICTs to Create a Culture of Transparency: E-government and Social Media as Openness and Anti-corruption Tools for Societies," pp. 264-271 in *Government Information Quarterly*, Vol. 27, No. 3.

Bi, J. (2001). "The Internet Revolution in China," p. 424 in *International Journal*, Vol. 56, No. 3.

Chang, G. (2001). *The Coming Collapse of China*. New York, NY: Random House.

Chase, M. and J. Mulvenon (2002). *You've Got Dissent!: Chinese Dissident Use of the Internet and Beijing's Counter-strategies*. Santa Monica, CA, Arlington, VA, Pittsburgh, PA: Rand.

Chen, T. and X. Luo (2011). "The Research of Chinese Cyber Politics: Progress and Debates," pp. 85-100 in *CASS Journal of Political Science*, No. 4.

Damm, J. and T. Simona (2006). *Technological Changes and Political Effects*. London, UK and New York, NY: Routledge.

Du, Z. and R. Zhang (2012). "Cyber Politics Development in China: Status and Strategic Vision," pp. 1-5 in *Journal of Beijing University of Aeronautics and Astronautics* (Social Sciences Edition), No. 3.

Fairbrother, G. (2011). "Forging Consensus for Implementing Youth Socialization Policy in Northwest China," pp. 179-186 in *International Journal of Educational Development*, Vol. 31, No. 2.

Hartford, K. (2000). "Cyberspace with Chinese Characteristics," pp. 255-262 in *Current History*, Vol. 99, No. 638.

Harwit, E. and D. Clark (2001). "Shaping the Internet in China: Evolution of Political Control Over Network Infrastructure and Content," pp. 377-408 in *Asian Survey*, Vol. 41, No. 3.

Hong, J. and H. Li (2005). "A Split and Swaying Approach to Building Information Society: The Case of Internet Cafes in China," pp. 377-393in *Telematics and Informatics*, Vol. 22, No. 4.

Huang, C. (December 27, 2009). "Don't Believe Corruption cannot be Eliminated, 95.8% Netizens are willing to Conduct Protracted War with Corruption" in *China Youth Daily*.

Kalathil, S. and T. Boas (2003). *Open Networks, Closed Regimes: the Impact of the Internet on Authoritarian Rule*. Washington, D.C.: Carnegie Endowment for International Peace.

Khalil, O. (2011). "E-Government Readiness: Does National Culture Matter?," pp. 388-399 in *Government Information Quarterly*, Vol. 28, No. 3.

Kluver, R. and J. Qiu (2003). "China, the Internet and Democracy," pp. 26-60 in I. Banerjee (ed.) *Rhetoric and Reality: the Internet Challenge for Democracy In Asia*. St. Davids, PA: Eastern Universities Press.

Lau, T., et al. (2011). "A Comparative Study of Online Privacy Regulations in the U.S. and China," pp. 603-616 in *Telecommunications Policy*, Vol. 35, No. 7.

Li, Y. (2007). "The Development Process of Internet Governance Policies in China," pp. 44-48 in. *Journal of Nanjing University of Technology* (Social Science Edition), No. 2.

Pan, X. (2011). De-bureaucracy: Re-Inspection of the Function of Internet in Chinese Political Communication," pp. 36-43 in *Zhejiang Social Science*, No. 1.

Qiu, J. (2000). "Virtual Censorship in China: Keeping the Gate between the Cyberspaces," pp. 1-25 in *International Journal of Communications Law and Policy*, No. 4.

Shie, T. (2004). "The Tangled Web: Does the Internet Offer Promise or Peril for the Chinese Communist Party?," pp.523-540 in *Journal of Contemporary China*, Vol. 13, No. 40.

Sussman, L. (1989). *Power, the Press and the Technology of Freedom: the Coming Age of Integrated Systems Digital Net*. Lanham, MD: University Press of America.

Tang, W. (June 20, 2008). "General Secretary Hu Jintao Communicates with Netizens Online via the Forum of Powerful Nation in People's Daily Online, p. 7 in *People's Daily*.

Taubman, G. (1998). "A Not-So World Wide Web: The Internet, China and the Challenges to Nondemocratic Rule, pp. 255-272 in *Political Communication*, Vol. 15, No. 2.

Ting, T. and F. Yi (2012). "ICT Policy for the ''Socialist New Countryside'' - A Case Study of Rural Informatization in Guangdong, China," pp. 626-638 in *Telecommunications Policy*, Vol. 37, No. 8.

Tobey, R. (1996). *Technology as Freedom: the New Deal and the Electrical Modernization of the American Home*. Berkeley and Los Angeles, CA: University of California Press.

Wang, S. and J. Hong (2010). "Discourse behind the Forbidden Realm: Internet Surveillance and its Implications on China's Blogosphere," pp. 67-78 in *Telematics and Informatics*, Vol. 27, No. 1.

Xiong, G. (2008). The Promotion of China's Political Development by the Rise of Cyberpolitics," pp. 43-47 in *Journal of Shandong University of Technology* (Social Science Edition), No. 3.

Yang, F. (2007). "Internet is the Gift of Modern Politics," pp. 24-25 in *People's Tribune*, No. 7.

Yang, K. (2007). "A Comparative Study of Internet Regulatory Policies in the Greater China Region: Emerging Regulatory Models and Issues in China, Hong-Kong SAR, and Taiwan," pp. 30-40 in *Telematics and Informatics*, Vol. 24, No. 1.

Yin, D. (2009). "Illusion and Reality: Internet's Role in China Democracy," pp. 136-142 in *Comparative Economic and Social Systems*, No. 1.

Zheng, Y. and G. Wu (2005). "Information Technology, Public Space, and Collective Action in China," pp. 507-536 in *Comparative Political Studies*, Vol. 38, No. 5.

Index of Subjects

Index of Names

Arbeit, Bildung & Gesellschaft
Labour, Education & Society

Herausgegeben von Prof. Dr. György Széll, Prof. Dr. Heinz Sünker, Dr. Anne Inga Hilsen und Dr. Francesco Garibaldo

Bd. 1 György Széll (ed.): Corporate Social Responsibility in the EU & Japan. 2006.

Bd. 2 Katja Maar: Zum Nutzen und Nichtnutzen der Sozialen Arbeit am exemplarischen Feld der Wohnungslosenhilfe. Eine empirische Studie. 2006.

Bd. 3 Daniela De Ridder: Vom urbanen Sozialraum zur kommunikativen Stadtgesellschaft. 2007.

Bd. 4 Heinz Sünker / Ingrid Miethe (Hrsg.): Bildungspolitik und Bildungsforschung: Herausforderungen und Perspektiven für Gesellschaft und Gewerkschaften in Deutschland. 2007.

Bd. 5 Anja Bastigkeit: Bildungsbiographie und elementarpädagogische Bildungsarbeit. 2007.

Bd. 6 Antônio Inácio Andrioli: Biosoja versus Gensoja. Eine Studie über Technik und Familienlandwirtschaft im nordwestlichen Grenzgebiet des Bundeslandes Rio Grande do Sul (Brasilien). 2007.

Bd. 7 Russell Farnen / Daniel German / Henk Dekker / Christ'l De Landtsheer / Heinz Suenker (eds.): Political Culture, Socialization, Democracy, and Education. Interdisciplinary and Cross-National Perspectives for a New Century. 2008.

Bd. 8 Francesco Garibaldo / Volker Telljohann (eds.): New Forms of Work Organisation and Industrial Relations in Southern Europe. 2007.

Bd. 9 Anne Marie Berg / Olav Eikeland (eds.): Action Research and Organisation Theory. 2008.

Bd. 10 György Széll / Carl-Heinrich Bösling / Ute Széll (eds.): Education, Labour & Science. Perspectives for the 21st Century. 2008.

Bd. 11 Francesco Garibaldo / Philippe Morvannou / Jochen Tholen (eds.): Is China a Risk or an Opportunity for Europe? An Assessment of the Automobile, Steel and Shipbuilding Sectors. 2008.

Bd. 12 Yunus Dauda: Managing Technology Innovation. The Human Resource Management Perspective. 2009.

Bd. 13 Jarmo Lehtonen / Satu Kalliola (eds.): Dialogue in Working Life Research and Development in Finland. 2009.

Bd. 14 György Széll / Werner Kamppeter / Woosik Moon (eds.): European Social Integration – A Model for East Asia? 2009.

Bd. 15 Benedicte Brøgger / Olav Eikeland (eds.): Turning to Practice with Action Research. 2009.

Bd. 16 Till Johannes Hoffmann: Verschwendung. Philosophie, Soziologie und Ökonomie des Überflusses. 2009.

Bd. 17 Denis Harrisson / György Széll / Reynald Bourque (eds.): Social Innovation, the Social Economy and World Economic Development. 2009.

Bd. 18 Werner Weltgen: Total Quality Management als Strukturierungsaufgabe für nachhaltigen Unternehmenswandel. 2009.

Bd. 19 György Széll / Ute Széll (eds.): Quality of Life and Working Life in Comparison. 2009.

Bd. 20 Francesco Garibaldo / Volker Telljohann (eds.): The Ambivalent Character of Participation. New Tendencies in Worker Participation in Europe. 2010.

Bd. 21 Richard Ennals / Robert H. Salomon (eds.): Older Workers in a Sustainable Societey. 2011.

Bd. 22 Christoph Sänger: Anna Siemsen – Bildung und Literatur. 2011.

Bd. 23 Nam-Kook Kim: Deliberative Multiculturalism in Britain. A Response to Devolution, European Integration, and Multicultural Challenges. 2011.

Bd. 24 Mirella Baglioni / Bernd Brandl (eds.): Changing Labour Relations. Between Path Dependency and Global Trends. 2011.

Bd. 25 Rüdiger Kühr: Japan`s Transnational Environmental Policies. The Case of Environmental Technology Transfer to Newly Industrializing Countries. 2011.

Bd. 26 Francesco Garibaldo / Dinghong Yi (eds.): Labour and Sustainable Development. North-South Perspectives. 2012.

Bd. 27 Francesco Garibaldo / Mirella Baglioni / Catherine Casey / Volker Telljohann (eds.): Workers, Citizens, Governance. Socio-Cultural Innovation at Work. 2012.

Bd. 28 Simone Selva: Supra-National Integration and Domestic Economic Growth. The United States and Italy in the Western Bloc Rearmament Programs 1945-1955. Translation by Filippo del Lucchese, revision by Simone Selva. 2012.

Band 29 György Széll / Roland Czada (Hrsg.): Fukushima. Die Katastrophe und ihre Folgen. 2013.

Band 30 Siqi Luo: Collective Bargaining and Changing Industrial Relations in China. Lessons from the U. S. and Germany. 2013.

Band 31 Litsa Nicolaou-Smokoviti / Heinz Sünker / Julia Rozanova / Victoria Pekka Economou (eds.): Citizenship and Social Development. Citizen Participation and Community Involvement in Social Welfare and Social Policy. 2013.

Band 32 Christ'l De Landtsheer / Russell F. Farnen / Daniel B. German / Henk Dekker / Heinz Sünker / Yingfa Song / Hongna Miao (eds.): E-Political Socialization, the Press and Politics. The Media and Government in the USA, Europe and China. 2014.

www.peterlang.com

www.ingramcontent.com/pod-product-compliance
Ingram Content Group UK Ltd.
Pitfield, Milton Keynes, MK11 3LW, UK
UKHW021831100926
8556IPUK00004B/268

9 783631 628348